Administering Active Directory

G000143916

Mark Wilkins

McGraw-Hill
New York   Chicago   San Francisco   Lisbon   London
Madrid   Mexico City   Milan   New Delhi   San Juan
Seoul   Singapore   Sydney   Toronto

McGraw-Hill

A Division of The McGraw-Hill Companies

1 2 3 4 5 6 7 8 9 0   AGM/AGM   0 5 4 3 2 1

ISBN 0-07-212722-8

The sponsoring editor for this book was Michael Sprague and the production supervisor
was Daina Penikas. It was set in New Century Schoolbook by Patricia Wallenburg.

Printed and bound by Quebecor/Martinsburg.

This book is printed on recycled, acid-free paper containing
a minimum of 50% recycled, de-inked fiber.

Contents

Contents

Contents

Contents

Contents

Understanding Active Directory

This chapter provides an introduction to Active Directory, discussing:

- Benefits of using Active Directory services
- Windows 2000 and Active Directory features
- X.500 conventions and attributes
- Lightweight Directory Access Protocol (LDAP)
- Microsoft Management Console (MMC)

In the Beginning:
Before Directory Services

Remember when you had one server and a few clients, and in hindsight, network administration was easy? Then the server's hard drives became full, so a second server was added, and each user had to remember two passwords and login names. Over time with many servers, the end user and support staff became unhappy with the complicated network they had to use, administer, and share.

In 1993 Microsoft released NT with support for a single logon point using multiple servers employing *domain architecture* for a shared security database between multiple servers as shown in Figure 1.1.

Figure 1.1
The multiple master domain was common in NT design.

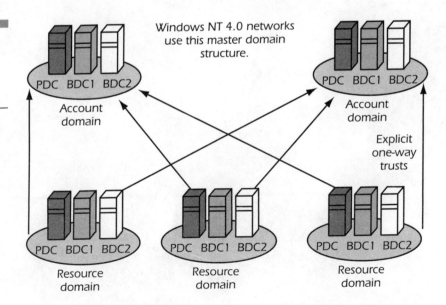

In the subsequent NT 3.51 and 4.0 versions, the security system was (and still is) stored and maintained on a domain controller called a primary domain controller, and replicated in read-only format to any available backup domain controllers.

Once any primary or backup domain controller within the users' defined domain authenticated the known user with a valid user account, that user could logon to the network. Another advantage that Microsoft enjoyed was perfect timing; the emergence of NT 3.51/4.0 was its integration with TCP/IP as the use of the Internet began to explode. One-way trusts were then used to link separate domains, creating potentially large network environments where the rules could and did change from domain to domain.

The major problem with the available domain structures supported by NT was that security was applied only at the domain level, making it impossible to delegate security effectively to other sub-administrators for control of the security principals user and group accounts, and computer accounts. The end result was a large sprawling network topology with multiple master domains with many one-way trusts left to manage and maintain; in many cases it just wasn't working well, especially in the network environments linked across Wide Area Network (WAN) links.

Novell NetWare and NDS

Novell was the first vendor with a large network market share to offer an X.500 directory service. Currently there are over 70 million NDS users worldwide. NDS can also run on any combination of NetWare, Windows NT, Linux, Solaris, IBM's AIX, and OS/390 and can be accessed from DOS, Windows, UNIX, Linux, and Macintosh systems. As a result, Microsoft began to feel threatened, since NT was not as scalable as NDS. In 1995, the availability of Novell NetWare Version 4.0 introduced the network directory service (NDS), though it had no initial native support for TCP/IP. The other problem area for Novell was marketing NDS properly; NetWare had a very important directory service structure that would eventually be copied by Microsoft, but Novell couldn't seem to educate the masses about the benefits of using NDS.

Instead, a majority of NetWare 3.X network administrators and companies began drifting toward Microsoft's applications, browsers, and NOS. With the current version of NetWare 5.1, TCP/IP, rather than IPX can now be the native protocol used, and the many new NetWare solutions appearing are based on the initial directory service model: DirXML Metadirectory, eDirectory, and NDS Corporate Edition.

However Windows NT 4.0 now controls the small and mid-size network market that NetWare had locked up for years. And Active Directory will probably be the final nail in the coffin for NetWare's dominance of the mid-size networking market as a one-stop solution provider.

Active Directory Structure

The basic design and layout of Active Directory is based on the X.500 schema (think of a blueprint, or a building code as an analogy for the schema) just as NDS is. Microsoft adds many additional object classes, objects, and attributes into the schema once Exchange 2000 is deployed on top of Windows 2000; in fact, the size of the schema is more than doubled, and this is for just one application! Active Directory services are scalable and can be deployed in both mid-size and large enterprise network environments; however, the smaller network with just a few servers will also benefit, especially if Exchange is the preferred mail server.

Active Directory Provides Central Control

Using a directory service allows your organization's administrators to manage all supported network resources across the entire directory structure. Through a single point of access, the administration of a worldwide Windows 2000 network is very doable. It all depends on your company's current administrative practices and preferences. Certainly central control is a huge administrative benefit. And with Active Directory, security can be enforced across the entire directory structure, protecting resources, network services, and data files from the outside public world and also from users on your network by many granular security levels from one location. However, there are thousands of security settings that can be deployed, from the site level down to the single object and attribute level, so the setting of security is a huge job. At least we now have the ability to handle security properly, and we couldn't say that with NT 4.0. Active Directory can also be distributed across a large network and WAN hierarchy, incorporating forests and trees of domains at multiple sites; these concepts will be discussed fully in the chapters to follow.

Improved Fault Tolerance

Multimaster directory replication between multiple domains supported by multiple domain controllers allows a much higher level of fault tolerance, and improved network traffic flow we could only dream about back in the NT 4.0 world. In Windows 2000, Domain Controller roles are now combined into one model, the Domain Controller (DC), since *Primary Domain Controllers* (PDC) and *Backup Domain Controllers* (BDC) are not used in native Windows 2000 networks. All Windows 2000 servers with Active Directory installed are *Domain Controllers*. However, Windows 2000 Domain Controllers can emulate the PDC role for the support of NT 4.0 BDCs, allowing replication of security information in the default mixed mode to a down-level NT 4.0 network; this permits Windows 2000 servers and NT 4.0 servers to co-exist during the migration process.

Industry Support

Active Directory also has ever-growing industry-wide support. Microsoft has relationships with many hundreds of hardware vendors and software developers who have bought into the Active Directory concept. This level of third-party support is something that NetWare never managed to achieve; however, Microsoft has developed into both an application developer and a network operating system provider that is proving impossible to stop. The key relationship to watch is Microsoft and Cisco. They are currently in a hush-hush relationship, and some of the most important security features of Windows 2000 (Quality of Service [QoS] and IPSec) were integrated and designed with Cisco's help. Think of it this way: Microsoft wants to be your network plumbing. What better way to accomplish this task than to partner with the existing network plumber, Cisco? Once Windows 2000 is inside routers, it can then control your telephone system, alarm system, in fact any integrated system. Read the white papers on **www.microsoft.net**; you may be surprised. The takeover of the desktop and Internet browser will seem like child's play a few years from now. This is a 20-year plan that's just starting, and the first step is entrenching AD as the corporate network structure.

Application Software and Active Directory

Many versions of Microsoft's popular application software will first support, then integrate with, and eventually require, Active Directory and Windows 2000 fully to deploy and provide all of their features. Exchange Server 2000, SQL Server, Proxy Server, and Systems Management Server 3.0 (Code named Emerald) are but the first wave.

- **Exchange Server 2000**—The next version of Microsoft Exchange, code-named Platinum, uses Active Directory in place of the Exchange Directory Service.
- **SQL Server**—In future releases of SQL, server security will integrate completely with Active Directory.
- **Proxy Server**—Future versions of Proxy Server integrated with Active Directory security will be a big plus since the replicated active directory database combined with Kerberos security will provide a system-wide security level.
- **Systems Management Server 3.0**—It's hard to imagine just what SMS 3.0 can offer—software deployment, remote access, and software licensing are all part of Windows 2000. Inventory control is not, however.

NOTE

Exchange Server 2000 will be backward compatible with Exchange 5.5. Microsoft offers a directory migration tool to migrate the contents of the Exchange folder to the Active Directory folder.

Active Directory Features

Group Policy

The biggest feature of AD is group policy, a bizarre name, considering it is deployed for users and computer systems. *Group policy* (GP) works on many levels of control, from the site level, which may be your entire company, down to the domain level, then at the organizational unit level and, if desired, also at the local workstation level. You may be familiar with system polices that were available with Windows NT 4.0; these settings, plus a lot more, can be controlled and managed with group policy.

GP can be installed on a local Windows 2000 Professional node, but it is much more powerful when it is deployed through Active Directory as shown in Figure 1.2.

Figure 1.2

Group policy settings for the domain.

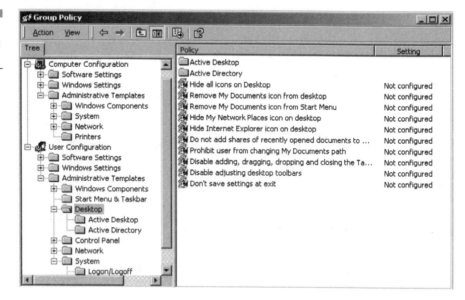

As mentioned, group policy can be deployed at several administrative levels: starting at sites, then in domains, and finally in organizational units. This order of deployment through inheritance is very important. Group policy can be deployed to take advantage of the areas of Windows 2000 shown in Table 1.1.

TABLE 1.1

Group policy options.

Feature	Details
ADM	Administrative templates similar to NT 4.0 system policy settings but with enhancements
Applications	With the Windows Installer advertisements, applications and operating system updates can be performed automatically
Files	Files can be deployed to the client at logon
Machine	Contains settings and changes for the computer
Scripts	Startup and shutdown scripts can be used for computer configuration. Logon and logoff scripts can be use for the end user; they can be written in VBScript, Jscript, batch files, and WSH (Windows Scripting Host)
User	Contains settings and changes for the user and group of users

NOTE

There are over 1,000 possible settings that can be deployed through group policy for the Windows 2000 operating system alone.

Folder Redirection

To a network client, a folder may appear to be locally stored on a Windows 2000 Professional client, when in fact it could be located on a network server as detailed in Figure 1.3.

Figure 1.3
The My Documents folder can be automatically replicated to the network.

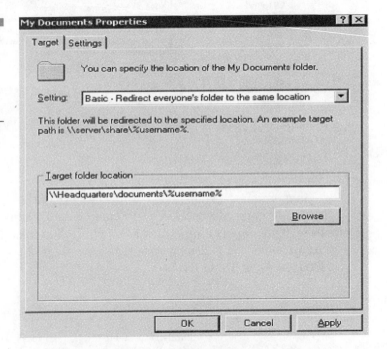

Off-line folders and roaming folders are two major features of group policy. When a client logs off the network for the day, defined folders and files can be configured to move automatically to a local hard drive location. When the user comes back into work and logs onto the network once again, the off-line folders can be automatically synchronized and updated with the network copies. Folder policy can be deployed in one of two methods: basic, which redirects every user to the same network location; and advanced, where each group's folders can be redirected to a specified network location. The environment variable %USERNAME% can also be used for more control.

Terminal Services

Terminal services will be the ultimate feature-set of Windows 2000. Most of us want email, word processing and, in general, very low processing power for the generic corporate application. The power applications such as games, CAD, or programming will still need their local processing but the rest of us don't. Terminal services execute on a remote server location and just the video, mouse, and keyboard changes are updated on your terminal server client. The TS client can be a standard PC; however, the emergence of instant-on net PCs, and ever-increasing bandwidth across corporate networks means that terminal services are a bonus for administration since the end-user can't change anything because all components are server based.

Active Directory Services Interface (ADSI)

ADSI is Microsoft's open offering to independent software vendors to write scripts and applications that will hook into the active directory service using this single set of interfaces. Any application that is ADSI compliant will be able to access Active Directory Service. The present directory-service structure is driven by a specific application programming interface (API) for communicating with AD clients and servers. ADSI objects are component object models (COMs)—objects that are either container or leaf objects as listed in Table 1.2.

TABLE 1.2

AD objects used with ADSI scripts.

Container Objects	Leaf Objects
Namespaces	User
Country	Alias
Locality	Service
Organization	Print Queue
Organizational Unit	Print Device
Domain	File Share
Computer	Session
Group	Resource

Distributed File System

The distributed file system (Dfs) used throughout Windows 2000 is hosted by Active Directory to track and automatically replicate files that can even be stored on different servers across the enterprise network, as shown in Figure 1.4. Service pack 1 allows this feature to work. The end result is that the reference point is not a drive letter but a folder.

Figure 1.4
Dfs can be deployed for automatic file replication throughout the directory.

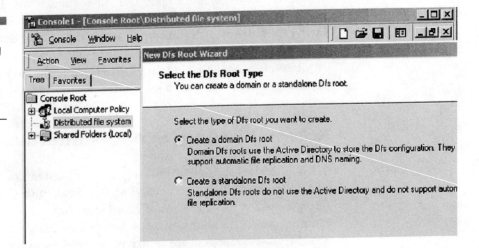

The Metadirectory: The Present and the Future

At this point in time, directory services can be split into two basic levels, starting at the system-specific components and ending up at the complete global or enterprise level sometime in the future. The reality is that all countries will probably not be able fully to work together, but the design principles of X.500 that Windows 2000 are actually built upon are hoping for the best. The key term is the *metadirectory*. Right now we are approaching level one in terms of integration as shown in Figure 1.5.

- **Level 1**—Firewalls, email, routers, networks, and Web sites.
- **Level 2**—This will use a metadirectory service to store together all the separate objects found in Level 1 so they can all be centrally managed and modified worldwide. Cisco and Microsoft hope to be the glue for the network of the future.

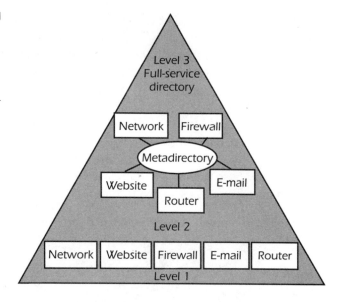

- **Level 3**—This is the metadirectory that would exist if all countries and people agreed to work together in the same manner. (Don't hold your breath.)

In an effort to fill in the holes, independent hardware vendors Cisco, Lucent, 3Com, and many others are already manufacturing directory-enabled devices like hubs, switches, and servers that can communicate using the standard LDAP protocol employed by all directory services. Each directory-enabled device can take advantage of the ability to extend the directory database structure through the schema, adding its own object identifiers and attributes that then become part of the directory. These devices could then also be administered like any other object stored in AD.

Under the Hood: Active Directory Structure

Active Directory is structured as a *directory service* used as unique identification of all users and resources found across an internetwork, linking them together. The Manhattan Yellow Pages, or the Who's Who Internet Listing are two examples of a public directory services that can be used in an alphabetical name format to search for and retrieve information. These existing Internet services use DNS (Domain Name System) as the locator mechanism. Each Windows 2000 server that implements the Active Directory service also offers shared network resources to any Windows 2000 Professional Client coincidentally using DNS as the locator service. Active Directory includes both the *directory*—the location(s) where the network resources are stored—and the *network services*. Network services are the driving force for Windows 2000, executing in the background to provide network support and access to the Active Directory resources. The Active Directory database is a central database that looks the same to the clients in Japan or in Toronto as shown in Figure 1.6.

Figure 1.6
The Active Directory database appears the same to many locations.

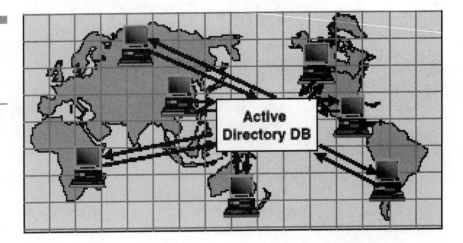

All resources are stored in the Active Directory database as objects and then populated (or replicated) throughout the network to every domain controller running Windows 2000 Server and Active Directory in the tree or forest.

Exchange Server 5.5 was the initial model for the Active Directory database.

NOTE

Active Directory Single Point of Access

With a single point of access required for both user access and administration, an administrator with the appropriate permissions can log onto the network anywhere and administer all objects and network resources as shown in Figure 1.7. The active directory database is also fully replicated; any changes made to the Active Directory database will automatically update all other replicas through multi-master replication.

Figure 1.7
Using ADUC,
administration can be
performed on all
domains in the forest.

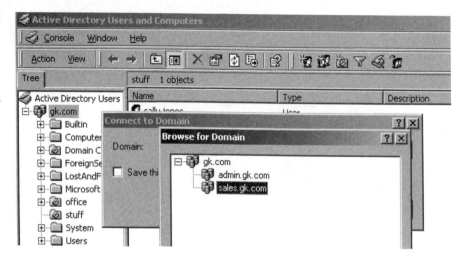

Scalability

The architecture of AD is modeled after Exchange Server 5.5's directory structure and storage engine. Each AD structure can support database stores that can contain millions of objects per forest.

Integration

Windows 2000 Server(s) (Server, Advanced Server, and Data Center Server) and Windows 2000 Professional are fully integrated once Active Directory is installed and all servers are running in native mode. The important concept to remember is that emerging software applications will integrate with the system information stored in the directory. All upcoming Windows 2000 NOS features will require and embrace Active Directory in one way or another, taking advantage of the security and the central storage.

Open Standards

Microsoft has wisely decided to embrace existing standards instead of creating a completely new propriety model. Active Directory is joined at the hip with DNS, using it for its name system for locating network services like the global catalog server and domain controllers. It can also exchange data with any application that supports the LDAP protocol. Other common name formats are supported as shown in Table 1.3.

Name Format	Details
RFC 822	Uses the format of an email address username @domain
HTTP URL	Formatted in **http://domain/path**
UNC	Uses the format **\\gk.com\doc\newfile.doc**
RFC 1799	Uses the format LDAP://server.gk.com/CN=FirstnameLastname, OU=system, OU=division, DC=development

Multi-Master Replication

Since we know that there are multiple copies of the Active Directory database, we should ask how they stay up to date with each other. The answer is, multi-master replication that monitors and replicates any changes made to a Domain Controller's replica of the database, then propagates the changes to all other domain controllers. Replication provides a large measure of fault tolerance and redundancy, plus distributed administration, since most changes need not be made at a specific DC, they can be performed at any DC in the tree or forest and replication will then update the other replication partners (other DCs that are also hosting the domain).

The Parts of the Active Directory Database

There are three main categories or parts to the database/schema of Active Directory:

1. **Resources**—all devices that are physically attached to the network, which can be accessed by a user at their computer including:
   - File server hard drives
   - Software applications

- Folder(s) containing data files
- Modem(s)
- IP addresses of network devices
- CD-ROM towers

   In order for a resource to be accessible by any user at any location across the network, each network resource must also be shared.

2. **Services**—a service is a system network application running and executing in the background of the server and the workstation. In the Control Panel, the Services icon lists the executing network services. Most, if not all, installed network services directly relate to the resource that they are hosting, as shown in Table 1.4.

TABLE 1.4

Services are linked to the supported resource.

Network Resource	Associated Network Service
Software Application	Terminal server
IP Address	DHCP
Printer	Printer service
Folder	File service
Hard Drive Partition	File service

3. **User Accounts**—A current user account is obviously necessary before any object can be accessed in the Directory. The user must supply a valid logon ID and password before accessing a resource in the directory.

Objects and Attributes

Active Directory references everything viewable in the Windows Explorer shell by the word *object* or *attribute*.

   The directory is a collection of these objects; printers, files, folders, fax servers, file servers, databases, computer systems, and user accounts, as shown in Figure 1.8.

   When a user wants to access an object stored in the directory, the access can be controlled by layers of security that define the level of access allowed at a specific point in the directory. Each object can be searched and located either by the name of the object, or by the attributes of the

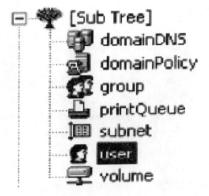

object itself. Suppose that a user in the accounting department wanted to find the location of clipart for a certain type of presentation; he could request, "All business clipart." If a color laser printer were needed fast because the known local printer was on the fritz, the user could request, "Find all color printers on the main floor."

These two examples illustrate the use of *attributes*. An attribute describes the named object; the more attributes, the easier it is to search for a specific object, as detailed in Figure 1.9.

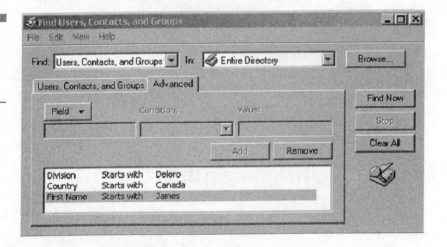

What's X.500?

X.500 is an industry-wide standard for the design of directory services; it was first defined and published in 1988 by the International

Telecommunications Union (ITU). Design modifications were made in 1993, and the latest updates in 1997. The X.500 standard defines the model to be used, complete with defined object classes and protocols. The same standard is also published and maintained by another standards body, the ISO, which you may have heard of with regard to the OSI network layers.

The defined X.500 protocols are the delivery mechanism for delivering the required data stored in the directory itself.

- Directory Access Protocol (DAP)
- Directory Service Protocol (DSP)
- Directory Information Shadowing Protocol (DISP)
- Directory Operational Binding Management Protocol (DOP)
- Lightweight Directory Access Protocol (LDAP)

The above protocols are defined by X.500; however, if they were all implemented at the same time they would consume a ton of bandwidth. The only one currently used by Active Directory is LDAP.

Lightweight Directory Access Protocol

Lightweight Directory Access Protocol (LDAP) is the protocol used to add, modify, delete, query, and retrieve data stored in Active Directory. LDAP provides the basic communication service of locating information in the directory. It defines how a directory client can access a directory server and access and share directory data. LDAP is used to store and retrieve information from Active Directory that could be distributed across multiple Windows 2000 servers containing multiple system services and software applications.

It also puts in place a "platform-neutral" common structure for information services required by today's network operating systems and database applications. It is used to store and retrieve information for other Windows 2000 system services, such as DNS, DHCP, and erberos, which is stored in the directory.

LDAP Components

Client-to-Server

By holding common system information used by Windows 2000, LDAP simplifies the management of system information and also greatly reduces unnecessary duplication, as shown in Figure 1.10.

Figure 1.10
LDAP and
client-to-server
communications.

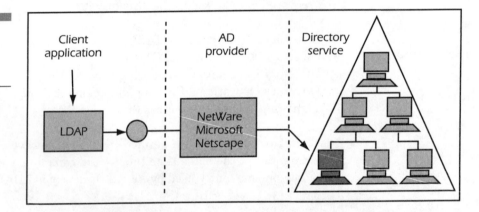

The client-to-server communication allows a user-installed application to make contact with a Windows 2000 server running Active Directory and to create, retrieve, modify, and delete data records.

Server-to-Server

Server-to-server communications define how servers share the contents of the directory tree and how they perform updates and replication amongst themselves as shown in Figure 1.11.

Most vendors, including Microsoft, deploy the client-to-server communications in a standard format. However, for Windows 2000 the server-to-server communications is a Microsoft mix of the proposed LDAP standard plus their own enhancements.

LDAP and Data Retrieval

LDAP is a protocol to retrieve requested data; it can be used to retrieve information from the directory in three distinct methods:

1. **As a service protocol**—Used by different applications or user requests to retrieve the desired information they require. For exam-

Figure 1.11
LDAP and
server-to-server
communications.

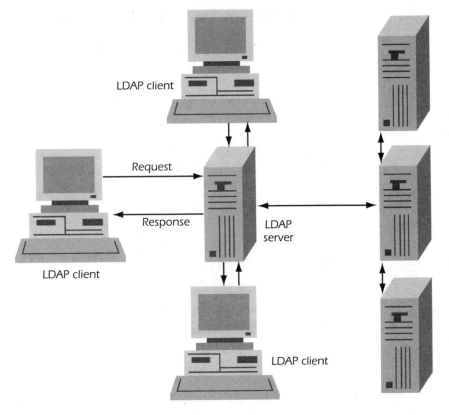

LDAP client

Request

Response

LDAP
server

LDAP client

LDAP client

ple, a user creates a query, which is then sent to a search engine; the query is matched against an LDAP server, and this points to the place where the actual data are located.

2. **As a application data exchange interface**—Used by one software application to exchange data with another. For example, a Lotus Notes database can store records into an LDAP server so that an LDAP-supported client such as a Microsoft Outlook client can then retrieve it.

3. **As a system service protocol**—Used by the operating system to communicate information between its different components. For example, an LDAP server can contain the access rights of user accounts that are referenced by the login system and by the installed file system.

*For more information on LDAP version 3, search on the Internet for RFCs 2251–2256 at **www.ldapcentral.com**.*

NOTE

The LDAP Functional Model

The LDAP structure is based on six functional models, as shown in Figure 1.12.

Figure 1.12
The six layers of LDAP design.

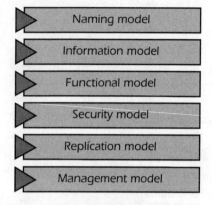

The Naming model
Information model
Functional model
Security model
Replication model
Management model

The Naming Model

This model details how the tree of data is laid out so that you can build a tree-like representation of your entire organization. The tree is also called a DIT or a directory information tree; the Active Directory database file is called NTDS.DIT.

Each entry can correspond to any type of object—a file, a user account, a printer, a DNS resource record, a user's desktop preference, etc. Each node in the LDAP tree can be of any type and can have any number of child nodes of different varieties; there are no limitations. The naming model also defines how each entry can be accessed within the context of the entire directory information tree.

The Information Model

This model defines the attributes of each entry and the data types of these attributes. For example, for a user account there must be a definition of how the account name is represented; usually by a string of characters. The information model defines the supported data types (strings, binary data, Boolean values, integers, and floating point values).

The Functional Model

This model defines how data are accessed from the directory system and what LDAP commands can be used. The commands listed in Table 1.5

can be grouped into useful tasks such as: search and compare; add, delete, modify, and rename; and session control operations of bind, unbind, and abandon.

TABLE 1.5

LDAP commands.

LDAP Command	Description
Search	Search the directory for matching directory objects
Compare	Compare one directory object to a set of data
Add	Add a new directory object
Modify	Modify a particular directory object
Delete	Delete a particular directory object
Rename (Modify DN)	Rename or modify the distinguished name of a directory object
Bind	Start a session with an LDAP server
Unbind	End a session with an LDAP server
Abandon	Abandon an operation previously sent to an LDAP server
Extended	Extended operations command

The Security Model

This model defines how the directory is secured. Security can be established by sub-tree, by individual entry, or by an attribute within an entry. Under LDAP version 3, there is a common authentication framework known as the Simple Authentication and Security Layer (SASL); it works with Secure Sockets Layer (SSL), Transaction Layer Security, Secure MIME, Kerberos, and other security systems and protocols deployed in Windows 2000.

Active Directory, Netscape's Directory Server, and NDS all use access control lists to provide security down to the directory objects and their attributes.

The Replication Model

This model is detailed for multi-server environments and defines how the directory information tree (DIT) is then replicated across servers.

The Management Model

This model defines how the tree is managed, either as a whole or in parts.

Both Active Directory and Novell's NDS, allow you to assign specific jobs to administrators so that they can manage selected subdomains or organizational units (OU).

NOTE

Active Directory Interoperability

Active Directory supports standards to provide a degree of interoperability with Microsoft products and third-party vendors.

Application Programming Interface

There are two APIs that can be used to access data stored in Active Directory: the Active Directory Service Interface (ADSI) and the LDAP C API.

ADSI

Active Directory Service Interface (ADSI) supports access to the objects stored in Active Directory. The new access method is also referred to as Component Object Model (COM) objects. COM began life as DDE and OLE for the object linking and embedding of data records across a network between clients and server locations.

The classic example is the manager who doesn't know how to use computers that well, yet needs to know how the company is doing. A spreadsheet could be created for the manager so he or she can view it with summarized data pulled from different departments, and network locations throughout the company. Using OLE and DDE, a master spreadsheet could be linked with several other spreadsheets stored in different locations around the network. When the manager started up his spreadsheet, in the background his computer queried the other linked spreadsheets and provided an updated view of the company's data.

OLE and DDE became the component object model (COM), allowing us to perform linking and embedding across the network and across the Internet, with security features added in.

COM then became DCOM, the Dynamic Component Object Model that allows for distributed applications in the active directory world of Windows 2000. With Active Directory, the choices of objects we can link with are much more than just spreadsheets or documents. Since everything in our 32-bit world is a defined object, we can link and embed with almost anything using COM as a communication tool. For COM access, "providers" are available for NetWare's NDS, Windows NT, Windows 95/98, LDAP, and the IIS metabase.

LDAP C API

The LDAP C API is a set of low-level C language APIs linked to the LDAP protocol. It is supported on all Windows platforms.

Synchronization

Directory synchronization services are provided with Windows 2000 for synchronizing Active Directory with the applications listed in Table 1.6.

TABLE 1.6

Synchronization services.

Application	Service Provided
Exchange 5.5	Active Directory Connector
Novel NDS	Services for NetWare 5.0
Lotus Notes	Supported when Exchange 2000 ships
GroupWise	Supported when Exchange 2000 ships

Backward Compatibility

Windows 2000 Servers are installed in a default mode called a mixed mode configuration that supports both Windows NT backup domain controllers and Windows 2000 domain controllers. Active Directory also supports mixed mode for the purpose of both NT 4.0 servers and clients authenticating with the Windows NT LAN Manager authentication protocol. As a result, older Windows 95/98 and NT 4.0 clients can log on and access resources in a Windows 2000 Domain.

Microsoft Management Console (MMC)

Active Directory Tools are contained as a "snap-in" component. This new interface is used for all Windows 2000 tools and utilities and was first used in Internet Information Server 4.0 administration, as detailed in Figure 1.13.

Figure 1.13
The Microsoft Management console (MMC).

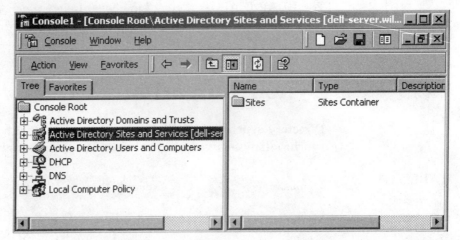

Although the initial introduction to the MMC with the term "snap in" can be confusing, it's actually a slick idea. Microsoft provides the empty shell of a utility called the "tool host" in official development lingo, and you fill in (snap in) each software component you want to use. The current version of MMC is 1.1 and can be activated by typing in MMC using the run option from the Start menu. After filling up your MMC console you can save your electronic toolbox as a console file with the .msc extension. This file can then be sent to other administrators at different locations for their use.

Administrative Solutions: Creating Custom MMCs

Using the MMC is the only framework for using Windows 2000 utilities. There are several default MMC consoles included with Windows 2000 and others can be easily created from the UI. The extension used to save all MMC consoles is .MSC.

Creating an MMC for Local Administration

1. Click the **Start** button select **Search** and **For Files or Folders**.
   A. Search for files with the .MSC extension—you will find several consoles displayed.
   B. Double-click on the file devmgnt.msc—this will open the Device Manager.
   C. Try several others, for example compmgmt.msc and msinfo32.msc.
   D. Close the Search Results screen.
2. Click the **Start** button and select **Run**.
   A. Enter the text **mmc** and click **OK**. An empty console called Console1 will open.
   B. Maximize the Console1 and Console Root window.
   C. To check on the currently configured options click the **Console** button and select **Options**.
      The default operating mode when creating custom MMCs is Author mode. Take a few moments to select and read the description for the four console modes. You can choose the User mode that limits any changes from being made to MMCs that you create for other users or administrators.
   D. Make sure that the Author Mode is selected and then click **OK**.
   E. Click the **Console** button and select **Save As...**.
   F. In the File Name: box type **Disk Management** and then click **Save**.
   G. From the Console menu select **Exit**.
3. Click **Start**, point to Programs I Administrative Tools and select **Disk Management**. Your MMC that was just created should load.
   A. From the top left corner, click the **Console** button and select **Add/Remove Snap-in...**. The Add/Remove Snap-in dialog box is displayed.

    B.   Since this is the first custom MMC to be created, all snap-ins must be added to the Console Root.

    C.   Click **Add** to display the Add Standalone Snap-in screen.

    D.   Scroll through the list of displayed options and first select **Disk Defragmenter** and click **Add**. Your choice will be added to the Add/Remove Snap-in Standalone tab.

    E.   Click **Add** to display the Snap-in choices.

    F.   Select **Disk Management** and click **Add**. MMC displays the Choose Computer dialog box, allowing you to select the computer to administer. Make sure the Local computer is selected and click **Finish**.

    G.   In the Add Standalone Snap-in dialog box, click **Close**.

    H.   In the Add/Remove Snap-in dialog box, click **OK**.

    I.   From the Console menu select **Exit** and click **Yes** to save your console settings.

Creating Custom MMCs

Custom MMCs can be created for local users and then customized by modifying the available extensions of the snap-ins selected and by changing the mode of operation of the MMC.

1.   Click the **Start** button and select **Run**.

    A.   Enter the text **mmc** and click **OK**. An empty console called Console1 will open.

    B.   Maximize the Console1 and Console Root window.

    C.   Click the **Console** button and from the menu select **Add/Remove Snap-in**.

    D.   From the Standalone tab click **Add**. The Add Standalone Snap-ins: appears.

    E.   Click **Add** and select the snap-in Computer Management.

    F.   From the Computer Management splash screen select **Local computer** and click **Finish**.

    G.   Click **Close** and then **OK**.

    H.   Expand Computer Management and note the preconfigured System Tools Device Manager and Local Users and Groups. By removing extensions, particular tree items can be removed, allowing you to create a custom console with limited functionality.

2.   Click the **Console** button and from the menu, select **Add/Remove Snap-in**.

A. Click to highlight Computer Management (Local) and then select the **Extensions** tab.

B. Clear the Add all extensions check box, and from the Available extensions box clear the Device Manager and Local Users and Groups check box.

C. Click **OK**.

D. Expand Computer Management and note the removal of the System Tools Device Manager and Local Users and Groups.

E. Click the **Console** button and from the menu select **Options**.

F. From the Options splash screen change the Console mode to User mode—full access. Take a moment to review what this mode of operation removes.

G. Click the **Console** button and from the menu select **Save as**.

H. From the Save in dialog box select **Desktop**.

I. Save this custom console as Local Toolset.

J. Click the **Console** menu and select **Exit**.

K. Click the **Desktop** shortcut beside the Start button to display the Desktop.

L. Double-click the **Local Toolset** to launch the MMC.

M. Click the *Console* button and attempt to add a snap-in. Can you? You shouldn't be able to.

Active Directory Architecture

Chapter topics include:

- Windows 2000 Server architecture and Active Directory components
- Objects, organizational units (OU) and attributes
- Naming conventions used in Active Directory
- Active Directory components
- Logical and physical structure
- Replication issues
- Global catalog servers
- DNS and namespace rules

Active Directory Architecture

The importance of understanding both the logical and physical pieces of Active Directory cannot be overstated. The architecture and components of AD determine the effectiveness of the design of your initial directory structure; long-term support and maintenance of your Windows 2000 network require that these concepts are fully understood.

Figure 2.1
Windows 2000 and Active Directory architecture.

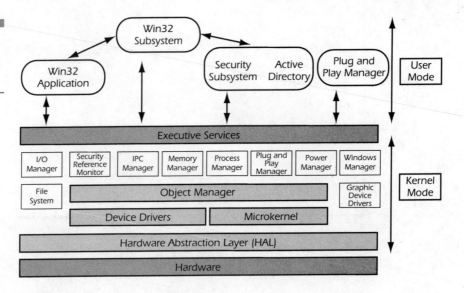

Security Subsystem

The security subsystem is located in the user module where Active Directory executes, as detailed in Figure 2.1. The user mode has several components called *environment subsystems*. Software applications written for the 32-bit Windows 98/NT world and 32-bit utilities that execute at the command prompt are supported by one of the subsystems, the Win32 subsystem. All application programming requests (APIs) for services first start in user mode, but are then transferred to the kernel mode where each service is located, and run in protected mode. Think of each subsystem as a created world supplying the required environment for supported software and services to execute successfully.

Directory Access

In kernel mode, the security reference monitor is responsible for enforcing the security for Windows 2000 and Active Directory and the type of access control assigned to each object. A software application will not be allowed access to a resource located in Active Directory without proper authentication and authorization, key terms to understanding the security used in Windows 2000 and throughout the directory.

- **Authentication**—Any access to a directory object will require proper proof that you are a valid user or network service; this is determined by the security subsystem.
- **Authorization**—The next step is the validation of your access permissions; it is carried out by the security subsystem along with the security reference monitor.

Security Subsystem Architecture

Windows 2000 security uses Kerberos security software components that create the Windows security model for Active Directory and domain controllers. The security subsystem tracks and mandates the security policies and active user accounts that are active within each domain controller. The security policies and user accounts are stored and referenced in Active Directory as shown in Figure 2.2.

Security Subsystem Components

Four subsystem components make up the security subsystem.

Figure 2.2
Security architecture.

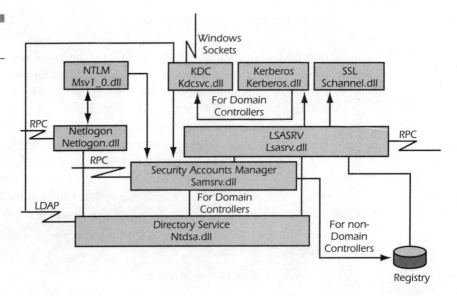

1. **Local Security Authority**—The management of the local security policy.
2. **Security Accounts Manager.**
3. **Secure Sockets Layer**—Secures network connections.
4. **Kerberos v5.0 authentication protocol**—Authenticates Windows 2000 users, hosts, and trusts between domains.

LOCAL SECURITY AUTHORITY (LSA)   The LSA runs as a protected subsystem in kernel mode and performs many functions, including the generation of access tokens for authenticated users and identifying the users allowed system access and privileges. When you enter your logon information (username and password) in the standard logon dialog box, the LSA is asked for verification for the user attempting to log on. Once LSA has verified your account, either locally or by communicating to the domain where your user account was created, the requested logon proceeds.

SECURITY ACCOUNTS MANAGER (SAM)   The SAM service is used for storage of all local user accounts on Windows 2000 Professional Clients, member servers, and standalone servers where Active Directory is not installed. In the NT 4.0 network, each domain controller or standalone NT workstation contained a Registry hive, also called SAM, for storage of user account information. In Windows 2000, the SAM is still available but is used only for local authentication, if Active Directory is installed and functioning. If problems prevent Active Directory from functioning, then the only way to log on to a domain controller is to use the security information stored in the local registry SAM hive.

SECURE SOCKETS LAYER (SSL)   The SSL service allows secure network connections over nonsecure network connection using a security handshake involving public-key encryption.

KERBEROS   Kerberos version 5.0 is the security process used by Windows 2000 to identify users and hosts through the authentication service. Kerberos uses "shared secrets" to authenticate and verify users. The basic concept is this: If you know a secret, and tell one other person the secret, either of these two people can verify the secret to another party. If I share a password with Janice, say cravethirst, for sending email between us and no-one else knows this password, then either Janice or I can use this password to verify all email messages.

This simple example is taken to the next level with Kerberos, where a password must be verified without revealing the actual password. This is done through a process called secret-key cryptology. Instead of sharing the password, a shared key is used to both encrypt and decrypt information. Each participant uses the knowledge of the key to verify or prove someone's identity; however there are three parties involved in Windows 2000: the client, the server, and a trusted third party called the KDC (the key distribution center). In Greek mythology, Kerberos, also known as Cerberus, was a three-headed dog that guarded the Greek underworld.

The KDC runs as a network service on every domain controller containing account information for every security principal in its world, the local domain. A security principal is a user, group, or member server. What the KDC does is store a cryptographic key known to itself and each security principal. When a Windows 2000 client sends its logon security credentials to a domain controller, it and the server will each receive a unique session key from the KDC to communicate with each other. The server decrypts the user's information with its own secret key and can verify the end-user's identity. IP security (Ipsec) and the quality of service (QoS) Admission Control Service also use Kerberos for authentication.

Directory Service Architecture

The security subsystem has been enhanced for Windows 2000 with three service layers providing the support for Active Directory security as shown in Figure 2.3.

Figure 2.3
Security subsystem
levels.

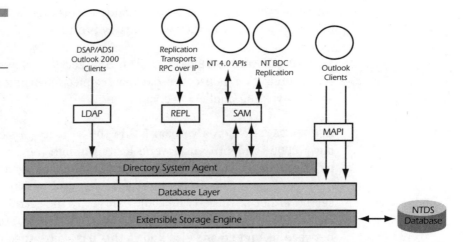

- **The Directory System Agent (DSA)**—This provides directory access calls to the physical copy of the directory stored on the local hard drive. The DSA contains a directory partition that holds domain data, plus two nondomain directory partitions that contain forest-wide data.
- **Database Layer**—This layer accepts calls from applications that are in turn passed to the directory database itself.
- **The Extensible Storage Engine (ESE)**—This stores and can access each record (stored as an object) in the database. The indexing engine for Active Directory is similar to the ESE used in Exchange Server 5.5.

Directory System Agent Functions

Some of the other functions provided by the directory system agent (DSA) are:

IDENTIFICATION OF OBJECTS Objects stored in Active Directory are identified by a GUID (Globally Unique IDentifier). This is an identifier that is always unique and never reused. You may have seen them used in the Windows 98 and NT 4.0 Registry to identify objects uniquely.

UPDATES TO THE SCHEMA An update to the schema adds or changes objects, classes, and attributes and is performed as a single-master operation, to only one domain controller. Changes are then replicated, and these changes can never be deleted, just disabled.

ENFORCEMENT OF ACCESS CONTROL   The DSA tracks and enforces security by reading the SIDs on the access token in order to verify proper access.

REPLICATION   The DSA performs replication services when updates occur.

REFERRALS   If required, the DSA performs all cross-referencing of the directory across the installed hierarchy of multiple domains.

NOTE

The directory is stored in a file called NTDS.DIT found in the WINNT\NTDS folder on a domain controller. The database can be up to 16 terabytes in size.

How Do We Access Active Directory?

Access to Access Directory is normally through one of the following four methods (Figure 2.4):

1. Lightweight Directory Access Protocol (LDAP)
2. Message API (MAPI)
3. Security Accounts Manager (SAM)
4. Replication (REPL)

LDAP

Lightweight Directory Access Protocol (LDAP) is the core protocol for Active Directory, which runs directly over TCP/IP or UDP transports. LDAP is a protocol, not a directory specification; there is no such thing as an LDAP directory. LDAP was developed as a preference of Directory Access Protocol (DAP), the defined protocol for exchanging information with an X.500 directory service. The primary reason for LDAP's development was to be able to use TCP/IP for the network transport; DAP specifies that the Open Systems Interconnection stack must be used for transport. Windows 95/98, NT 4.0, and Windows 2000 client software are examples of the LDAP client software; a Web browser is another.

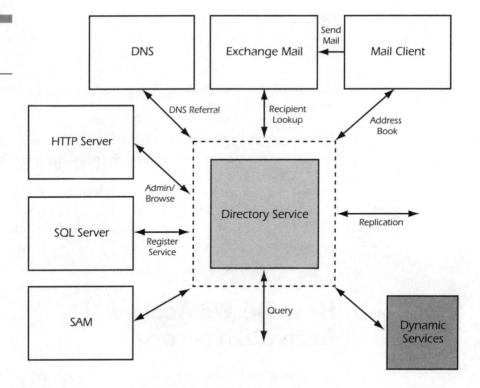

Figure 2.4
Active Directory
access.

Messaging API (MAPI)

Messaging API (MAPI) clients are, for example, Outlook clients that communicate with active directory through the directory system agent (DSA) with the MAPI RPC address book interface.

Security Accounts Manager (SAM)

Windows 4.0 clients use the Registry SAM API interface to communicate with the DSA.

Replication (REPL)

Replication (REPL) is used by Active Directory through the DSA to perform domain controller directory replication throughout the directory through remote procedure calls.

How Does Active Directory Function as a Directory Service?

When all three of its essential components are operational and in synchronization (Figure 2.5):

1. The Internet Domain Naming System (DNS) is available for locating the directory (Active Directory).
2. X.500 naming standards are respected as they apply to Windows 2000 and LDAP access to the directory.
3. LDAP is used for directory access as the core protocol.

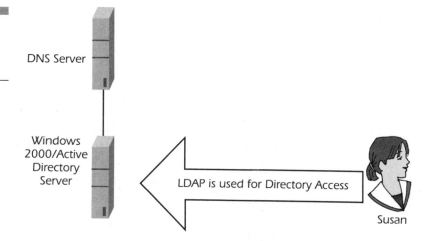

Figure 2.5
DNS, LDAP, and Active Directory work together.

DNS Server

Windows 2000/Active Directory Server

LDAP is used for Directory Access

Susan

Active Directory Components: Objects and Attributes

When objects are created in Active Directory they are created in a hierarchical structure in containers that branch down from the root container, similar to the roots of a tree as shown in Figure 2.6. Objects considered leaves can include shared resources such as printers, folders, servers, shared volumes, network users, applications, security, and just about anything you can think of that is used and shared across your network topology. Active Directory stores objects and information about objects found across a network hierarchy of domains and domain controllers that create a tree or a forest.

Figure 2.6
A sample company's
structure.

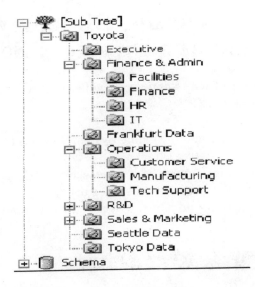

Accessing a Windows 2000 network and the resources stored in Active Directory normally requires a defined user object in the directory. Two types of objects can be created: *containers* and *leaves*. Objects called containers can also contain other objects. An example of this is a Domain, which is defined as a container object containing users, groups, and computers. Leaves are called *noncontainers*, since they cannot hold other objects. A user cannot be placed inside another user; it is called a *leaf object*. The user account object is shown in Figure 2.7.

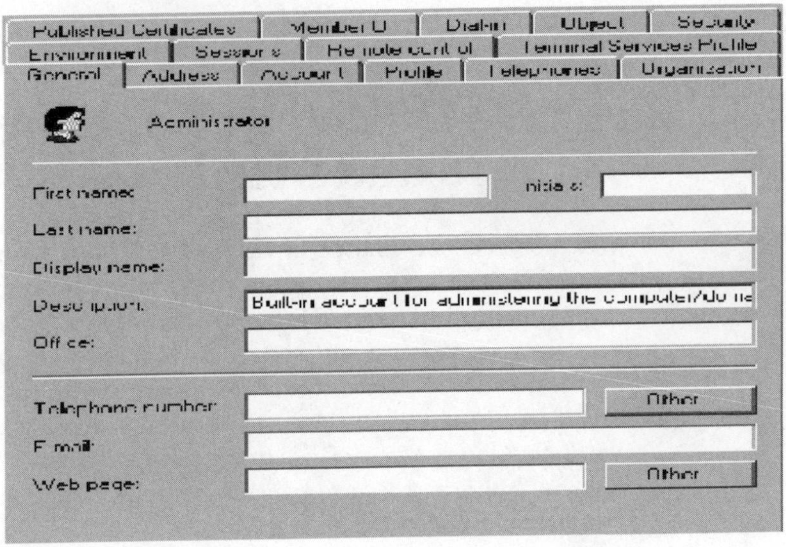

Figure 2.7
A User Account is a
leaf object.

Attributes

An attribute is a method or way of identifying a defined object stored in the directory. Although the normal way to find a user object in the directory is to search using the name, another user's attributes could also be utilized to locate the desired user. The user account's attributes are "characteristics" that describe the user's account. It is important to enter as many object attributes as possible when creating a new object in the directory. Human nature is to enter as little as possible, which may suffice if your network is small. As your directory increases in size and scope the attributes that define each object become very important. Other optional attributes will be used depending on the object created in the directory. For example, for a user object, the user's phone number and email address would be common attributes. Each class of object in the Active Directory database structure, called the *schema,* has both mandatory and optional attributes.

Mandatory Attributes

Each object has mandatory attributes that ensure each object is uniquely identified in the Directory. Microsoft has retained compatibility with the standards maintained by LDAP for directory object names by importing the entire X.500 base attribute set into Active Directory. As shown in Figure 2.8, when a network printer is installed, some attributes will be automatically configured. Some of these objects will be mandatory, such as a port to print to, or a paper tray, depending on the actual printer type. These attributes can be used to locate the printer in Active Directory.

Active Directory Physical and Logical Components

Active directory can be viewed as logical or physical components. The logical view is for the design aspect of Windows 2000 and Active Directory; the goal is a directory structure that works with your company or organization. The physical view is the network components where Active Directory and Windows 2000 execute.

Logical Components

Used to mirror the logical structure of your company, these include domains, trusts, trees, forests, containers, and organizational units.

Figure 2.8
A printer will have
several mandatory
attributes.

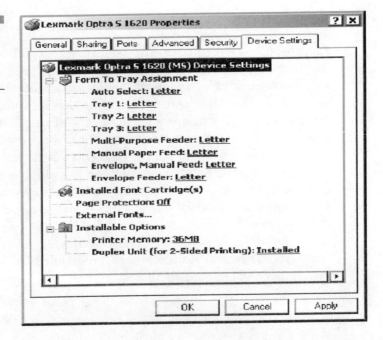

Physical Components

Used to develop a directory structure that mirrors the physical structure of your company, these include Domain controllers, subnets, and sites (collections of physical subnets).

Containers

Inside Active Directory is a hierarchical structure of containers, since every object has to be contained by something, a container. Containers you will create on a regular basis to hold users and groups are called *organizational units* (OUs). There are also special kinds (classes) of containers created by the operating system, such as DNS-based domain containers for holding server components or default groups and containers such as Built in, Computers, and Lost and Found. When a Windows 2000 server has Active Directory added by executing DCPROMO, the server becomes a domain controller, and the operating system creates a number of default containers, as shown in Figure 2.9, through the Active Directory Sites and Services console.

Figure 2.9
Default containers
created after
DCPROMO executes.

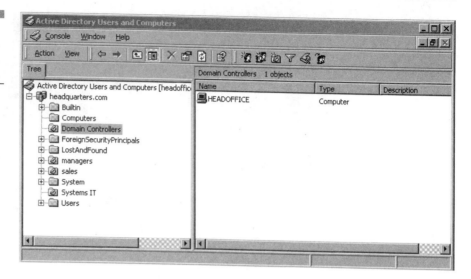

Each domain contains a child container called *configuration*; the configuration container also has a child container called *schema*.

NOTE

Containers cannot be created from the GUI; we create containers called organizational units rather than containers to contain objects. Scripts could create containers; however the operating system is normally the only process where a container is created.

Organizational Units (OU)

Organizational units (OU) are logical containers that you can create using the Active Directory Users and Computers, as shown in Figure 2.10, to place objects such as user accounts, groups, computers, printers, file shares, and other organizational units. An OU is the smallest unit to which you can assign or delegate administrative authority with a wizard. OUs cannot contain objects from other domains. Each OU is like an "electronic container" used in Active Directory to organize each domain into a logical grouping that represents your company structure. An OU is a container with additional attributes for specifying address, phone, and email information about the department, division, project, or whatever is contained inside the OU.

Each OU is also an administrative boundary that can link to group policy objects (GPOs), the powerful replacement for system policies assigned

Figure 2.10
Creating an OU with
ADUG.

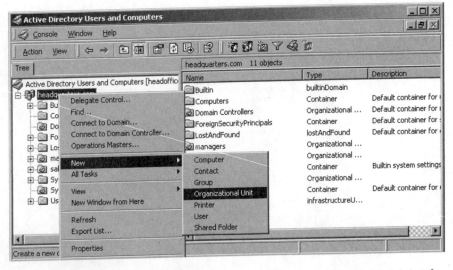

to all users and computers contained (directly or by descendants) in the OU. This also provides a method for delegating administration.

Delegation of Administration

Active Directory supports the delegation of administration of containers and subtrees to other users and groups, as Figure 2.11 details. With OUs, a complete hierarchal structure can be created that mirrors your company's real structure. You could then create a tree of OUs and delegate authority for certain parts of the OU tree to specific users or groups.

Logical Structure: Domains

The basic unit of logical structure for Active Directory is the domain. Each domain can store millions of objects. A domain is a defined administrative and security boundary used in Windows 2000 networks as detailed in Figure 2.12. The rules of operation and delegation have substantially changed from Windows NT 4.0 networks; a domain is an administrative boundary for a collection of objects and containers such as OUs. Permissions can be inherited from OU to OU, and from OU to object, based on containment in the domain, just as files can inherit folder permissions within a partition or volume.

Figure 2.11
Delegating
administration
through OUs.

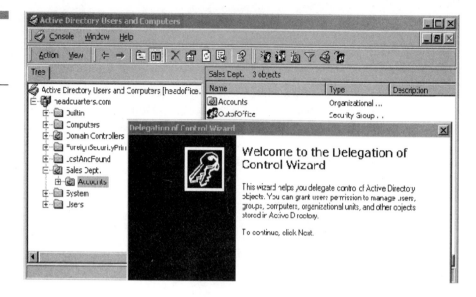

Figure 2.12
Domain structure.

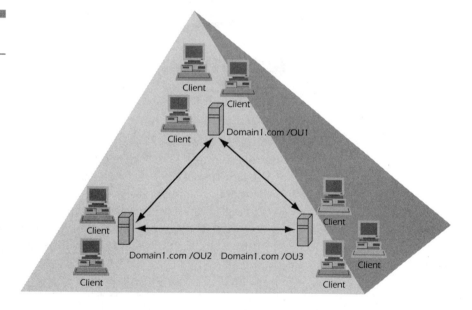

A proper design makes use of all the logical and physical parts of Active Directory; a typical structure is a logical domain containing a number of organizational units. Objects stored in the OU are the resources required for your users to carry out their day-to-day tasks. Just as files and folders are the main objects of interest to users, objects and containers (such as OUs) are the main focus of users for navigating the directory.

Domains Aid Administration

Domains can be used to define administrative permissions that do not go across domain boundaries. Security policies and settings will not cross from one domain into another domain by default. Administrative authority can be delegated either by the domain or by organizational unit, reducing any one administrator's authority across the entire domain unless so desired. Other concepts of domains in Windows 2000 networks are detailed in Table 2.1.

TABLE 2.1

Windows 2000 logical domain concepts.

- The clustering of organizational units together creates a domain.
- The suggested practical number of objects stored in a domain is one million (per domain).
- All network objects exist within a domain.
- Each domain stores only the information about the objects contained.
- Once implemented, Active Directory contains at least one domain.

Logical Structure: Domain Trees

Several domains that form a seamless contiguous namespace construct a domain tree. For Windows 2000, a tree is a set of one or more domains with contiguous names. The first domain in a tree is called the root of the tree; the additional domains in the same tree are called *child* domains. The domain immediately above a domain in the same tree is called the *parent* of the child domain. The domain name of the child domain is the relative name of the child name appended with the name of the parent domain. In Figure 2.13 gk.com is the parent domain and us.gk.com and uk.gk.com are its child domains. The child domain of uk.gk.com is abc.uk.gk.com.

Domain Tree Rules

- Domains in a single tree share a contiguous namespace.
- Domains in a single tree share a single schema.
- Domains in a single tree share a global catalog—the central location for all information about all objects in the tree.

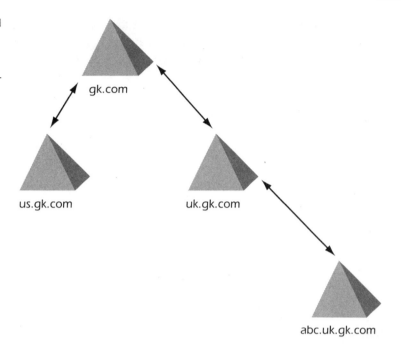

Figure 2.13
Domain and
subdomain naming.

- An administrator in a parent domain is not automatically made an administrator of a child domain.
- Once a hierarchy of domains has been created within a logical tree structure, security can be delegated to a single domain of the tree or to a single OU.

Logical Structure: Forests

An Active Directory forest is a distributed database with one or more trees, as shown in Figure 2.14. A forest is a set of one or more trees that do not form a common namespace. The Directory database is made up of many partial databases distributed among multiple computers installed as domain controllers. Two forest-wide administrative groups are created by default in the forest root domain: *enterprise administrators* and *schema administrators*.

All domain controllers in a forest host a copy of the forest configuration, the schema container, and one domain database. The local domain database contains the directory objects (user, computers, and groups) that can be granted or denied access to the network resources. Multiple domain trees within a single forest do not form a contiguous namespace; they have noncontiguous DNS domain names. For example, globalknowledge.com, arg.com, and globalknowledge.ca must be in separate trees.

Figure 2.14
Active directory forest structure.

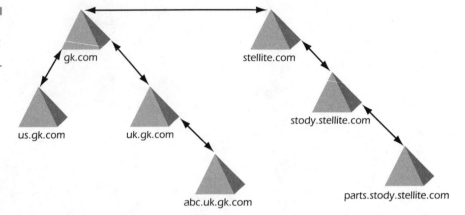

Root Domain Rules

- The forest has a singe root domain called the forest root domain.
- By default the forest root domain is the first domain created in the forest.
- Trees share a common set of cross-relationship objects and Kerberos trust relationships known to the member trees in the forest.

Domain Concepts: Brain Twisters

- A domain is the smallest unit of partitioning and the smallest unit of authentication.
- If your company has a single domain structure, remember:
    - The single domain can contain just one OU.
    - The single domain is also one forest.
    - The single domain is also one forest containing one tree.
- The initial install of Windows 2000 contains a default number of containers and OUs; you could decide to use one additional organizational unit to hold all of your company objects.
- You can nest OUs within each other, creating a hierarchical structure.
- Each domain can have its own hierarchy of OUs, or the OU hierarchy can be identical in each domain. However, an OU cannot be extended across domains.

The Schema

The schema is the formal definition of all object classes, attributes, and syntax that make up the defined object classes that can be stored in the Active Directory. The schema describes the object classes and attribute types in Active Directory, as shown in Figure 2.15. Each attribute type is defined once but used in many different classes. The schema definitions are stored as class schema objects and attribute schema objects. The attributes in each class of objects found in the schema guarantee unique identification of each object in the directory data store.

Figure 2.15
The schema console allows you to view the schema.

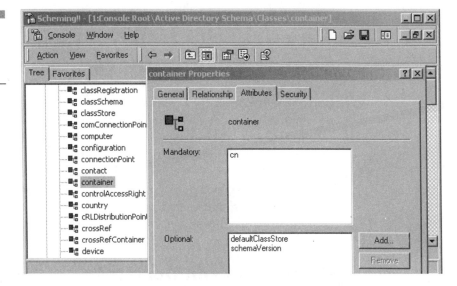

Each object in Active Directory is an instance of one or more of the classes in the Directory. For example, a user cn=Janice exists as an instance of the User class. Rules are defined about what type of data can be stored in an attribute. For each class of object, the schema defines the attributes the object will have, the additional attributes it may have, and the object class that can be its parent.

Object classes that can be defined include users, groups, computers, domains, organizational units, and security policies.

Editing the Schema

When Windows 2000 is first installed, a set of basic classes and attributes is included. The schema can be extended to include new classes and attributes. However, any additions made to the schema cannot be deleted, only deactivated. Microsoft recommends that the changes be made through Application Directory Service Interface (ADSI).

Other administrative tools such as the LDAP Data Interchange Format utility (LDIFDE) and the MMC Active Directory Schema snap-in can also be used (with caution.) For example, in your company you may have a definition that is not included in the basic schema, such as asset tags; you could add this to the schema. Proper planning and testing on a test machine or network is strongly advised before changing any settings in the schema. At this point in Windows 2000, schema editing is not common.

Physical Structure: Domain Controllers

Each domain controller can host exactly one domain. Domain controllers automatically update changes through the process of multi-master replication with the other domain controllers for their domain. Having more than one physical domain controller in a domain provides fault tolerance and localized access. Trust relationships between all domains are transitive two-way trusts unless manually changed to one-way trusts. Each Windows 2000 domain controller stores and replicates a copy of the domain directory throughout the domain tree.

Replication and Domains

A domain contains at least one or more domain controllers; therefore all domain controllers within the domain will have a complete copy, or replica, of the local domain's portion of the directory. Domains within Active Directory use a new domain model: the multi-master peer-control model. Domain controllers in a domain automatically replicate all objects in the domain among themselves using multi-master replication.

Fault Tolerance

Having more than one physical domain controller in a domain provides fault tolerance—if one domain controller goes off line another domain controller can provide all required operating system functions.

Trusts

All domains that are in trees are associated with each other by two-way transitive trust relationships. A trust relationship is now "transitive and hierarchical," which means if Domain A trusts Domain B, and Domain B trusts Domain C, Domain A will also trust Domain C, as shown in Figure 2.16.

Figure 2.16
Kerberos transitive trusts between domains.

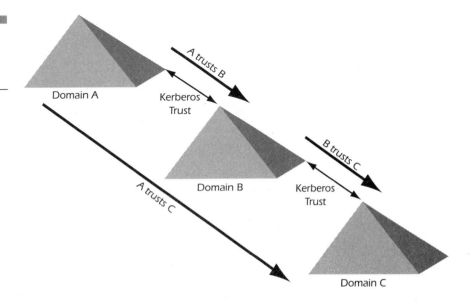

Physical Structure: Sites

In a Windows 2000 network, a site is a set of computers in one or more TCP/IP subnets. Sites are defined as one or more TCP/IP subnets connected using a local area network, as shown in Figure 2.17. Sites map the physical structure of your network, whereas domains map the logical structure of your company. Computers within a site are usually well connected as compared to the communication links between separate sites, which are connected with slower WAN links. The sites themselves are not part of the Active Directory namespace. A site contains only computer objects and connection objects for replicating between sites.

Figure 2.17
Three sites in one
domain.

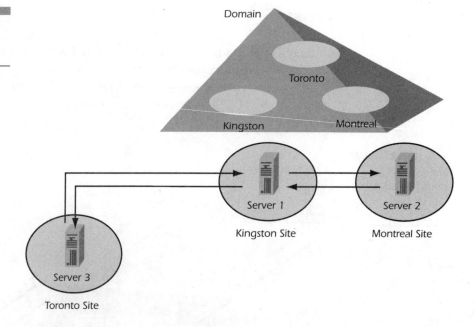

The Global Catalog

The global catalog holds directory information from all objects in a tree or forest. It is created automatically on the first domain controller in the forest and is known as the *global catalog server*. Universal group membership information is also stored in the global catalog.

The global catalog is required to complete the logon authentication process for a native-mode Windows 2000 network. If the global catalog were not available, logon would only be allowed onto the local node for the Domain Admins group. The global catalog works on an attribute search that is carried out across domains to find the desired object.

The global catalog stores a full replica of all the object attributes in the directory for its host domain, and also a partial replica (some attributes) of all objects for every other domain contained in the forest, as shown in Figure 2.18. The partial replica stores the most frequently used attributes, such as user's first and last name, or logon name. With the Active Directory Schema console, attributes can be added to the global catalog.

Figure 2.18
Global catalog
contains a partial
replica from all
domain controllers in
the forest.

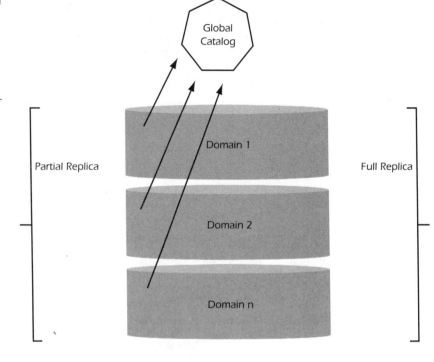

Partial Replica

Full Replica

Replication Details

Replication is the process that ensures that directory information is available to all Active Directory users and services at any time. Each server within a domain running Active Directory stores and maintains a complete copy of the domain directory. Any time information is changed at one of the domain controllers running Active Directory, it is replicated to the other servers through a process called "multi-master replication." Information stored in the directory is split into three categories and each of these categories is called a directory partition.

Directory Partitions

Each directory partition is an actual unit that will be replicated based on three types of information being stored in each directory on each domain controller: schema, configuration information, and domain data.

- **Schema Information**—Objects and attributes that are common to all domains in the domain tree or forest.
- **Configuration Information**—How the current Windows 2000/ Active Directory installation is set up and maintained (pertaining to domain setup and replication).
- **Domain Data**—Domain-specific data describe all the current objects, users, and groups created in a domain. These data are not replicated to other domains but only to other domain controllers in the same domain.

A subset of the domain data containing every object but a limited number of attributes is also stored in the global catalog server for searches across the domain tree or forest. Active Directory replicates information more frequently within a site, automatically generating a topology for replication between the domain controllers using a ring structure, as shown in Figure 2.19. The ring structure guarantees two replication paths from one domain controller to another.

Figure 2.19
Replication paths between domain controllers.

One Site Replication

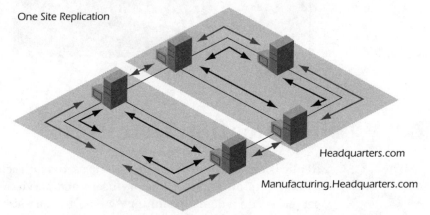

Headquarters.com

Manufacturing.Headquarters.com

Replication between sites across a WAN link requires that site links be manually created for the replication method used, including such factors as the replication protocol, cost, and when the link is available.

Naming Conventions Used with Active Directory

Names used to identify directory objects and their placement in Active Directory include Fully Qualified Domain Name, Distinguished Name, Relative Distinguished Name, and User Principle Name.

Fully Qualified Domain Name (FQDN)

A fully qualified name leaves no room for error when identifying a network object. With an FQDN, the exact location of the object can be identified.

As an example, user JohnW is located in the headquarters domain in a company called gk.com. JohnW's FQDN is johnw.headquarters.gk.com. When John prints to his printer, the printer will also have a FQDN, Printer1.headquarters.gk.com

If a computer system called System1 is located in the marketing domain of the gk.com tree its FDQN is, System1.marketing.gk.com

Relative Distinguished Name (RDN)

An RDN, as shown in Figure 2.20, identifies an object within the OU where it is located. Duplicate RDNs can be used for Active Directory objects, but two objects cannot have the same RDN in the same OU. As an example, user John must be unique in the Manufacturing OU where he is located, there can't be another user account called John in the same Manufacturing OU; there could be another user called John in another OU within the directory hierarchy.

Figure 2.20
A relative
distinguished name.

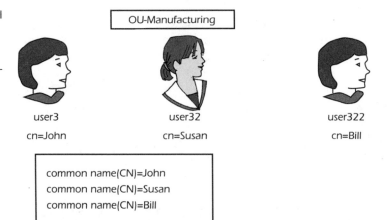

Distinguished Name (DN)

A DN, shown in Figure 2.21, is based on the X.500 naming conventions and is used to orient an object uniquely within the entire directory tree.

Within Active Directory, distinguished names use a prefix to identify an object's placement in the directory. Objects with the same duplicate RDN names can exist in separate OUs because they have different DNs.

Fig 2.21
Distinguished name.

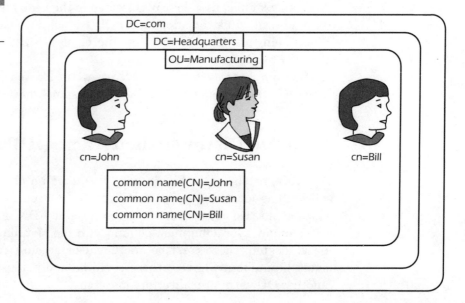

DC (domain component) is used for the domain DNS object class. OU is used for the organizational unit class. CN (common name) is used for the user object class.

NOTE

The distinguished name (DN) must be unique in the directory. The relative distinguished name (RDN) must be unique in the OU. Think of the objects real physical location when writing out a distinguished name.

User Principle Name (UPN)

The UPN is the one name you are most familiar with—your logon name is a UPN. It is created from the user's logon name and the domain name where the user object is located, as shown in Figure 2.22. Using the example of user Susan in the domain headquarters.com, the user principal name is susan@headquarters.com.

Figure 2.22
A user principle
name.

User logon name:

| Susan | @headquarters.com ▼ |

User logon name (pre-Windows 2000):

| HEADQUARTERS\ | Susan |

Logon Hours...   Log On To...

Globally Unique Identifier (GUID)

A GUID is a unique 128-bit number assigned to an object when the object is created in AD. Once created, the GUID for an object never changes, even if the object's name is changed later. Active Directory is "identity based." This means that objects are known internally by their identity, the assigned GUID, and not by their current name. The GUID is stored in a protected attribute called an objectGUID that is present on every object within the directory, as shown in Figure 2.23. It cannot be changed or removed. In Figure 2.23, the gPLink shows the GUID. When a reference to an object within Active Directory is stored in an external database like SQL Server, the objectGUID will be used as the reference, not a DN or RDN that could be changed.

Figure 2.23
GUIDs are always
unique.

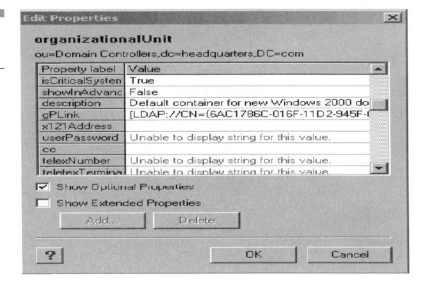

Edit Properties   ✕

organizationalUnit
ou=Domain Controllers,dc=headquarters,DC=com

Property label	Value
isCriticalSystem	True
showInAdvanc	False
description	Default container for new Windows 2000 do
gPLink	[LDAP://CN={6AC1786C-016F-11D2-945F-(
x121Address	
userPassword	Unable to display string for this value.
co	
telexNumber	Unable to display string for this value.
teletexTermina	Unable to display string for this value.

☑ Show Optional Properties
☐ Show Extended Properties

Add...   Delete

?   OK   Cancel

Domain Component (DC)

The common naming scheme for Active Directory is to use the DNS naming scheme for identification of objects. DNS is a required component of Active Directory, since domain component naming is used to locate objects, as shown in Figure 2.24.

Figure 2.24
Domain component
naming is required.

```
drawing1.ldf - Notepad                                          _ □ X
File  Edit  Format  Help

cn: cn=Users,DC=headquarters,DC=com
changetype: add
objectClass: top
objectClass: container
objectCategory: CN=Container,CN=Schema,CN=Configuration,DC=headquarters,DC=com
instanceType: 4
cn: Users
whenCreated: 2000/05/04 14:51:11
whenChanged: 2000/05/04 14:51:11
uSNCreated: 1314
uSNChanged: 1314
systemFlags: -1946157056
name: Users
distinguishedName: CN=Users,DC=headquarters,DC=com
isCriticalSystemObject: True
showInAdvancedViewOnly: False
description: Default container for upgraded user accounts
```

See the following examples:

FQDN: johnw.headquarters.gk.com
In DC notation: cn=JohnW,dc=headquarters,dc=gk,dc=com
FQDN: Printer1.headquarters.gk.com
In DC notation: cn=Printer1,dc=headquarters,dc=gk,dc=com
FQDN: System1.marketing.gk.com
In DC notation: cn=system1,dc=marketing,dc=gk,dc=com

DC in this context does not stand for domain controller.

NOTE

LDAP ADPaths

Access to Windows 2000/Active Directory objects occurs through LDAP system calls. The LDAP standard also defines what operations are performed, and in what order, when querying the directory or a specific directory object. LDAP paths are called ADPaths and all directory services can be accessed through ADPaths. Active Directory tools included with Windows 2000 do not show the LDAP syntax for the attributes being searched:

LDAP Syntax: LDAP:// dc=mycompany.dc=com

If a company's domain is **europe.headquarters.gk.com**
the ADSPath is **LDAP://dc=Europe,dc=headquarters,dc=gk,dc=com**.

Configuring Network Services

This chapter provides details on preparing for the deployment of Active Directory and describes the common network service infrastructure that must be present:

- Windows 2000 and TCP/IP changes
- Active Directory and Dynamic DNS
- DCHP and Dynamic DNS
- Resource record types
- WINS

Future Planning

Planning for the expansion of your current network hierarchy cannot be assumed to be a small component of Active Directory. In the next few years Active Directory could very well be integrated into the foundation of most corporate networks and even the Internet.

These changes could have a huge impact in the years to come as Windows 2000 integrates network services, protocols, and users to a degree not seen before in a network operating system. Active Directory will include the network hardware, application and operating system software, and security components.

With an NT 4.0 background, the mindset for the older legacy design was based on many architectural realities not required in the native Windows 2000/Active Directory networking world. But some of us will be working in what's called a mixed mode for the first few years, using Windows NT 4.0 and Windows 2000 servers. If this is your predicament this will be an important chapter. Windows 2000 must have DNS and TCP/IP in order to support Active Directory.

TCP/IP and Networking Services

TCP and IP are the best known of the protocols, so it has become common to use the term TCP/IP or IP/TCP to refer to the whole family of protocols and utilities shown in Figure 3.1. With the release of Windows 2000, the current version of Windsock supported is version 2.2. This version is backward compatible with older versions of Winsock. At the time of this writing Windows 2000 does not have an IPv6 stack; however, it

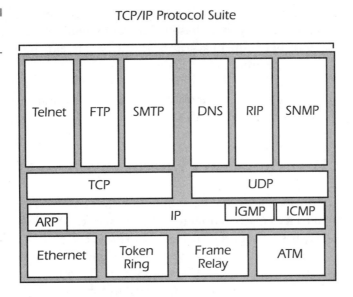

Figure 3.1
TCP/IP components.

will have one in the future that will work side by side with the current IPv4 stack.

All TCP/IP knowledge is in the public forum; the most up-to-date Internet location for RFCs is **www.rfc-editor.org**/. Some of the most common documents are shown in Table 3.1.

TABLE 3.1

RFCs for TCP/IP.

RFC #	Details
791	IP protocol
793	Transmission Control Protocol
1034	DNS Concepts
2131	Dynamic Host Configuration Protocol (DHCP)
2136	Dynamic Updates in DNS (Dynamic DNS)

Windows 2000 TCP/IP Features

- Windows 2000 supports the Routing Information Protocol (RIP) and the Open Shortest Path First (OSPF) protocol for exchanging routing tables with other routers.
- Generic quality of service (GqoS) allows network applications to reserve bandwidth required between a client and server using a width-reservation protocol called RSVP.

- Enhanced security is provided at the IP layer through IPSec, which uses cryptography-based security to monitor the paths between hosts, and between hosts and gateways. It can be assigned locally or through group policy using Active Directory.
- The TCP receive window, which specifies the amount of receive data, can be tuned automatically—the default window size is twice the size of NT 4.0 (16K vs. 8K).

Transmission Control Protocol (TCP)

TCP provides reliable, full-duplex connections between two hosts. It is called a connection-oriented delivery service; this means a connection must have been established between two hosts before data can be exchanged.

Each segment transmitted is assigned a sequence number, and an acknowledgment (ACK) verifies that the other host received the data. Each TCP connection is initialized in three steps confirming the synchronization of the sequence and acknowledgment numbers from both hosts.

1. The client sends a segment to the server containing the initial sequence number for the connection plus details of the buffer size at the client.
2. The server replies with a segment containing its initial sequence number, an acknowledgment of the client's sequence number, and the buffer size at the server.
3. The client sends a segment back to the server containing an acknowledgment of the server's sequence number. The key fields in each TCP datagram header are shown in Table 3.2.

TABLE 3.2

TCP Header fields.

TCP Header Field	Details
Source Port	TCP port of the sending host
Destination Port	TCP port of the destination host
Sequence Number	Specifies the first byte of data
Acknowledgment Number	Specifies the next byte of data to be received
Window	Size of the TCP buffer on the sending host
TCP Checksum	Performs an integrity check of the header and the data

Internet Protocol (IP)

IP is also a connectionless protocol used for routing packets between hosts. A session is not established before data are exchanged and data delivery is not guaranteed, although IP always makes the "best effort" to deliver a packet. Certain fields in the IP header, shown in Table 3.3, help describe IP operation.

TABLE 3.3

IP Header fields.

TCP Header Field	Details
Source IP address	IP address of the source node
Destination IP address	IP address of the final destination node
Protocol	The destination protocol used: TCP, UDP, or ICMP
Checksum	Verifies IP header's integrity
Time to live (TTL)	Defines the number of networks this packet is allowed to travel before being a discarded by a router

User Datagram Protocol (UDP)

UDP is a protocol used for transmitting data contained inside the TCP/IP protocol suite. Each data unit is sent with complete source and destination IP addresses and port numbers that identify the application-level processes involved in the data exchange, as shown in the TCP/IP architecture detailed in Figure 3.2.

UDP is called a connectionless transport protocol because it does not use a pre-established connection to transmit data; data can be sent without requiring that a data circuit be already established. As a result, UDP requires less overhead than TCP.

UDP does not, however, guarantee that data arrive in the order in which they are sent; TCP guarantees that messages are assembled in the order in which they are sent.

A big advantage of UDP over TCP is that it is more suited for applications that require broadcast data. A single datagram can be broadcast on the network by specifying a broadcast address on the destination address. UDP is popular in many LAN-based applications that are broadcast based and do not require the complexity of TCP.

Applications that use UDP are NFS, DNS, WINS, and SNMP. For example, a WINS server uses UDP for resolving NetBIOS names. In

Figure 3.2
TCP/IP architecture.

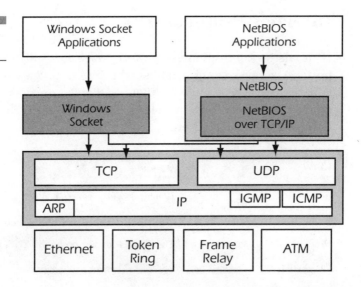

order to use UDP, the network service or application must provide the IP address and the UDP port number for the destination application or service. Table 3.4 lists well-known UDP ports.

TABLE 3.4

UPD ports.

UDP Port Number	Details
53	Domain Name System (DNS)
69	Trivial File Transfer Protocol (TFTP)
137	NetBIOS name service
161	SNMP

Network-Layer Addressing

32-bit numbers called IP addresses represent the internetwork-layer addresses. Each network interface in a node that supports an IP stack must have an IP address assigned to it. The IP address is a logical address independent of the underlying network hardware or network type. It consists of two parts: a network ID (netid) and a host ID (hostid). The most significant bits are used to determine how many bits are used for netid and hostid. Five address classes are currently defined: A, B, C, D, and E. Of these 5 classes, A, B, and C addresses are assignable. Class D is reserved for multicasting and is used by special protocols to transmit messages to a select group of nodes. Class E is reserved for future use. The netid portion of the IP address identifies the network uniquely. Interconnected networks must each have a netid.

Installing TCP/IP

TCP/IP is installed from the network and dial-up connections program group. Selecting the properties of the Local Area Connection displays TCP/IP from the listed protocols shown in Figure 3.3. If you are installing a Windows 2000 client, perhaps DHCP will be an option for automatically assigning IP addresses. The default for a client install of TCP/IP is DHCP. Obviously, for a file server installation, a static IP address must be chosen. DHCP details are found later in this chapter.

Figure 3.3
Installing TCP/IP.

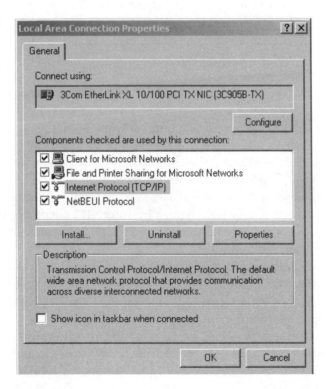

The beauty of installing most Windows 2000 network services is that you don't have to reboot.

TCP/IP and Non-Routable Addresses

If your current network will not be connected directly to the Internet but will instead be shielded from the public world by a firewall or proxy server, a special set of reserved numbers should be used. The use of these numbers saves an incredible amount of publicly assigned numbers. If your network computers are invisible on the Internet, using these special classes for your internal IP addresses keeps your network private, since routers will not route these numbers. These addresses are further defined in RFC 1918 and are listed in Table 3.5.

TABLE 3.5

Non-routable IP addresses.

1 class A network: 10.0.0.0 through 10.255.255.255

16 contiguous class B networks: 172.16.0.0 through 172.31.255.255

256 contiguous class C networks:192.168.0.0 through 192.168.255.255

Subnets and Subnet Masks

If you are connected to a large network spread out over a wide geographical area, there are probably routers lurking in the background that have divided the large network into several smaller subnets. This division will optimize network performance and also make it easier to troubleshoot and isolate network problems. If your company has been assigned a network address by InterNIC, then a process called subnetting has possibly been employed to divide a single IP address into smaller logical subnetworks.

Subnetting uses a host portion of an IP address to create a subnet address. A Class B subnet address will use the first two bytes to refer to the network address. All machines on the network, regardless of their particular subnet, share this network address.

For this to work, every computer on the network must know what part of the host address will be used as the subnet address. To accomplish this goal, each computer is assigned a subnet mask. The ones represent the network or subnet address. The zeros represent the host address, as shown in Figure 3.4.

Figure 3.4
Subnet addresses
define the network
and host ID.

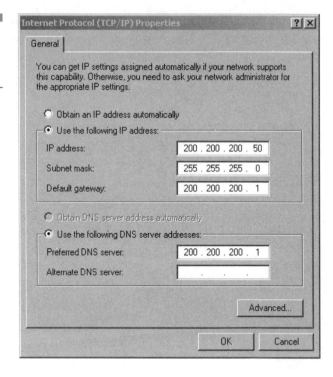

NetBIOS Over TCP/IP

In NT 4.0, using NetBIOS to map workstation and server names was a necessary task. However, with Windows 2000 networks, NetBIOS (also referred to as NetBT) may not be required, since it is not used for name resolution once Active Directory is enabled. Instead, DNS takes its place, and all network communications are sent with TCP using the TCP port 445 and not the NetBIOS session TCP port.

The Windows 2000 services listed below are NetBT clients and do respond to NetBIOS requests from older Windows clients. NetBIOS requests are still used if DNS is not available; however, this does not suggest that the DNS is not required; in fact, DNS is mandatory for network communications with Active Directory.

- Workstation
- Server
- Browser
- Messenger
- NetLogon

You may also have used Microsoft's NetBIOS name server WINS on your NT network. WINS may be nearing the end of its life on native Windows 2000 networks, but the age of your software applications and mail servers may dictate that NetBIOS and WINS stay a while longer. More details on WINS are found later in this chapter.

NOTE

The disabling of NetBIOS can be performed through the advanced properties of TCP/IP. Make sure any client/server software applications no longer require NetBIOS over TCP/IP before it is disabled.

Domain Name System (DNS)

In general, users can more easily remember symbolic names for the identification of hosts. The alternative is to remember the IP address of the host. The IP address of a host name is a 32-bit number, which most people find difficult to use and remember.

Figure 3.5
DNS communication steps.

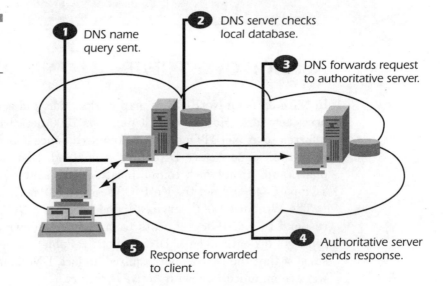

Any symbolic name used by the TCP/IP application service is translated to the equivalent 32-bit IP address. This translation is performed by the Domain Name System (DNS), which essentially acts as a names database (also called a *name server*). When given a host name, DNS translates it to an IP address, as detailed in Figure 3.5. DNS can also do reverse translations (also called *pointer queries*). This means that when given an IP address, DNS can return the host name registered for that IP address. DNS is implemented as a distributed database for looking up name-to-IP address associations.

Static Host Files

Another way of performing the name lookup is to keep the name-to-IP address information in a static file. On UNIX systems, this static file is the /etc/hosts file. On Windows NT computers, this static file was kept in the \drivers\etc\hosts file.

Windows NT computers can also use the LMHOSTS files for Net-BIOS over TCP/IP applications. The following sample host file shows an organization:

```
# Local network host addresses
# # ident "@(#) hosts 1.1—99/11/17"
 # 127.0.0.1 local lb localhost loopback
144.19.74.1 sparc1 sp1
144.19.74.2 sparc2 sp2
144.19.74.3 sparc3 sp3
144.19.74.4 sparc4 sp4
144.19.74.5 sparc5 sp5
```

The IP address 127.0.0.1 is a special address called the *loopback address*. Packets sent to this address never reach the network cable. The loopback address can be used for diagnostic purposes to verify that the internal code path through the TCP/IP protocols is working. Host files in a Native Windows 2000 network are no longer required due to the new dynamic feature of Microsoft's DNS service.

DNS Root Servers

The 13 name servers that currently manage the domain names at the root domain are listed below.

```
A.ROOT-SERVERS.NET 198.41.0.4 BIND (UNIX)
B.ROOT-SERVERS.NET 128.9.0.107 BIND (UNIX)
C.ROOT-SERVERS.NET 192.33.4.12 BIND (UNIX)
D.ROOT-SERVERS.NET 128.8.10.90 BIND (UNIX)
E.ROOT-SERVERS.NET 192.203.230.10 BIND (UNIX)
F.ROOT-SERVERS.NET 192.5.5.241 BIND (UNIX)
G.ROOT-SERVERS.NET 192.112.36.4 BIND (UNIX)
```

```
H.ROOT-SERVERS.NET 128.63.2.53 BIND (UNIX)
I.ROOT-SERVERS.NET 192.36.148.17 BIND (UNIX)
J.ROOT-SERVERS.NET 198.41.0.10 BIND (UNIX)
K.ROOT-SERVERS.NET 193.0.14.129 BIND (UNIX)
L.ROOT-SERVERS.NET 198.32.64.12 BIND (UNIX)
M.ROOT-SERVERS.NET 202.12.27.33 BIND (UNIX)
```

In the current public setup, the COM domain has one or more DNS servers that know the names of all commercial organizations in the COM domain. Within the COM domain, a subdomain such as IBM.COM will have its own DNS servers for its own domain. On Windows 2000 networks, hosts within a domain, domain tree, or forest query a specified DNS server for the domain to resolve names and provide essential network services.

DNS Details

In the naming scheme used in DNS, names are organized into a hierarchical tree. At the top of the tree is the root domain named by the period symbol (.)

The period is omitted when specifying the hierarchical root name in most TCP/IP applications. Below the root domain are top-level domains. These reflect how names are organized. The two-letter designations are assigned to a country as per the CCITT (now called ITU) standards and the ISO-3166 standard (except for Great Britain, which uses UK rather than the designated GB). These are the same country designations used for specifying country objects in NetWare Directory Services (NDS). Below the top-level domains are middle-level domains. Each name is separated from another by use of the period (which can never be used as part of the name of a domain). An example of a complete domain name is: archie.ans.net.

A name cannot exceed 255 characters. In the name archie.ans.net, the name of the host is archie. The domain is named ans.net. If another host, named wilkins, were in the same domain, its fully qualified domain name (FQDN) would be wilkins.ans.net.

Common Top-Level Domain Names

COM	Commercial organization
EDU	Education institution: universities, schools, etc.
MIL	Military
GOV	Government, U.S.A.
NET	Network provider

Middle-Level Names

Many of the public middle-level names refer to names of organizations. An organization is free to, and probably will, define subdomains within its own organization. If it does this it will need to provide appropriate DNS name services to resolve names in these subdomains for Active Directory.

Consider, for example, the organization SCS that has been given the following domain name: SCS.COM. If this organization has separate networks for its corporate, marketing, and research arms, it could define three separate subdomains named CORP, MKTG, RESCH, and provide a DNS server or a number of DNS servers to resolve names on its networks. The domains, in this case, would be named CORP.SCS.COM, MKTG.SCS.COM, and RESCH.SCS.COM.

Domain Name Details

As local government agencies, schools, and community colleges join the Internet, the public domain name organization under the U.S. domain has become more complex.

Membership in the U.S. domain is open to any computer in the United States. Over time, the U.S. domain has grown; it currently registers hosts in federal and state government agencies, technical/vocational schools, K-12 schools, community colleges, private schools, libraries, city and county government agencies, as well as in businesses and homes. The U.S. domain hierarchy is subdivided into states, and then localities (city or county), and then organizations, computer names, and so on.

The state codes are those assigned by the U.S. Postal Service. Within the state name, locality names such as cities, counties, or other local names are used, but incorporated entities are not.

Registered names under localities can be of the following types:

- hostname.CI.locality.state.US (for city government agency)
- hostname.CO.locality.state.US (for county government agency)
- hostname.locality.state.US (for businesses)

For example, the code of CI is used for a city government, and CO is used for a county government. Businesses are registered under the locality name. If a county and a city have the same locality name, uniqueness still is maintained because of the use of the CO or CI keyword.

Cities

Cities can be designated by their full names (spelled out with hyphens replacing spaces, as in San-Francisco or New-York), or by a city code. The preference should be to use the full city name. If it makes sense, you can also use a well-known city abbreviation known throughout a locality. It is desirable, however, for all users in the same city to use the same designator for the city. That is, any particular locality should have just one DNS name. For example, the fire department of Middle County in Montana (MT) could have the following DNS name: Fire-Dept.CO.Middle-County.MT.US. The state code is the postal code MT for Montana. The locality is Middle County. The keyword CO designates that this a reference to the county government. Fire-Dept is the name of the department in the Middle County government.

Understanding DNS and Windows 2000

The Domain Name System (DNS) is designed around the same hierarchical tree structure called a *domain namespace*. On the Internet this namespace is well known, and even if your background in DNS is limited, we've all heard of the .com address, one of the top-level Internet DNS domains along with .edu, .org, and .ca, among others. Within your company's private network .com may be not visible on the Internet; however, Windows 2000 has taken advantage of DNS structure. In fact, Windows 2000 must have DNS services running before a Windows 2000 server can be promoted to be a domain controller.

Fully Qualified Domain Name (FQDN)

The Domain Name System (DNS) requires a name format that matches its hierarchical structure. This is called a fully qualified domain name (FQDN) and is the name of the host that includes each level of the hierarchy from the host up to the root of the DNS tree, with each separated by dots, as shown in Figure 3.6. The fully qualified a domain name of the headquarters server in the gk.com domain under the commercial (.com) domain would be headquarters.gk.com.

Figure 3.6
A FQDN of a
Windows 2000
server.

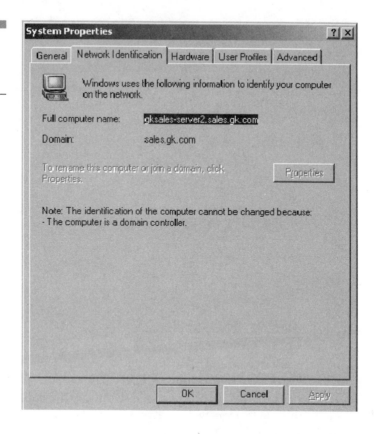

All DNS host names have periods in them. These types of names use a hierarchical naming convention from the specific to a general class. FQDNs also have naming restrictions that limit user to the characters a–z, A–Z, 0–9, and the dash or minus sign.

The use of the period is allowed only between domain names and also at the end of the FQDN. If the periods are not entered correctly, your DNS services will not work reliably, if at all.

NOTE

DNS Service Components

The following components provide the DNS service:

DNS Servers

These are computers running a DNS server program. This can be a Windows 2000 server running Microsoft's DNS server, or a third-party version. The function of the DNS server is to resolve (solve) a client's request for the location of a domain controller or network service. If the queried DNS server can't solve the user' request, it can point the user to another server that might help, and reply that it does not have that information.

DNS Resolvers

Resolvers are small utility programs that can query remote or local DNS servers for the required information.

Resource Records

These are records of information, stored in the DNS database, which point to a network resource. Each DNS server is typically in charge (authoritative) of a portion of the defined DNS namespace. DNS servers can also work together as a team, as in primary and secondary DNS server arrangements.

Zones

A zone is a contiguous portion of the DNS namespace of which the server is in charge (authoritative).

Zone Files

Zone files are text files containing resource records for the servers in authoritative zone. The zone file defaults to the zone name with a DNS extension. For example, if your zone were called gk.com, the default name is gk.com.dns. The zone name is based on the highest domain in the network hierarchy—in effect the "root" for that domain.

DNS and Name Resolution

The DNS system was developed to overcome the problems of name resolution on a large IP network. It provides a distributed database of names and IP addresses used predominantly for resolving host names for the TCP/IP protocols. TCP/IP application software can also be configured to use DNS to resolve names. When a TCP/IP application encounters a host name, it sends a query to a network service, usually running on the host computer, called the *name resolver* to translate the name to an IP address, as shown in Figure 3.7. If the name resolver cannot find the answer, it sends the query to a known name server. If the name server cannot find the answer, the query can be sent to another name resolver on the TCP/IP network.

Figure 3.7
DNS operation.

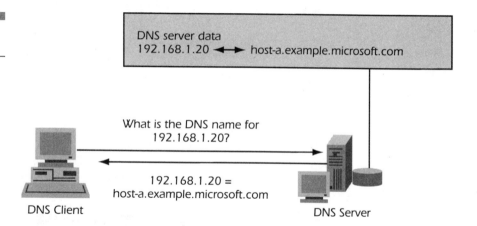

DNS and UDP

The DNS system relies on a query/response type of behavior and uses the UDP protocol as the transport protocol. The UDP protocol is best suited for applications that are query/response-based because there is no overhead of maintaining a connection for transmitting data.

NOTE

The most widely used implementation of DNS is the Berkeley Internet Name Domain (BIND) server, originally made available on BSD UNIX, but now available on most UNIX platforms. BIND 8.2.2 patch level 5 is the latest version of ISC BIND 8. On UNIX systems, it is often called the named (name daemon) program.

Lookup Queries

The DNS name server resolves both forward and reverse lookup queries.

A forward lookup query resolves a name to an IP address; the reverse lookup query resolves an IP address to a name. A name server can only resolve a query for a zone over which it has authority—for example, the name server on a local network can only resolve addresses within its local database. When a name server cannot resolve the query, it is passed to a name server it hopes can resolve the query.

What Is a Zone?

Zones are supported by the DNS service, which allows the dividing up of the namespace into one or more zones, as shown in Figure 3.8. Although you may be used to DNS storing the IP data type, in fact DNS can store much more information. This information is called a *resource record*, in short form RR. The simple host name-into-IP address association is called an Address (A) RR. Clients query DNS severs for services they are trying to locate, such as an Internet mail server [(MX) RR]. DNS uses name servers to maintain information about the domain tree structure. Each server contains a subset of the domain information, called a zone, which is then automatically distributed to redundant name servers, or, in English, more than one DNS server. Each zone would then store name information for one or more DNS domain(s).

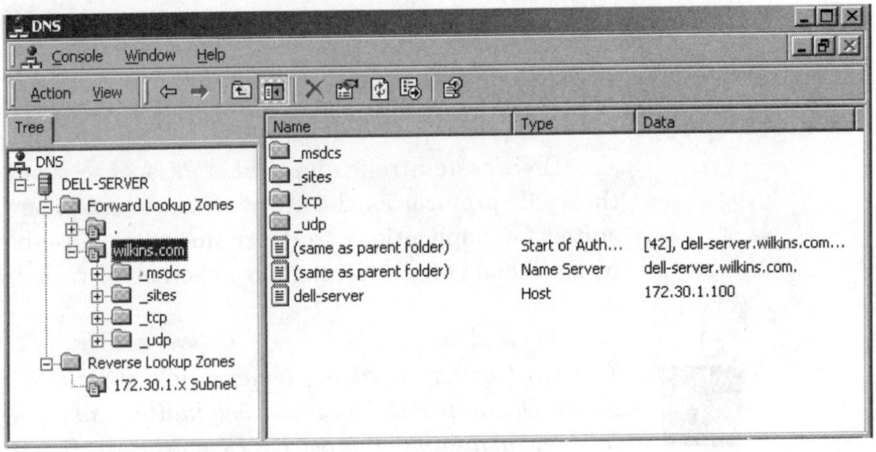

Figure 3.8
DNS zones.

Forward Lookup Queries

To resolve a forward-lookup query—resolving a host name to an IP address—a client passes the queries to a local name server. The local server can either resolve the query, or it queries another name server for resolution, as shown in Figure 3.9.

Figure 3.9
Forward lookup
query details.

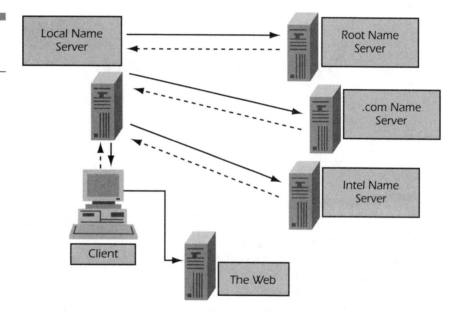

Resolving a Forward Lookup Query to Microsoft.com

1. A Windows 2000 client passes a forward lookup query for www.Microsoft.com local name server on the network.
2. The local name server on the network looks in its own database file to figure out if it contains the name-to-IP address mapping for the client's query.
3. Since the local name server does not have the authority for the Microsoft.com domain, it passes the query to one of the DNS root servers requesting resolution of the host name.
4. The route name server sends back a referral, pointing to the .COM name servers.
5. Next, the local name server sends a request to the .COM name server, which responds with a referral to the Microsoft name servers.
6. Now the local name server sends a request to the Microsoft name server.

7. Since the Microsoft name server has authority for that particular portion of the domain name space, it sends back the IP address for www.microsoft.com to the local name server.

8. The local server now sends the IP address for www.Microsoft.com back to the client.

9. The successful name resolution is complete; the client can access the desired Web site.

Reverse Lookup Queries

What happens when you have an IP address and you have to look up the host name? A process called a reverse lookup is used. A reverse lookup query maps an address to a host name. The DNS database is indexed by name and not by IP address, therefore a reverse lookup query would require a search of every domain name listed.

Also a DNS name starts with a specific component and ends at the general, starting with a host name and ending with the root of the domain. An IP address is exactly the opposite, starting at the network and moving to the node. A unique second-level domain called in-addr.arpa was created and is used for reverse lookup queries based on IP addresses.

The in-addr.arpa. domain is the reverse tree for IPv4 addresses. The name derives from Inverse (IP) address; ARPA was one of the organizations behind the creation of the Internet. In the in-addr.arpa domain, the octets of an IP address are reversed with in-addr.arpa added to the end of the IP address. For example, the IP address 10.240.232.229 would be queried as the 229.232.240.10 in-addr.arpa. The query then finds the new resource record (RR) type PTR (pointer) that is then used to map an address in the reverse lookup zone to the A record (address) of the desired host. The A record is located and the associated DNS name is returned to the client.

NOTE

In order for an Internet Service Provider (ISP) to offer this name service for machines under its care, it has to put these two pieces of information, known as BIND data records, into tables on its Internet domain name servers. These two data records are: A (address) and PTR (pointer). The address returns a numeric IP address when given an Internet name; the pointer returns an Internet Name with provided with an IP address.

Name Server Caching

As a name server processes a query for a client, it may have to send out several queries to find the final answer. Each query discovers more name servers; the name server caches these query results, reducing network traffic and increasing its knowledge. All cached query results have specific parameters for how long the cached information is stored by the local name server.

Figure 3.10
Name servers cache
query results.

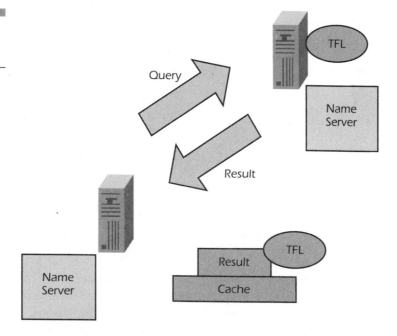

1. The name server caches the query result for a certain amount of time, called time to live (TTL).
2. The authoritative zone that actually provided the query result to the name server will specify the TTL, usually 60 minutes.
3. When the TTL expires, the query result is deleted from the name server cache.

NOTE

With the DNS console, the TTL value can be changed from the default value. However a shorter TTL value increases the network load on local name servers since it must more frequently rely on other name servers for its information.

Dynamic DNS

Windows 2000 adds several new features into the DNS service. The most important is the new standard called DDNS or dynamic domain name system. In Windows 2000 and third-party versions of DNS software that support dynamic updates, using a static host file is history, since zones can be automatically updated from Windows 2000 workstations directly, and also from DHCP and WINS servers. Indeed, the zones can also be stored in Active Directory in a format called secure dynamic updates, allowing only authorized users to make changes to DNS zones.

Older down-level clients cannot take advantage of DDNS.

NOTE

Configuring the DNS Service

Before actually configuring the DNS service, first modify the TCP/IP properties of the computer that will be the DNS server:

1. From the Desktop right-click on **My Network Places** and select **properties**.
2. Right-click on the **Local Area Connection** and select **properties**.
3. Select **TCP/IP** and click the **properties** button.
4. Enter the static TCP/IP address of your server.
5. At the DNS section select "Use the following DNS server addresses" and enter the local IP address.
6. Click **Advanced**.
7. Select the DNS tab and ensure the "DNS suffix for the connection" is the DNS domain you are about to create, as shown in Figure 3.11.
8. Click **OK** and close the local area connection.

Next check that the computer's primary suffix is set properly.

1. Right click on **My Computer** and select **properties**.
2. Select the **Network Identification** tab and click the properties button.
3. Click the **More** button.

Figure 3.11
DNS suffix
information.

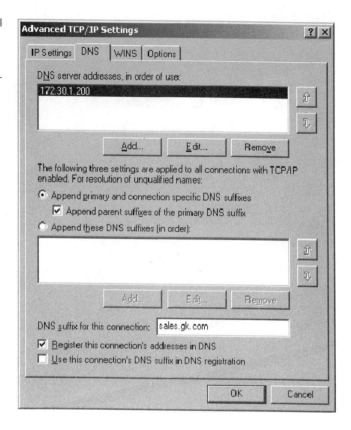

4. Ensure Primary DNS suffix of this computer is set to the DNS domain you are about to create, as shown in Figure 3.12, and click **OK**.
5. Click **OK** to all dialogs to close all windows.
6. Click **Yes** to restart the computer.

Installing the DNS Service

1. To install the DNS service, open the Control Panel and select **Add/Remove Programs**.
2. Select **Add/Remove Windows Components** and select the component **Network Services**.
3. Click the **Details** button, add DNS, and click **Next**.

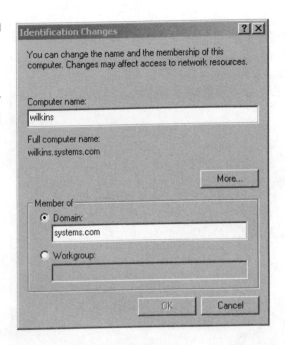

Figure 3.12
Computer name and
DNS suffix
information.

Configuring the DNS Service

1. Start the DNS console in the Administrators program group.
2. Right-click on the **DNS** icon and select **Connect to Computer**. Select This computer and click **OK**. Your node will then appear in the tree.
3. Right-click on the node present and select **Configure** the server—this will launch the Configure DNS Server Wizard.
4. Select one or more DNS servers are running on this network and enter the IP address of the root server installed in step 1: 192.168.10.10 and click **Next**.
5. Select "Yes, add a forward lookup zone" and click **Next**, as shown in Figure 3.13.

Configuring Zones

If your network is composed of multiple servers, there may be a real need to divide one large DNS zone into multiple smaller zones. Two zone lookup types can be created: forward and reverse. On name servers, at

Figure 3.13
DNS forward lookup zone.

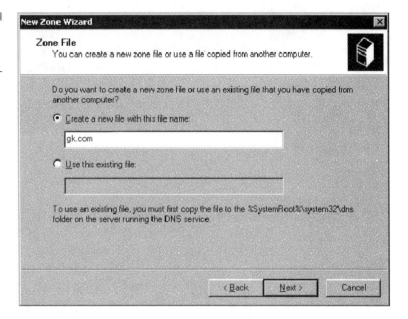

least one forward zone must be configured for the DNS service to work. When Active Directory is installed, and the wizard is allowed to install and configure your DNS server, a forward zone is automatically configured based on the DNS name provided to the server. There are three choices for the types of zones that you can define:

- **Active Directory integrated**—This type of zone uses Active Directory to store and replicate all zone files. It is a master copy of a new zone and can only be created after Active Directory has been installed on your domain controller.
- **Standard Primary**—The master copy of the new zone is stored in a standard text file. Maintenance is performed on the computer where the primary zone is created and stored.
- **Standard Secondary**—A standard secondary zone is a replica of an existing zone. A secondary zone is read only and also stored in a standard text file. Primary zones must first be created before a secondary zone can be created.

1. The zone type is selected: Select "Standard primary" and click **Next**.
2. Enter the name of the zone to match your domain name and click **Next**.
3. Select "Create a new file with this file name" and click **Next**.
4. Select "Yes, add a reverse lookup zone" and click **Next**.

5. Select "Standard primary" and click **Next**.
6. Enter your subnet address, for example, 172.30.1, and click **Next**.
7. Select "Create a new file with this file name" and click **Next**.
8. Review the summary splash screen and click **Finish** to complete the installation.
9. Expand the DNS server and then expand the reverse lookup zone.
10. Highlight and right-click the reverse lookup zones and select New Pointer.
11. Enter the FQDN of your computer in the host name, as shown in Figure 3.14.

Figure 3.14
Reverse lookup zone
FQDN.

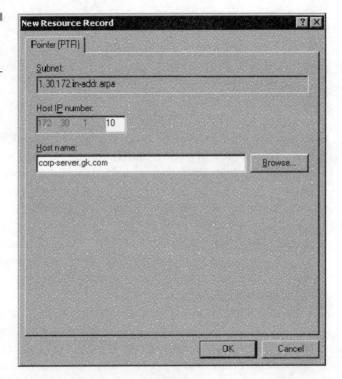

Enabling Dynamic Updates

The last procedure is to enable the zones to allow dynamic updates; this permits hosts to add records automatically to the DNS server records.

1. Highlight the DNS server and the forward lookup zones and select the domain just created.
2. Right-click on the domain and select **Properties** from the context menu.

3. Choose **Yes** from the "Allow dynamic updates?" dropdown box and click **OK**.
4. Expand the reverse lookup zones and select the reverse lookup zone. 192.168.10.X Subnet.
5. Right-click the zone and select **Properties** from the context menu.
6. Choose **Yes** from the "Allow dynamic updates?" dropdown box and click **OK**, as shown in Figure 3.15.

Figure 3.15
Allowing dynamic updates.

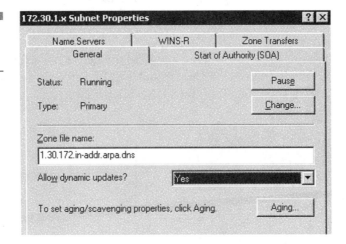

7. DNS is now configured for your domain.
8. Highlight and right-click the DNS server and select **Properties**.
9. Select the **Monitoring** tab.
10. Test the operation of DNS by right-clicking your server name and selecting **Properties** from the context menu.
11. Select the **Monitoring** tab and select the test "A simple query against this DNS server's."
12. Click the **Test Now** button—the test results should pass.

Benefits of Active Directory Integrated Zones

With Active Directory integrated storage, all dynamic updates are conducted established on the multi-master update model. Any DNS server, for example a Windows 2000 domain controller (DC) running the DNS server service, is a primary source for the zone.

The master copy of the zone is stored in the Active Directory database and replicated to all domain controllers. In addition, security is deployed through the Directory so access control lists can control all dynamic DNS updates.

Zone Replication and Active Directory

Whenever a new zone is added to an Active Directory domain it is automatically replicated throughout the Directory, as shown in Figure 3.16. Active Directory simplifies DNS planning.

Figure 3.16
Active Directory integrated zones.

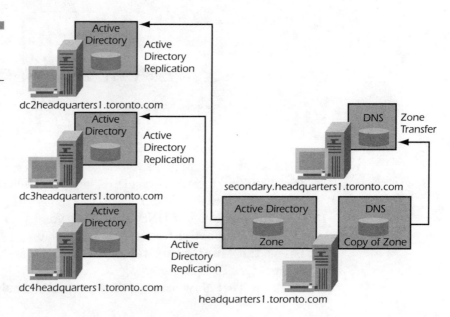

Integrated DNS storage in Active Directory means all the integrated zones are stored at each domain controller, yet you can centrally administer DNS through Active Directory.

Faster Replication

Only relevant changes made to DNS are propagated through the Directory.

Fault Tolerance Issues

In order to achieve a high degree of fault tolerance, DNS should be available from more than one server on the network. If a single server were to be used for DNS services and the server failed, all queries in the zone could fail. Zone transfers are required in order for proper replication and synchronization of the copies of the zones used at each server. This necessitates multiple Windows 2000 servers as DNS servers for proper replication and transfer.

Additional DNS Servers

The more DNS servers, the higher the zone redundancy and the higher the success ratio for resolving queries for DNS clients. Additional DNS servers reduce DNS network traffic. If WAN links are part of your network, then DNS servers on each side of the WAN link will greatly reduce traffic. Further secondary servers can also be used to reduce traffic loads on primary servers for a zone.

Incremental Zone Transfers

In earlier implementations of DNS, a zone update mandated a transfer of the entire zone database. Windows 2000 supports incremental zone transfers (IXFR), which use queries that allow the secondary server to pull only the zone changes needed to synchronize its copy of the zone with its defined source, either a primary or secondary copy of the zone maintained on another DNS server. A zone transfer between servers follows an exact order depending on the following parameters:

1. When the DNS service is started on the secondary server for a zone
2. When the refresh interval time runs out for the zone
3. When changes are made to the primary zone and a notify list is generated.

Secondary Servers

Secondary DNS servers for the zone always initiate all zone transfers. A request is sent to the DNS server defined as the secondary site server's source for the zone. When the source server receives a request for the zone update, either a partial or full transfer of the zone takes place. After a new configuration has been set up, the destination server sends a transfer request for the zone to the DNS server defined as its source for the zone. The source server responds with a full zone transfer to the destination server.

Depending on the serial number contained in the zone records, the next update that occurs, at the default rate of every 15 minutes, will be full or partial depending on whether the serial number of the source server is the same as or higher than that of the destination server.

DNS and Resource Records

When a client logs onto Active Directory, DNS is used to locate the Domain Controllers by means of resource records. Service locator resource records (RR) are used by the NETLOGON service to register and locate domain controllers in the DNS namespace.

Resource records are records in the zone database file that links DNS domain names to data records for specific network resources. When a zone is first created, DNS automatically creates two resource records, as shown in Figure 3.17. The first is called the *start of authority* (SOA). The second is called the *name server* (NS).

Start of Authority (SOA)

Every zone has a start of authority (SOA) resource record at the beginning of the zone. The fields are detailed in Table 3.6.

Resource Records (NS)

A name server resource record lists the servers authoritative for the zone. The information lists both primary and secondary servers and any servers for any delegated zones. Every zone must contain at least one NS zone record at the root.

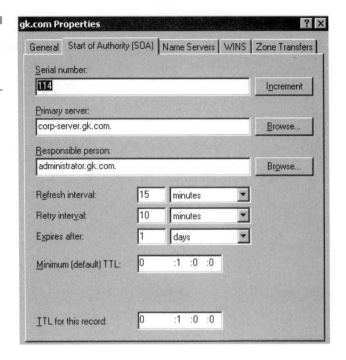

Figure 3.17
Resource records detail the location of network resources.

TABLE 3.6	Owner	The name of the DNS domain to which this RR belongs.
Start of authority details.	TTL	Time to live—it can be left blank.
	Class	One of four classes—usually INT for Internet.
	Type	Identifies the type of RR.
	Authoritative server	The primary DNS server authoritative for the zone.
	Responsible person	The email address of the Administrator responsible for the zone.
	Serial number	Shows how many times the zone has been updated. When the serial number of the master is higher than the serial number of the secondary, a zone transfer occurs.
	Refresh	How often the secondary server checks to see when the zone has been changed.
	Retry	The length of time the secondary server waits for a response from the master server.
	Expire	The time period a secondary waits before discarding its own zone.
	Minimum TTL	Value used if the TTL field is empty. The server sends back a resource record with a minimum time to live.

Resource Record

An address record points a fully qualified domain name (FQDN) to an IP address. This helps the resolvers request the corresponding IP address for a FQDN.

PTR Pointer Resource Record

A pointer resource record maps an IP address into a FQDN.

Canonical Name Resource Record (CNAME)

The canonical name resource record creates an alias for the specified FQDN. This alias name allows you to hide structural details of your network from the network clients.

For example, if your FTP server name is called a canonical name of FTP1.raleigh.gk.com, it could be moved to another server location and only the CNAME would have to be changed. There can be only one canonical name per alias.

MX Resource Record

The mail exchange resource record details a mail exchange server for a DNS host name. The mail exchange server can process or forward mail for the DNS domain name.

If there are multiple mail exchange servers in one DNS domain, multiple MX resource records are allowed.

SRV Service Locator Record

SRV records are used to find Active Directory DC.

This special type of *resource record* (RR) permits multiple servers that allow the same service to be referenced from a single DNS query. An Active Directory client uses the LDAP protocol to locate domain controllers through TCP port 389.

An SRV RR would be formulated in the manner described in RFC 1700 and Table 3.7.

SRV Examples

- **_Ldap._tcp.DnsDomainName**—This SRV record permits a client to find a server running the LDAP service in the domain named by DnsDomainName.

TABLE 3.7

SRV details.

_Service	The service name
_Proto	The transport protocol used: TCP or UDP
Name	The DNS domain name
TTL	The time to live—this field can be left blank
Class	One of four classes—IN for the Internet is common
Priority	A number between 0 and 65,535; this details whether the target host has the lowest number and therefore the highest priority
Weight	A number between 1 and 65,535 is used to load balance two or more target hosts
Port	The transport protocol port
Target	The host's DNS domain name that is providing the service

- **_Ldap._tcp.gc._msdcs.DnsForestName**—This SRV record allows a client to locate a Global Catalog (gc) for the named forest.

Less-Common Resource Records

There are many experimental resource records that are in a constant state of testing and accreditation. Some of the current experimental records are listed in Table 3.8.

TABLE 3.8

Experimental resource records.

Record Type	Details	RFC
AAAA	Address records that map a host to an Ipv6 address	1886
AFSDB	Provides the location of the Andrew File System (AFS) cell database server	1183
HINFO	Identifies a host's hardware type and operating system	1035
ISDN	Maps an FQDN to an ISDN address	1183
MB	A DNS host is specified with the mailbox record	1035
MG	A mail group resource record	1035
MINFO	A mailbox responsible for a specified mailing list	1035
MR	A mailbox that is an alias of another mailbox	1035
RP	The responsible person for the DNS domain or host	1183

continued on next page

	Record Type	Details	RFC
TABLE 3.8 continued	RT	The route resource record is used with ISDN and X.25 RR to route packets to a destination host	1183
	TXT	Text resource record holding details on an item in the DNS database	1035
	WKS	Services provided by a protocol on a specific interface	1035
	X.25	Maps an FQDN to a X.121 address	1183

Dynamic Host Configuration Protocol (DHCP)

For TCP/IP networks, the Internet Engineering Task Force (IETF) has developed several autoconfiguration protocols, such as Boot Protocol (BOOTP) and Dynamic Host Configuration Protocol (DHCP). A Windows 2000 server can also be configured as a DHCP server. This simplifies the configuration of TCP/IP devices (workstations, servers, routers, etc.) on the network. DHCP can also be used for dynamic configuration of essential TCP/IP parameters for hosts (workstations and servers) on the network and for updating DNS records, as shown in Figure 3.18. The DHCP protocol consists of two elements: a mechanism for allocating IP addresses and other TCP/IP parameters and a protocol for negotiating and transmitting host specific information.

The TCP/IP host requesting the TCP/IP configuration information is called the DHCP client, and the TCP/IP host that supplies this information is called a DHCP server.

On a Windows 2000 network, the DHCP clients are Windows NT workstations, Windows 95/98 clients, or other NT servers, but the DHCP server can only be a Windows 2000 server.

IP Address Management

In the dynamic allocation method, DHCP assigns an IP address to a DHCP client on a temporary basis. The IP address is on loan or leased to the DHCP client for a specified duration. On expiry of this lease, the

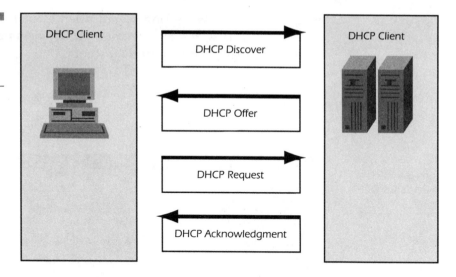

Figure 3.18
The DHCP client request TCP/IP parameters.

DHCP Client

DHCP Discover

DHCP Offer

DHCP Request

DHCP Acknowledgment

DHCP Client

IP address is revoked, and the DHCP client is required to surrender the IP address. If the DHCP client still needs an IP address to perform its functions, it can request another one. If the DHCP client no longer needs an IP address, such as when the computer is being shut down, it can release the IP address to the DHCP server. The DHCP server can then reissue the same IP address to another DHCP client making a request for an IP address.

DHCP States

When the DHCP ACK from the DHCP server is accepted, three timer values are set, and the DHCP client moves into what is called the BOUND state. The first timer, T1, is the lease renewal timer; the second timer, T2, is the rebinding timer; the third timer, T3, is the lease duration. The DHCP ACK always returns the value of T3, the lease duration.

The values of timers T1 and T2 can be configured at the DHCP server, but if they are not set, default values are used based on the duration of the lease.

DHCP and Dynamic DNS

As we have mentioned, Windows 2000 supports the integration of DHCP with Dynamic DNS, as shown in Figure 3.19. This automatically allows the updating of a client's DNS record when a client receives a new IP address from a DHCP server. Windows 2000 clients can send dynamic updates for three types of network adapters:

1. DHCP Adapters
2. Statically configured adapters
3. Remote access adapters.

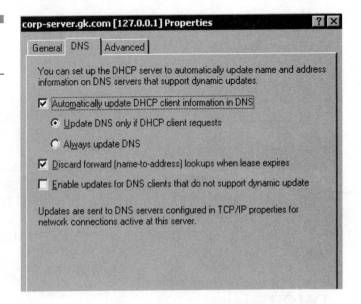

Figure 3.19
Dynamic DNS/DCHP options.

The DHCP client runs on all Windows 2000 clients, whether or not they have been configured as DHCP clients. A dynamic update is performed by the dynamic DHCP client every 24 hours or whenever one of the following events occurs:

- The TCP/IP configuration is changed.
- The DHCP address is renewed or a new lease is obtained.

If your company still uses static DNS servers across your network, WINS will need to be enabled to provide WINS lookup for older DHCP clients that use NetBIOS, in order to avoid failed DNS lookups.

NOTE

Installing DHCP

The DHCP server can only be installed on Windows 2000 Servers and not on Windows 2000 Professional Workstations. If routers separate DHCP servers, each router must be configured to forward BOOTP messages. The following is an outline of the procedure for installing a DHCP Server on a Windows 2000 server.

1. Log on to the Windows 2000 server as an Administrator.
2. To install the DNS service, open the Control Panel and select **Add/Remove Programs**. Select **Add/Remove Windows Components** and select the component **Network Services**. Click the **Details** button, add **DNS**, and click **Next**.
3. Double-click on the **DNS** icon in the Administrative Tools program group.
4. If this is the first time you have started the DHCP Manager, you should see that the DHCP Manager shows the local computer.
5. After the first startup, the DHCP Manager screen shows the DHCP servers to which the DHCP Manager is connected and their existing scopes.
6. Connect the DHCP Manager to a DHCP Server by choosing (right-clicking) the DNS tree and selecting **Add Server** menu. You should see the Add Server to dialog box, as shown in Figure 3.20.

Figure 3.20
Adding a DHCP server.

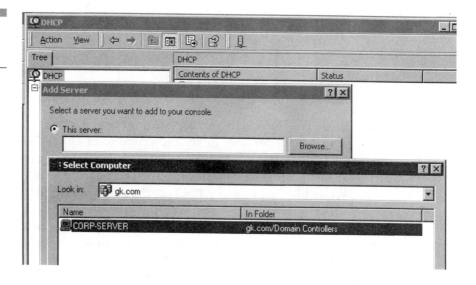

7. Add the IP address of the DHCP server to which you want to connect. This should be the IP address of the DHCP server you want to administer. Choose **OK** when you are finished making changes.

You should be back to the DHCP Manager screen showing the DHCP server or servers added to the DHCP server list. Next a DHCP *scope* must be defined. A DHCP scope is a grouping of DHCP client computers; it must be created for each IP subnetwork on your network. The DHCP scope defines parameters for that subnet, such as a subnet mask and lease duration values. The DHCP scope is identified by a DHCP scope name created at the time of defining the scope.

8. Right-click the displayed server in the DHCP Manager screen and select **New Scope** to initiate creating a DHCP scope. The New Scope wizard should appear.
9. Enter a name in the Start Address and End Address fields to define the range of IP addresses available to the DHCP clients. In the Subnet Mask field, enter a valid subnet mask for the group of DHCP clients and click **Next**.
10. In the Exclusion Range group of fields, specify any IP addresses to be excluded from the IP address range pool that you specified in step 9.
11. Right-click the created scope and select **Activate** to start the assigning of IP addresses.

Windows Internet Name Service (WINS)

Microsoft's WINS server, which can be installed only on Windows NT and 2000 servers, is an implementation of the NetBIOS Name Server (NBNS) described in RFCs 1001 and 1002 and detailed in Figure 3.21. WINS provided NetBIOS computer name mappings to IP addresses; this has been replaced by DNS services that match the DNS computer name to the assigned IP address. However, if you are using NT 4.0 and Windows 95/98 clients WINS still has a place on your network. WINS is installed from Network Services, where the DNS and DHCP were installed (as described earlier in this chapter).

Figure 3.21
The WINS resolution process.

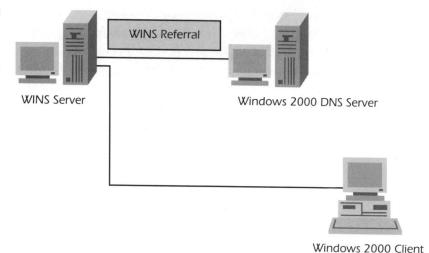

WINS Server

Windows 2000 DNS Server

Windows 2000 Client

WINS Integration with DHCP and DDNS

In Windows 2000, the WINS server can also interact with DHCP and with Dynamic DNS. DNS can provide name resolution for any names that it learns from the WINS service. If DHCP is used automatically to generate IP addresses for Windows NT computers, the IP addresses assigned using DHCP are updated automatically in the WINS database. If Active Directory is not installed, then WINS will be required to create the network browse list. NetBIOS and WINS can be discontinued if:

1. There are no Windows for Workgroups, Windows 95/98, and Windows NT 4.0.
2. No legacy applications are relying on NETBIOS.

Name Resolution Using WINS

The name resolution steps for a Windows 2000 Server are:

1. Windows 2000 client attempts any name resolution from the client cache.
2. If the attempted resolution from the client cache fails, next the client attempts resolution through Dynamic DNS.
3. If the DDNS resolution fails, the client then attempts resolution using the service.

4. If the WINS server does not respond or is unable to resolve the name query, the name registration and query requests are broadcast via UDP datagrams in the h-node.

5. If a computer is configured to use a WINS server, its name registration request is sent directly to the WINS server. The WINS server examines the registration request and accepts or rejects it based on the information in its database.

6. If no challenge to the new registration request is made, the WINS server accepts the registration request and adds it to its local database.

Designing Active Directory Topology

This chapter concentrates on the preparation, planning, and design of Active Directory. Topics include:

- Getting ready for Active Directory deployment
- Planning logical and physical designs
- Inventory of your physical network
- Planning organizational units
- Planning for forests and domains

Corporate Networks and Active Directory

Once Active Directory is deployed throughout your company it could very well influence how your company performs. The foundation of your network and corporate software applications, (word processing, email, and contact management) will be supported by Windows 2000 running Active Directory Services. Once Active Directory is as successfully integrated as Windows NT, email services (Exchange 2000), Office Suite Software (Office 2000), Inter-Office Communications (Outlook 2000), and network routing services (Cisco/Microsoft) could dictate how successfully the mission statement of your company is carried out.

Since your entire infrastructure is more than ever dependent on Microsoft, the pros and cons of Active Directory will influence your bottom line. If you think about it, the real cost of running a network these days is not even tabulated properly. Remember the last virus that hit your company? Perhaps it was the latest Outlook or Palmtop virus. It doesn't matter which example we use; for a moment, roughly calculate how many hours you and your support staff spent determining and fixing the problem. Several hours at least, right? What if Active Directory replication problems required you to force replication manually to complete a forest-wide installation of required software; or, heaven forbid, a schema update messed up your entire schema for a period of time?

These examples illustrate how we are becoming even more reliant on Active Directory; therefore, the proper design and implementation of AD is also now an administration responsibility.

Wal-Mart is deploying Windows 2000 nationwide; their cash registers will be Terminal Server clients. Hand-held computers running Windows CE Terminal Server client will be used for inventory throughout the store. The ability of Wal-Mart to carry out its mission statement depends on the stability and reliability of the network.

Documenting Your Network Infrastructure

The most overlooked task is documenting your current network environment including both the physical and logical topology (Figure 4.1).

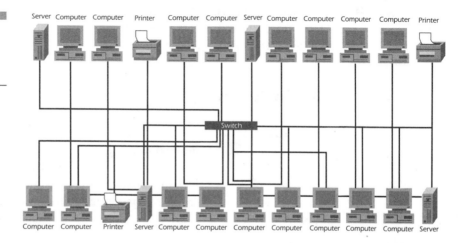

Figure 4.1
Documenting your network pieces is essential.

Without proper current network documentation, Active Directory cannot be deployed, and forget about troubleshooting a nondocumented Windows 2000 network successfully. A successful Active Directory installation also depends on understanding the current physical topology and bandwidth available just for AD. Replication of domain, schema, and configuration information is the lifeline of a Windows 2000 network. Read Chapters 8–10 for further details on replication traffic.

Hardware and Software Components

Documentation of your network infrastructure must include both hardware and software components. Hardware components describe the physical structure of routers, hubs, switches, and bridges; software components itemize the use and configuration of the network services and protocols deployed. Both physical and logical networked diagrams should also be generated, since Active Directory deployment requires both physical and logical viewpoints. For example, it's great to have a networking drawing of multiple domains, but the more important issue is how many domain controllers host each domain and what essential local network services, such as DNS and global catalog servers, are available to service local user requests.

Network infrastructure is one of the most important components to consider; your current bandwidth may not be sufficient for Active Directory's replication needs. As we will see in the coming chapters, proper network design and a great deal of bandwidth form the glue that keeps Active Directory functioning properly.

NOTE

Network Stability

Your current network must also be stable before a Windows 2000/Active Directory deployment takes place. TCP/IP subnets and network services must be properly designed and in place before AD is deployed. Upgrading to a new network operating system on an already unstable network means any problems that develop will be almost impossible to trace and fix.

Physical Network Documentation

Your physical documentation (Figure 4.2) should include the following information:

- **Communication links**—Cable length, grade, and physical paths of wiring: T1, Analog, Fiber, and ISDN lines
- **Servers**—Computer name, IP address, server role, domain membership.
- **Location**—The physical location of network devices such as modems, switches, hubs, routers, bridges, printers, or proxy servers
- **WAN Bandwidth**—List all communication links and the approximate bandwidth between each site during peak and off-peak times
- **LAN Bandwidth**—Test the approximate bandwidth across the local network during peak and off-peak times.

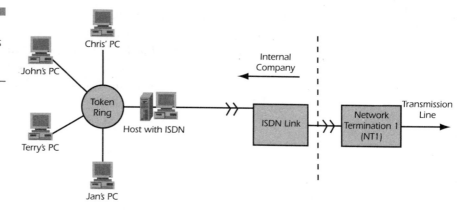

Figure 4.2
Physical components define your existing infrastructure.

Documenting Logical Network Structure

Although Active Directory automatically assigns transitive two-way trusts, you may require down-level NT 4.0 domains as part of your network for months or years to come. Many organizations, are deciding to migrate their client base to Windows 2000 Professional, and then upgrade their PDCs to Windows 2000 servers, leaving their BDC structure in place. Your plans may or may not follow this path; however it's essential to document your current plan before your new plan is implemented. (See Figure 4.3.)

Figure 4.3
A logical network diagram details the functional roles of network servers and the existing trusts assigned.

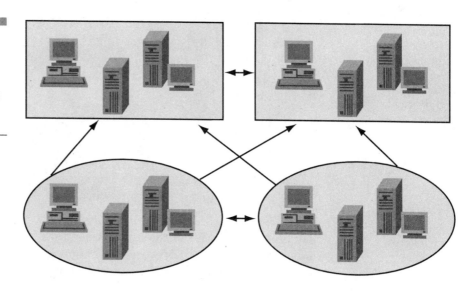

Logical network structures that must be documented are:

- Domain architecture showing the existing domain hierarchy including server names.
- The roles of the servers including primary and backup domain controllers, DHCP servers, and WINS servers.
- All configuration details of all member servers include data storage, print, and Web servers.
- All trust relationships, including one-way and two-way trust relationships.
- How NT 4.0 or Windows 95/09 system policy has been deployed.

NOTE

Until both clients and servers are Windows 2000 based, taking advantage of Active Directory and Windows 2000 features is not possible.

Hardware and Software Inventory

Software inventory should include all software applications and network services used on all servers (member servers, PDCs, and BDCs) including any upgraded DLLs used with the software applications/network services deployed on your network (Figure 4.4).

Figure 4.4
Hardware and software inventory must be carried out for all your servers and client computers on your network.

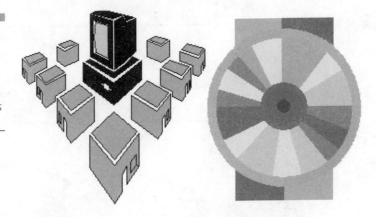

Pay careful attention to the applications that run on each server; for example, you may have a software application that must run on a domain controller. Record all modems, routers, and any other hardware subsystems such as RAID arrays or RAS server hardware. Up-to-date details on BIOS settings and any special settings for any peripheral devices can be very important for maintaining compatibility with Windows 2000.

Pay careful attention to:

- Driver versions and other software and firmware versions; these should be notated for any discrepancies that appear after installation
- Any service packs; these should be documented if they have been applied to the operating system and/or applications, as should the order in which they were successfully applied. If you have not personally installed all network applications and services on your servers, assume that there was a correct way to install all applications; this order will have to be tested again on Windows 2000.

Documentation

The following checklist can be used to begin your documentation process:

Physical Locations
- Links between physical locations
- Link speed
- Measure your bandwidth
- IP addresses of network devices
- Routers
- Switches
- Hubs
- Servers
- Firewalls

Network Infrastructure
- Hardware and software
- File and print servers
- Web servers
- Directory services architecture
- Security
- Business applications

Existing Network Architecture
- Servers
- Desktops
- Network devices

Required Protocol Standards
- NetBIOS
- NetBEUI
- IPX/SPX

- TCP/IP
- Remote Access

Network Services
- DNS
- DHCP
- WINS
- TCP/IP

Cabling Standards
- Coaxial
- 10/100 MB
- Fiber

Server Hardware Inventory
- Vendor name
- Processor
- Memory
- Disk capacity
- Disk subsystem
- Disk configuration
- File system
- Network adapter

Software Inventory
- Application software
- Operating system version
- Service pack
- Patches
- Hot fixes
- Application software
- Services
- Drivers

Testing and Other Issues
- Are your network services network compatible?
- What types of clients exist?
- Where is critical data stored?

Existing Naming Standards
- Users
- Groups
- Servers
- DNS
- DHCP
- TCP/IP
- WINS

Security Review

Your current security standards and policies should be reviewed and notated. Available security levels for files and folders and all objects hosted by Active Directory are greatly expanded. Questions you should ask and document include:

1. Who creates users and groups, and sets password policy? One of the new features of Active Directory is the delegation of administration at every level—sites, domains, and most important, OUs. Security tasks can now be delegated to trusted subadministrators, managers of departments, or to the help desk.

2. What types of users and groups do you wish to deploy? Are local and global groups sufficient for your company or are universal groups more appealing due to their flexibility and nesting abilities? This also brings up the question of mixed or native mode; if you have NT 4.0 domains mixed with Windows 2000 domains, then universal groups may not apply now; they could be on the agenda once NT 4.0 is history.

3. Do you have third-party consultants who work with your company on a daily basis? Do they need special rights? Try to use the Power User for all consultants initially; this may not be enough depending on the task at hand.

4. Do you restrict access to specific network applications or devices? Active Directory objects, by default, assign read access to all objects. The type of install you select can also allow anonymous access to Active Directory and assign the Everyone group full permissions on all hard drives.

5. Has a security audit been performed on existing users and groups for duplication or information that should be removed? Now is the time to remove user accounts and groups that are outdated.

Planning Your Active Directory Structure

The design criterion for Windows 2000 networks has been replaced with many major changes and much new terminology. Organizational Units, Domains, and Forests are the new terms to understand fully. Other design concepts are summarized in Table 4.1.

Planning with Organizational Units (OU)

The container used to create structure within Active Directory is called an *organizational unit*. Through the creation and nesting of organiza-

TABLE 4.1

Design
terminology.

NT 4.0 Design	Windows 2000 Design
Geographical locations	Sites and replication
NT 4.0 trusts	Transitive trusts
Multi-master domain	Single domains or a smaller number of domains
Trust relationships are manual	Trust relationships can still be manually set but the default is transitive two way trusts
PDC / BDC Domain Controllers	Domain Controllers
Stand-alone servers	Member servers
DNS namespace may not be used	DNS is mandatory
WINS may be essential	WINS may not be required

tional units you can create a tree-like OU structure in Active Directory, as shown in Figure 4.5.

Figure 4.5
The nesting of OUs allows a flexible design model for administration and group policy.

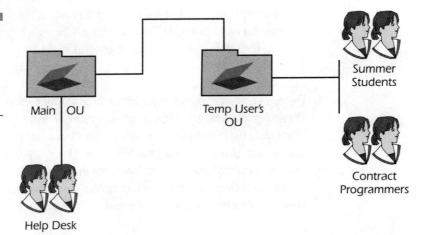

Main OU

Temp User's OU

Summer Students

Contract Programmers

Help Desk

Once your Active Directory design involves OUs and the nesting of OUs, the administration of the objects contained inside the OU can be delegated. If OUs were not used, all of your defined users and groups would be contained in the Users container and all delegation of administration and assigning of group policy would remain at the domain level, just as in NT 4.0.

Organizational Units and Security Principles

An organizational unit is not a security principle; however, it *contains* security principles—users, groups, and computers; in fact, an OU cannot be made a member of a security group, only users and groups can. For this version of Windows 2000, each OU begins life as an empty container created by the administrator or script; any user or group assigned to an OU does not have permissions assigned directly to the OU; these are assigned to the user or group. Microsoft had to leave the existing NT 4.0 group structure intact for Windows 2000 in order to have an upgrade path from NT 4.0.

An OU is therefore created for three purposes:

1. Grouping security principles for the purpose of administration
2. Grouping security principles to delegate administration of the OU's contents to a trusted user or group
3. Grouping security principles for the purpose of assigning group policy.

The following objects can be created in an Organizational Unit:

- Domain User
- Local, global, or universal groups
- Computers
- Printers (NT 4.0 printers)
- Contacts
- Published folders
- Organizational unit

NOTE

OUs are used for the successful managing and administration of security principles and the common objects required for users to do their jobs. However, a user still authenticates to the domain.

OUs and the Delegation of Administration

The delegation of administration can now be carried out through assigning the administration of an organizational unit to a trusted user or group. Delegating administration allows you to control or assign the support personnel who require high levels of access across the domain or forest. For example, your management department can be granted the ability to create user objects in a certain OU but nowhere else. Help desk personnel could be granted the ability to reset the passwords of users in a particular OU but not the right to create users. To delegate administration, you modify the access control list of the OU. The easiest way to perform this task is by using the delegation of control wizard. Common tasks to consider delegating are listed in Table 4.2.

TABLE 4.2

Plan to delegate the following tasks.

Organizational Unit Tasks You Can Delegate
Create delete and manage user accounts
Reset user account passwords
Create, delete, and manage groups
Read all user information
Modify group membership
Manage, create, and delete printers
Manage Group Policy links

Group Policy and Organizational Units

A group policy object (GPO) can be associated with a specific OU as shown in Figure 4.6 or with a top level OU that then would apply to all other organizational units in the nested tree. For example, you could mandate desktop settings for all users at the topmost OU in the tree and leave each computer system to be controlled by each specific OU group policy object. Suppose that you had three departments, Sales, Design, and Management for which you wished to define global settings for all desktops; you also wished to leave the management of the desktops to each OU administrator. You could the create four OUs, one for each of the departments under a global OU called Main, as shown in Figure 4.7. In the main OU, the global desktop settings for all users could be defined for the main OU; these settings would then propagate to each sub-OU. Each of the other sub-OUs could also have separate GPOs for each of the users' computer objects.

NOTE

Because group policy can be applied to sites, domains, and OUs, consider the actual scope that should be used for every policy item. As the structure of the directory (with respect to sites, domains, and OUs) is planned, specify and document the site, domain, or OU to which each policy item applies.

OUs could also be used to group shared folders or printers; then assign the administration of all shared folders or printers to a specific administrator. The beauty of designing with OUs is that within the domain, all objects can be moved. The disadvantage of OU design is that OU objects cannot be moved easily between separate domains; scripting or cryptic command line utilities such as MOVETREE must be deployed.

Figure 4.6
Group policy can be
applied directly to
each OU.

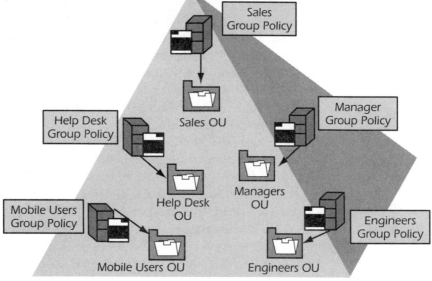

Granular Group Policy

Figure 4.7
Levels of control can
be defined with
group policy.

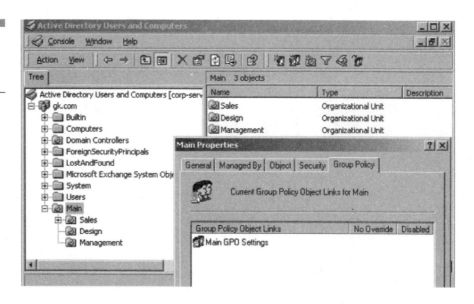

The OU Planning Process

The OUs you create should help you to manage your users. Every time you are about to add an OU, ask yourself why? The goal is to try to eliminate unnecessary structure. OUs can be used to create an exact structure that matches your company, its departments, and divisions. Is this valid for how your network is administered?

Let's take another example of centralized administration. Several administrators take care of all the users across the company and are divided into several OU divisions. What happens when a user transfers from one division to another? If the divisions were Sales, Management, and Engineers, as shown in Figure 4.8, how efficient would it be to have organizational units for each division? What happens when somebody from Sales transfers to Management? The Administrator now has to move the user's account from the Sales OU to the Management OU. Would it not have been better to create a single OU structure that contains all user accounts in the company? In that case, if the user transfers from one division to another, nothing needs to be done.

You also may have divisions within your company on a per-project, or divisional basis where resources are to be assigned to a user based on a particular job or function. OUs could be created on a per-project or function basis.

Figure 4.8
The location of user account depends on the type of company and clients you administer.

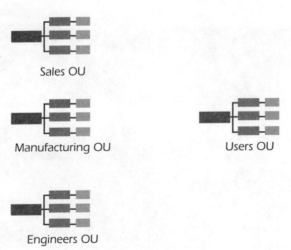

Sales OU

Manufacturing OU

Users OU

Engineers OU

Planning for Domains

The AD is a distributed database composed of many partial databases spread across all domain controllers in the forest. Each partial database consists of the schema and configuration partitions, forest-wide components that must be kept up to date when changes occur through the automatic process of replication. Within each domain, the domain partition remains local to all domain controllers within each domain. Another way of saying this is that domain objects created within a domain stay locally within the domain, with the exception of global catalog updates that could also be within the domain but in all probability will be located outside the domain as well. Updates to each domain controller within each domain, and any global catalog server within and outside the domain, are also kept up to date through the process of replication. If you are thinking "how much replication traffic is there?" there are several ways to analyze this.

First, replication traffic is the cost of running a fault-tolerant Windows 2000 network; if you create users, groups, and other objects you expect them to update automatically all the other domain controllers within the domain. When you install software and add other domains, or domain controllers, you would also expect that operating system to take the necessary steps to update all other domain controllers in the tree or forest. This is the cost of running Windows 2000. Exact details on the size of replication traffic can be found in Chapter 10. For now I will summarize the replication traffic size.

Within a site (an area defined as a network with good connectivity), replication data are not compressed and can be large; however, since we have good connectivity, the network will be able to handle it.

Between sites (areas defined a being connected through WAN links), replication traffic is well compressed to 85 percent of its original size. More details on sites can be found in Chapters 8 and 9.

Domain Components

Each domain will have the following domain components:

DOMAIN CONTROLLERS   Any Windows 2000 server that hosts a domain database is a domain controller and each domain controller can host exactly one domain. Changes to objects within a domain can be performed at any domain controller—the changes will then be replicated to all domain controllers in the domain. Domain controllers running Windows 2000 are all domain controllers. All domain controllers can accept updates and authenticate users across the forest.

AUTHENTICATION   Each domain database contains objects called *security principle objects*. Although an OU can contain security principles, domains host OUs that can also contain security principles. A security principle authenticates to a domain and each security principle object is unique: it is granted or denied access to the network resources (authorization) based on credentials obtained through an authentication process performed by a domain controller for the domain, regardless of where the security principle objects are located: in the Users container within a domain or in an OU defined within the domain. With Active Directory domains, there is no effective limitation on the number of user accounts. Millions of objects per domain are allowed.

ADMINISTRATION AND POLICY BOUNDARIES   Each domain has a domain administrators group that has full control over every object in the domain directory. These administrative rights are valid only within the domain; they do not spread to other domains. Any group policy defined for a particular domain also does not automatically spread to other domains or child domains in the forest unless explicitly linked.

SECURITY POLICY ACCOUNTS   Security policies that apply to domain user accounts can only be defined per domain. These security policies are:

- **Password policy**—Password rules that apply per domain.
- **Account lockout policy**—Rules for intruder detection per domain.

DNS DOMAIN NAMES   All domains are identified by DNS namespace throughout Active Directory. Namespace considerations depend on your company's current use of DNS and any assigned Internet domain names.

DELEGATION OF ADMINISTRATION   Administration can be delegated within a domain using organizational units to organize objects (users, groups, computers) into logical subgroupings.

GROUP POLICY   Group policy can be applied to the domain through a GPO defined at each domain level. Group policy is also applied to each domain controller that hosts each domain defined on the Domain Controller OU itself.

How Many Domains?

Many factors have changed in creating Windows 2000 domains as opposed to domain creation in Windows NT 4.0. With your background in Windows NT 4.0 domain structure and planning, you can be excused for thinking multiple domains are a necessity for your company. Of course, you could be right; but start your planning process assuming that a single domain will do. If you are lucky enough to be in a company where administration is centralized, and all network subnets are linked with high-speed connections, then grouping users, groups, printers, files, and shares into OUs hosted by one domain may be an acceptable design to follow.

However, you may have the classic multiple-master design with two one-way trusts linking account domains together, or large geographic boundaries separated by WAN links; in this case even Microsoft recommends that two domain be created and then all resource domains be relaunched as OUs within the applicable domain.

If politics or state laws mandate that your networks remain separate, then multiple domains may be the mandated design model; this is not a problem as long as you recognize the boundaries of administration and group policy presented in this chapter. You will find more details on multiple domains below.

Multiple Domain Creation

Additional domains are created when you require the ability to:

PRESERVE EXISTING WINDOWS NT 4.0 DOMAINS   If you currently have Windows NT 4.0 domains, the timeframe until you upgrade all domains to Windows 2000 may be months or years. The application software you must use also may not work with Windows 2000, although this is unlikely.

ADMINISTRATION PARTITIONING   You may wish certain users to submit to a security policy that is distinct from the standard policy applied to the typical user. For example, a particular group may be involved with custom software application development, or highly sensitive data; both these situations may involve placing each group of users in a separate domain.

PHYSICAL PARTITIONING   If your company is divided into many small divisions, dividing your Windows 2000 network into a hierarchy of smaller domains within a single forest may best reflect the reality of how your company operates and is administered.

Choosing the Forest Root Domain

Once it has been decided how many domains will be placed in the forest, decide which domain will be the forest root domain. The forest root domain is always the first domain created in a forest. In the root domain, two important groups reside: the enterprise administrators and schema administrators.

On a large network, creating a dedicated domain whose sole purpose is to act as the forest root can be a bonus for fault-tolerant design.

Benefits include:

- The domain administrator in the forest root domain will control the membership of the enterprise administrators and schema administrators groups. Place members in these groups only when forest-wide administration is required.
- The only role this domain will have is to serve as the forest root; the end result is that the root domain will be small, easily replicated, and stable since there will be few changes.
- No other software or network tasks will be assigned to the root domain so it will not risk becoming obsolete.
- If your company is undergoing mergers and major changes, using child domains for company divisions may make sense. You could also argue that using OUs for these company divisions makes even more sense; sometimes company politics are the final decision makers.

Rules for Windows 2000 Domain

1. It is a simple task to add new domains to a forest; however you cannot move existing Windows 2000 Active Directory domains between forests.
2. After a tree root domain has been created you cannot add to the forest a domain with a higher-level name than the root domain. You can only create a child domain.
3. Demoting a domain controller for a domain to a member server removes the domain from a forest and deletes all domain information, including all user accounts.
4. The ability to split a domain into separate domains, or to merge two domains into one does not exist at this point with Windows 2000. However you could split a domain by first adding an empty domain

to a forest, and then moving objects into the new domain from other domains.

5. A domain cannot be renamed or moved within a forest.

Planning for Forests

A forest is a collection of Active Directory domains and child domains. A forest can take advantage of global directory database, simplifying the users navigation of a large network. Key components of the forest are a single schema, the configuration container, transitive trusts (Figure 4.9), and the global catalog shown in Figure 4.10.

Figure 4.9
Forest structure creates transitive trusts.

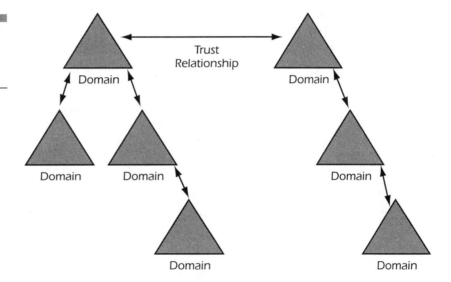

Single Schema

The single schema is made up of existing objects and attributes and is replicated to every domain controller that is part of the forest stored on the schema partition on each domain controller.

Configuration Container

A single configuration container, which also contains the complete forest structure, is replicated to every domain controller in the forest.

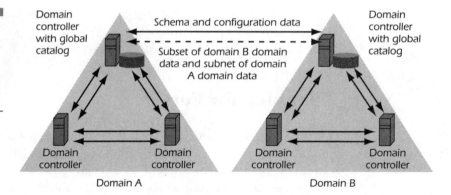

Figure 4.10
Global forest components include the schema and the configuration partitions.

Transitive Trusts

All domains that are part of the forest are automatically linked with transitive, two-way trust relationships. Any member computer in the forest will recognize any user and group from any domain.

Global Catalog

A global catalog contains a copy of every object from every domain in the forest, but only a subset of the attributes from each object. The global catalog allows searches that cross the entire forest; in effect the existing directory structure becomes transparent to any end user. The global catalog also allows a user to log on to any domain controller within the single forest and be authenticated, even though the user account may not be physically located in the domain from which the authentication request started.

Planning for Single or Multiple Forests

Plan with a single forest model as the goal. Although your organization may require multiple forests, start your planning as simply as possible. Single forest advantages are: simpler maintenance; all users see a single directory–schema; no manual trust configuration is required when adding new domains; configuration and schema changes are applied once and affect all domains.

Multiple Forests

Since all elements in the forest are shared, all domains sharing the forest must also share the contents and administration. If your organization is a mixture of partnerships and consolidated companies, you may not have or want a central decision-making process. Multiple forests could also increase the administrative overhead. The Windows 2000 product should not be tasked with multiple forests for the majority of installations. For example, the entire Compaq Windows 2000 worldwide network is built with four domains within one forest.

More than one forest may have to be created if:

- **Domain administration must be kept separate**—Domain administrators may not know and therefore may not trust each other.
- **Schema and configuration changes cannot be agreed upon**—If the network is expanding with new domains and changes that are not appropriate across the forest
- **Trust relationships must be limited**—In a secure environment you may not want transitive trusts; in fact, your company's need may demand explicit trust relationships. You may also wish to separate your production network from a domain or forest that is connected to the Internet.
- **Increased overhead**—Each additional forest needs at least one domain. In real terms this also means you need additional domain controllers. Each forest must also be managed separately
- **Additional configuration**—For any user residing in one forest, to be able to access resources in another forest, an explicit trust must be created between the two domains. Explicit relationships are one-way and not transitive. Users must be trained to query directly domains outside the default forest where they reside. Although data from other domains can be imported into the user's default forest, they are not automatically updated when the source information changes.

NOTE

The biggest factor in multiple forests is that the joining together of two separate forests with one-way trusts does not create transitive trusts. Only the operating system can create transitive trusts.

Making Changes to the Forest

Keep in mind that your Active Directory forest could be deployed worldwide. Configuration and schema changes have a forest-wide impact. Consider the following:

CONFIGURATION CHANGES The members of the enterprise administrators group hold full control over the configuration container replicated throughout the forest.

SCHEMA CHANGES The members of the schema administrators group hold full control of the schema within a forest.

Documentation for schema and configuration changes should be written down and include:

- The name or the team of administrators making changes.
- Documentation guidelines.
- A mandated process for requesting, changing, and evaluating all changes.

Changing the Forest Plan

When a domain is first created, it can be joined into an existing forest. By default, the domain administrator group of the forest root domain is the schema administrator group for the entire forest.

A domain, once created, cannot be moved between forests; it will always remain a member of the original forest.

Installing and Removing Active Directory

In this chapter the process of promotion and de-promotion with DCPROMO, and metadata cleanup with Ntdsutil are detailed. Topics covered include:

- Promoting the root domain controller
- Adding domain controllers to existing domains
- Creating multiple tree forests
- Demoting a domain
- Performing a metadata cleanup

Using Dcpromo to Install Active Directory

When a Windows 2000 member server is promoted, the end-result of the promotion can be described in two different ways that have exactly the same outcome:

1. Installing Active Directory creates a Windows 2000 domain controller
2. Promoting a member server to a Windows 2000 domain controller installs Active Directory.

Dcpromo is the installation wizard included with Windows 2000 server products for promoting member servers to active directory domain controllers as shown in Figure 5.1. It can also de-promote an Active Directory domain controller back to a member server role. You should be aware that the use of dcpromo is a bit tricky since the several options available can be confusing at first. If the wrong choices are made, there is no turning back once the promotion has started; your only choice is to de-promote the server.

NOTE

You should also be aware that dcpromo is quite unstable at times. If you are promoting on a busy network, the promotion process can fail quite regularly.

Figure 5.1
Dcpromo is the wizard used to install Active Directory.

Before Promotion Starts

Before you start the process of promoting your server to a domain controller there are some key decisions you must make and implement. These relate to:

1. **DNS services**—In order for a member server to become a domain controller, it must have access to a current DNS server on the network, or DNS services must be installed on the member server before dcpromo is executed, as shown in Figure 5.2.

    A third option, which I don't recommend, is to let the dcpromo promotion process install DNS services automatically. The reason for not recommending that the wizard handle DNS services is that only a forward lookup zone is created, the bare minimum for Active Directory services. It is tempting to let the wizard handle DNS, especially if you are not familiar with installing and configuring DNS. My advice is to get to know DNS completely. If DNS services fail, so does Active Directory. DNS services have to be rock-solid, in fact much more solid and reliable that the current Microsoft version. If you are using BIND DNS, the version that supports the DNS requirements for Windows 2000 domain controllers is version 8.12.

2. **DNS namespace**—Your member server should have its domain name in place before the promotion process begins, as shown in Fig-

ure 5.3. This is also a mandated requirement for every domain controller. You can make the decision during the promotion process; however, this is not the time to make a quick naming decision, because you can't change it later on after the promotion is complete, unless you completely reinstall from the beginning.

3. **NTFS partitions**—NTFS partitions are required for the installation of Active Directory. The key is to plan for future size requirements; these are dealt with in Chapter 10. The *minimum* partition size is 200 MB, but, we need lots of space and RAID hardware subsystems for Windows 2000.

NOTE

If at all possible, don't upgrade your NT 4.0 PDCs to Windows 2000 domain controllers. Try to perform a clean Windows 2000 install and promotion on a freshly wiped system. The speed of a newly installed Windows 2000 domain controller versus an upgraded NT 4.0 PDC is almost twice as great because of loads of older system DLLs and other system components that remain behind after an upgrade.

The First Domain Controller is the Boss

The first domain controller to be installed can be referred to as the first DC in the new forest, new site, and new root domain. As the first domain controller in the forest, it is the single most important DC in your entire enterprise—if this DC fails so does your entire Active Directory hierarchy. Cover yourself adequately; never have just one domain controller in the forest root domain; a minimum is two. Hardware vendors will rejoice because for the first domain in the forest, several essential services are installed during the promotion process, and since they are essential, they have to be installed on the first domain controller; there is no other DC yet available to share the load of essential active directory services, which are:

- **FSMO Roles**—The first domain controller in the forest hosts two forest-wide single-operation master roles: the schema master (the schema can only be written to and updated on the physical domain controller where the schema master role is present) and the domain-naming master. Only at this physical domain controller location in the forest can the configuration information describing all domain controllers in the forest and the trust relationships between them be written and updated.
- **Global Catalog server**—By default, the first domain controller in the forest hosts the first global catalog server for the entire forest.

You will have numerous global catalog servers since every domain controller has the capability to perform the global catalog role.

- **Trusts**—As the first domain controller in the forest, the root DC forms the start of each Kerberos transitive trust with every child domain that is added to the forest below it, and with each additional root domain in the forest. If these trusts become damaged, the game is over. Are you starting to appreciate the importance of the first domain controller in the forest?

- **Default First Site**—The first domain controller in the forest is installed into the first site in the forest, called the default site. Initially there is only one site for the entire forest of domain controllers. Since the root DC is also the first domain installed in the default first site, it is also assigned the role of the InterSite Topology Generator. This role manages the network topology for both intra-site and inter-site replication.

The First Domain Controller in a Domain

The very first domain controller in the forest is also the first DC in the domain. As other subdomains are added to the forest, each domain will initially have a "first domain controller" in each separate domain. The first DC also has important system roles you should be aware of; three domain-wide operations masters roles are assigned to the first domain in the forest: the PDC emulator role, the RID master, and the infrastructure master. More details on these roles are found in Chapter 6.

Promoting the First Domain Controller

Starting the promotion process is as simple as clicking the **Start** button and choosing **Run** and then typing **DCPROMO** and clicking **OK**. Clicking **Next** presents the first decision you must make, as shown in Figure 5.4: whether to create a new domain controller for a new domain, or to create an additional domain controller for a new domain. Since this is the very first domain controller in the forest, the first option "Domain controller for a new domain" is selected.

Figure 5.4
Choosing the domain controller type with dcpromo.

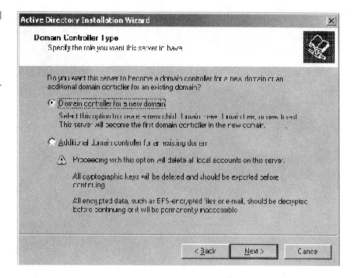

Tree or Child Domain

The next screen is titled "Create tree or child domain, as shown in Figure 5.5. Terminology used at this point is confusing; we were just talking about creating a forest, and now the question asks about a tree. However, once you have created the first root domain controller this screen makes more sense.

The first option, "Create a new domain tree," will be chosen since we are creating a new domain tree starting at the root. We are also creating the first forest and the first site as well. Once this promotion is complete we would then add a second domain controller to the domain just created.

New or Existing Forest

Since this is the first domain controller in the forest, tree, and site, the first option presented in Figure 5.6 will be to select "Create a new forest of domain trees." In the future, this option will have other ramifications if you already have another existing Windows 2000 forest installed. Choosing the first option in this case would create another root domain controller in a completely different forest that would not be linked in any way, shape, or form to the first root domain you created. You think to yourself, I'll create a one-way trust at the root level on each root domain controller linking the two roots together. This could be accomplished, but the one-way trusts pointing both ways do not combine to

Figure 5.5
Creating the first
domain tree with
dcpromo.

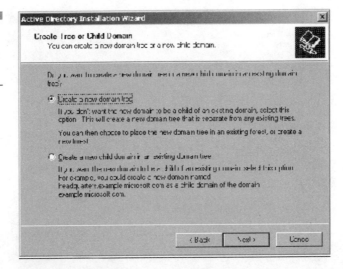

create a Windows 2000 transitive trust, they are NT 4.0 one-way trusts. They cannot and will not become transitive trusts; they must be managed as NT 4.0 trusts.

Figure 5.6
Creating a new forest
with dcpromo.

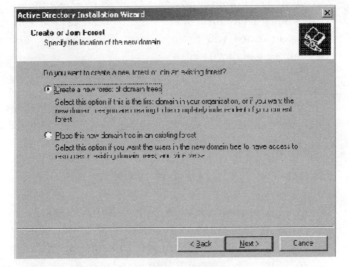

Naming Your Domain

This next screen, displayed in Figure 5.7, asks you to enter the DNS name of your domain and not the name of the domain controller. Installing the first domain controller means that the DNS name will be something on the order of mybusiness.net, or corp.com. Make sure that the name you use is the proper name—after promotion there is no undo for a misspelled or wrong DNS name.

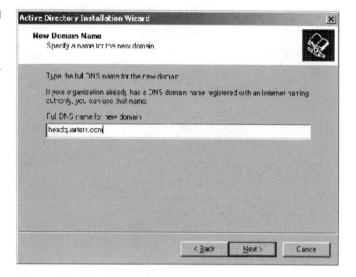

Figure 5.7
Enter the new DNS domain name.

NetBIOS Naming

After a short period of time the wizard will prompt you to OK its selection of the NetBIOS name as shown in Figure 5.8. The name must be less than 15 characters, and you will be prompted if the name is incorrect. Down-level 95/98 and NT 4.0 clients require this name to be able to find the new domain; WINS and browser registration also require this name as well. I would leave the name the same as in the first part of your DNS domain.

Database and Log Locations

Location of the two main components of Active Directory, the NTDS.DIT database file, and its associated LOG files, can be indicated at this time, as detailed in Figure 5.9. The best results will be obtained if the database and log files are located on separate spindles. This can be accomplished in the future using the command line utility Ntdsutil, which is covered at the end of this chapter.

Figure 5.8
Accept the NETBIOS
name.

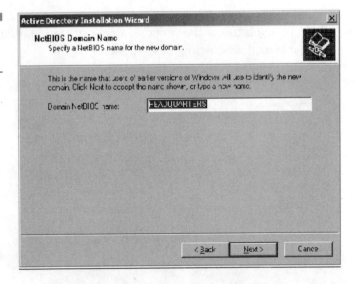

Figure 5.9
Database and Log
file locations for
Active Directory.

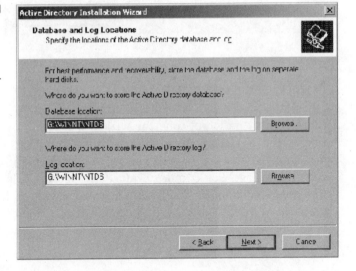

Shared System Volume

The wizard now prompts you for the location of the shared system volume, as presented in Figure 5.10. The SYSVOL volume will automatically replicate with all other domain controllers in the domain and its partition format must be NTFS version 5. Finally, the location of the SYSVOL volume cannot change after the promotion process is complete.

Figure 5.10
SYSVOL is replicated
to all domain
controllers in the
domain.

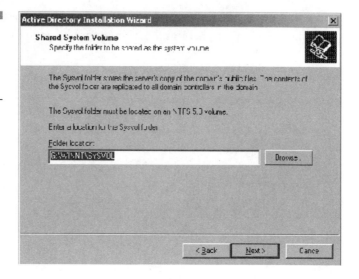

Calling DNS

At this point in the promotion process, DNS services are contacted. It's easy to forget to point your server to the desired DNS server, so if the message shown in Figure 5.11 appears, first check your TCP/IP properties. This can be done without exiting the wizard. Or, you may see the message "The wizard cannot contact the DNS server ....." because you have planned to use the wizard to install DNS services. This can work, but I don't recommend it! Clicking OK presents the Configure DNS splash screen shown in Figure 5.12, which forces you to make a choice: let the wizard install DNS or stop the promotion process and install DNS manually and then run dcpromo once again.

Figure 5.11
Where are DNS
services?

The normal course of events that can also unfold is that DNS is installed properly on the local member server being promoted, or the member server already correctly points to a current DNS server on the network. So Figures 5.11 and 5.12 may not be seen at all.

Figure 5.12
DNS choices are
made here.

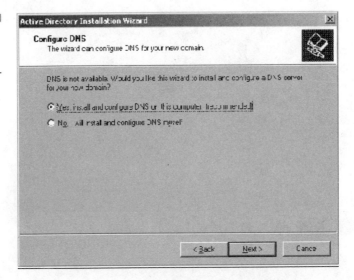

Deciding on Permissions

Now the wizard asks you to select the default permissions for user and group objects, as displayed in Figure 5.13. If you are using network services on other NT 4.0 servers that allow authentication with NULL credentials, such as NT 4.0 RAS, you probably don't want anonymous users to be able to authenticate to your Windows 2000 servers and be able to access files. Selecting the first option in Figure 5.11, "Permissions compatible with Windows 2000 servers" adds the Everyone group to the local group "Pre-Windows 2000 Compatible access" allowing everyone read access across the Windows 2000 server. Choosing the second option, "Permissions compatible only with Windows 2000 servers," removes this security loophole.

Directory Services Restore Mode Password

The screen presented in Figure 5.14 is easy to skip over and forget. Don't do that; this password is not the local administrator's password; this is the password you must supply when your domain controller has failed, or you want to enter a special mode of operation called Directory Services Restore Mode. WRITE THIS PASSWORD DOWN AND LOCK

Figure 5.13
Permissions compatible with Windows 2000 remove anonymous access.

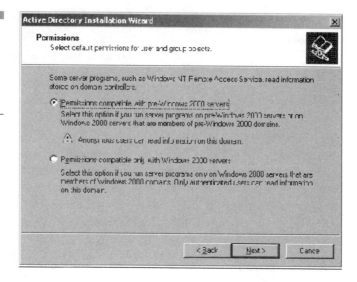

IT IN A SAFE OFF-SITE LOCATION. THERE IS NO WAY TO RETRIEVE THIS PASSWORD IF YOU FORGET IT. Although you can change this password later using DSRM, you first need the password to be able to change it.

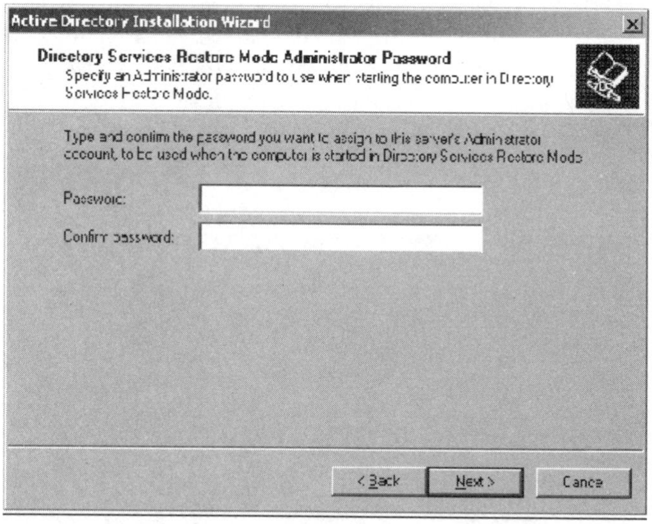

Figure 5.14
This password is required for Directory Services Restore Mode.

Finalizing Before Promoting

A summary screen similar to Figure 5.15 will now be displayed summarizing your choices. Click **Next** to start and complete the promotion process.

Figure 5.15
Summary information
as to how promotion
will proceed.

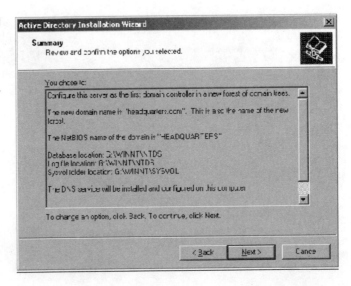

Figure 5.15
Summary information
as to how promotion
will proceed.

Promotion Details

During the promotion process, many system messages are shown on screen. Read them carefully; the details can be useful if you continue to have promotion failures. Noting where the failure occurs can help direct you to the same location in the WINNT\DEBUG dcpromo.log file that will detail the success or failure of dcpromo. Figure 5.16 shows the beginning of the promotion process.

Figure 5.16
Promotion details
about how
promotion is
proceeding.

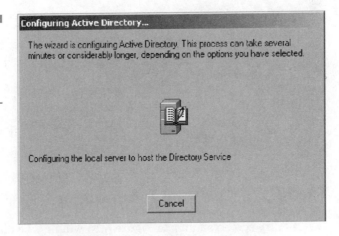

Successful Promotion

Once the promotion process is complete, a summary screen similar to Figure 5.17 will be displayed. After rebooting, your member server is now a Windows 2000 domain controller. When you log in as Administrator, the Administrative Tools will be updated with the Active Directory console tools for managing Active Directory.

Figure 5.17
Successful
promotion.

Adding a Domain Controller to an Existing Domain

Every Windows 2000 domain, other than a small remote domain, should be hosted by multiple domain controllers for reliability and fault tolerance. This promotion process is the simplest use of dcpromo with the fewest steps. Changing the fully qualified domain name of the member server, as well as pointing to existing DNS services on the local subnet, should be performed before running dcpromo.

Once dcpromo is started, the second splash screen is where the choices start once again, as shown in Figure 5.18. Adding a second or third domain controller requires the selection of the second option, "Additional domain controller for an exiting domain." But before clicking **Next**, re-read the splash screen as displayed in Figure 5.18. All local accounts will be deleted on this local server; the only accounts that will remain are the Administrator's account and IUSR and IWAM accounts used for

IIS anonymous access. If you have used the server as a member server for some time, there may be some user accounts deleted during the promotion process.

Figure 5.18
Adding additional
domain controllers.

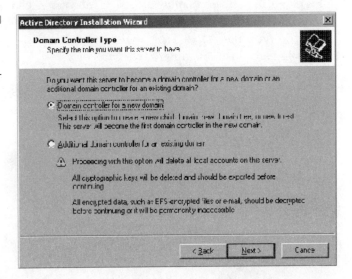

Figure 5.18
Adding additional
domain controllers.

Network Credentials

The wizard now prompts you for a valid set of network credentials, as shown in Figure 5.19, which verify that you are allowed to perform this promotion process. The local administrator and password of either the local domain you wish to join, or the root domain in the forest, are acceptable credentials to enter.

The next installation options are requested at the end of every dcpromo session; all promotions need to know the following information. Graphics for these steps are presented earlier in the chapter if you wish to review them.

NOTE

Database and Log Locations

Location of the two main components of Active Directory, the NTDS.DIT database file, and its associated LOG files, can be indicated at this time, as detailed in Figure 5.9. The best results will be obtained if the data-

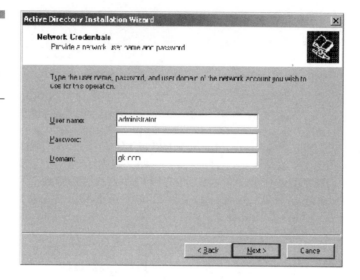

Figure 5.19
Proper network credentials are required to promote member servers.

base and log files are located on separate spindles. This can be accomplished in the future using Ntdsutil, which is covered at the end of this chapter.

Shared System Volume

The wizard now prompts you for the location of the shared system volume as presented in Figure 5.10. The SYSVOL volume will automatically replicate with all other domain controllers in the domain, and its partition format must be NTFS version 5. Finally, the location of the SYSVOL volume cannot change after the promotion process is complete.

Permission Choices

Now the wizard asks you to select the default permissions for user and group objects, as displayed in Figure 5.13. Selecting the first option, "Permissions compatible with Windows 2000 servers" adds the Everyone group to the local group "Pre-Windows 2000 Compatible access," allowing everyone read access across the Windows 2000 server. Choosing the second option, "Permissions compatible only with Windows 2000 servers," removes this security loophole.

Directory Services Restore Mode Password

The screen presented in Figure 5.14 is easy to skip over and forget. Don't do that; this password is not the local administrator's password; this is the password you must supply when your domain controller has failed, or you want to enter a special mode of operation called Directory Services Restore Mode. WRITE THIS PASSWORD DOWN AND LOCK IT IN A SAFE OFF-SITE LOCATION. THERE IS NO WAY TO RETRIEVE THIS PASSWORD IF YOU FORGET IT. Although you can change this password later using DSRM, you first need the password to be able to change it.

Finalizing before Promoting

A summary screen will now be displayed summarizing your choices. Click **Next** to start and complete the promotion process.

Monitoring the Promotion Process

Carefully monitor the promotion process it unfolds. As mentioned earlier in this chapter, the promotion process is sometimes quite unstable, possibly due to other network traffic and other unseen elements of Murphy's Law and the cosmos interacting. Whatever the reasons, there are critical steps in the promotion process to oversee. The first example displayed is Figure 5.20, which shows the first step in adding an additional domain controller to an existing domain as the domain membership of the member server is changed to the domain it will be hosting.

The other two system messages that will be displayed, regardless of the type of promotion being performed, are the replication of the configuration container and the schema container, as shown in Figure 5.21. If problems occur when this information is being replicated from the existing domain controller to the member server being promoted, you will receive a variety of error messages; a common error message is that the server is busy, as shown in Figure 5.22. The question is: doing what? Many times I have promoted a member server on a network with no other activity and the message will still appear, forcing me to start the promotion process once again.

Figure 5.20
System messages
detail the promotion
process.

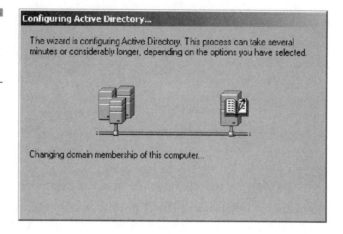

Figure 5.21
The configuration
and schema
containers must
replicate in a timely
fashion or the
promotion process
will fail.

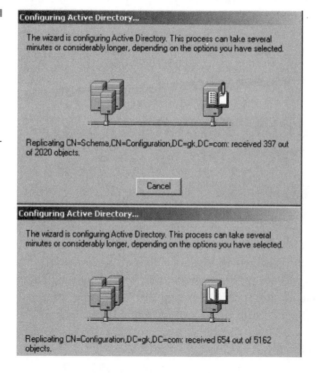

Successful Promotion

Once the promotion process is complete, a summary screen will be displayed. After rebooting, your member server is now a Windows 2000 domain controller that is sharing the hosting of the domain. When you

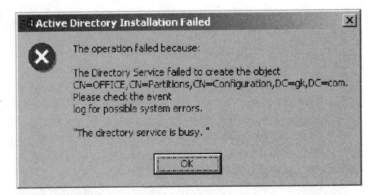

log in as Administrator, the Administrative Tools will be updated with
the Active Directory console tools for managing Active Directory. Every
additional domain controller added to an existing domain is not
assigned any of the three domain operations masters roles, or the role of
an additional global catalog server. These decisions and changes are
manual tasks. What the additional domain controller provides is additional fault-tolerance for the domain.

Adding Domains to an Existing Tree

Adding an additional domain to an existing forest is called making either a
child domain or subdomain; you could also choose to add a second or third
tree to the root of an existing forest (that option is covered later in this chapter). The naming of the new child domain must follow the DNS naming
already defined by the root domain and possibly other subdomains; it all
depends where the new domain will be placed. The new domain must also
have proper TCP/IP, DNS, and an FQDN in place before running dcpromo.

Once dcpromo is started, on the Create Tree or Child Domain splash
screen, select the second option "Create a new child domain in an existing domain tree," as shown in Figure 5.23.

Network Credentials

As before, to promote a member server to a domain controller, you must
supply a user account and password suitable for the task. Again, the
local administrator account for the root domain is sufficient.

Figure 5.23
A new child domain
is created in an
existing domain tree.

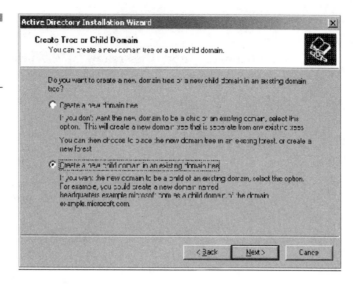

Naming the Child Domain

The wizard now requires the name of the new child domain. The DNS
namespace used to identify the domain must properly place the child
domain in the existing tree; your choices are directly off the root, as
shown in Figure 5.24, or as a child domain of another existing domain in
the tree.

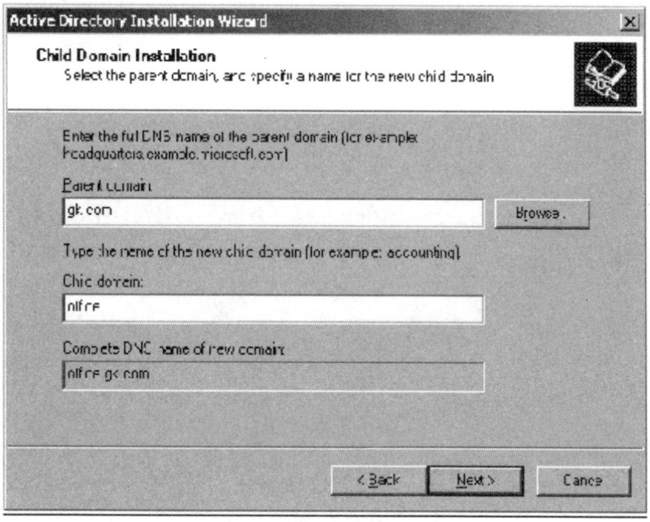

Figure 5.24
The placement of the
child domain
depends on the
parent domain
chosen.

Finishing the Promotion

The remaining steps in getting ready for the promotion of the child domain are:

1. Accepting the NetBIOS name
2. Assigning database and log file locations
3. Assigning a SYSVOL location
4. Getting permissions: compatible with pre-Windows 2000 servers, or only with Windows 2000 servers
5. Assigning a Directory Services Restore Mode password

Creating New Domain Trees in Existing Forests

The last task for which we can use dcpromo is to create a second tree that will be located in an existing forest. Since we are creating a new tree, the four components that must also be created are:

1. A new domain
2. A new domain controller to host the new domain
3. A new DNS name for the new domain
4. DNS services delegated to the initial root domain

New Domain Tree Concepts

The key point to understand here is that there is only one root domain in a single forest. However, there can be multiple trees created within a single forest that link directly to the root domain at the top of the initial tree created in the forest. We are not creating multiple forests; we are creating multiple trees within one forest, and each tree will have a unique DNS name. The first decision to make when running dcpromo is to create a new domain tree, as shown in Figure 5.25.

The next decision is to select "Place this new domain tree in an existing forest," as shown in Figure 5.26.

Figure 5.25
Creating a new
domain tree that
resides in an existing
forest.

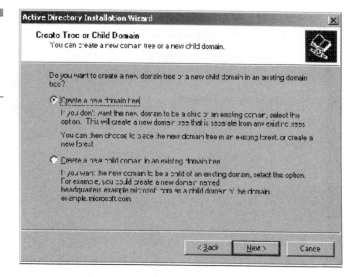

Figure 5.26
A new domain tree
will have access to
the initial trees
resources through a
transitive trust.

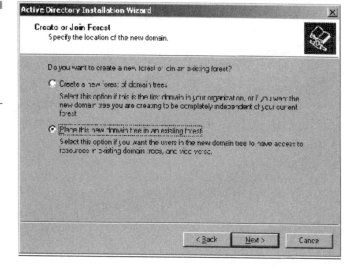

DNS Naming for the New Tree

Next you must name the new tree with a unique DNS name. It may
appear that you are creating a root, since the DNS name is similar in
scope; for example, if my root domain DNS name were headquarters.com,
my new tree could be named research.com, as shown in Figure 5.27. This
is not a root domain; however, it is joined to an existing root domain at

the top of its tree. Once the promotion process has finished, there will be a transitive two-way trust between headquarters.com and research.com.

Figure 5.27
The DNS name of the second tree must be unique.

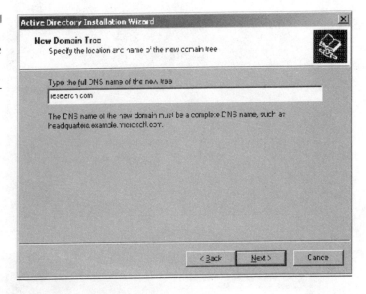

Finishing the Promotion

The remaining steps in getting ready for the promotion of the new tree are:

1. Accepting the NetBIOS name
2. Assigning database and log file locations
3. Assigning a SYSVOL location
4. Getting permissions: compatible with pre-Windows 2000 servers, or only with Windows 2000 servers
5. Assigning a Directory Services Restore Mode password

Summary

The summary of the creation of a new tree in an existing forest is presented in Figure 5.28, confirming the new domain tree and the trust link with the root domain.

Figure 5.28
Confirming the steps
that will be
performed in the
promotion process.

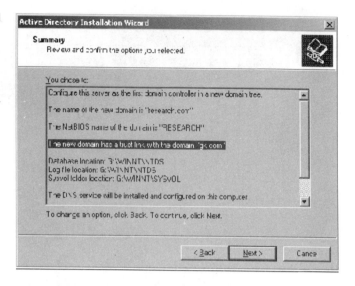

Dcpromo Creates a New Domain Structure

Every Windows 2000 domain controller has new files and folder structures that were added during the dcpromo process.

Dcpromo Logs

In the WINNT\Debug folder several log files are stored that deal with the dcpromo promotion process. DCPROMO.LOG is a summary log of the promotion process; DCPROMOUI.LOG is a complete step-by-step listing of the entire promotion process from beginning to end, including error messages. A partial listing of DCPROMO.LOG is shown in Figure 5.29.

Active Directory Database Files

Once promotion is complete, the WINNT\NTDS folder is created and populated with the database file NTDS.DIT and transaction log files, as shown in Figure 5.30. EDB.LOG is the master log file, and RES1.LOG and RES2.LOG are backups in case the hard disk becomes full. EDB.CHK is a pointer to the location in the log files where information has not been updated in the database.

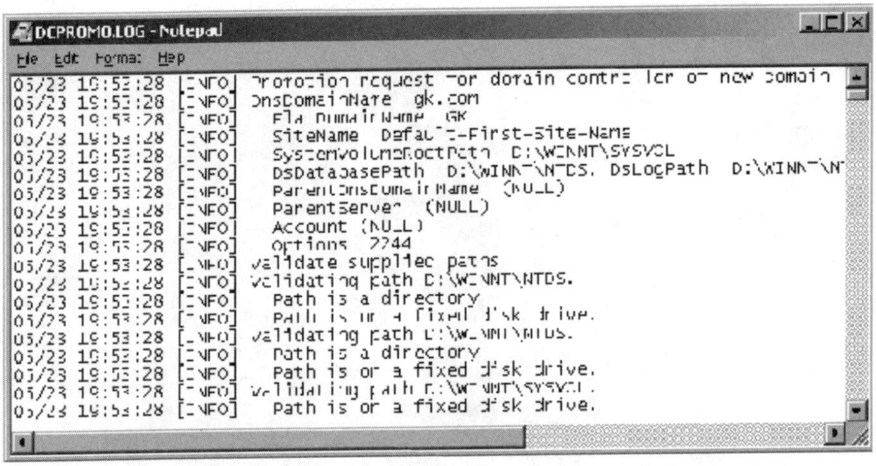

Figure 5.29
Log files are helpful for troubleshooting dcpromo.

Figure 5.30
Database and Log files created by dcpromo.

SYSVOL

Sysvol is the shared system volume, shown in Figure 5.31, that holds logon scripts and group policy settings automatically set to replication using the file replication service. Identical information is contained on every domain controller within a domain.

Figure 5.31
SYSVOL holds group policy and script settings.

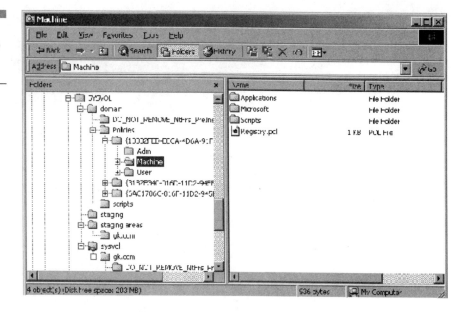

DNS Structure

After promotion has completed, you are prompted to reboot your server. Once the new domain controller comes online, the Netlogon service will create a text file called NETLOGON.DNS, which contains all the relevant DNS information used by the DNS service. This file is stored in the WINNT\SYSTEM32\CONFIG folder. If DNS is changed from standard primary to Active Directory integrated, the NETLOGON.DNS file contents will be copied and stored in Active Directory. As shown in Figure 5.32, the DNS service will have four new folders in its forward lookup zone indicating that Active Directory has successfully been installed: _msdcs, _sites, _tcp, and _udp.

The Registry

The Registry is updated with essential local settings for each domain controller, as shown in Figure 5.33. Important settings include: DNS naming, global catalog promotion details, and the defined replication schedule, all located in HKLM\System\CurrentControl\Services\Services\NTDS\Parameters. In addition to these settings, the Diagnostics folder also allows you to set the level of reporting detail sent to the event log. See the Troubleshooting chapter for further details on the Registry setting that can be changed.

Figure 5.32
DNS records are
updated after
promotion to a
domain controller.

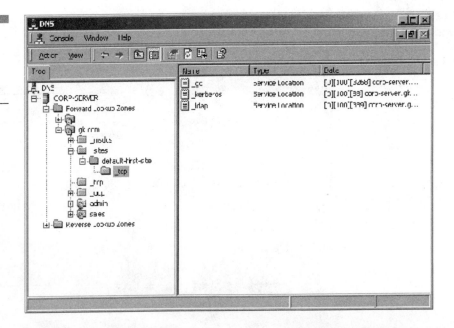

Figure 5.33
Key active directory
settings are stored in
the local registry.

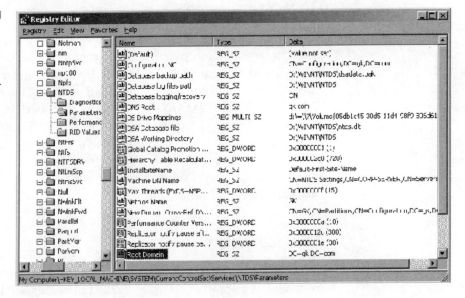

Default Containers

After the dcpromo process, several default containers are added to each
domain controller. These are mandatory; they cannot be moved or deleted. See Figure 5.34.

Figure 5.34
Default container
structure after
installation.

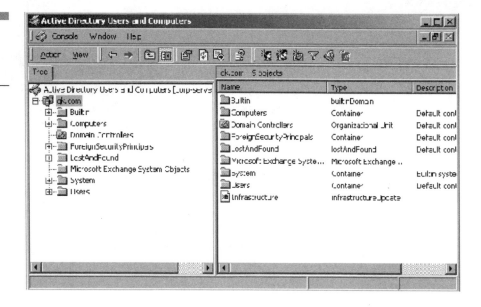

Builtin

The builtin container is where the eight NT 4.0 local groups plus one additional group, Pre-Windows 2000 Compatible Access, are located. When an NT 4.0 primary domain controller is upgraded, the eight local groups are migrated to this folder.

Computers

This container holds Windows 2000 computer accounts when they join the domain. When an NT 4.0 primary domain controller is upgraded, all existing computer accounts will be migrated to this folder.

ForeignSecurityPrinciples

This container holds the groups that are controlled and populated by the operating system; Anonymous Logon, Batch, Creator Group, Creator Owner, Dialup, Enterprise Domain Controllers, Proxy, Restricted, Self, Service, System, Terminal Server User, Authenticated Users, Interactive, Network, and Everyone.

Users

The Users container contains the users and groups by default. If an NT 4.0 primary domain controller in-place upgrade is performed, all the existing NT 4.0 domain user accounts are migrated to the Users container. The Users container cannot have its own group policy object on its own; it is subject to the domains group policy object.

Domain Controllers OU

This container contains all Windows 2000 domain controllers that host the domain. If an NT 4.0 primary domain controller in-place upgrade is performed, all the existing NT 4.0 domain controllers in the domain are migrated to the Domain Controller's OU container. They are then controlled by the Domain Controller's OU default group policy.

Lost and Found

Objects that become lost due to mix-ups in replication end up in the Lost and Found folder. For example, let's say you delete an OU called Executive because it is not being used. Somewhere else in the current domain, a few minutes later, another administrator creates a user in the Executive OU called Mark. In the normal process of replication, the OU would get deleted, and then the user would be created, except there is no Executive OU into which to place the user. The solution is the Lost and Found container, where Mark will reside until someone notices that Mark is homeless and takes pity and moves Mark to his new home.

System

The System container (viewable with the Advanced Features view turned on) shows the system features that have their hooks and links into Active Directory, as shown in Figure 5.35. Some administrative tasks are performed here; for example, in order to change the default operation of the file replication service, you must select the File Replication Service\Domain System Volume (SYSVOL share) properties. Since the container operates 24 hours a day, 7 days a week there is usually no reason to change the default values.

Figure 5.35
The System Container is hidden by default.

Demoting a Domain Controller with Dcpromo

Dcpromo has another duty: to remove Active Directory from a domain controller, returning it to a member server role. It would be wonderful if dcpromo could always de-promote quickly and efficiently; it just doesn't. When you perform a de-promotion there are usually old metadata left behind at the root domain that can cause problems when you re-promote the member server using the same name as before. Launching dcpromo on a Windows 2000 domain controller results in the wizard's launching once again, as shown in Figure 5.36, but with only one choice: the removal of Active Directory.

After clicking **Next**, we can get down to business. The only choice on this screen (shown in Figure 5.37) is whether or not the domain controller being removed is the last domain controller in the domain; if it is, then check the box "This server is the last domain controller in the domain." Note that all user accounts, cryptographic keys, and encrypted data will also be deleted.

NOTE

If you have installed Certificate Services, they will also need to be removed using the Control Panel applet Add/Remove Programs.

Figure 5.36
Dcpromo is also used to remove Active Directory.

Figure 5.37
Removing a domain controller can also delete many system components.

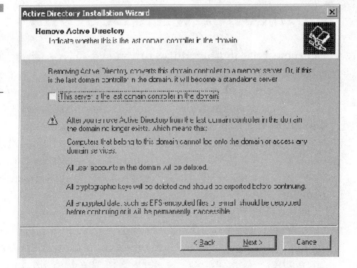

When you click **Next**, the wizard prompts you to enter network credentials of a user who has been assigned Enterprise Administrator privileges; this will usually be the root domain administrator. Then the local domain administrator's username and password must also be entered.

After you again click **Next**, a summary screen (shown in Figure 5.38) is displayed, warning you that the current domain will no longer exist after this process is complete.

Figure 5.38
Last warning before the domain controller is demoted.

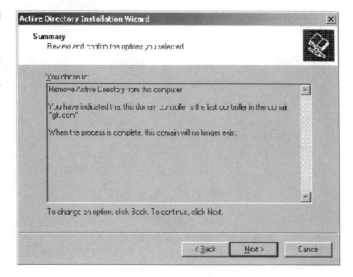

Metadata Cleanup

After you have demoted your domain controller, you are left with a member server. However, as far as the root domain is concerned, it may still have fragments of the just-deleted domain and the domain controller stored in the configuration container. For example, as shown in Figure 5.39, the sales domain has been removed using dcpromo, yet the root domain still thinks it exists. If this happens, and it does fairly regularly, we must dig into our toolbox of command-line tools to remove old metadata components. Depending on what has been left behind this process could take minutes, or hours.

Using Ntdsutil

Ntdsutil has many functions for Active Directory; one of the most important is metadata cleanup. To clean up old metadata located on your root server these are the essential steps.

Figure 5.39
Old metadata may
have to be removed.

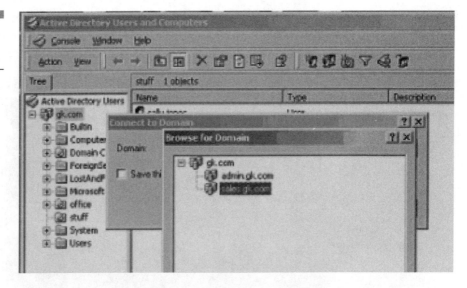

1. Exit to the command prompt and execute Ntdsutil.
2. At the Ntdsutil prompt, enter **Connection** to enter the Connection menu as shown in Figure 5.40. Use the command "Connect to server." After you have successfully bound to your root server, type Quit to move back to the metadata cleanup menu.

Figure 5.40
A connection to the
root domain is
required.

3. Next type **Select Operation target**. At the prompt, enter List domains, as shown in Figure 5.40. The domains will be listed numerically starting at 0.

4. Select the domain you wish to remove and type select domain <number>. In Figure 5.40 I have selected domain 1, the sales domain, to remove.

5. Type **Quit** to return to the metadata cleanup menu.

6. Next type **Remove** selected domain, as shown in Figure 5.41; you will be prompted with the warning "Are you sure?" Click **Yes** to continue the process.

7. The metadata will be removed, as detailed in Figure 5.41. Exit from Ntdsutil and you're done.

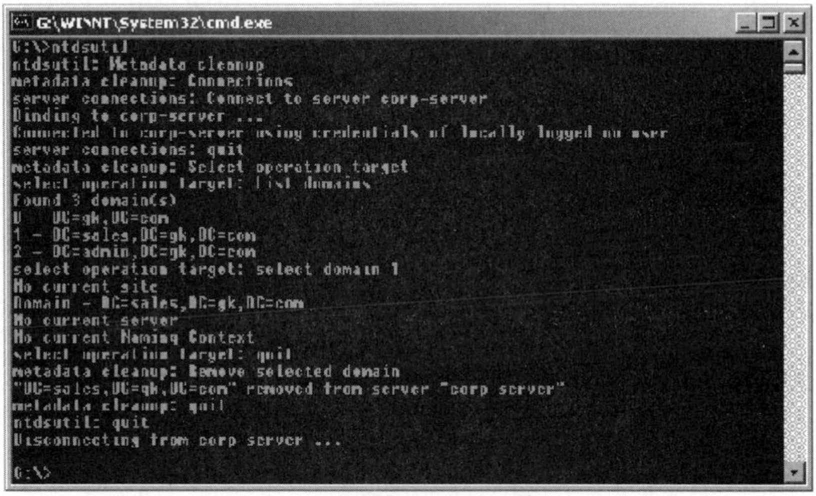

Figure 5.41
Removing metadata
can be a time
consuming task.

Administrative Solutions: Getting Ready for Promotion

Active Directory requires an NTFS 5 partition.

1. You may have to create an NTFS partition for Active Directory; start by navigating Start\Programs\Administrative Tools and selecting MMC Disk Management.

   A. Select the Disk Management folder in the Computer Management tree.

   B. Right-click the portion of your hard drive to create a new partition and select Format.

   C. Format the partition with these parameters:
      – NTFS selected

        – Default allocation unit size

        – The checkbox Perform a Quick Format is checked.

    D. Close the MMC Hard Disk Management.

2. From the Desktop right-click on My Network Places and select **Properties**.

    A. Right-click on the Local Area Connection and select **Properties**.

    B. Select TCP/IP and click the **Properties** button.

    C. On the General tab enter the static TCP/IP address of your server and subnet mask.

    D. Click **OK** three times to close the Local Area Connection properties.

Now check that your fully qualified domain name is correct.

3. From the Desktop, right-click My Computer and select **Properties**.

    A. Select the Network Identification tab and click the **Properties** button.

    B. Click the **More** button.

    C. Ensure that the "Primary DNS suffix of this computer" is set properly.

Write down your computer's FQDN:

_____._____._____.com

  Computer Name   sub-domain root

Installing Active Directory Creating a Child Domain

1. Select **Start | Run** and enter the text DCPROMO; the Active Directory Installation wizard will launch; after each step, click **Next** to continue.

    A. At the Domain Controller Type splash screen, select "Domain controller for a new domain."

    B. At the Create Tree or Child Domain splash screen, select "Create a new child domain in an existing domain tree."

    C. For network credentials, enter the following valid values and click **Next**.

    D. The DNS name of the parent domain should be already filled in; add the name of the child domain you are creating.

E. Accept the Domain NetBIOS name as shown and click **Next** to continue.

F. At the Database location and Log location enter the desired location and click **Next** to continue.

G. At the Shared System Volume, change the location to the desired location.

H. On the Permissions screen select the desired Permissions and click **Next**.

I. For the Directory Services Restore Mode Administrator password, if you enter a password, write it down; click **Next**.

J. Read the summary screen to review and click **Next** to start the promotion process.

K. The promotion process should take 15–20 minutes.

Read the messages displayed on the Configuring Active Directory splash screen as your domain is created and Active Directory is installed.

L. Reboot when prompted.

M. Check the existing network structure using the Active Directory Domains and Trusts console found in the Administrative Tools menu. You should see the root domain gk.com and the subdomains listed below.

N. Open the log file dcpromo.log found in \WINNT\DEBUG.

O. Review the promotion details for your subdomain.

Use DCPROMO to Remove a Domain

1. Click **Start | Run** and enter DCPROMO and click **OK**.

A. Click **Next** and on the Remove Active Directory splash screen check the checkbox "this server is the last domain controller in the domain" if it is applicable; click **Next**.

B. Enter the network credentials and click **Next**.

C. Accept the splash screen summary and click **Next** to start the demotion.

D. Once demotion is complete, reboot your server and log in as Administrator.

Promote an Additional Domain Controller for an Existing Domain

1. Select **Start | Run** and enter the text DCPROMO; the Active Directory Installation wizard will launch.

   A. At the Domain Controller Type splash screen, select "Domain controller for an existing domain."

   B. For network credentials enter valid network credentials and click **Next**.

   C. Enter the full domain name of the existing domain (using the browse button you can also select the domain you will belong to).

   D. For the default database and log locations enter the desired location and click **Next**.

   E. For the shared system volume enter the desired location and click **Next**.

   F. For the Directory Services Restore Mode Administrator password, if you enter a password, write it down and click **Next**.

   G. Read the summary screen to review and click **Next** to start the promotion process.

   H. The promotion process should take 10–15 minutes.

   I. Reboot and log in as administrator. Check structure using Active Directory Domains and Trusts console. You should see your domain and the two domain controllers that are now hosting it.

Domain Structure

This chapter introduces both logical and physical domain and organizational unit design concepts through the following topics:

- Logical and physical domain structure
- Trusts
- Operations Masters roles
- OU design

Windows 2000 Domains

What is a Windows 2000 domain? A simple answer is that a domain is a logical grouping of *organizational units* (OU), as shown in Figure 6.1. However, that only answers the logical side of the question. A domain must also be viewed as a physical entity. In the logical sense, the domain hosts OUs; but what about the physical side of the equation? A domain controller is assigned to host a domain, and just one domain, containing OUs.

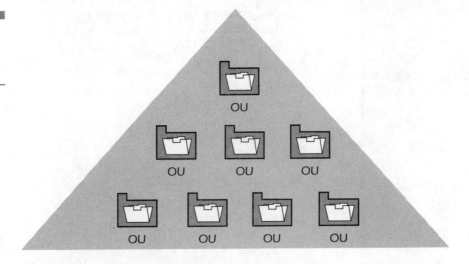

Figure 6.1
In the logical definition a domain contains OUs.

But in fact, the domain performs many other roles that must be addressed. The domain defines a security boundary for all the objects contained within its walls. Inside a typical domain will be familiar objects that define the network's resources: users, groups, printers, files and folders, software applications, file shares, and so on. These objects will then be grouped into containers called organizational units (OUs).

Defined administrative permissions do not expand to other domains. Each domain has a security policy that applies to all security accounts located within the domain's boundaries. The domain also defines a replication boundary; all domain objects defined within its walls are only replicated within the domain. When a new user is created at one domain controller, the other domain controllers will update their records through the normal process of replication. Keep in mind that a domain could be spread over a very large area, like North America. Replication could affect network performance at certain times: when password changes are carried out, or new users, groups, or software installation take place.

The central definitions of Active Directory domains are:

- **A unit of partitioning**—Each domain is identified by a DNS name, and each domain controller hosting the domain stores information about the objects contained within the domain.
- **A unit of authentication**—Each user must be known to the domain, in other words have a valid user account and password, to be successfully authenticated.

The central definitions of Active Directory domain controllers are:

- **Units of replication**—Replication of domain information occurs only within the defined domain.
- **Security boundaries**—Security policies, group policies, permissions, and ACLs stay within the domain.
- **Administrative boundaries**—Administrators of a domain define the security policy within the defined domain.

Domains and Trees

Domains installed in a tree are united by transitive trusts starting from the root domain and share a common DNS namespace, a common schema, and a common configuration topology. Since the schema and configuration information must remain the same on every domain controller in the tree, replication occurs both inside and outside each domain, keeping the global tree information up to date. In Figure 6.2, deloro.com is called the tree root domain; the child domains of deloro.com are sales.deloro.com and manufacturing.deloro.com. Transitive trusts are said to flow between multiple domains; in Figure 6.2, deloro.com trusts sales.deloro.com and sales.deloro.com trusts manufacturing.sales.deloro.com.

The domains sales.deloro.com and manufacturing.deloro.com are also called *child domains* or *subdomains*.

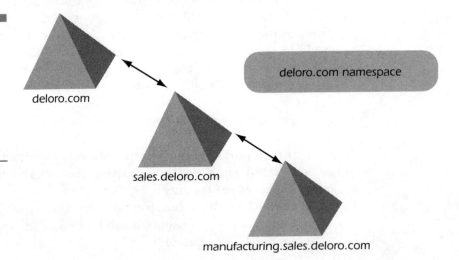

Figure 6.2
Windows 2000 domains can be arranged into a tree of one or more Windows 2000 domains with a contiguous namespace.

Domain Trees to a Forest of Domain Trees

A forest is a set of domain trees that share a common schema and global catalog that have been joined through the initial root domain using dcpromo. The domain trees trust each other using a transitive trust relationship established between the root domains of each tree. Remember, the root domain is the first domain installed in the forest. Each domain in Figure 6.3 has a direct transit trust with its parent and each of its children. If you come across the situation of two completely separate forests and want to join them together with transitive trusts, you won't be able to perform this task. You can join the forests with one-way trusts at the root of each tree. These are not the same as Windows 2000 transitive trusts; they are instead NT 4.0 one-way trusts, and as such must be managed just as we did in NT 4.0. You will find more details on trusts later in this chapter.

Searching in the Forest

Once a forest is created, a central read-only index called the *global catalog* is created automatically on the first domain controller in the root domain, as shown in Figure 6.4; it contains every object in the forest and

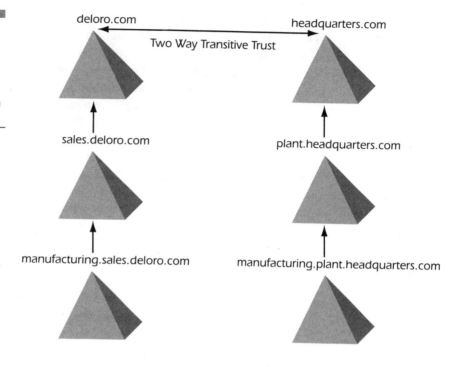

Figure 6.3
Multiple domains with a different namespace that share a single directory are called a forest.

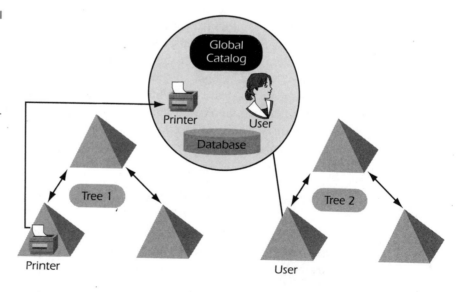

Figure 6.4
A user can search for any object in the entire forest which he/she has the permission to access.

a subset of the available attributes used to describe each object. So, every object defined within each domain must also be replicated to the global catalog. Therefore, the global catalog allows a full search of each object within the entire forest. Within a domain, each domain controller maintains complete information about the domain objects and attributes created and contained within their own domains. So, a search for an object or attribute that starts at a specific domain controller may not use the global catalog at all if the domain controller knows the answer to the query. In fact, Microsoft documentation states that for a single domain, a global catalog is not necessary. This is true only in a domain running in mixed mode; even then in a very large domain, for example a domain that spans North and South America, a global catalog is necessary to quickly resolve queries of a global nature for user logins, since all user principle names are also stored in the global catalog. You could argue that you won't be using UPNs, and then I would have to wonder why you wanted to use Windows 2000 in the first place. The real answer is that in a large Windows 2000 domain running in native mode, a global catalog is required for logons and universal group membership. More on group members and the global catalog's inner workings can be found in Chapter 7.

Domain Controllers are Physical

To support the millions of objects a forest can support, the forest must be partitioned into domains hosted by domain controllers. A domain can be hosted by one domain controller; however, for a measure of fault tolerance, several domain controllers should be used. Note the plural: domain controllers. Each domain should be hosted by a minimum of two DCs and the root should be hosted by a minimum of three DCs.

After all, we want multimaster replication and clustering to provide fault tolerance, don't we? This means many domain controllers. Domain controllers residing in the same domain contain the same domain, schema, and configuration information.

Directory Partitions

The *domain partition* contains a container holding the created users, groups, and computers for the domain. Updates to the domain container are only replicated locally within the domain; however, if a change has

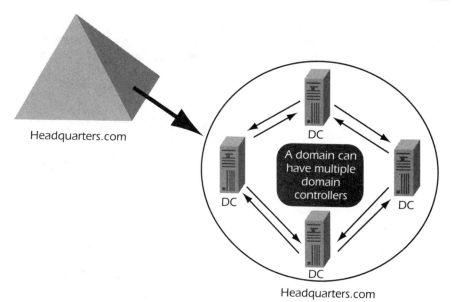

Figure 6.5
In the Windows
2000 environment, a
domain controller is a
computer that is
running Windows
2000 server and
hosting Active
Directory.

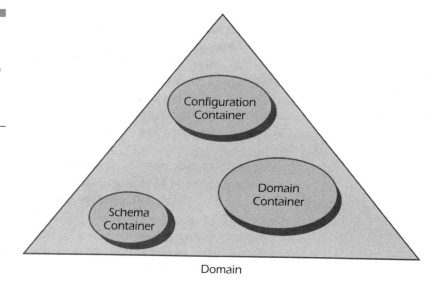

Figure 6.6
Each domain
controller stores dis-
tributed segments of
the directory
database called
partitions.

been made to an attribute replicated to the global catalog, then the GC will be updated as well.

The *schema partition* stores both class and attributes classifications for all existing Active Directory objects. Any changes to the schema container are then replicated to all domain controllers within the forest. The schema container can be viewed using the Schema console snap-in.

The *configuration container* stores configuration details on all domain controllers, directory partitions, sites, and services hosted somewhere in the forest. This information is also replicated to all domain controllers in the forest.

Domain Creation Rules

When you are creating a new domain the rules for creation are:

1. It must be added into an existing tree in a forest.
2. It must be added as a new tree in an existing forest.
3. It must construct a new tree in a new forest.

Domain Names and the DNS Namespace

A domain controller cannot even be promoted until it has a DNS namespace consisting of the server's name and the domain name, also called a *fully qualified domain name* (FQDN). All Windows 20000 server nodes on the network are part of the DNS domain naming hierarchy and the Active Directory hierarchy, as shown in Figure 6.7. Domain names for Active Directory follow the format of root.com. Domains sharing the same namespace as the forest root domain will be defined by a subdomain name of parent.root.com. Any further domains under them will use the subdomain format of child.parent.root.com, as shown in Figure 6.7.

A public .com domain is outside the boundaries of Active Directory; it is a top-level domain found on the Internet, as shown in Figure 6.8.

Within Windows 2000, DNS namespace mandates the following rules:

1. A child domain can only have one parent domain.
2. Two children of the same parent cannot have the same name.

NetBIOS Domain Names are Still Needed

During the domain promotion process, a NetBIOS name is created for your server based on the first portion of the soon-to-be DC's DNS namespace (Figure 6.9). Without the support for NetBIOS names, the older clients would not be able to identify and find a Windows 2000 domain.

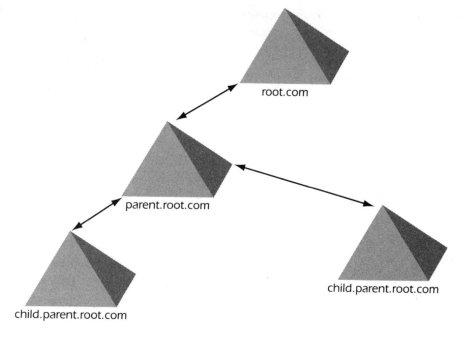

Figure 6.7
DNS naming
standards are used to
name computers and
domains.

root.com

parent.root.com

child.parent.root.com

child.parent.root.com

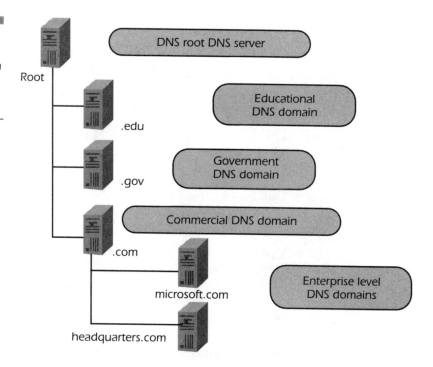

Figure 6.8
Every part of a name
that is separated by a
period (.) represents
an Active Directory
domain name.

DNS root DNS server

Root

Educational
DNS domain

.edu

Government
DNS domain

.gov

Commercial DNS domain

.com

microsoft.com

Enterprise level
DNS domains

headquarters.com

NetBIOS names are used in mixed mode, when you have NT 4.0 backup domain controllers and Windows 2000 Servers performing the PDC role. Mixed mode supports the NetBIOS name, so that Windows 2000 domain controllers can be identified as the "primary domain controller." Both NT 4.0 clients and Windows 9.x clients will still require the NetBIOS name to be able to locate a Windows 2000 controller in either mixed or native mode.

The NetBIOS name can be changed during the creation of a new Windows 2000 domain, but not after.

NOTE

Figure 6.9
NetBIOS names are still supported in Windows 2000 for backward compatibility with Windows NT 4.0 domains and older down-level network clients.

DNS Suffix and NetBIOS Computer Name	? X
Primary DNS suffix of this computer:	
gk.com	
☑ Change primary DNS suffix when domain membership changes	
NetBIOS computer name:	
WILKINS	
This name is used for interoperability with older computers and services.	
	OK Cancel

Resource Records are Used to Find Resources

Nodes and available services are identified through service records called *resource records* (RR). Service records are used to indicate which TCP/IP network services are available within the zone, as shown in Figure 6.10. Each Windows 2000 domain controller registers with DNS using a service record (SRV) and a Host Address resource record; its individual host address and the services that it hosts can be located by servers and clients throughout active directory. This emphasizes the absolute requirement that DNS must always be functioning properly for Active Directory to function. Every network request uses DNS: sites, DNS lookups, secondary servers, domain controllers, Exchange 2000 services; you name it and DNS is involved, since all these services must be hosted by a Windows 2000 server, as shown in Figure 6.11.

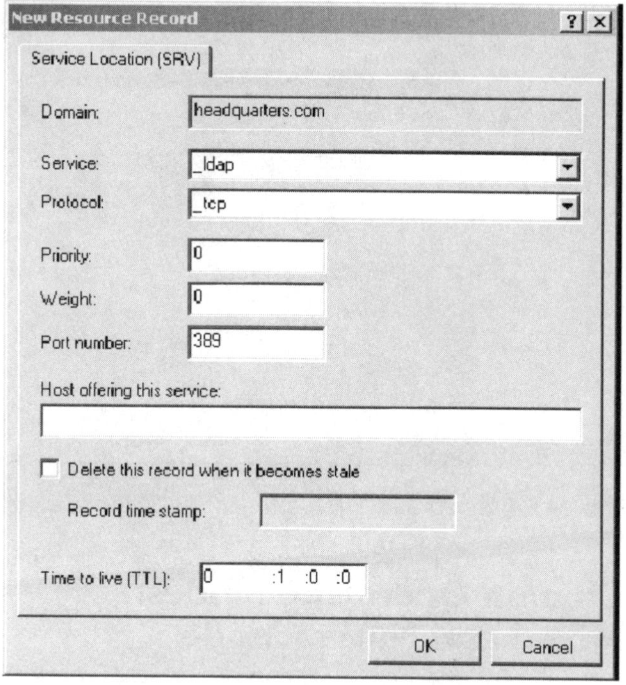

Figure 6.10

Domain controllers use DNS for node identification and Windows 2000 services—LDAP servers, domain controllers, and global catalog servers.

A Windows 2000 client supporting DNS can then send a request, for the server that is hosting a particular service within the defined zone, and receive a list of available servers. Typical service requests from a network client are for:

- Domain controllers that provide logon services
- Global catalog servers
- Network services.

Administrators can also take advantage of resource records by editing resource records to move or add services within the defined zone, as shown in Figure 6.11. Once DNS has been integrated into Active Directory, the DNS zones can then take advantage of multimaster replication. When an update is received by a domain controller, the update is written to Active Directory and then replicated to all other domain controllers. Any DNS server that queries Active Directory will receive the updated information.

Figure 6.11
The DNS forward
lookup zone is the life
blood of Active
Directory.

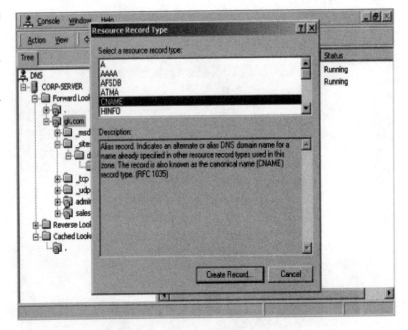

Domain Operating Modes:
Mixed and Native Mode

When a domain controller is first promoted to Windows 2000, it operates in a default mode of operation called mixed mode. Mixed mode allows the Windows NT 4.0 backup domain controllers located in the same domain as the Windows 2000 server to receive any changes that occur to the domain database on the Windows 2000 domain controller through the regular replication process expected by the BDC. Down-level replication happens because a Windows 2000 server, by default, performs the role of the PDC for NT 4.0 BDCs. In a mixed-mode network consisting of Windows 2000 servers and NT 4.0 BDCs, any changes made at the Windows 2000 server must replicate to the BDCs. This allows the older Windows NT 4.0 and Windows 95/98 clients to authenticate to any BDCs available using the down-level system information (NetBIOS, SAM, and LAN Manager authentication). Of course, Windows 2000 client computers can authenticate through a BDC as well. If the domain controller is the first domain controller in a new domain, then it is automatically assigned several of the flexible single-master operations roles. One role is as the PDC emulator. The roles performed by the PDC emulator in mixed mode for the older down-level clients are NT 4.0 style replication and a cloned PDC role.

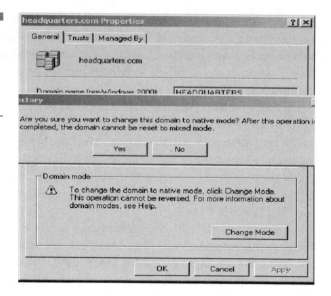

Figure 6.12
Windows 2000 domains have two modes of operation: mixed (which is the default) and native.

NT 4.0 Style Replication to all BDCs from the PDC Emulator

This role is assigned per domain, as shown in Figure 6.12. When you upgrade your PDC to a Windows 2000 domain controller, it knows about the existing backup domain controllers supported in the NT 4.0 world it just left; it will support them as long as it remains operating in mixed mode. However, what about other BDCs in other domains? The existing BDCs located in other NT 4.0 domains will have to be supported through the regular replication process by a mixed-mode Windows 2000 server. If you have a multimaster domain model, with two account domains joined via two one-way trusts, each of the account domains PDC once upgraded to a Windows 2000 mixed-mode server will inherently support the BDCs it knows about.

Performing the PDC Role

This is a done for down-level clients that change their computer account name, for users who change their password, and for NT 4.0 administrative tools (User Manager for Domains or Server Manager) that make changes at a BDC.

Changing to Native Mode

Again beware and be careful! If an administrator opens up Active Directory Users and, Computers and through the domain controllers properties, clicks the button to change to native mode, there is no turning back once the change is made. If there is an NT 4.0 BDC or several BDCs that are receiving updates from a Windows 2000 server running in mixed mode, if the switch is made in error to native mode they will never again replicate!

Even more ominous is the specter of a large domain spread out over a large geographical area. Let's say that the PDC role was assigned to the domain controller in San Francisco, and an Administrator performing maintenance in Boston on a domain controller within the same domain decides that "we aren't using NT 4.0 any more" and clicks the button changing the entire domain, including all domain controllers, to native mode. There is a big problem.

This setting should really be harder to set, in my opinion, but at least you now know the ramifications. Assuming that you want to switch to native mode and click the button making that choice, the down-level replication task is now removed, and that's all. As far as Windows 2000 domain controllers are concerned, just the replication support for NT 4.0 BDCs is affected. Older down-level clients can still log on to Windows 2000 servers and change passwords and computer names, but BDCs are now not involved. Other duties of the PDC emulator are covered in the FSMO section below. Table 6.1 summarizes some additional native and mixed-mode details

TABLE 6.1

Mixed and native mode comparison.

Process	Mixed Mode	Native Mode
Replication	PDC emulator updates BDCs Windows 2000 DCs use multimaster replication	All domain controllers use multimaster replication
Authentication	NT 4.0 clients use NTLM authentication, Windows 2000 use Kerberos	NT 4.0 clients use NTLM authentication, Windows 2000 use Kerberos
NetBIOS	Used for backward compatibility	Used for backward compatibility
Groups	Forced compatibility	Universal groups. Additional nesting options.

FSMO Roles

Active Directory is usually defined as a multimaster directory database; however, there are some changes to the database where one domain controller server acts as the single master. There are five flexible single-master operations roles also called FSMO roles. Three of the five prevail across each domain and two are enterprise in scope, across the entire forest. If a domain controller gets into trouble and becomes unavailable, and that particular domain controller is carrying out one of the FSMO roles, another domain controller is not automatically promoted to assume that role. The FSMO role must be assigned to a new owner (domain controller) as a manual task. These roles are described in the following sections.

Schema Operations Master (Forestwide)

This role belongs to the domain controller in the forest that is permitted to make originating changes to the schema. The first domain controller installed in the forest root domain is the schema master by default. It makes supreme good sense to leave it where most local administrators won't have access to the schema master. Also, properly document the location of the schema master. This means that the Schema Administrators group controls all schema updates carried out in the entire forest. These updates will not be a trivial matter, since any changes to the schema cannot be removed; if mistakes are made the mistakes stay, but they *can* be disabled. Most of you will experience, or already have experienced, the installation of Exchange 2000. This must be installed on the domain controller that is the schema master, since Exchange more than doubles the schema object classes and attributes. This means that schema administrators also will control true Windows 2000 software, which changes the schema before its installed. This is a good idea for controlling changes to the schema. Changing the schema master is done using the Schema console, as shown in Figure 6.13.

Domain Naming Master (Forestwide)

This role belongs to the domain controller that adds new domains and removes existing domains from the forest, and for adding or removing any cross-references to external directory services. The first domain controller installed in the forest is the domain naming master, by default. Again, it should be left here and properly documented so that Administrators know where the role is, or was. During dcpromo, the domain naming master is contacted for current configuration information to replicate to the new domain controller. To view the domain naming master, use Active Directory Sites and Services, as shown in Figure 6.14.

Figure 6.13
The schema master
role defaults to the
first root domain
controller.

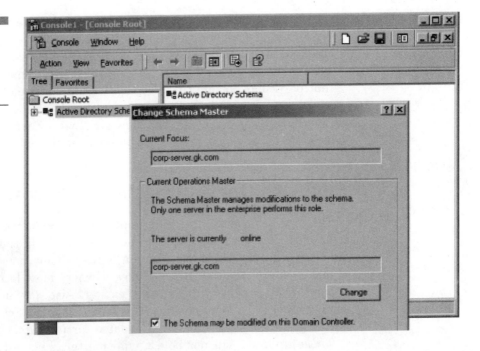

Figure 6.14
The domain naming
master is used during
promotion and
depromotion of
domain controllers.

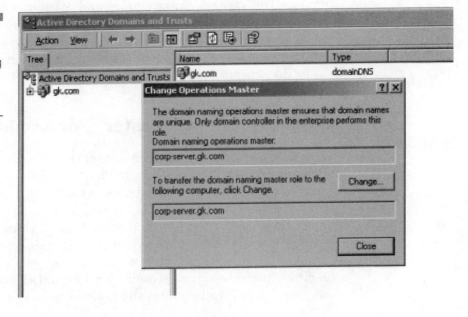

Domain FSMO Roles

The remaining three FSMO roles have a domain scope; that is, each domain will have a domain controller hosting the three roles or, within each domain, if there are multiple domain controllers, each domainwide FSMO role could be assigned to a specific separate domain controller. However, to be perfectly clear, there are only three domainwide FSMO roles; you can't have two PDC emulators, or two RID masters. There can only be one role per domain.

PDC Emulator (Domainwide)

Its scope is the domain and it is assigned to the first domain controller installed in a domain; its responsibility is providing the PDC role for down-level BDCs while running in mixed mode, plus a host of other system tasks. In mixed mode, the PDC emulator performs the following tasks:

1. The PDC role for NT 4.0 replication to existing BDCs.
2. Receiving all password changes immediately once the password has been changed on a Windows 2000 or NT 4.0 BDC domain controller within the domain.
3. Being the domain master browser in the domain.
4. Being the default time master for the domain.
5. Being the default domain controller when there are GPO changes and modifications for group policy in the domain.

A little more detail on password changes is useful: all password changes carried out by any other domain controllers are first sent to the PDC emulator. The PDC emulator is required to reprocess any password authentication requests for users and computers that fail at other domain controllers in the domain. All domain FSMO roles are viewable through Active Directory Users and Computers by selecting Operations Masters, as shown in Figure 6.15.

RID Master (Domainwide)

Its scope is also at the domain, and it is assigned by default to the first domain controller installed in a domain; its responsibility is to manage the Relative Identifier Pools (RIDs). Every domain controller in the domain can create security principals (users, groups, and computers). A RID is part of the Security Identifier (SID). Allotments of RIDs in 512

Figure 6.15
ADUC allows you to
change the FSMO
roles for the domain.

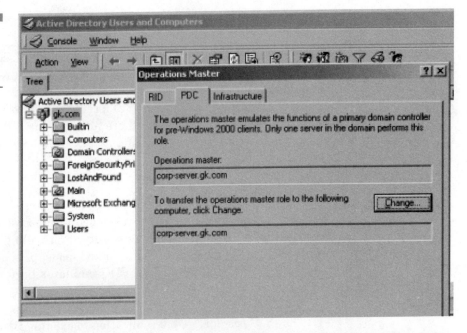

Figure 6.15
ADUC allows you to change the FSMO roles for the domain.

identifier "pools" are assigned to each domain controller at a time. The RID pool master assigns a pool of RIDs to itself and a pool to every other Windows 2000 domain controller in the domain. Once a domain controller has its RID pool allotment from the RID pool master, that DC can autonomously create up to 512 unique SIDs for security principals (e.g. users, groups, computer objects). Before a DC exhausts its allotment, it will request another pool from the RID pool master. A domain controller will completely exhaust the old pool before using any RIDs from the newly allocated pool.

Infrastructure Master (Domainwide)

Its scope is the domain, and it belongs to the first domain controller installed in the domain; its responsibility is to maintain "object consistency" throughout the domain and in remote domains. If a group or user name is changed, its responsibility is to replicate the changes locally in the domain to the domain controllers hosting the local domain. For example, if a user is added as a member of a group in another domain, or if a group in one domain is added as a member of a group in another domain, the infrastructure master in each of the domains makes sure that the two sides of the membership agree that the user is listed as a member of the group, and the group also has the user listed as a member.

In a forest with one domain, there are five operation masters roles; in a forest with three domains the number of operations master roles is 11.

Changing FSMO Roles

As the last section has shown, changing the FSMO roles can be carried out using Active Directory administration tools, when everything is working, of course. What happens when one of the FSMO roles stops working? Will we notice or even care until an assumed FSMO role is not being carried out due to a domain controller's being offline during maintenance, or system failure? In a domain spread across a large geographic area, this could be a problem. The consequences of an FSMO role's being unavailable are detailed in Chapter 15 on troubleshooting; for now rest assured that the command line utility Ntdsutil can be used by an administrator with sufficient permissions to transfer or seize any of the FSMO roles, changing the responsibility level of an online server without rebooting. Once the offline server comes back online, it is informed that it does not have the responsibility of performing an FSMO role.

Domain Trust Relationships

Initial transitive trust relationships in a Windows 2000 forest require no preplanning. A trust relationship is automatically defined between two domains: the trusting domain and the trusted domain. This allows users from a trusted domain to access resources in a trusting domain. Each trust relationship can be one of two types: *one-way* or *transitive two-way*.

One-Way Trust

A single one-way trust relationship is shown in Figure 6.16 where domain A (Trusting) trusts domain B (Trusted). Any authentication requests from users can be processed in one direction, from the trusting domain to the trusted domain. Windows 2000 domains can establish a one-way trust with:

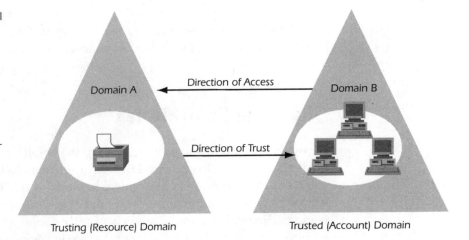

- Windows 2000 domains in a separate forest.
- Windows NT 4.0 domains.

Remember that a trust only allows the possibility *of access, it does not grant the access; that is the administrator's job.*

NOTE

Transitive Two-Way Trusts

All trusts created between Windows 2000 domains are by default two-way transitive trusts. A transitive trust is always two-way and is automatically created between a parent and the new child domain. Transitive trusts are only created between Windows 2000 domains in the same forest by the operating system during promotion of a member server to a Windows 2000 domain controller. There is no other time that a transitive trust can be created, ever. For example, if a new trust is created by the promotion process between a new second child domain in a forest and the existing forest root domain, it is always a transitive trust.

Transitive trusts in the Windows 2000 hierarchy are said to "flow" upward through the domain tree in the forest as they are created. Authentication also flows through the forest, following the trust paths as they are established. As a result, any accounts from any domain in the forest can be authenticated at any domain present in the forest, with the help of the global catalog that also contains all user accounts, User

Principal Names, and other account information used to locate the domain where the account was first created. This allows users to be created anywhere in the forest.

Nontransitive Trust

Creation of a nontransitive trust is always a manual administrative task By default, a nontransitive trust is one-way, although you could follow the exact same NT 4.0 conventions and create two one-way trusts. Any trust relationship created between Windows 2000 domains that do not reside in the same forest, or between a Windows 2000 domain and a Windows NT 4.0 domain are nontransitive (one-way) trusts, as shown in Figure 6.17.

Figure 6.17
A nontransitive trust does not flow to any other domain in the forest.

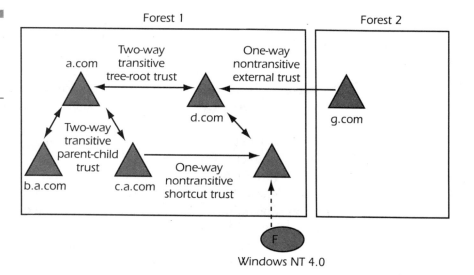

Shortcut Trusts

Shortcut trusts are still one-way trusts, though defined in new terms. However, there is the potential to decrease reliance on parent domains in the default forest trust hierarchy. Multiple trust paths can exist through a forest and also between forests. If the user's location is in a domain not in a parent–child relationship with the domain where the requested resource is located, a chain of authentication must be performed starting from the user's location in the network and going to the

Figure 6.18
A shortcut trust can be established to speed up authentication between a user and a network resource the user wants to access.

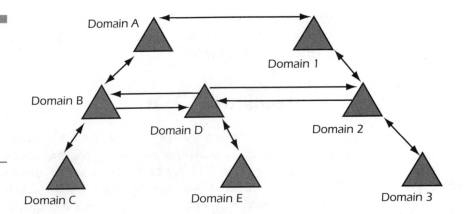

domain's location where the resource is located. Figure 6.18 shows shortcut trusts created between domain B and domain D and, between domain D and domain 2. By default, the root of a tree is a child of the forest root domain where they are joined.

Therefore, all authentication requests between any two domains in different trees must journey through the forest root. The addition of any shortcut trusts could decrease the reliance on intermediate domains such as the forest root (or any parent domain for that matter). Because transitivity is allowed only on the automatically created trusts within a forest, the trust routing rules are simple. If there is a shortcut directly from the current domain to the destination domain, create it properly and it will be used. Otherwise, use traditional tree and forest parsing rules to follow the hierarchical trust path through the forest to the destination. If domain controllers in the intermediate domains are inaccessible, the shortcut trust could also provide a short-term workaround to keep the system functioning. This is especially useful when domain controllers for different domains, which are not parent and child of one another, exist within the same site.

NOTE

Another way of looking at shortcut trusts is as a method to solve any design problems that may arise from multiple forests. Multiple forests may arise after ther merger of companies and place new network hierarchies under your control. It may not be perfect, but it may work.

Inside the Domain: Designing Organizational Unit Structure

An organizational unit is the container we use to place domains into logical administrative groupings for administration and for group policy. Your design depends on your company's direction and future plans. For example, your company:

1. May be structured in such a way that creating a logical representation of your company's structure with organizational units makes a lot of sense.
2. May want to subdivide your current network into smaller groups of users and groups, or users and resources.
3. Is expanding rapidly, with many changes coming out of nowhere, and with which you must contend.

The beauty of designing with organizational units (OUs) is their flexibility—unlike domains or forests, OUs can be created, moved, added, or deleted within the domain at any time.

Comparing OUs to Domains

Both domains and organizational units adhere to a hierarchy. The hierarchy of domains is the tree they belong to; the hierarchy of organizational units is defined inside the domain boundaries.

A domain can also be compared to a file system volume, and an organizational unit can be compared to a folder. Volumes contain information about the file system used: a domain contains core information about the domain's networked objects and the structure (disks and other system information about the files and directories stored on the volume itself).

Directories, or folders in a file system, are also really containers holding files or other subdirectories; a Windows 2000 organizational unit is also a container holding other objects or OUs.

An organizational unit is not part of the DNS namespace; the names of your organizational units can only be addressed through a query to the Directory. For example, if you had an organizational unit called Accounts in the sales.headoffice.Kingston.com domain, the OU is not addressed as part of the DNS namespace as accounts.sales.headoffice.Kingston.com.

The OU is not a part of a user logon name. Neither the pre-Windows 2000 compatible logon name (e.g. ACME\fred) nor the user principle name (UPN) (e.g. fred@acme.org) includes any OU designations.

OU Design Notes

Designing with OUs should be defined in levels. The goal of creating organizational units at the first level is to use names that won't change. If your company reorganizes, you don't want to have to rename your structure and cause havoc.

The *first level* has continental and geographical boundaries. In the *second level*, countries and cities should be defined, depending on the size of your company. Larger regional offices and sites could also be defined if your company is not based in multiple continents, but instead is nationwide. Depending on the design you've chosen for your organizational unit, you may have *third* and *fourth levels* for even more administrative control within your company.

Geographical Model

If you have a very large multinational corporation spread around the globe with no central administration, the geographic model may be useful, as shown in Figure 6.19.

The first level of organizational units could represent the continents where head offices are located, for example, North America, Europe, and Asia. The second level of organizational units would be named after the individual countries, for example: United States, Canada, Japan, Korea, Sweden, Denmark, and Germany. There could then be a *third* or *fourth level* of organizational units where the area of geography is defined into states, provinces, cities, or townships.

Departmental Model

The *first level* of organizational units would represent the different business functions, for example: sales, manufacturing, and administration. The second level of organizational units would become more specific. For example, there might be units called:

Figure 6.19
A geographic model organizes its OUs by their geographic location.

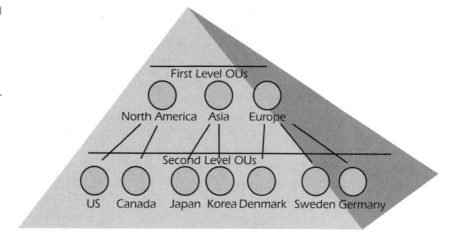

Figure 6.20
The structure of the departmental-based model is by department or business function.

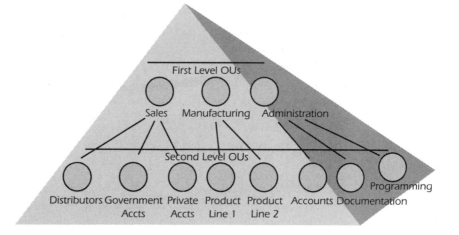

- **Sales**—Distributors, Government Accounts, Private Accounts
- **Manufacturing**—Product Line 1, Product Line 2
- **Administration**—Accounting, Documentation, Programming

Business Unit Model

If your company is divided into profit centers, a business-unit–based model holds each division of your company, as shown in Figure 6.21.

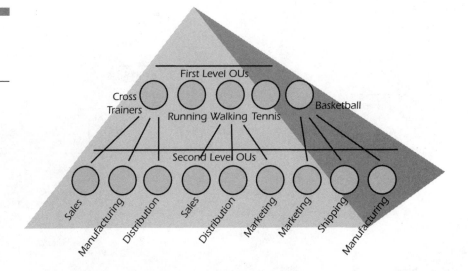

The *first level* of organizational units would represent each division. For example: Cross-trainers, Running, Walking, Tennis, and Basketball. The *second level* of organizational units would represent the departments that make up each division of the company, for example: sales, manufacturing, distribution, and marketing.

Project Based Model

A company might decide to base its networking structure on the product line, as shown in Figure 6.22, such as personal hovercraft devices (PHD), single-user spaceships (SUS), and electric cars (EC). This model treats each product as a cost/profit center.

The *first level* organizational units would be PHD, SUS, and EC. The *second level* organizational units could be engineers, marketing, and sales. This model is not static; as products change or go off market, your structure must also change.

Administrative Model

If information technology (IT) support is centralized within your company, and your company also happens to be a large multinational corporation, then the first level of organizational units could contain the IT departments on different continents, as shown in Figure 6.23.

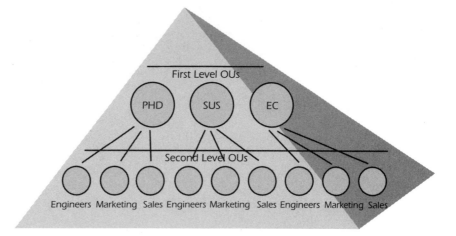

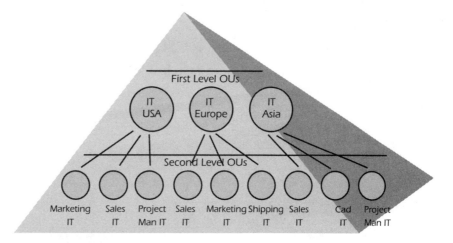

The *first level* of organizational units would be: IT USA, IT Europe, and IT Asia. The second level of organizational units would then be named after the IT divisions within the continents, reflecting the divisions within the company: Marketing IT, Sales IT, and Project Management IT, for example. Keep in mind that the administration model already in place within your company may not be the model you want or need.

Object-based Model

The *first level* of organizational units would store the primary group types that Active Directory supports, as shown in Figure 6.24, for example; Users, Computers, Applications, Groups, and Printers. The *second level* of organizational units would contain breakdowns of each first-level OU:

Figure 6.24
This model uses organizational units for storing the actual object types.

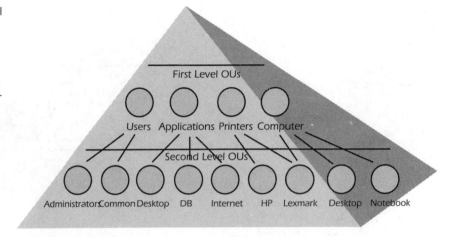

- Users could be linked to administrators and common users.
- Applications could be linked to desktop, database, and Internet.
- Printers could be linked to Lexmark and HP.
- Computers could be linked to desktop and notebook.

TABLE 6.2

OU designs: advantages and cisadvantages.

OU Model	Design Advantages	Design Advantages
Geographical	Resources are easy to find OUs at the first level would remain static	Structure may not match real organization seen by the end users Resources are not linked to business functions
Departmental	OUs at the first level would remain static	Resources are not easy to locate
Business unit	Works very well when each unit is totally independent	Users cannot be grouped into one OU if delegation of control is desired
Project based	Good logical separation	Projects may complete faster or drag on longer Renaming of projects as responsibilities shifted within an organization could cause confusion
Administrative	Administrators know where their resources are located and administered from. Easy to delegate administrative control	Users have no control of administration, which may be exactly what you want
Object based	Delegation is easy as the same object types are grouped in OUs ACLs are easy to setup as permissions are based on con tainers Reorganization of the Company is easier as the objects will be used.	Does not match any organizational structure object naming could be confusing Difficulty in identifying where resources are physically located

Active Directory Design for a Small Company

For a company with 1,000 users with three divisions, it may be best if a central group of administrators maintains the user and group information.

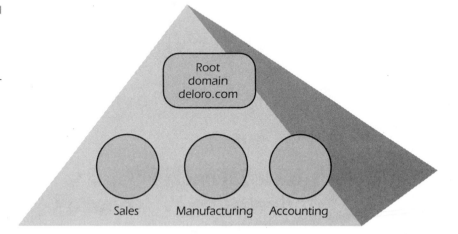

The *root name* should be the actual name of your organization, for example deloro.com. At the *first level*, create three OUs named for the actual divisions so that you can control each division separately.

At the *second level*, organizational units could be implemented later to delegate administration of users and resources with common needs.

Provincial or State Government

Government usually means many divisions of power. Examples would be a city, county, provincial or state agency, or a community college. The root domain should be the name of the government body, for example: ontario.gov.

First level organizational units are next created for each organizational division: city, county, and general. *Second level* organizational units would be named for the divisions within the government.

- City links to Toronto, Kingston, and Belleville
- County links to Frontenac and Leeds
- Legislative links to Courts and Public

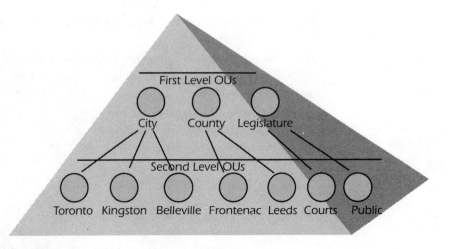

Figure 6.26
Group government
bodies by power
structure.

Administrative Tasks: Verifying SRV Records

One method of verifying that your domain created with DCPROMO is working is to check for the SRV records created during the promotion process.

1. At the command prompt execute nslookup.
   A. At the nslookup prompt type:

   ```
   > set type=srv
   > _ldap._tcp.<your domain or sub domain name here>
   ```

   B. You should get a response as shown in Figure 6.27.

2. Now use nslookup to view the other created SRV records on your domain controller and also at your root domain.
   A. At the nslookup prompt, use the server command to set the search to your domain controller, for example admin-server.

   ```
   > server admin-server
   ```

   B. Now enter the following SRV locations, inserting your domain for the syntax:

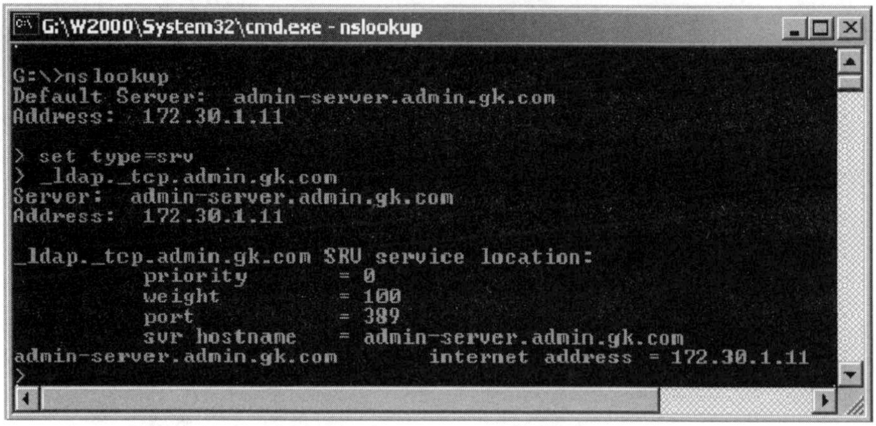

Figure 6.27
Nslookup results.

```
C:\ G:\W2000\System32\cmd.exe - nslookup                    _ □ ×

G:\>nslookup
Default Server:  admin-server.admin.gk.com
Address:  172.30.1.11

> set type=srv
> _ldap._tcp.admin.gk.com
Server:  admin-server.admin.gk.com
Address:  172.30.1.11

_ldap._tcp.admin.gk.com  SRV service location:
          priority       = 0
          weight         = 100
          port           = 389
          svr hostname   = admin-server.admin.gk.com
admin-server.admin.gk.com              internet address = 172.30.1.11
>
```

```
<domain controller> or <domainname>
```

This SRV allows clients to find LDAP servers for a specific domain:

```
_ldap._tcp. <domainname>
```

This SRV allows clients to find Kerberos Key Distribution Center (KDC) services for the domain:

```
_kerberos._tcp.<domainname>
```

This SRV allows clients to find Kerberos Change Password services in the domain:

```
_kpasswd._tcp.<domainname>
```

This SRV allows clients to find the global catalog servers using the Active Directory root domain:

```
_gc._tcp.<forestname>
```

C. Exit from nslookup and close the command prompt.

Changing your Domain from Mixed to Native Mode

From the Administrative Tools menu, start the Active Directory Domains and Trusts MMC snap-in.

A. Login to your domain as Administrator.
B. Expand your domain.
C. Right-click on your domain and select **Properties**.
D. Select the **General** tab and in the Domain Mode section click the **Change Mode** button.
E. Accept the warning dialog box and click **Yes**.
F. Your domain is now running in native mode.
G. Check the Event Log to see if the change was successful.

Directory Structure and the Global Catalog

This chapter provides details on Active Directory and the global catalog, including:

- Global catalog architecture
- Global catalog attributes
- SRV records and the global catalog
- Examination of replication paths of the global catalog
- Searching that uses the global catalog
- Changing the attributes replicated to the global catalog.

Tree and Domain Structure

Each Windows 2000 domain will be hosted by at least one domain controller (DC) but usually by several domain controllers, in order to provide the highest level of fault tolerance. The most common Windows 2000 networks will be designed as a forest of one or more trees consisting of one root domain and several child domains in various scenarios depending on your DN's namespace, as shown in Figure 7.1. By now, you are probably getting used to the fact that you will have fewer domains than your NT 4.0 network had. Domains within a domain tree have the following characteristics:

- They are connected by transitive trust relationships.
- They share and abide by a common schema.
- Forest configuration information is automatically shared.
- At a minimum, they share the use of the root global catalog (GC).
- The domain tree root defines the namespace.

Any additional domains created in a domain tree are called child domains since they are below the root domain. A domain immediately above a domain in the same domain tree is called a parent domain, yet the defined parent domain in this example could also be a child in another domain–child domain relationship. Following the rule of a contiguous DNS namespace, the domain name of a child domain will be the relative name of the child domain plus the name of the parent domain; for example, in Figure 7.1, stellite.deloro.com is a child domain of deloro.com.

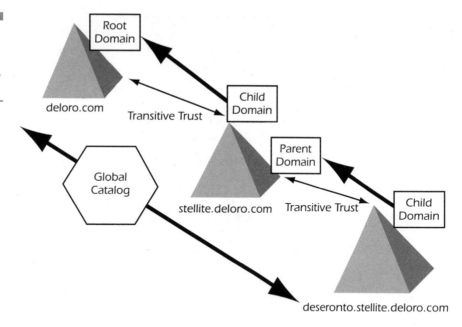

Figure 7.1
All domains shown
are joined together
by transitive two-way
trust relationships.

The transitive trust allows user authentication to occur within multiple domains and allows users to search the entire domain tree or forest for network resources that are outside the user's local domain. These benefits are provided by the global catalog, located by default on the first domain controller installed in the root domain. However, as the number of domains and transitive trusts increases, timing can become an issue for users authenticating to the domain, as can the time it takes to do a forest-wide search. Searching and authentication both depend on DNS and the location of the global catalog server.

Forest Structure and the Global Catalog

First let's look at the structure of a global catalog server and how it's created and deployed throughout the forest. As we know, the forest is a set of one or more domain trees with a common configuration, global catalog, and schema. When two trees are linked to create a forest, the trust is created at the root between the two root domains of each tree. The two domain trees and all child domains trust each other using Kerberos

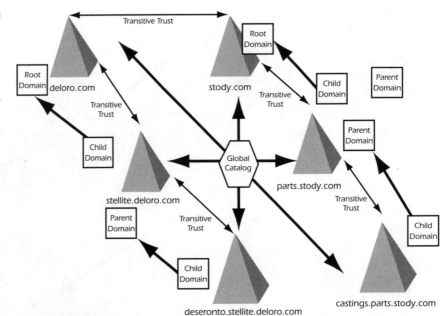

Figure 7.2
A single global catalog will not be sufficient for a large tree or forest of trees.

transitive trusts. Again, the global catalog takes advantage of the defined trusts to carry out its role of forestwide searches and user logons. In Figure 7.2 the global catalog server could be in the root domain or it could be somewhere else in the forest. Each forest needs, at a minimum, one global catalog server; the reality is that you will have multiple domain controllers performing the role of global catalog server.

Global Catalog Servers (GC)

The global catalog contains a replica of each object in the directory and a partial list of attributes describing each object. The end result is that each global catalog server contains a partial replica of every domain's domain naming context found in the forest, its their own full local domain-naming context. The word partial refers to the partial list of attributes stored in the global catalog; the object list is a complete forestwide listing. In the Internet world, partial is also called *fractional*.

The global catalog server is always created on a domain controller and any domain controller can be configured to collect, store, and respond to global catalog queries.

NOTE

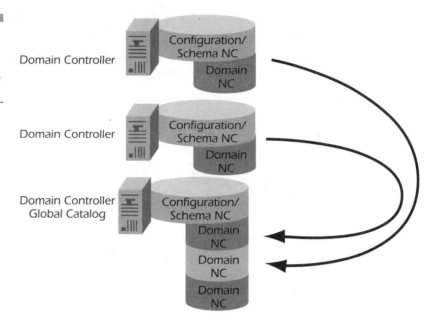

Figure 7.3
The global catalog is a read-only instance of every object in the directory.

Global Catalog Architecture

The directory partitions on a global catalog server (configuration, schema, and domain NCs) are all stored in the Active Directory database file NTDS.DIT, as shown in Figure 7.4. The formats of the database partitions (as they apply to users of the network) are listed in Table 7.1. Of course, the operating system treats the global catalog as a read-write partition, since updates are carried out through the replication process. We can also define additional attributes to add to the global catalog, but to the end-user it is a read-only index.

Each forest has a global catalog automatically created on the first domain controller in the forest through the initial dcpromo process. Complete details describing the root domain and the entire forest are stored in the root domain's configuration NC. When a new domain is added, during promotion of the server to a domain controller using dcpromo, these details are then replicated to the new domain controller in the new child domain through a service called the *knowledge consistency checker* (KCC). This executes every 15 minutes, checking and verifying replication paths. The KCC on the child domain initiates replication after an initial period of time, pushing the partial domain replica from the new local domain controller to the global catalog server, or multiple global catalog servers, if they exist. The knowledge consistency checker on the local domain controller is always responsible for the regular replication of any changes made to the local directory partition to the domain controller or controllers that host the global catalog service.

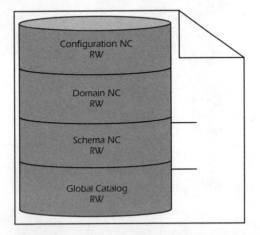

Figure 7.4
The GC is a part of the NTDS.DIT file.

NTDS.DIT

TABLE 7.1

Directory partitions.

Directory Partition	Format
The Configuration NC	Read / Write
The Schema NC	Read / Write
The Domain NC	Read / Write
The Global Catalog	Read only

Global Catalog and Domain User Logons

"A functioning global catalog server is required for Windows 2000 user authentication." This is the standard statement made in many books and the Windows 2000 Server Resource Kit because you won't be turning off the global catalog operation as a normal procedure. But what if you did, or a global catalog was not available? When you attempt to log in to the domain where your user account was created while running in native mode, since the domain where your account was created holds all of your user account information, you would log in successfully. However, if you are running in native mode, even within your own domain, the global catalog must be available for successful authentication; therefore your login would fail. You would be able to log on only to the local computer system and not the domain. In native mode you have the opportunity to use universal groups that can contain users and resources from any domain in the forest. A potential security hole would exist if your universal group membership were not checked out and verified at every log in, as shown in Figure 7.5. The only exception to this is that users who are members of the domain administrators (Domain Admin) group would be able to log on to the network even when a global catalog was not available.

NOTE

Mixed-mode domains do not require a global catalog query for logon.

Figure 7.5
Logins require global catalog servers for UPNs and universal membership.

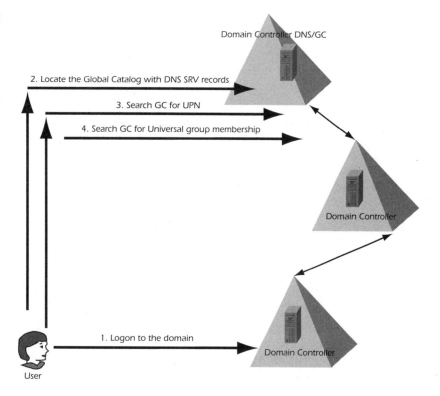

UPN and Global Catalog Support

All user principle names (username@DNSdomainname) are resolved by the global catalog server database for logins outside the user's local domain, or when operating in native mode. As a result logon is allowed to the forest from any domain in the forest. In fact, not just users but every security principle object authenticating to Active Directory must reference the global catalog server, including every computer that boots up. The global catalog server then resolves the user principle name for the domain tree or forest to the proper user account. Recall that the suffix used in a UPN does not need to be the name of the domain in which the user account resides. The information in the global catalog points to the proper domain in which the user account actually exists. When a user attempts to log into a domain, the authentication process also must determine what universal groups the user belongs to.

A global catalog is also needed if the user logs on with a non-default user principle name and the user's machine account is in a different domain from that of the user's user account. Instead of accepting the default DNS domain name as the UPN suffix (when user accounts were created, a global UPN suffix was given; for example all UPNs end with @gk.com so that the user then becomes simply username@gk.com), the user provides a single UPN suffix that is used for all users; a global catalog is required for logon.

Active Directory Domains and Trusts console is used to manage UPN suffixes for a domain.

NOTE

Universal Group Membership is Stored in the GC

Universal group membership is stored in the global catalog containing the names of the universal groups along with each user name in the group. Therefore, global catalog security must determine whether the user is indeed a universal group member. Universal group membership is stored in the GC along with the domain-naming context indicating where the universal group was created. It is then replicated to the global catalog. Again, the reason the global catalog is involved with storing universal group information is that the global catalog contains the full set of universal groups that could contain users from every domain in the forest. If a directory object's access control list contains an access control entry for a universal group, then the user's access token must contain that information. Otherwise rights could be granted to a user based on other assigned group memberships; if the universal group information were present, any Deny Access permissions assigned through a universal group would be read and applied to the user's token. Reading universal group membership from the global catalog is also more efficient; a global catalog server is only needed to build the authenticating user's membership to universal groups. It need not communicate with each domain controller in the entire tree or forest at every login.

Even when a global catalog is not present, users who are members of the Domain Admin group will be able to log onto the local domain.

NOTE

Searches that Use the GC by Default

The global catalog is searched when an application or utility specifies port 3268; during the logon process when a user principle name and universal group membership is accessed; when the "Entire Directory" is selected using the Search utility.

The scope of the search initiated determines whether the global catalog or the domain is searched. A search limited to a domain's local domain partition can answer any local query; a search of the forest can be resolved to any domain partition using the global catalog.

Searching the Global Catalog

The GC is a complete "read-only" listing of all objects found in the forest containing a "most-used" list of attributes used when searching to find an object or objects. The GC allows users, services, and applications to search and find objects stored in the directory without having to know the exact location of the object. The *access control list* (ACL) for all objects is also stored in the global catalog, ensuring that if a search request finds an object for which the user has no read permissions, the object will not be shown.

Figure 7.6
Global catalog searches are searches outside the domain where the search was initiated.

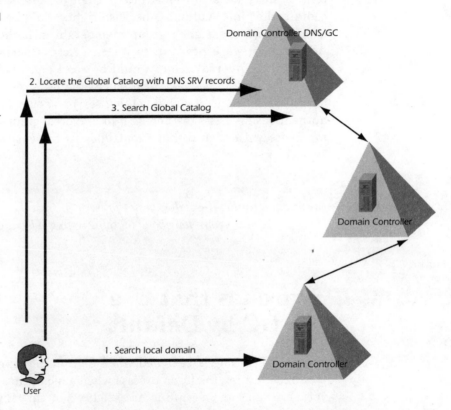

When a search is started in a local domain for a network resource, the local domain controller will first attempt to answer the query, as shown in Figure 7.6. If the query fails because the domain controller does not have the required information, next the global catalog is searched. When searches for network resources on the entire network are performed, query traffic is sent first to the domain controller or controllers storing the global catalog replica. The location of the domain controller in a single site is stored at the root server and is part of the configuration information.

If the global catalog cannot locate the object being searched for, the search is passed back to the Active Directory database in the domain where the search was started. There are just two reasons that a search could fail in the global catalog: time and space. Both intra-site and inter-site replication delays could result in attributes not being found in a specific global catalog for a finite period of time; but they could still be found in another GC within the forest. This is not a normal situation. Also, since every attribute is not stored in the GC, just the "catalogable" attributes, using a specific search filter for attributes not stored in the GC could also fail.

Who Decides What's in the Global Catalog?

A core set of attributes of all objects is initially replicated to the global catalog. A checkbox setting in the schema on each attribute type establishes what attributes are forwarded, no matter what object those attribute types are used in. As a member of the Schema Administrators group you can select which attributes are replicated to the GC using the schema console shown in Figure 7.7.

Figure 7.7
The schema console is used to add attributes to the global catalog.

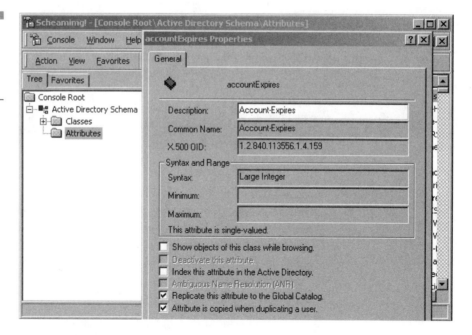

An attribute is chosen for replication to the GC when the option **Replicate this value to the Global Catalog** is checked.

Internally, the selected value in the attribute is changed to TRUE. During the next schema naming context (NC) replication cycle, all other global catalog servers will be updated with any new attributes that need to be replicated to the global catalog. See Table 7.2.

TABLE 7.2

Default global catalog attributes.

cA-Certificate	mSMQ-Routing-Services
cA-Certificate-DN	mSMQ-Service-Type
certificate-Templates	mSMQ-Sign-Certificates
domain-Component	mSMQ-Sign-Certificates-Mig
description	mSMQ-Sign-Key
distinguished-Name	mSMQ-Sites
dNS-Host-Name	mSMQ-Transactional
driver-Name	mSMQ-User-Sid
dS-Core-Propagation-Data	ms-RRAS-Attribute
flags	netboot-Machine-File-Path
frs-Computer-Reference	nT-Security-Descriptor
fRS-Member-Reference	object-Class
gP-Link	partial-Attribute-Deletion-List
home-Phone	partial-Attribute-Set
instance-Type	pKI-Critical-Extensions
ip-Phone	pKI-Default-CSPs
is-Deleted	pKI-Default-Key-Spec
manager	pKI-Enrollment-Access
meetingBlob	pKI-Expiration-Period
meetingDescription	pKI-Extended-Key-Usage
meetingName	pKI-Key-Usage
meetingProtocol	pKI-Max-Issuing-Depth
member	pKI-Overlap-Period
mSMQ-Authenticate	poss-Superiors
mSMQ-Base-Priority	print-Color
mSMQ-Dependent-Client-Services	print-Duplex-Supported
mSMQ-Digests-Mig	printer-Name
mSMQ-Ds-Services	print-Max-Resolution-Supported
mSMQ-Encrypt-Key	print-Media-Ready
mSMQ-Ds-Services	print-Pages-Per-Minute
mSMQ-Foreign	print-Share-Name
mSMQ-In-Routing-Servers	print-Stapling-Supported
mSMQ-Journal	proxied-Object-Name
mSMQ-OS-Type	range-Lower
mSMQ-Out-Routing-Servers	range-Upper
mSMQ-Privacy-Level	repl-Property-Meta-Data
mSMQ-Queue-Journal-Quota	repl-UpToDate-Vector
mSMQ-Queue-Name-Ext	reps-From
mSMQ-Queue-Quota	

continued on next page

TABLE 7.2

Default global catalog attributes (continued).

reps-To		system-Poss-Superiors
server-Name		telephone-Number
service-Binding-Information		user-Cert
service-Class-ID		user-Certificate
service-Class-Info		user-SMIME-Certificate
srvice-Instance-Version		USN-Last-Obj-Rem
short-Server-Name		version-Number
signature-Algorithms		well-Known-Objects
st		when-Changed
street		when-Created
sub-Refs		winsock-Addresses

Designating Additional Global Catalog Servers

The first domain controller in a forest is the automatic default location of the global catalog; however, any domain controller can be made a global catalog server. One or more global catalog servers should be added to each site. In a site with over 500 users, a second global catalog server should be added. Note that this means adding an additional domain controller to that site if there isn't already more than one; you can't have a GCS that is not also a DC. If you open the NTDS settings using the Sites and Services console, as shown in Figure 7.8, the checkbox on the general tab can select or deselect the domain controller as a global catalog server.

Figure 7.8

Every domain controller can become a global catalog server.

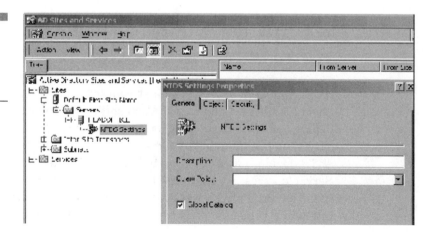

Once selected, the domain controller is added to the global catalog replication schedule as the NTDS settings object attribute hasPartialReplicationNCs is added to the Configuration partition.

It could take several replication cycles before the new global catalog server is added to the forest.

Increasing Replication Traffic

Adding additional global catalog servers increases forestwide replication traffic, putting an increased load on the network. The tradeoff, however, is that while the replication traffic may be increased, local users may be able to search a local global catalog rather than one on a far subnet or across a WAN. Also, each global catalog will potentially be less busy. Having a local global catalog (not just per site, but per LAN segment) can also reduce inter-subnet traffic since the local subnet can now be used for forestwide searches using the local GC.

Once the global catalog has gotten its replicas of the domains in the forest, consider the following guideline: what is the ratio of changes to objects in the forest to the number of searches?

This calculation could be made separately for each LAN. Because new changes to catalogable attributes will cause subsequent GC replication (and of course, regular full replication to other DCs in the same domain as the change), this ratio helps to gauge the tradeoff of network traffic.

Exchange 2000 Requirements

All Exchange 2000 clients must contact a global catalog server for the Global Address List (GAL). Microsoft's general rule for global catalog deployment is that there should be no more than four Exchange 2000 servers per individual GC server.

To decide how busy a global catalog server will be with Exchange Server queries, a general estimate of the number of daily user queries must be calculated. Base this on the number of client searches, email messages sent each day, and the amount of public folder access by

Exchange users. Since the root domain is the location of the Exchange server, all queries to the global catalog by Exchange users outside the root domain would have to travel up to the root; this would not be acceptable on a large network or necessary, since other local domain controller in each domain could also be initiated as global catalog servers.

For example, if your client base were 15,000 users, the global catalog server would have to support between 400 to 600 queries per second. This figure is derived from Microsoft tests that indicate the summary values of the average user:

- Exchange 2000—450 queries per second
- General searches—6 queries per second
- Future applications and growth—50 queries per second

Keep in mind the integration of Exchange Server 2000 with Active Directory and the following use of Exchange:

- The number of messages sent per day
- The number of replies, forwards, meetings
- Browsing for contacts

In the near future, Active Directory applications will also place additional stress on global catalog servers and the overall environment; the effect of this cannot now be predicted.

The GC and the Infrastructure Master FSMO Role

Remember the infrastructure master? Its role is to keep the domain up to date with any user and group changes. Then the infrastructure master distributes its updates using multimaster replication. What happens when a domain controller is assigned the infrastructure role and the global catalog role? Do not assign the infrastructure master role to the domain controller that is also hosting the global catalog. If you do, the infrastructure master will not function. Since all domain controllers in a domain also host the global catalog, all domain controllers have current data and therefore the infrastructure master role is not needed.

Removing the Global Catalog

A global catalog server can be removed by editing a key in the DC's local registry at the location HKEY_LOCAL_MACHINE\System\Current ControlSet\Control\Lsa\IgnoreGCFailures. This may be helpful in remote offices where it is not feasible to have a global catalog due to poor network links; however, the domain must be in mixed mode—this setting will rarely be used.

SRV Resource Records and the Global Catalog

When a domain controller first starts operation, the Net Logon service registers SRV resource records in DNS. SRV records within each site identify the location of the global catalog server. The SRV record is used to map the name of the LDAP service to the computer system that is providing the global catalog service. A workstation from which the user logs onto the domain queries DNS for the SRV records in the following format:

```
service. protocol. DNS subdomain. domain
```

Figure 7.9
SRV records are used to locate global catalog servers.

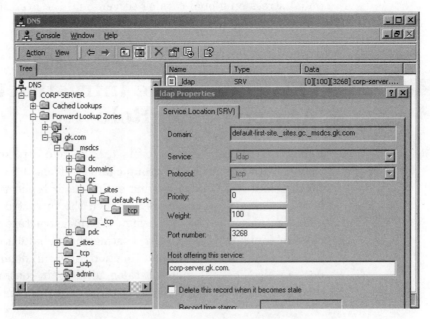

In addition to this required information, a prefix (_msdcs) is used to identify the computers functioning in a specific Windows 2000 role. The prefix is reserved in DNS as a subdomain for locating domain controllers; therefore the global catalog must be located on a DC.

_ldap._tcp.gc._msdcs.*DnsForestName*

The information in this SRV record allows a client to locate the global catalog server for this forest. Each domain controller hosting the global catalog server in the forest entered in DNSForestname registers this SRV record in DNS.

_ldap.tcp.SiteName._sites.gc._msdcs.*DnsForestName*

This record allows a client to locate the global catalog server for this forest in the site entered in SiteName. Each domain controller hosting the global catalog server in the forest entered in DNSForestname registers this SRV record in DNS.

When an application requests access to Active Directory, an Active Directory server (domain controller) is located by a mechanism called the locator, an algorithm that runs in the context of the NetLogon service and finds domain controllers on a Windows 2000 network by using DNS names for IP/DNS-compatible computers or by using NetBIOS names for older clients.

1. On the client PC looking for a domain controller, the Locator is started as a remote procedure call to the local NetLogon service.
2. The client assembles the information needed to select a domain controller and passes the information to the NetLogon service by using the DsGetDcName API; this in turn calls the DnsQuery API to read the Service Resource (SRV) records and A records from DNS.
3. The available domain controllers respond to the NetLogon datagram to indicate that they are online and returns the information to DsGetDcName.
4. The NetLogon service returns the information to the client from the domain controller that responds first.

The NetLogon service caches the domain controller information so that subsequent requests need not repeat the discovery process.

Caching this information advances the consistent use of the same domain controller and network services such as global catalog servers.

Administrative Tasks

Add Global Catalog Duties to a Domain Controller

Log onto your domain as administrator.

A. From the Administrator tools menu open Active Directory Sites and Services.
B. Open the Default-First-Site-Name and expand your server.
C. Highlight the NTDS Settings.
D. From the Action menu select **Properties**.
E. On the General tab check the box Global Catalog and click **OK**.
F. Log onto your root domain as Administrator.
G. Open the DNS console and look in the gk.com forward lookup zone and highlight the _msdcs\gc folder.
H. You should see a Host record for your global catalog server.
I. Check the Event Viewer to see if your server became a global catalog server.
J. It may take several minutes to replicate.

Enable Additional Attributes to be Replicated to the Global Catalog

Log onto the domain controller where the schema operations masters role is defined for schema master as Administrator.

A. Click **Start\Run** and enter **mmc** and click **OK**.
B. Add the Active Directory schema to the console and save as Schema.mmc.
C. From Administrative tools load the schema console; expand the Active Directory schema tree.
D. Highlight the Attributes folder and double-click any attribute in the Details pane.
E. Double-click the selected attribute and check the box "Replicate this attribute to the Global Catalog" and click **OK**.

Replication Fundamentals

This chapter is an introduction to replication fundamentals. The understanding of the process of replication is essential for the proper planning of sites and troubleshooting of Active Directory. Topics to be covered are:

- Goals of replication
- Connection objects
- High watermark and up-to-dateness vector
- Updating sequence numbers
- Replication steps

Goals of Active Directory Replication

The process of replication attempts to use available network bandwidth as efficiently as possible for updating all domain controllers in the forest when changes are made. The replication process on a day-to-day schedule is much more efficient than it was in NT 4.0 and Exchange 5.5. The other times when replication occurs should be thought as the cost of running Windows 2000. These times are when:

- Passwords are changed
- The global catalog is updated
- Additions or modifications are made at a DC
- Windows 2000 Software is installed
- The schema is changed

Replication efficiency is maintained by replicating only the changes—a phone number change only replicates the attribute changed. Replication between sites using WAN links uses data compression very effectively—about 85 percent. There is also a choice of protocols that can be used for replicating across WAN links; RPC over either IP or SMTP can be used.

Replication Details

Any change made on any domain controller with a read-write replica of the domain *naming context* (NC) will then replicate these changes to its replication partners, if they exist. On each domain controller a process called the *knowledge consistency checker* (KCC) automatically generates the replication connections within each site. The changes will eventually be updated throughout the tree or forest through replication using the connection objects automatically created by the KCC.

There are four areas of replication to consider:

1. Domain NC
2. Schema NC
3. Configuration NC
4. Global catalog updates

Windows 2000 and Exchange 5.5 Comparison

Windows 2000 is the plumbing for Exchange 2000. Although it works well as a server, the majority of corporations are deploying Windows 2000 only because their next step is Exchange 2000. A comparison of how replication has changed and improved is shown in Table 8.1.

TABLE 8.1

Windows 2000 provides efficient replication.

Exchange 2000	Active Directory
Object-based replication when any changes occurred	Attribute-based replication when changes occur
Limited access control	Flexible access control
Multimaster within site	Multimaster within the domain
Limited schema extensibility	Full schema extensibility
Objects were not renamed safely	Objects are all unique since GUIDs are assigned

Objects

Exchange 5.5 replicated on a per-object base. This meants if one attribute was changed on an object, the entire object must then be replicated. In Active Directory, replication is attribute based.

Access Control

Exchange's access control was limited to the object. Active Directory can set fine granular rights on the object and specific attributes.

Replication Boundaries

The boundaries of replication are also different for Exchange and AD. Exchange used multimaster replication at the site level whereas AD uses multimaster replication to the domain boundary.

Schema Extensions

The schema for Exchange can be extended only by predefined extension attributes, whereas the schema model for AD allows full extension by any objects and attributes desired.

Object Naming

With Exchange, the distinguished name of the object was its identity—if the object's name changed, it lost its ability to be referenced. Active Directory references all objects with unique GUIDs that can never be changed. Even if the name, the DN, and the RDN of the object is changed, the GUID remains the same.

Defining the Naming Contexts

There are three naming contexts on each domain controller used by Active Directory: configuration, schema, and domain, as detailed in Figure 8.1. There can also be a fourth, the global catalog, but this is not considered a naming context by strict definition, although the GC can be a large part of the replication process.

Configuration

The first NC is the configuration that holds all the configuration information about the directory service along with how many sites and domains are currently defined and how they communicate. Other network services that now or soon will add their information to the configuration container include the *file replication service* (FRS) and Exchange 2000.

Schema

The second NC is the schema that contains all the attributes and objects that can be used in Active Directory. Whenever the schema is extended, the changes have to be replicated to all the other domain controllers.

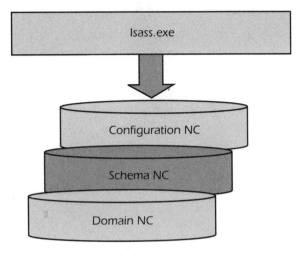

Figure 8.1
The Directory is
stored and separated
into naming
contexts.

Domain

The third NC is the domain that holds the objects such as OUs and security principles.

Global Catalog

Each object, and a minimal set of attributes stored in the domain-naming context, is also replicated to each defined global catalog server that could be located in the different domains throughout the forest. By default, the root domain will be a global catalog server.

The scopes of the three naming contexts are different: the configuration and schema always have an enterprise context, the domain-naming context is relative to the domain. The domain-naming context is replicated locally within the domain. If there are multiple domain controllers hosting the same domain, then the domain controllers replicate the entire contents of the domain-naming context to each other. Both the configuration and the schema-naming context will be replicated across the tree or forest to all domain controllers.

Naming Context in the Domain Namespace

The first domain in the enterprise is the root domain and the naming context is identified through the assigned FQDN of the domain.

Deloro.com is the root of the domain, as shown in Figure 8.2 and thus is the root of the domain-naming context.

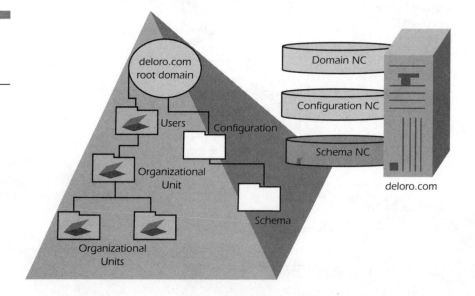

Figure 8.2
Each domain controller has three naming contexts.

Replication Fundamentals

Multimaster replication dictates that when a change is made at one domain controller, it is then replicated to its replication partner in an orderly fashion.

Any originating update can only happen at one domain controller in the forest.

NOTE

NT Used Single-Master Replication

Windows NT used a single-master replication model so that changes were made at one location, the PDC, and then replicated to all BDCs. The PDC was the only server that talked to the BDCs, so location was very important in a large network with WAN connections. If the PDC was in North America and several BDCs in Europe were connected with a slow WAN connection, the PDC had to talk to the first BDC and then the second, and so on. For updates with a network with four BDCs, the WAN link would have to be crossed four times.

What Triggers the Replication Process?

Three main operations will trigger replication in AD: object creation—a new object; object manipulation—a change is made; and object deletion—an object is removed from the database.

Object Creation or Manipulation

When changes are made at a domain controller at the local AD database by a user, application, or service it is called an *originating update*. All other domain controller(s) will receive the change as a *replication update*. The replication update can occur from any domain controller, but the originating update happens only on the domain controller where the change occurred.

Between 5 and 15 minutes after a change is made, the replication cycle begins.

NOTE

Deleting Objects

All object deletions create *tombstones*. When an object is deleted, the tombstone is then replicated to the replication partners.

Replication is Now Transitive

In Active Directory replication is *transitive*. This means that when a change is made in North America, the local Windows 2000 domain controller replicates the changes to the domain controller in Europe, which then replicates the changes to another domain controller in Europe, and then to the next DC if it exists. This is called a *store and forward* mechanism for the information to be replicated among domain controllers. Since replication can originate on any domain controller, a mechanism must be put in place to make sure that replicated changes are not replicated many times to the same domain controllers. This process is called *propagation dampening* and is discussed later in this chapter.

Creating Replication Topology

The replication topology is created using global unique identifiers (GUIDs) for the objects that are involved in the replication process: the server and the directory database. When a Windows 2000 server is promoted to a domain controller, a GUID for the server is created in the configuration container identifying each domain controller and the database.

State-Based Replication

Active Directory replication is state based; a domain controller always remembers the *state* in which its replication partner has been left. The database GUID is used in replication calls to identify the domain controller and to find out whether changes have been made that must be replicated.

Domain Controller Failure

If a domain controller fails and has to be restored from a backup tape, then the current state of the domain controller is not in the state its replication partners assume. When an Active Directory database is restored, the database GUID is also changed, signaling to the domain controller's replication partner to replicate any changes that have occurred since the failure.

Replication Architecture: Update Sequence Numbers (USN)

Every time a change is performed in the Active Directory database, the change is assigned to a transaction and assigned an USN number, as shown in Figure 8.3. An update sequence number is a 64-bit value. USNs are used to find out if there have been any changes on a replication partner and also to identify and find the changes quickly. Each object in AD carries two USNs:

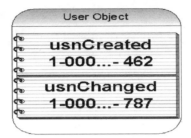

Figure 8.3
Each object is
identified with two
unique identifiers
called update
sequence numbers.

- usnCreated—Indicating when the object was created.
- usnChanged—Indicating the last change on an object.

USN Details

As long as the object is not deleted, the usnCreated value will remain the same; however, changes will be reflected with the usnChanged. If a user changes a password, the usnChanged will change to a higher value, indicating change has occurred. USNs are only used for replication and to determine what is to be replicated and when this is to happen. Once the transaction is completed successfully, then a USN is assigned to the attribute change. The value of usnChanged will be the highest USN of all attributes on the object. If the transaction is not completed, then the assigned USN is not used; it is discarded, and the next transaction USN will be increased to a new value.

System clocks and timestamps are not used unless the version numbers are equal. For replication, only update sequence numbers are used.

NOTE

User Object Creation

When a request is made to create the new user, the domain controller first updates its USN from 4710 to 4711.

1. Next the domain controller starts the transaction, creating the object.
2. The object is created and the USN 4711 is applied to usnCreated and usnChanged.

Figure 8.4
The domain
controller is called
DS1 and it has an
update sequence
number of 4710.

USN: 4710 ———————————————➤ USN: 4711						
Object: usnCreated: 4711				Object: usnChanged: 4711		
Property	Value	USN	Version #	Timest.	Org. DB GUID	Org USN
P1:	Value	4711	1	TS	DS1 DB GUID	4711
P2:	Value	4711	1	TS	DS1 DB GUID	4711
P3:	Value	4711	1	TS	DS1 DB GUID	4711
P4:	Value	4711	1	TS	DS1 DB GUID	4711

3. Any user attributes that were also filled in are also assigned the USN 4711.
4. Every attribute also has a version number; every time we change the attribute we also change the version number.
5. Next, a timestamp is set on each attribute along with the originating database GUID.
6. Because the new user was created on DS1, the domain controller's originating GUID is used.

The Replication Process: Step 2

The user object is replicated from DS1 to DS2. DS2 has a completely different set of USNs; it is currently at 1745.

1. Once the user object request is replicated over to DS2, the first task performed by DS2 is to change the USN from 1745 to 1746. Then the user object is created in the database of DS2.
2. Since the user object is newly created, both the usnCreated and the usnChanged are assigned the USN 1746.
3. The property values of the newly created object on DS2 are also assigned the USN 1746 with a version number of 1.

Figure 8.5
Now the new user
must be replicated to
the domain
controller's
replication partner.

DS1 USN: 4711				DS2 USN: 1745 ──→ USN: 1746			
Object: usnCreated: 1746				Object: usnChanged: 1746			
Property	Value	USN	Version #	Timest.	Org. DB GUID	Org USN
P1:	Value	1746	1	TS	DS1 DB GUID	4711
P2:	Value	1746	1	TS	DS1 DB GUID	4711
P3:	Value	1746	1	TS	DS1 DB GUID	4711
P4:	Value	1746	1	TS	DS1 DB GUID	4711

NOTE

In the heading Org. DB GUID in Figure 8.5 note that the listing shows where the object originated, that is, where it was first created; in this case DS1 is listed along with the original USN where the originating write was performed.

Modifying an Object

Changing the password is also a transaction, so the DS2 domain controller upped the UPN of the password attribute from 2001 to 2002. The user object created in the database has a UPN of 1746 and this remains untouched. However, the attribute that has been changed receives the UPN 2002, in this case property P2.

Since this is also a change from the original password, the version is changed from version 1 to 2 and timestamped as well.

In the field for the originating database GUID (Org. DB GUID), the domain controller where the originating write operation was made is entered, along with the UPN 2002.

Figure 8.6
The user changes
his/her phone
number on the
domain controller
DS2.

| DS1 | | | | DS2 | | |
USN: 5039 ⟶ USN: 5040				USN: 2002		
Object: usnCreated: 4711				Object: usnChanged: 5040		
Property	Value	USN	Version #	Timest.	Org. DB GUID	Org USN
P1:	Value	4711	1	TS	DS1 DB GUID	4711
P2:	Value	5040	2	TS	DS2 DB GUID	2002
P3:	Value	4711	1	TS	DS1 DB GUID	4711
P4:	Value	4711	1	TS	DS1 DB GUID	4711

Changes Replicated: Step 2

1. DS1 has performed some other operations and its UPN is 5039; the first order of business is to increase the UPN to 5040.
2. With the USN changed, the transaction is performed and the value usnCreated is entered as 5040.
3. The new phone number is entered and because this is a change, the version is increased to 2 and a time stamp is again set.
4. In the field for the originating database GUID (Org. DB GUID), the domain controller where the originating write operation was made is entered along with the UPN 2002.

What's a High-Watermark Vector?

The high watermark is a table on each domain controller with two fields detailing the replication partners and the highest known USN sent from the replication partners. The high watermark is used to detect any recent changes from the DCs replication partners. The high watermark is used when replication is initiated to find out whether partners have any information to replicate.

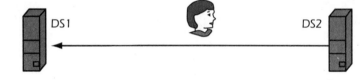

Figure 8.7
Now the changes
must be replicated
back to the
replication partner
domain controller
DS1.

DS1 USN: 5039 ⟶ USN: 5040				DS2 USN: 2002		
Object: usnCreated: 4711				Object: usnChanged: 5040		
Property	Value	USN	Version #	Timest.	Org. DB GUID	Org USN
P1:	Value	4711	1	TS	DS1 DB GUID	4711
P2:	Value	5040	2	TS	DS2 DB GUID	2002
P3:	Value	4711	1	TS	DS1 DB GUID	4711
P4:	Value	4711	1	TS	DS1 DB GUID	4711

1. In Figure 8.8, domain controller DS4 has two replication partners, DS1 and DS3. The fourth domain controller DS2 does not directly communicate with DS4.
2. The high-watermark vector contains the DSA GUID for the two domain controllers DS1 and DS3.
3. The USNs are the highest values that DS4 has seen from its two replication partners DS1 and DS3, 4711 from DS1 and 1217 from DS3.

Preparing for a Replication Cycle

In replication, changes are always pulled from the replication partner. Information is sent in preparation for replication to the replication partner through an initial notification process. The replication partner then uses this information to determine whether or not it contains any changes that need to be replicated. Changes are requested for the naming context: schema, configuration, or domain partition. Next the maximum number of object update entries and values requested is sent.

The default number of values and objects that can be requested and sent is 100 changes at a time, so as to not swamp the network. It also takes a period of time for the domain controller to carry out the updates

Figure 8.8
The high -watermark
vector is used to
detect updates.

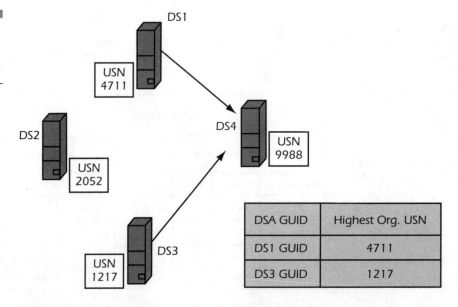

DSA GUID	Highest Org. USN
DS1 GUID	4711
DS3 GUID	1217

and changes. A bit is set at the end of the object and value update from
the replication partner, indicating if there are additional updates to
replicate.

1. If there is more information, then replication is initiated once more
   with the next batch of changes pulled from the replication partner.
2. Then the high USN changed-value, from the naming context we
   requested changes, is sent to the replication partner.
3. Then the complete up-to-dateness vector (also called the *state vector*)
   is sent.

Up-to-Dateness Vector

The up-to-dateness vector has only two entries:

1. The originating DC-GUID (Database GUID) of domain controllers.
2. The highest originating USN of known domain controllers.

Domain controllers are added only if originating updates have been
received from them. If the version numbers are the same, then the timestamp is used as a tiebreaker. If the version numbers and the timestamp are the same, then GUID of the originating value is used as a

tiebreaker. Using DS4 as the example, only DS1 and DS2 have performed any originating write operations. DS3 has only performed replicated write operations.

Figure 8.9
The up-to-dateness vector is a second table holding a list of pairs.

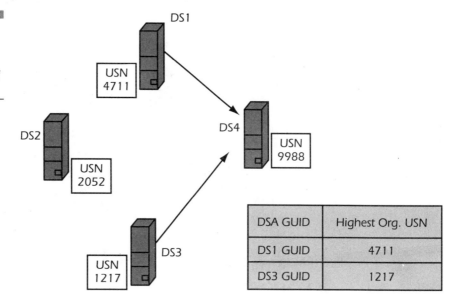

DSA GUID	Highest Org. USN
DS1 GUID	4711
DS3 GUID	1217

Following the Replication Process: Step 1

This example will use the domain controller DS4 to track replication through the replication topology.

1. The Administrator creates a user object on DS2.
2. DS2 increases its update sequence number (USN) to from 2052 to 2053 and then creates the new object and all the desired attributes.

On DS4 we have the high-watermark vector with entries for DS1 and DS3. Therefore DS1 and DS3 are DS4's replication partners.

The highest known USN from DS1 is 4711. The highest known USN from DS3 is 1217; therefore the creation of the user on DS2 does not affect DS4 at this moment.

The highest originating USN seen on DS1 was 4711 and on DS2 was 2050. DS3 has not performed any originating write operations.

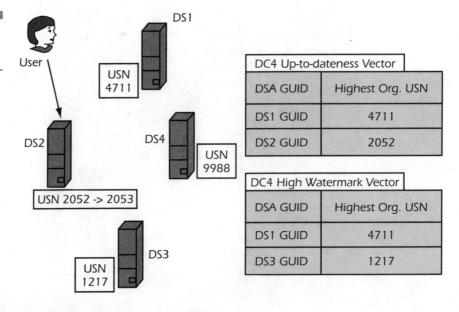

Figure 8.10
Step 1: A user object
is added to DS2.

Following the Replication Process: Step 2

1. The new user object is now replicated from DS2 to DS1.
2. DS1 now updates its USN from 4711 to 4712 and then writes the new object to the database.
3. On DS1 all the created attributes are stamped with the updated USN, 4712.
4. On DS1, the originating database GUID will be stamped with DS2's database GUID and the originating write USN value with DS2's GUID, 2053.

Following the Replication Process: Step 3

Now DS4 starts the replication process with DS1. Information sent to DS1 in preparation for replication includes:

- The highest USN seen from DS1, which is 4711, from the high-watermark table.

- The next 100 changes.
- The next 100 values.
- The up-to-dateness vector table.

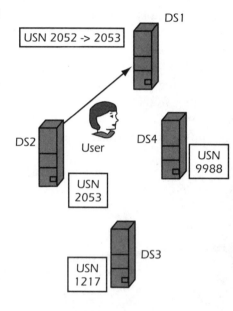

Figure 8.11
Step 2: The user object is replicated to DS1.

USN 2052 -> 2053

DS1

DS2

User

DS4

USN 9988

USN 2053

USN 1217

DS3

DC4 Up-to-dateness Vector	
DSA GUID	Highest Org. USN
DS1 GUID	4711
DS2 GUID	2052

DC4 High Watermark Vector	
DSA GUID	Highest Org. USN
DS1 GUID	4711
DS3 GUID	1217

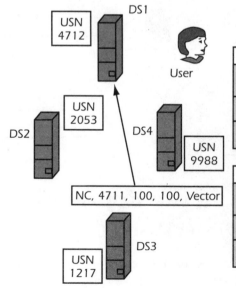

Figure 8.12
Step 3: DS4 starts replication with DS1, sending the NC, USN, objects, values, and up-to-dateness vector.

USN 4712

DS1

User

USN 2053

DS2

DS4

USN 9988

NC, 4711, 100, 100, Vector

USN 1217

DS3

DC4 Up-to-dateness Vector	
DSA GUID	Highest Org. USN
DS1 GUID	4711
DS2 GUID	2052

DC4 High Watermark Vector	
DSA GUID	Highest Org. USN
DS1 GUID	4711
DS3 GUID	1217

Following the Replication Process: Step 4

1. DS1 then replicates the new user to DS4, sending the data, last-object changed USN, and state data (the up-to-dateness vector).
2. DS4 now updates its USN from 9988 to 9989 and performs the transaction in its database.
3. DS4 also updates its high-watermark vector to 4712, indicating that DS4 has seen the change stamped with the USN 4712.
4. The object replicated from DS1 to DS4 has its original write operation on DS2.
5. As a result, the up-to-dateness vector on DS4 is also updated.

DS4 now knows that the highest originating write operation it has seen on DS2 is USN 2053.

Figure 8.13
Step 4: DS1 now detects that it has a new user object that has not been replicated over to DS4.

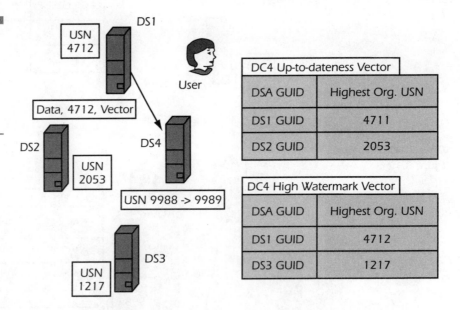

DC4 Up-to-dateness Vector	
DSA GUID	Highest Org. USN
DS1 GUID	4711
DS2 GUID	2053

DC4 High Watermark Vector	
DSA GUID	Highest Org. USN
DS1 GUID	4712
DS3 GUID	1217

Following the Replication Process: Step 5

Remember that the user object was first created on DS2. Now DS2 starts the replication process with DS3.

1. Information is pulled to DS3 in preparation for replication.
2. DS3 increments it's USN from 1217 to 1218.
3. DS3 now creates the new object in its database.

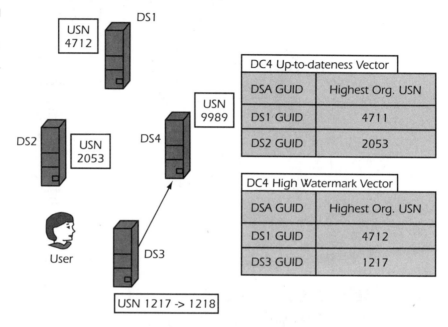

Figure 8.14
Step 5: DS2 replicates the new user to DS3.

DC4 Up-to-dateness Vector	
DSA GUID	Highest Org. USN
DS1 GUID	4711
DS2 GUID	2053

DC4 High Watermark Vector	
DSA GUID	Highest Org. USN
DS1 GUID	4712
DS3 GUID	1217

Following the Replication Process: Step 6

The time has now come in the replication cycle for DS4 to talk with DS3. DS4 initiates replication with DS3 and in preparation for replication it sends DS3 the following information:

- The naming context
- The highest-known USN from DS3
- The number of objects and values
- The up-to-dateness vector

Figure 8.15
Step 6: DS4 starts
replication with DS3
sending the NC,
highest-known USN
from DS3 for this NC,
objects, values, and
up-to-dateness
vector.

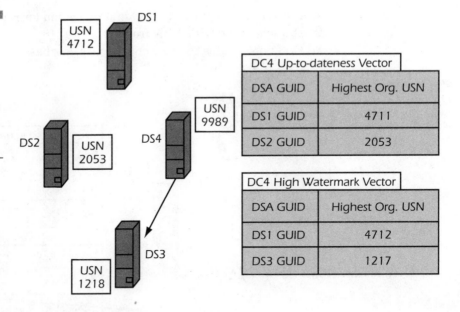

DC4 Up-to-dateness Vector	
DSA GUID	Highest Org. USN
DS1 GUID	4711
DS2 GUID	2053

DC4 High Watermark Vector	
DSA GUID	Highest Org. USN
DS1 GUID	4712
DS3 GUID	1217

Following the Replication Process: Step 7

DS3 will send the last-object changed USN and the up-to-dateness vector, but no data. DS3 knows that it has one change in its database that has not been replicated over to DS4. This is the change that carries the USN 1218.

1. DS3 takes the up-to-dateness vector that DS4 sent.
2. DS3 checks if this change might already have reached DS4 on a different route by comparing the originating write database GUID and the USN.
3. DS4 has already seen the change stamped with the USN 2053 from the domain controller DS2.
4. Therefore, DS3 knows that it doesn't need to replicate this change over to DS4. DS4 will use DS3's high-watermark vector 1218 to update its high-watermark vector.

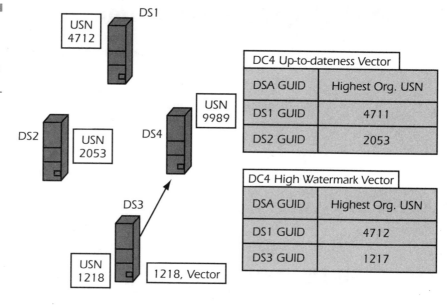

Figure 8.16
Step 7: DS3 sends its replication reply indicating that DS4 is already up to date.

DC4 Up-to-dateness Vector	
DSA GUID	Highest Org. USN
DS1 GUID	4711
DS2 GUID	2053

DC4 High Watermark Vector	
DSA GUID	Highest Org. USN
DS1 GUID	4712
DS3 GUID	1217

Solving Conflict Resolution

When an attribute is changed on an object, in this case the user object, the version number is increased. The next time an additional change is made, the version number will increase one digit.

Attribute Value Conflict

Let's suppose that a user changes his/her phone number on the domain controller DS1, through client software attached to DS1. However, the Administrator on DS2 also changes the user's phone number. When replication occurs between DS2 and DS2 the domain controllers will discover that the same attribute has been changed on both domain controllers.

When there is a conflict, the version number of the attributes will be compared and the higher version number always wins. If the version numbers are the same, then the timestamp is used as the tiebreaker. This is the only time that the timestamp is relied on.

What happens if the version numbers and the timestamps are the same? The GUID is used on the domain controller where the write operation originated and the higher GUID wins. If the version, timestamp and GUID are the same, then it is the same value because GUIDs are always uniquely created.

Urgent Replication

Urgent replication is initiated by the SAM hive or LSA and not by LDAP writes:

- Replicating a newly locked-out account
- Changing an LSA secret (trust account passwords used between DCs)
- Changing the RID Manager state

These actions trigger an immediate replication cycle within the site. Notification is sent to all domain controller replication partners to replicate right away.

Password Replication

When a user arrives at work and forgets his password he may call the help desk. The help desk resets the password on a domain controller that may not be the same domain controller at which the user is located. If the user tries to log on immediately, the login fails until the password is normally replicated; this could take some time. The solution in the Windows 2000 network is a special domain controller role called the PDC role owner (also called the PDC advertiser), one of the FSMO roles assigned to domain controllers. When a password is changed on any domain controller, the DC will push the password change immediately to the PDC role owner. Then when the user tries to log onto the network, internally, the password request will first fail, then the DC checks with the PDC role owner and the logon will succeed.

Administrative Solutions: Using Repadmin to Trace Replication

Repadmin.exe is a Windows 2000 Resource Kit tool that is a command-line interface to Active Directory replication. Use Repadmin.exe to determine your server's direct replication partners.

Exit to the command prompt and type the following command:

```
C: \ >repadmin /showreps dc=<yourdomain>,dc=gk,dc=com
```

A. Once the target server is reached, it will display a similar output, as shown in Figure 8.17.
B. You should be able to see the domain controllers located in your domain.
C. Under the Inbound Neighbors section of the output, the direct replication partners for each directory partition will be identified, along with the status of the last replication.

Figure 8.17

Repadmin displays both inbound and outbound neighbors.

Use Repadmin.exe to Get All Changes that Have Been Replicated

Exit to the command prompt and type the following command:

```
C: \ >repadmin /getchanges dc=<yourdomain>,dc=gk,dc=com
> changes.txt
```

Edit changes.txt with EDIT-; you will see the groups and users that you have created.

Check the High Watermark with Repadmin

Exit to the command prompt and type the following command:

```
C:\ > repadmin /showreps /verbose >highwater.txt.
```

The high watermark is shown in Figure 8.18: USNs: #### / OU.

Press **ALT–ENTER** to exit to a full screen and find the high-watermark values for your domain's domain controllers.

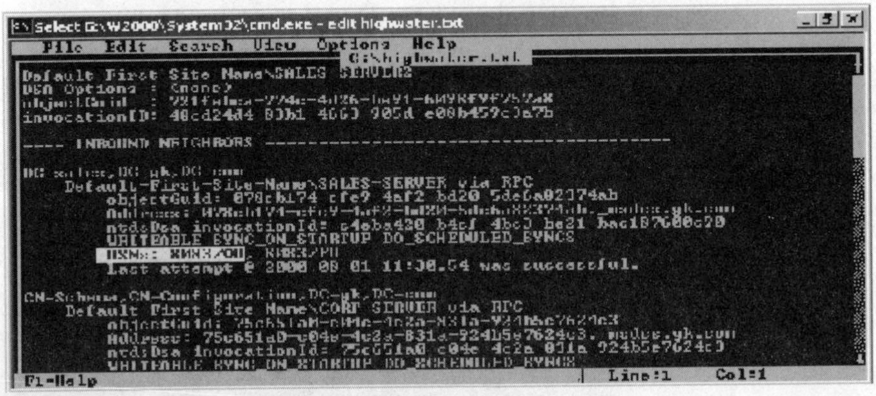

Figure 8.18
Use repadmin to view the high watermark vector.

Use Repadmin to View the Up-to-Dateness Vector

Exit to the command prompt and type the following command:

```
C: \> repadmin /showvector dc=<yourdomain>,dc=com
```

The output will list the up-to-dateness vectors for your domain, for example: Default-First-Site-Name\SALES-SERVER2 @ USN 4774Default-First-Site-Name\SALES-SERVER @ USN 8026.

Sites and
Replication
Administration

This chapter provides details on intra- and inter-site replication, discussing topics including:

- Sites
- Site links
- Connection objects
- Intra-site replication
- Inter-site replication
- Planning inter-site replication
- Understanding intra- and inter-site replication
- Creating sites and site links
- Establishing replication costs and schedules

Planning Sites

Planning for sites in Windows 2000/Active Directory is the most important task to carry out when planning and deploying Active Directory, and potentially the hardest. Essential network tasks must be completed before sites and services can even be attempted.

1. If you have not defined your TCP/IP subnet structure or it is in the process of upheaval or change, you will first have to decide on your structure and get it in order.
2. Your DNS namespace must be fully developed and deployed. As we know, DNS is the locator service for servers, global catalog servers, and network services.
3. The location of your Exchange 2000 server must be defined.
4. Local DNS and global catalog servers must be defined.
5. Multiple domain controllers per domain must be defined and deployed.

Only when these tasks have been deployed and well documented are you ready to deploy sites.

What is the Role of Sites in Active Directory?

To define the physical structure of your network, you must configure one or more site objects in Active Directory. If areas of your network are connected by WAN links, these links will be slower than the normal local network bandwidth, typically 10 MHz or 100 MHz. In these situations you may decide to create sites, or multiple sites, as shown in Figure 9.1.

Figure 9.1
Sites are associated with subnets.

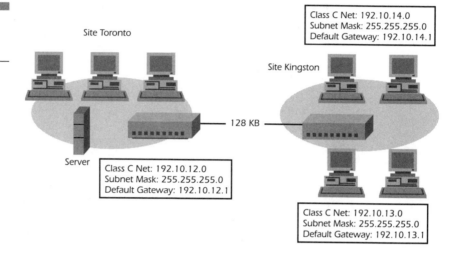

Site Toronto

Site Kingston

Class C Net: 192.10.14.0
Subnet Mask: 255.255.255.0
Default Gateway: 192.10.14.1

128 KB

Server

Class C Net: 192.10.12.0
Subnet Mask: 255.255.255.0
Default Gateway: 192.10.12.1

Class C Net: 192.10.13.0
Subnet Mask: 255.255.255.0
Default Gateway: 192.10.13.1

To configure a site object in Active Directory completely, you must associate it with one or more TCP/IP subnets. The subnet or subnets linked to a site object must share a high enough bandwidth for replication across the subnets.

When a domain controller is first installed, it is placed into a default site called the DEFAULT-FIRST-SITE, as shown in Figure 9.2. The subnet associated with the first domain controller in the site has not yet been defined using Active Directory Sites and Services and linked to the DEFAULT-FIRST-SITE.

Sites are mainly used to configure sites for Windows 2000 and Active Directory to control replication between sites. However, there are also other valid reasons you will use multiple sites: to control replication traffic; to isolate network logon traffic; and to identify network resources by immediacy.

To Control Replication Traffic

Sites are also used for in-site replication between domain controllers and global catalog servers. SYSVOL replication, where group policy settings are stored, is also based on sites. Sites are used by the directory

Figure 9.2
The default site
initially contains all
domain controllers
after promotion.

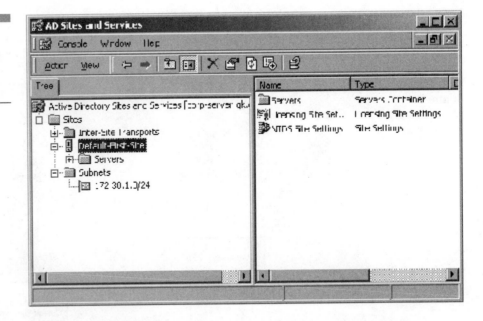

service to locate services closest to the client or server for example printers, member servers, and the *distributed file system* (DFS).

A site can have multiple subnets, but a subnet can be in only one site—in Figure 9.1, the Toronto site has one Class C subnet and in Kingston, the site has two Class C subnets. Each domain and subdomain, created in your company's tree or forest, hosts a separate domain partition within the directory. This domain partition, or *naming context* (NC), stores the values for every object in the domain and each of its defined attributes. To synchronize changes to each object and/or attribute, every domain controller in the same domain replicates the domain partition on a defined schedule with a replication partner, using multimaster replication. Replication traffic within the domain is not compressed; as a result, on a large network where domains can span several sites, you can control when replication updates will be sent across the domain. The amount of replication traffic on a day-to-day basis may be a non-issue if your network is stable and changes are minimal. However, "the cost of running Windows 2000" can involve large amounts of replication traffic when software installations occur that require schema updates to propagate across the domain or forest, or that demand a large-scale deployment of users and groups.

Isolating Network Logon Traffic

Site objects can also be defined to isolate logon traffic. During the logon process, a workstation examines the site objects in Active Directory to find a domain controller in its local site. The TCP/IP subnet the client machine belongs to defines the local subnet where it will attempt to find a domain controller to log onto the network, DNS services, and global catalog services. Sites should contain the closest domain controllers and the global catalog for client authentication. When a user attempts to log onto a domain that is a part of his/her workstation, Windows 2000 attempts to locate a Domain Controller and global catalog services using DNS resource records in the local site. In addition, DNS needs to be able to perform a reverse lookup of the site by specifying an IP subnet.

Active Directory passes the client query to the Net Logon service running on the domain controller. The client then receives a list of available domain controller IP addresses from the DNS query response.

The client's IP address is matched to the subnet/site on which the client resides and information on the closest DC is returned to the client. The client looks up the subnet objects in the configuration NC that most closely matches its own subnet.

Then the client takes the site name attribute from its subnet object and asks DNS for a list of servers in its site. Based on the weights presented for each server and associated resource record, a server is chosen. The server may not be physically the closest to the client but through site design and the location of servers and defined subnets, the real availability of network resources can be defined by the site administrator. Other site and domain controller locations will be returned to the client if there is not a DC located in the site where the client is located.

NOTE

By defining different sites in the same physical location, you can more closely control the logon process as long as DNS, a global catalog, and a domain controller are present locally within the site.

This could be quite helpful in universities and other large campus-style networks. For example, if the west campus administrators would like to isolate that campus completely from the East Campus logon requests, two sites, East Campus Site and West Campus Site, could be configured for the campus network. When network users in the East Campus site log on, their workstations look to Active Directory within the locally defined site to find a local DC and GC, and DNS services.

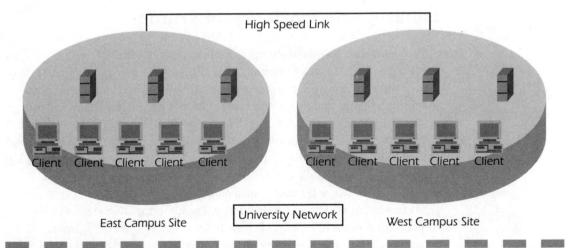

High Speed Link

Client Client Client Client Client   Client Client Client Client Client

East Campus Site   University Network   West Campus Site

Figure 9.3   This domain is split into two separate sites; therefore the West Campus can be isolated from the East Campus logon requests.

To Identify Network Resources by Immediacy

Sites are also used to find a variety of other resources within close proximity. The DFS is another resource that offers site-enabled location services. When attaching to a DFS Tree, a workstation examines the site objects stored in Active Directory to find a DFS child node in close proximity. Accordingly, Microsoft is planning to use the concept of sites in Exchange 2000 as detailed in Figure 9.4, certificate servers, RAS, and many other network services.

Sites Host Network Services

The site that is defined as your local logon site should host the required network services including: domain controllers, DNS services, DHCP services, global catalog servers, and DFS; and in the near future: Exchange 2000 services, Mailboxes, and proxy server information.

Sites can also take advantage of the following features:

- **Delegating administration**—This can make sense when a subnet, network, or a set of subnets/networks corresponds to the area of intended delegation but an existing domain or OU boundary does not.

Figure 9.4
Exchange 2000 installs service components into Active Directory.

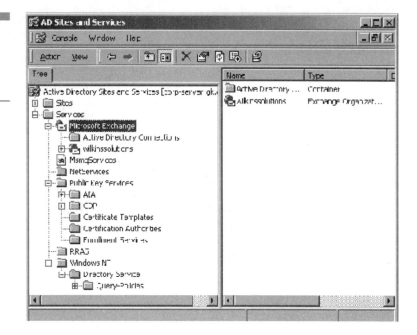

- **Assigning group policy per site**—Remember group policy can also be assigned at both domain and OU levels and these options should be fully explored first.

Controlling Network Queries

How much traffic does an LDAP query for access to an Active Directory objects(s) generate? The LDAP query starts in the domain where the query was generated by an application, service, or user request. If an LDAP client queries information located in a sister domain these are the steps taken:

1. The LDAP client first queries DNS for the location of an LDAP server in the current domain.
2. DNS responds with a Domain Controller located in the current domain or local site, as long as the network resource is properly located in the site location.
3. The LDAP client queries the Domain Controller for the desired information on the Active Directory object.
4. The Domain Controller then refers the client to the parent domain.

5. The LDAP client queries DNS for an LDAP server in the parent domain.
6. DNS responds with a Domain Controller in the parent domain.
7. The LDAP client then queries the parent Domain Controller for the desired information about the Active Directory object.
8. The parent Domain Controller refers the client to another of its child domains.
9. The LDAP client queries DNS for an LDAP server in the sister domain.
10. DNS responds with a Domain Controller in the sister domain.
11. The LDAP client then queries the sister Domain Controller for the information about the desired Active Directory object.
12. The sister Domain Controller finally responds to the client's request.

If a client routinely has to query network services located on remote sites, the time lag and the network traffic could be substantial.

Planning for Site Deployment

Evaluate your company's physical environment and document relevant information for your site design, including:

- Physical locations in your company that can form a single domain.
- Areas of your network that will be created as individual sites.
- The physical network links between your sites.
- The names of your company's site link objects.
- Assigning a cost and replication schedule to each site link object created.
- Configuring a site link bridge for added redundancy over your secondary links.

Site Identification

Identify the site where a domain controller is located in the Configuration container as a site object in cn=Sites, cn=Configuration, dc=ForestRootDomain container. Each subnet is an addressed segment within a site; in fact, it may be the only segment, and it is defined by an object in the cn=Subnets, cn=Sites, cn=Configuration, dc=ForestRootDomain container.

Any site that is to function autonomously needs certain services at the site level: domain controller(s), a global catalog server, and DNS (name resolution services).

For example, if you had a small branch office off a main branch network, the creation of a site for the branch office would allow you to control the replication traffic across the slower link. If you had offices in the United States and at international locations, sites could be created to control replication, delegate authority, and apply group policy at the site level.

NOTE

Replication traffic may be a moot point on your network if there are not a lot of changes. How often are objects added, modified, and deleted? What type of objects— for example universal groups— are they?

Creating a Site

Having the proper permissions is crucial to having the ability to create sites. This makes sense since all site work is performed on the root domain controller. Enterprise Admins group normally has permissions to be able to create a site at the root level; other local administrators do not, by default.

To create a site:

1. Open the Active Directory Sites and Services.
2. Right-click the Sites folder and select **New Site**.
3. In the New Object-Site dialog box enter the name of the new site, as shown in Figure 9.5.
4. Select a site link object.
5. Choose the protocol, either IP or SMTP.

Once the site has been created several administrative tasks must also be performed:

1. Add subnets for the sites to the Subnets container.
2. Link the site to other sites with a site link.
3. Move domain controllers into the site to provide site coverage.

Figure 9.5
Sites are created with
AD Sites and Services.

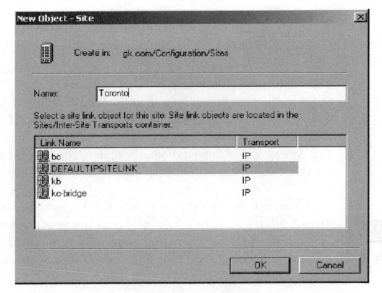

Creating a Subnet

Computers on a TCP/IP network are assigned to sites based on their location within a subnet. The subnet will contain both client and server computers. A subnet must be created and associated with a site.

To create a subnet:

1. Open the Active Directory Sites and Services.
2. Right-click the Subnets folder and select **New Subnet**.
3. In the New Object Subnet box enter the subnet identifier and subnet mask, as shown in Figure 9.6.
4. Choose the site to associate with this site and click **OK**.

The servers moved into the subnet will provide site coverage for the clients within the sites.

What if There Is No Domain Controller?

Each site need not contain a domain controller—there may be situations where a small branch office is linked with ISDN or a 56K connection.

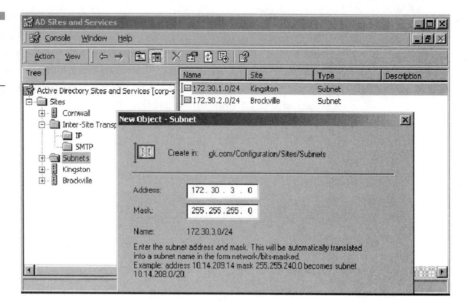

Figure 9.6
Creating a subnet requires association with an existing site.

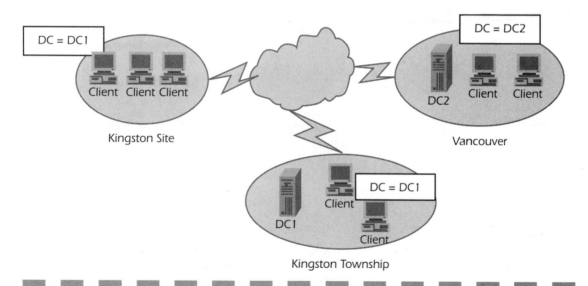

Figure 9.7 Small branch sites can rely on domain controllers in another site to provide site coverage.

The users within this site need the same network services (DC, GC, and DNS) to be able to authenticate properly. Every site, by default, will have a list of domain controllers available through a process called site coverage. By default, every site will also have a listing of all sites and the domain controllers in each site even if one site doesn't have a DC. Every domain controller, by default, checks all the sites in the forest to make sure that each site has access to a DC for the purpose of authentication. If the DC finds that it is the best location based on the WAN topology, it then registers a DC DNS entry pointing to the closest site location with a domain controller, i.e. the cheapest route. It will then be published within DNS as if it were in the site.

For each domain controller in the forest, DNS follows this procedure:

1. A list of target sites that have no DCs for the domain is created.
2. A list of candidate sites that have DCs for the domain is created.
3. It chooses the candidate site with the largest number of domain controllers available at the least cost.
4. It registers target-specific SRV records for the winning domain controller.

Sites and Replication

Two types of replication are used by AD: intra-site (within a site) and inter-site (between sites). Table 9.1 summarizes terms I will define in the next few pages.

TABLE 9.1

Replication terminology.

	Intra-Site Replication	Inter-Site Replication
Transport	RPC	RPC or SMTP
Topology	Ring	Spanning Tree
Schedule	Frequency Schedule	Availability Schedule
Replication	Notify and Pull	Pull/Store and Forward
Compression	None	Full

Replication Transport

Transport within a site defaults to RPC, also called Replication RPC. Between sites, RPC (remote procedure calls) or Simple Mail Transfer Protocol (SMTP) can be used for configuration, schema, and global catalog replication. In the situation where connectivity between sites is unstable at best, SMTP can be used; the normal protocol for replication between sites that have acceptable connectivity is RPC over IP.

Replication Topology

Replication topology within a site is ring based, and between sites is based upon a minimum-cost spanning tree. The spanning tree is calculated by the KCC, based on the information provided when multiple sites are created.

Replication Schedule

The replication schedule within a site is driven by change; between 5 and 15 minutes after a change has occurred, a trigger will notify the DC's replication partners that changes have happened in the directory. A schedule for final notification within the site happens every six hours to ensure that all changes have been sent and ratified by all online domain controllers.

The Process of Replication

Within a site, once a DC has been notified, it pulls the changes from its replication partner; in inter-site replication changes are also pulled, but on a set schedule defined between sites. Replication within a site will normally have no bandwidth concerns, whereas replication between sites can be scheduled based on location and bandwidth. The replication schedule between sites is based on replication windows of availability scheduled at 15-minute intervals.

Compression of Replication Data

Within a site, replication data are not compressed; between sites compression is used very effectively—up to 85 percent.

How is Replication Topology Created?

There is a topology generator called a knowledge consistency checker (KCC) that runs on each domain controller. The KCC is a local DC service that computes the topology and creates connection objects for replication. The KCC is actually a local DLL process running on all domain controllers that reviews and maintains replication data stored in Active Directory in response to any changes that may occur with respect to local-site, or between-site, connectivity. Within the site boundaries, the KCC automatically creates and maintains connection objects.

The KCC's two main functions are:

- Configuring replication connections (called *connection objects*) between domain controllers within a site and, if chosen, acting as the KCC within a site responsible for inter-site connections
- Accepting inbound connection objects from other domain controllers and updating the local replication data.

The KCC Monitors the Replication Topology

There is a replication topology for naming context (NC) that the KCC considers when it calculates the replication paths and creates connection objects. NCs per domain controller have different scopes. The Domain NC is replicated to all domain controllers for that domain in the site; therefore the topology is different from the Configuration or Schema NC. The schema and configuration will be replicated to all domain controllers in the forest regardless of the domain in which they are located. The KCC automatically builds replication topology:

- **Within Sites**—For each naming context NC, a bidirectional ring is automatically built by the KCC.
- **Between Sites**—For each naming context NC, a spanning tree topology is automatically built based upon the existing network connectivity.

Replication Topology: Intra-Site

Within a site, a bidirectional ring is created by the KCC. This means a connection is created in each direction on each domain controller in the site for replication. The ring is optimized using a process called *optimizing edges*. The optimizing process is an algorithm followed by the KCC. As the number of domain controllers in a site increases, if it becomes necessary, the KCC calculates and adds extra connections that match an average of three tree hops between every replication path in the site. The average latency from one DC to another in any direction is maintained at three hops.

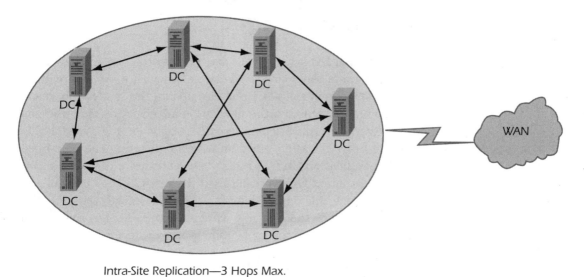

Intra-Site Replication—3 Hops Max.

Figure 9.8   The KCC creates the intra-site topology.

Once the number of domain controllers meets or exceeds six or equals seven or more DCs within a site, the KCC will deploy the extra rings required to keep the replication latency low and optimize the replication path.

The KCC works within the following mandate every 15 minutes:

- Every DC must remain within three hops from every other DC.
- The maximum time before replication occurs is 5 minutes.
- The maximum time (also called the *maximum convergence*) for an update to reach all DCs is 15 minutes.

The maximum convergence is set on each replication connection object, whether or not that object was manually or automatically generated. It could be set to once, twice, or four times per hour within the 24/7 grid.

Constructing the Inter-Site Replication Ring

Any newly installed DC is promoted using dcpromo. Then the new DC is placed in the domain controller container so other DCs are aware of the new domain controller's existence and can update the replication topology changes. Through dcpromo the new DC is added to the ring and new *connection objects* for replication are created, as shown in Figure 9.9. The DC waits one full replication schedule before replicating the new information in the replication ring. For intra-site replication, the domain controller's naming context GUID, also called the replica ID, is used to construct and optimize the replication ring. The KCC sorts the available GUIDs and determines the DC's replication partners within the site for the purpose of determining the replication order within the basic ring.

Figure 9.9
Each DC's GUID is used for identification within the replication ring.

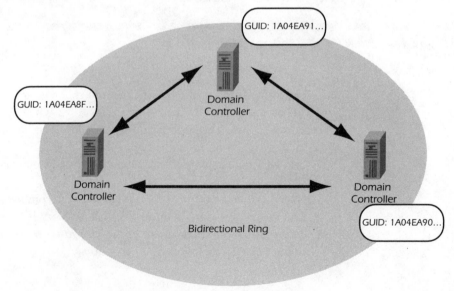

Connection Objects

A connection object defines the replication partners. Connection objects are unidirectional; you need two replication paths between two domain controllers to create a replication ring. Connection objects have two attributes: the source partner and the schedule of replication.

Connection objects are created automatically by the KCC based on the network topology it knows about. The connection object defines a replication partner along one path, from the target DC where the information resides to the destination DC that will pull the replicated information.

Figure 9.10
Each connection object is unidirectional.

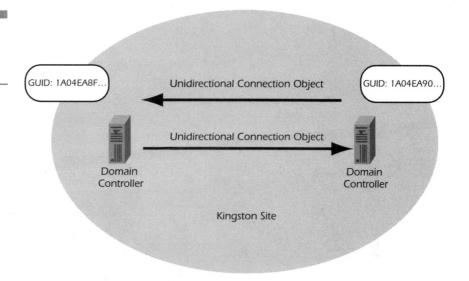

How are Intra-Site Connection Objects Created?

Once you define your site boundaries using the MMC snap-in Active Directory Sites and Services (ADSS), the KCC creates the site topology for the domain controllers within the site. It is generated by default automatically by the KCC within each site. The creation of connection objects is performed after you describe your network topology to the KCC. The same connection object transports the schema, configuration, and domain replication between domain controllers.

Once a site, subnet, and domain controllers have been added to the site, the KCC uses this information to determine what domain controllers to talk to and in what order replication will occur. If you manually add connections, the KCC will not remove them; they are permanent until manually removed. Microsoft recommends that the KCC be allowed to create the replication paths unless a special replication path is required.

Rings of Replication within one Domain

In this example, DC1 was the first domain in the site. Next a second domain was added using dcpromo. The schema and configuration was then downloaded to the new DC. DC1 is now aware of DC2 and each domain controller will have connections automatically created by its local KCC service. When DC3 is added, connections will be made with both DC2 and DC1, forming a replication ring. Finally, when DC4 is added, it too will create connection objects and replication partners for replicating domain, schema, and configuration information.

Figure 9.11
Rings of replication within a domain.

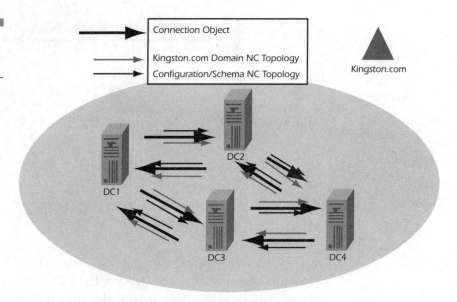

Rings of Replication with Two Domains

What happens with the replication paths if a second domain is added? When the sales domain DC1 is added to the site by running dcpromo, it becomes the first DC for the domain sales within the site. DC1 will receive configuration and schema information from one of the DCs in the Kingston domain. This forms a new replication topology and the connections will be established by the KCC. Since replication topology is for each naming topology, there are two replication paths: one for the domain NC and one for the configuration/schema naming topology.

DC1 adds itself into the replication topology and the rings are formed as detailed in Figure 9.12. When DC2 in the sales domain is added and initialized, the end result is that there are three rings: one for the Kingston domain NC, one for the Sales domain NC, and one for the configuration/schema.

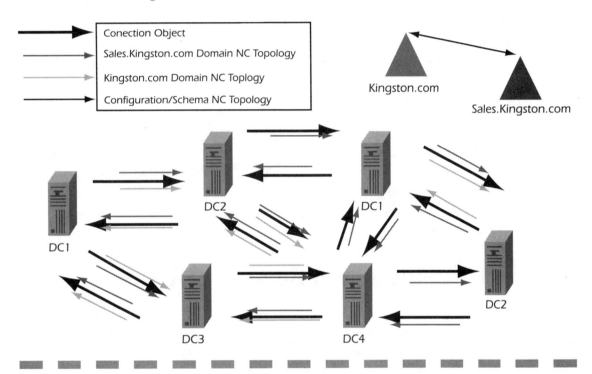

Figure 9.12 Two domains require additional connection objects.

Inter-Site Replication

For replication to occur between two sites, a site link must be established between the sites, as detailed in Figure 9.13. Note that a site link can have more than just two sites defined. With inter-site replication, the connection objects represent incoming replication communications just the same as in intra-site replication. Inter-site replication is controlled based upon the connection objects created and stored in the Directory. The KCC automatically makes decisions about what connection objects must be created for the site links. As mentioned, when Active Directory is first installed on the first DC in the forest, a default site link object called Default_First_Site_Name is automatically added to the Site container. As sites are added, each site will be automatically added to the site link, establishing network connectivity between the sites.

NOTE

The default site and defaultipsitelink name can be renamed to suit your environment.

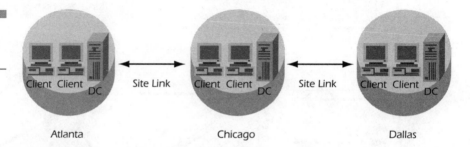

Figure 9.13
Site links are created manually.

Bridgehead Servers (BH)
========================

A *bridgehead* is the point where a connection enters or leaves a site. When the KCC creates the connections between sites, the domain controller that stores the connections linking the two sites is called a bridgehead server (see Figure 9.14).

A server that has a connection object pulling replication data from another site is called a destination bridgehead. A server acting as a source for a connection to another site is called a preferred bridgehead server. A bridgehead server must be able to handle the increased replication between sites. If the KCC has selected the bridgehead server automatically, which is the default, if failure occurs after two hours since the last replication cycle, the KCC will select another bridgehead server to take its place.

Figure 9.14
Bridgehead servers can be viewed with Active Directory Sites and Services.

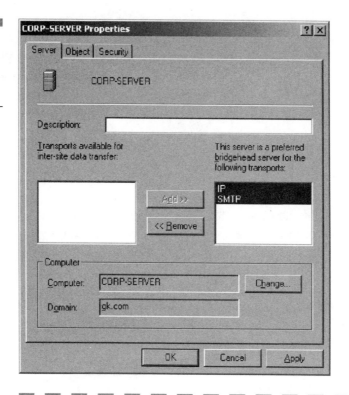

NOTE

You can select a bridgehead server manually; however, if failure occurs, the KCC will not automatically select another bridgehead server to take over.

Inter-Site Topology Generation

The KCC runs on every domain controller as a local service and controls the in-site replication. However when the KCC decides to replicate between sites, the creation of the connection objects is done on only one DC in the site. An algorithm is used to decide who gets to create the inter-site creation topology. The first server added to the site becomes the inter-site topology generator (ISTG). The ISTG server refreshes an NTDS site-setting object announcing that it is still alive and in charge of the inter-site replication. All other domain controllers in the site continually read that object. If the ISTG server stops updating the object, then a new ISTG server will be automatically promoted, taking over the inter-site topology role based on the GUID of the server.

Therefore there is always one server within the site monitoring and creating inter-site topology connections when these are required for out-of-site communications. Although it is similar to an FSMO role, the role transfers automatically. The inter-site topology generator server also creates connection objects for all bridgehead servers in the site.

Site Links

A site link is a collection of two or more sites that need connectivity to each other. The cost value defined on each site link has an impact on the choice of one site link versus another, when the same sites are defined with different site links. Different replication schedules could also then be defined for both a daytime and nighttime schedule between the same sites.

Once site links have been defined using ADSS, the KCC is notified that these two sites have physical network connectivity to each other and a cost is established for the defined link. The default cost factor is set at 100; the lower the number the higher the priority of replication. For example the cost of a T1 link could be set to the default of 100, while the cost of a dial-up link could be set to 150.

Another method used to set the cost factor would be to set a value of 1 for site links that are part of the backbone network, and cost = 100 for any sites linking to a slow connection to a branch office.

This would ensure that a DC in a branch office would always replicate with a DC on the corporate backbone and not with another branch office, since the cost factor of 1 is the highest-priority link. Since the KCC is trying to make efficient use of all replication paths between sites, the cost value is a huge factor in the path of replication chosen by the KCC. Site links are also defined as transitive or bridged, as shown in Figure 9.15, so the best path can be chosen across multiple site links if they exist, with the costs added together to find the actual cost factor.

Site-Link Schedule

A site link is associated with a schedule for replication. The schedule opens a replication window that defines when replication can take place. A common replication window timeframe between two sites connected by a site link is necessary for replication to occur. Multiple site links must have multiple replication windows. There must be a common win-

Figure 9.15
Site links are by
default bridged
together.

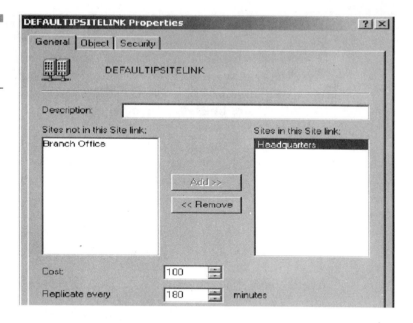

dow in order for the connection to be made available for replication, or replication will not take place.

If the schedule is thought of as a 15-minute window, in 24 hours we have an array of all the 15-minute intervals available for replication. The replication interval can be set from 15 minutes to a maximum of a week (10,080 minutes); the default is 180 minutes, as shown in Figure 9.16.

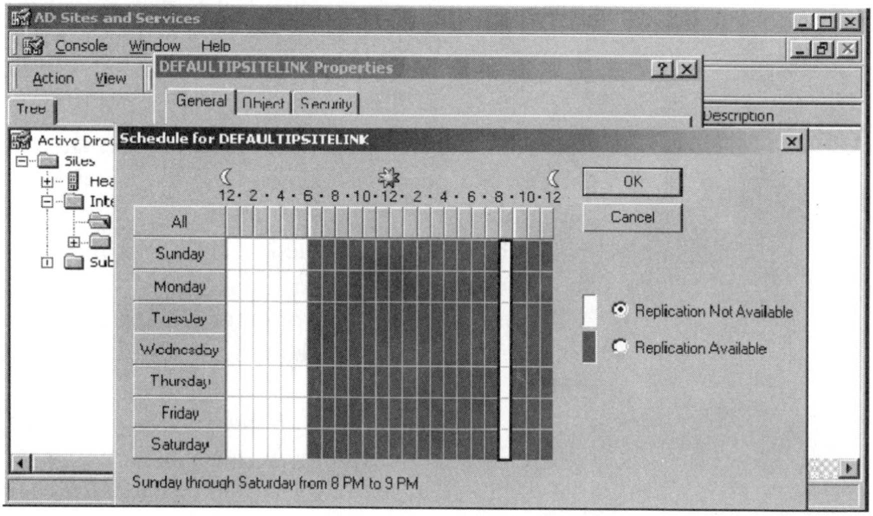

Figure 9.16
Each site link requires
a schedule for
replication.

Controlling Topology and Scheduling

The available topology is controlled through setting the costs on site links. The replication periods are controlled through setting the replication period on site links. Link availability is defined by setting the schedule on site links—for example blocking replication traffic during certain business hours.

The KCC can automatically set up all the costs and schedule; it may not be necessary manually to set any values. When the KCC creates a connection object, the replication period is set to a maximum time period based on the minimum cost path. However, we are dealing with replication, and this service is but one of many processes that utilize network bandwidth. Careful monitoring of the KCC decisions should be maintained so changes in your WAN are reflected in your replication schedule. For example, certain links may not always be available 24 hours a day; this will have to be considered when setting your replication schedule.

You may also want to set all your replication paths manually; this can be done through the use of site-link bridges, described later in this chapter.

NOTE

Assigning a Cost Value

A cost factor is used for the generation of the replication topology. Suggestions are listed in Tables 9.2 and 9.3. Integer values are used to define and calculate the cost. The cost value can also define the availability of a link.

- Backbone servers are directly connected; they can talk to each other as often as necessary. Therefore the backbone link should have the lowest priority.
- Any hubs directly attached to the backbone will also talk to the backbone servers directly.
- A T1 connection from a remote office to the backbone is still fast, but not as fast as the backbone link; therefore its cost value should be higher.
- A 56-K link is slower that the T1 link. However the office connected by this link should possibly have a higher priority than an international link since the office is still considered local—it just doesn't have

TABLE 9.2

Defining cost integers.

Network Type	Speed
Very slow	56 Kbps
Slow (typical in Europe)	64 Kbps
ISDN	64 Kbps or 128 Kbps
Frame relay	Between 56 Kbps and 1.5 megabits per second (Mbps)
T1	1.5 Mbps
T3	45 Mbps
Asynchronous Transfer Mode (ATM)	Between 155 Mbps and 622 Mbps
Gigabit Ethernet	1 gigabit per second (Gbps)

TABLE 9.3

Replication topology integers.

Replication Topology	Integer Value
Backbone link	1
T1 backbone	200
56 K link	500
Branch Office	1000
International Link	5000

good connectivity, so replication won't be as frequent due to the poor speed of the connection.

- An international link is only used when necessary to maintain the replication topology; it is assigned a much lower priority.
- A branch office, depending on the connection speed, may be assigned a cost value to minimize unnecessary multiple replication paths.

Look at your WAN and decide how you want to replicate your sites across the existing wide-area connections based on the assigned cost factor. The main factor in assigning the cost value is the bandwidth of each site link; therefore, a higher bandwidth link should be assigned a lower cost. There may be political reasons for assigning costs also. For example, you may have two links with equal speeds; one is an international link and the other is a backbone link. Assigning the international link a higher number than the backbone link can ensure that replication will take place first between the servers on the backbone and then between the branch offices or international sites on a less-frequent schedule.

Global Catalog Server Replication

The global catalog is created by default on the first domain controller in the enterprise. The global catalog is the data repository for queries holding specific information about all objects in the domain tree. There is usually one global catalog per site, since it is needed for logon and storage of universal group information. Global catalog replication is calculated based on every naming context in the enterprise. The KCC on a global catalog server builds a list of all the domain controllers in the enterprise and calculates the ring topology needed for that site based on its location in the site. If there are other GCs located in that site, the GCs will share topology information among themselves. Therefore, each GC calculates that topology where it is a part of the ring for each naming context locally, without having to go across the WAN to learn about the topology outside the site.

Site-Link Bridges

A site-link bridge is a manual connection that allows you to specify a replication path between two sites. In a complex environment you may not have WAN connectivity to all sites. By default, when a site link is created it is transitive; the assumption is that all sites can link to each other for a replication topology.

What if you had 10 sites that could talk to each other, but you had two sites somewhere else in the world that couldn't directly talk to each other? A site-link bridge could be defined on one common site to define replication between the two sites. A site-link bridge is not necessary if you have IP connectivity between sites.

Disabling Transitive Site Links

The transitive nature of site links must be disabled in order to enable site link bridges. To disable transitive site links:

Figure 9.17
Site link bridges provide additional fault tolerance.

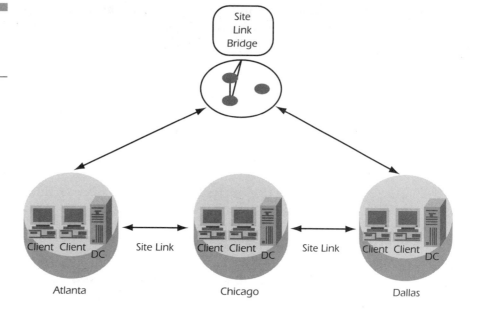

1. Open the MMC snap-in AD Sites and Services.
2. Right-click on the IP folder in the Inter-Site Transports and select **Properties**.
3. Uncheck the checkbox "Bridge all Site Links," as shown in Figure 9.18.

Figure 9.18
Bridging must be disabled before site link bridges are used.

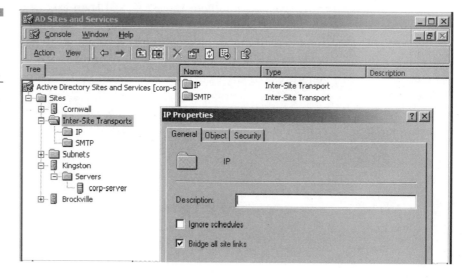

Since site links are no longer transitive, or working together, you must now manually define all replication paths from the DC. The bridging object must contain all the sites you wish to replicate together across the WAN.

Inter-Site Topology Creation: Summary

There are three ways for inter-site topology creation to occur:

- **Manually**—Turn off the KCC for inter-site replication and create connection objects manually.
- **Fully Automated**—Leave site-link transitiveness enabled and let the KCC figure out the connection objects that must be created.
- **Give the KCC hints about your preferences**; leave site links non-transitive and add site-link bridges to enforce certain routes.

Putting the KCC to Work

The KCC will do the rest, taking the site and site-link information provided, as shown in Figure 9.19. If you have left the default site-link transitiveness enabled, the KCC will then create connection objects. To summarize, subnets are created and placed in sites. Next we create site links describing the logical network topology. Then the KCC takes this logical representation of sites and the connections between them and generates the physical connections for replication.

The KCC can handle failover, assuming there is another defined path that can be utilized.

NOTE

Figure 9.19
The KCC uses the
supplied information
to calculate and
maintain replication
paths.

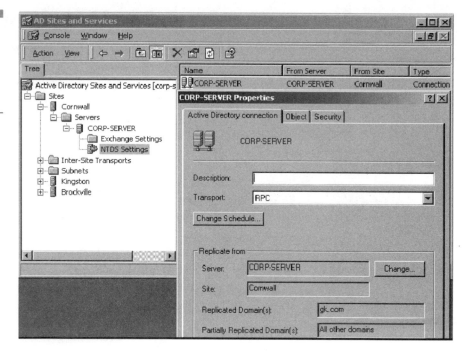

Figure 9.19
The KCC uses the
supplied information
to calculate and
maintain replication
paths.

Evaluate Your Company's Physical Environment

To create your site design, you must document your company's physical characteristics using the following criteria. Once this information is known you will have the necessary information you need to create a well-organized site structure.

- Available WAN links
- Speed of the WAN links
- Bandwidth available during normal/peak periods
- Locations in which your company has offices
- Speed of the local networks in each office
- TCP/IP subnets in each office
- Organization of links between offices
- Reliability of links

Case Study: Saint Mary's of the Lake Group

Figure 9.20 shows the physical locations for St. Mary's of the Lake Medical Group, an HMO operating in the Midwest. St. Mary's of the Lake Medical Group has a single domain shared by four locations: Chicago, Detroit, Green Bay, and Saint Paul.

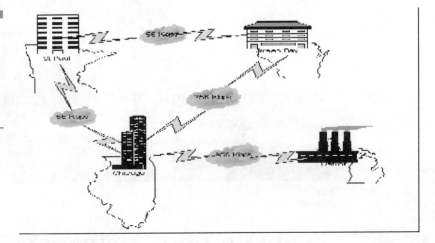

Figure 9.20
The Chicago office is the headquarters for St. Mary's of the Lake Medical Group and the main hub of the company's WAN.

All the company's locations have installed 10MB switched Ethernet from the desktop linked to a 100MB backbone. Several frame relay and fractional T1 links connect Detroit, Green Bay, and Saint Paul to the center of operations in Chicago. Local bandwidth is not a problem; however, most of the company's wide-area links are well utilized. The physical characteristics of St. Mary's of the Lake Medical Group are described in Table 9.4.

Defining the Network Areas to be Created as Individual Sites

To determine whether a network area should be defined as a site, consider the area's needs:

- Does the area of your company's network require scheduled replication?

TABLE 9.4   Physical characteristics of St. Mary's of the Lake Medical Group.

	Chicago	Detroit	Green Bay	St. Paul
TCP/IP	10.10.x.x	10.20.x.x	10.30.x.x.	10.40.x.x
Subnets	10.31.x.x	10.41.x.x		
Remote Links	Primary: 256 Kb to Green Bay	Main link: 256Kbps to	Main link: 256Kbps to Chicago	Main link: 56Kbps to Chicago
	Secondary: 56 Kb to St Paul	Chicago	Secondary: St. Paul to Green Bay	
Remote Link Utilization	40 %	75%	60%	80%

- Does the area of your company's network require control over the logon process?
- Does the area of your company's network require the identification of resources by immediacy?

Analysis

The sites and associated TCP/IP subnets for St. Mary's of the Lake Medical Group are shown in Figure 9.21. St. Mary's of the Lake Medical Group requires a site for each of its locations for better control of replication and logon traffic and to identify local resources. Each site object is named for the physical location it represents. The site objects created include Chicago, Detroit, Green Bay, and Saint Paul.

Identify the Network Links between Sites

If one of your sites is connected to another with two network links, classify each link as either primary or secondary. Your primary links are the network links between sites with the highest available bandwidth. If just one network link connects two of your sites, that link is a primary link.

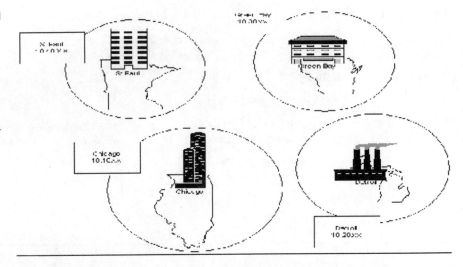

Analysis

The following site links for St. Mary's of the Lake Medical Group are named for the physical connections they represent: Detroit-Chicago; Green Bay-Chicago; and Saint Paul-Chicago.

Assigning a Cost and Schedule to Site Links

Your next task is to assign a cost and replication schedule to each site link. The default cost of a site-link object set is 100; the lower the number the lower the cost and the higher the priority. When multiple site-link objects are created to connect to two separate sites, replication occurs over the lowest-cost link. The default replication between sites occurs once every 3 hours, 24 hours a day, 7 days a week. The default replication schedule should almost always be used. If you set the schedule of inter-site replication to a 3-hour window and the site link were not available during that time period due to failure, replication would not be attempted for another 24 hours. You also may need to replicate updates more frequently if an application or group of users depends on having the latest changes to directory data. A dial-up link connecting two sites, which may be unavailable during certain time periods, could be a situation where less-frequent replication updates are acceptable. During business hours, if the physical link joining the two sites is overused, you may also decide to define a less-frequent replication schedule.

Configuring Site Link Bridges

Your final task is to configure a site-link bridge over your secondary physical links to provide redundancy for replication traffic. Figure 9.22 shows the primary and secondary physical links in the St. Mary's of the Lake Medical Group network WAN.

Figure 9.22
The redundancy plan allows replication to occur in the event of a physical link failure.

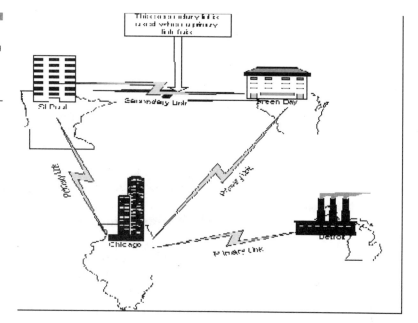

Employing a Secondary Link with Site-Link Bridges

Three site-link objects have been defined for the primary links connecting Detroit, Green Bay, and Saint Paul to Chicago. The connection between Green Bay and Saint Paul should be defined as a backup link for replication traffic. If the primary physical link between Green Bay and Chicago or Saint Paul and Chicago fails, replication traffic can travel over the secondary physical link. Fault tolerance for replication traffic between Green Bay, Saint Paul, and Chicago can be implemented by creating a site-link bridge. The goal is that the backup replication path, defined by the site link bridge, is used only when a failure occurs on a primary physical link. The desired behavior when failure occurs is:

- If the primary physical link between Green Bay and Chicago fails, replication traffic must travel from Green Bay to Saint Paul and then from Saint Paul to Chicago.
- If the primary physical link between Saint Paul and Chicago fails, replication traffic must travel from Saint Paul to Green Bay and then from Green Bay to Chicago.

Steps in defining a site-link bridge:

1. Define the physical backup link between Green Bay and Saint Paul as a site-link object.
2. Next create a site-link bridge object representing the physical secondary path of Green Bay-Saint Paul.
3. Add the Saint Paul-Chicago, Green Bay-Chicago and Green Bay-Saint Paul site-link objects to the site-link bridge.

Figure 9.23 and 9.24 show this fault-tolerance configuration in more detail. The site-link bridge object can use the physical connection between Green Bay and Saint Paul as a backup path for replication. The replication cost of the site-link bridge object is the sum of the Saint Paul-Chicago, Green Bay-Chicago, and Green Bay-Saint Paul site links, or $100 + 100 + 120 = 320$. When multiple pathways connect two separate sites, replication always occurs over the lowest cost link.

Replication Partner Failure

If the KCC detects a replication failure it will generate a new temporary connection to ensure replication continues. This connection is based on two thresholds: the number of failures and the period of time since the last replication. For example, if there were two replication failures within three hours, the KCC would create a new temporary topology connection. The original connection remains, for when the usual link is re-established. To change the thresholds for servers that stop responding, the following registry entries can be modified in HKEY_LOCAL_MACHINE\SYSTEM\CurrentControlSet\Services\NT DS\Parameters.

- InterSiteFailuresAllowed—default is 1.
- MaxFailureTimeForInterSiteLink—default is 2 hours.

The detailed
replication
redundancy plan for
St. Mary's of the Lake
Medical Group.

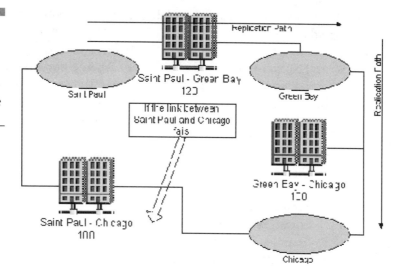

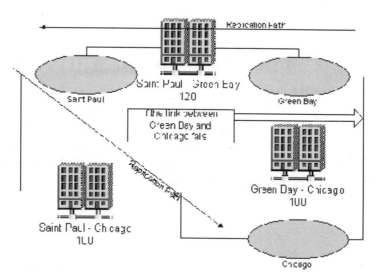

Administrative Tasks:
Analyze Your Default-First-Site

The first site is set up automatically when you install Windows 2000 Server on the root domain controller in your enterprise. The first site is always called default-first-site. To display any valid sites within your network:

Click Start\Programs\Administrative Tools\Active Directory Sites and Services.

A. Expand the Default-First-Site. All the servers for this forest were added to the default-first-site when they were promoted.
B. Display the servers that participate in the DEFAULTFIRSTSITE by expanding the Servers folder; your server will be displayed in the details pane.
C. View the connections for your server by expanding your server and displaying its NTDS Settings. For each server, there are connections and schedules that control replication to other servers in this site created by the KCC.
D. View the properties for each connection.
E. Double-click one of the replication paths.
F. Click the Change Schedule button to see the current replication schedule.

Create Sites with Active Directory Sites and Services (ADSS)

Suppose you have been tasked to set up a server site somewhere in the country to replicate with a remote server in the default-first-site site. This walk-through will take you through the basic steps you would perform to set up multiple sites.

Logon to the your domain as Administrator.

A. Click Start\Programs\Administrative Tools\Active Directory Sites and Services.
B. Expand the default-first-site site folder and highlight the Servers folder; all the installed servers network are in this site if sites have not been created.

Create a New Site

My site name is: _____
My subnet is: _____ _____ _____

My subnet mask is: ____ ____ ____ ____

1. Highlight the Sites folder and from the Action menu select New Site.
   A. In the New Object-Site dialog box enter the name of the new site.
   B. Since there are no other site links created at present, the DEFAULTTIPTSITELINK must be selected.
   C. Highlight the DEFAULTTIPTSITELINK and select **OK**.

Move Your Server into Your Site

2. Highlight your server icon in the Raleigh\Servers folder.
   A. Right-click your server and select **Move**.
   B. Select the site created and click **OK**.

Define a Subnet for a Your Site

3. Highlight the Subnets folder.
   A. On the Action menu, click **New Subnet**.
   B. In the New Object–Subnet box, enter the subnet address and subnet mask numbers.
   C. In the lower pane, select your site object for this subnet and click **OK**.

Create a Site Link

For scheduled replication to occur between multiple sites, both sites must agree on a transport to communicate, and site links must be created.

4. Expand the Inter-Site Transports folder and highlight the IP folder.
   A. From the Action menu, select **New Site Link**.
   B. In the New Object-Site Link dialog box, enter the name to the site link.
   C. The name should be <Site you created> to <Site already created>, for example Chicago to Raleigh.

My site link name is: _____ to _____
D. Add your sites from "Sites not in this Site link" to the right-hand column "Sites in this Site link", then click **Add**.

Configuring Inter-site Replication and Site-Link Attributes

In the Inter-Site Transports folder, highlight the IP folder.

A. Highlight the site link you created in the details pane and from the Action menu select **Properties**.
B. In the General tab there are three settings to configure:
   – Cost: Default at 100
   – Replicate every: 180 minutes
   – Schedule: Click **Change Schedule** to set the replication window.

Manually Configure Replication Objects

Highlight your server's NTDS Settings.

A. From the action menu select New Active Directory Connection.
B. Select a domain controller for the connection and click **OK**.
C. Name the manual connection Sample Manual Connection.
D. Edit the properties of the manual connection.
E. Click the **Change Schedule** button to see the current replication schedule.
F. Right-click the manual site link. What task could you force?

User and Group Accounts

This chapter provides details on managing users and groups, discussing such topics as:

- When to use local and domain user accounts
- Distinguish between local, global, and universal groups
- When to use built-in users and groups
- Why to use Run As

Managing User Accounts

In Windows 2000, user and group accounts are used to implement security for network access to resources, just as in NT 4.0. The user account allows a user to log on to a domain and gain access to network resources in the Directory or to log on locally and gain access to the local computer only. OUs are then used for administrative control and the deployment of group policy of user and group accounts. Three types of user accounts in Windows 2000 help gain access to resources:

- **Local User Account**—Access to local resources on a specific computer Windows 2000 Professional node.
- **Domain User Account**—Access to network resources in the Directory database.
- **Built-in User Accounts**—For performing administrative tasks.

Windows 2000 Groups

Groups may seem outdated in the Windows 2000 network; however, they are an essential component of user security becasue they aid in authentication and the assigning of permissions to resources throughout the network. The bottom line is that Microsoft did not have enough time to rewrite the operating system kernel to exclude groups from Windows 2000. The upgrade path to Windows 2000 would have been severely limited if large NT networks could not have upgraded their current user and group accounts.

Each created user and group account has unique characteristics that either allow or deny access to resources on the network.

Although user accounts could be used to define the access to network resources, groups containing user accounts are mostly used for implementing Windows 2000 security by grouping like users together and then assigning permissions to resources to the desired groups.

NOTE

From the viewpoint of the administrator the organizational unit provides a way to delegate administrative control and apply group policy. A user assigned to an OU gains no additional access or permissions just because of the particular OU or location in the domain where the user or group account is located.

Domain User Accounts

A domain user account allows a user access to network resources anywhere in the forest once he or she has been successfully authenticated. Each user who has been authenticated at the domain level receives an access token holding information about the user and assigned security levels to be used for the duration of their session. A new domain user account is created in the default User container or, in a specific organizational unit (OU) by using the Active Directory Users and Computers MMC snap-in.

Once created, the account is replicatd to all domain controllers in the domain. Built-in domain user accounts included with the installation of Windows 2000 are Administrator and Guest. Guest is always disabled and Administrator should always be renamed, for additional security.

Security Principle Details

A Windows 2000 user, group, service, and computer account is defined as a security principal. The capabilities of a security principal are sometimes defined by its identity, for example built-in users Administrator, or Domain Administrator, have built-in rights and permissions that exceed the defined rights of a basic user in the domain. The system identity of users, groups, and computers is uniquely defined to the operating system by a security identifier called an SID when it is first created.

The security subsystem monitors user and group requests for resources, through the security principal's access token.

All executing software applications or network services (processes and threads) have users and groups that are allowed or denied access defined through user or group SIDs. Each logged-on user is assigned an access token, which provides the security context for the user's actions on the local computer or through the Directory.

The context of all user activities within Windows 2000 is defined by the security context of the user account used.

NOTE

Access Tokens

The access token contains:

- The user's SID.
- The SIDs of groups to which the user is a member.
- Any privileges assigned to the user account.

Security Identifier (SID)

The SID is a unique number generated by Windows 2000 when a new user or group account is first created. The first section of the SID associates the domain where the SID was issued, as shown in Figure 10.1.

Figure 10.1
Using Regedit, the SID and the RID can be viewed.

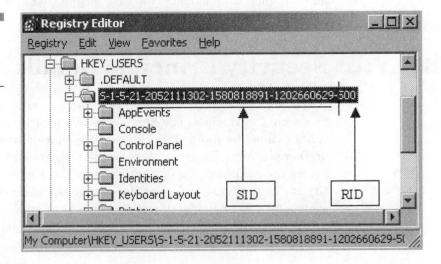

The second SID section is called the relative security identifier (RID) and identifies an account object within the domain relative to where the SID was issued. A SID is never reused; even deleting and recreating a group of the same name results in a different SIDs being assigned. The SID for the local account or group is produced by the local security authority on the computer and stored in the registry. The SID for a domain account or group is generated by the domain security authority and stored as an attribute of the User or Group object in Active Directory.

Security Descriptor Details

Each object in the Directory contains a unique header called a security descriptor that identifies the access permissions assigned to the object.

- **Owner security ID**—The user or group who owns the object.
- **Discretionary Access Control List (ACL)**—The users and groups who are either denied or granted specific access permissions through two ACLs—AccessDenied or AccessAllowed.
- **AccessDenied**—Overrules all AccessAllowed.
- **A system access control list**—Maintains a log of auditing messages generated if auditing is enabled using the SystemAudit ACL.

The Access Control List (ACL)

The ACL is a list of Access Control Entries (ACEs) that either deny or grant the users and groups detailed access rights or permissions to an object by identifying the SIDs for each access right or permission. If you give a user or group permission to a printer, that user or group's SID is noted in the access control entries that are part of the access control list assigned to the printer.

The Access Control Entry

An access control entry has an access mask that lists all possible actions by which an access right can be applied to an object, either singly, collectively, or by special grouping. When the user makes an attempt to access a network object, the SIDs are compared in the user's access token with the discretionary ACL for the network object. When one of the user's SIDs is present in the ACL, the user is allowed access to the object.

Rules for Creating User Accounts

The best way to create user accounts is to use LDF scripts. Example scripts for you to experiment can be found at the end of this chapter with. Regardless of the method used, the more attributes defined when a user account is created, the easier it will be to find the user through Active Directory.

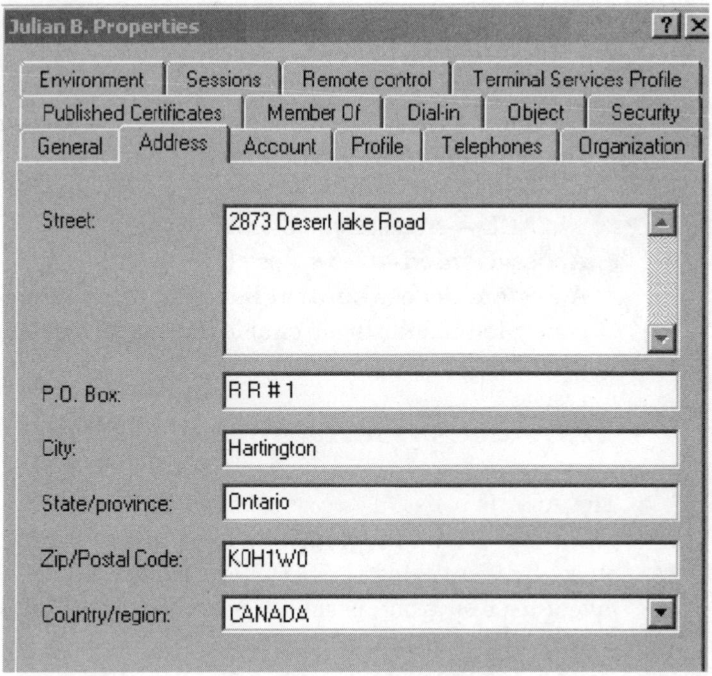

Figure 10.2
Define as many attributes as possible for all user accounts.

Julian B. Properties

Environment	Sessions	Remote control	Terminal Services Profile
Published Certificates	Member Of	Dial-in	Object	Security
General	Address	Account	Profile	Telephones	Organization

Street:	2873 Desert lake Road
P.O. Box:	R R # 1
City:	Hartington
State/province:	Ontario
Zip/Postal Code:	K0H1W0
Country/region:	CANADA

Each additional attribute entered allows for much greater success in searching for resources across the directory.

Specific rules you should consider for user accounts are given below.

Local User Accounts

User account names must be unique on the computer where they were created—try to make them unique at all times.

Domain User Accounts

The user's login name (DN) must be unique to the directory. Also, the user's full name (RDN) must be unique within the OU where the user account was created. Windows 2000 allows only 20 characters maximum for a login name. The login name is not case sensitive and passwords can be up to 14 characters.

Account Options

These define logon hours and the computers from which the user can log onto the domain.

Account Expiration

Seasonal or temporary workers should have expiration dates for their user accounts.

Naming User Accounts

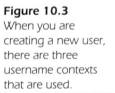

Figure 10.3
When you are creating a new user, there are three username contexts that are used.

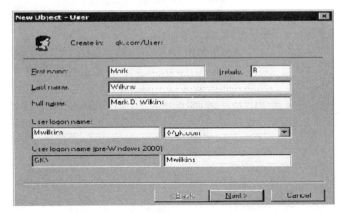

User Account Full Name

The user account full name must be unique within the context (normally the OU where it was created). It can be up to any length of upper- and lowercase characters, except for / \ [ ] : ; ! =,+ * ? < >.

User Principle Names (UPN)

New to Windows 2000 is the user principal name (UPN), a user-naming format that combines the domain name as part of the username. The

UPN format is user@domain.com. Length can be up to 64 characters except for / \ [ ] : ; ! =,+ * ? < >. UPNs must be unique across the forest. If Bob Clark and Bill Clark were both allowed to use a UPN of BClark@headquarters.com, there would be a name conflict at the global catalog.

Down-Level Name

Also called the SAM account name this name, is the comparable to NT 4 naming conventions. The down-level name must be unique within the domain. It can contain up to 20 upper- or lowercase characters except for / \ [ ] : ; ! =,+ * ? < >.

The Local User Profile

A user profile is created when a user is first authenticated to a Windows 2000 Professional non-networked PC or when a user is first authenticated to a Windows 2000 domain. The user's local user profile folder contains the user's own local Registry (NTUSER.DAT) plus the folders and shortcuts that define the users desktop and preferences, as shown in Figure 10.4. The local user profile is stored on the local computer in the folder Documents and Settings\< users_logon_name> on the defined local system drive, usually drive C: The next time the user logs onto the local PC or domain he will receive the user profile settings from the local profile location. The advantages of having a user profile are:

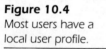

Figure 10.4
Most users have a local user profile.

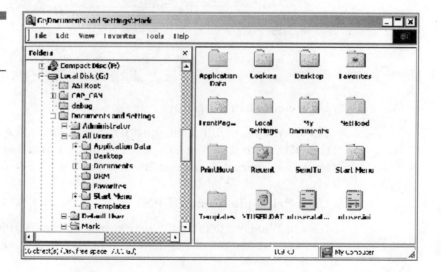

- More than one user can share a PC using individual settings.
- Customizations by one user do not affect another user.
- User profiles can be locally stored, mandated by the administrator, and stored in a network location, moving with the user around the network, called a *roaming user profile*.
- Software application settings can be retained for Windows 2000 certified products.

Roaming User Profiles

Just the addition of a path in the domain user's account in Active Directory Users and Computers can change the default action of the user's local user profile to a roaming user profile. A roaming profile is set up and stored at a shared network location so that it is available to the user whenever and wherever she logs onto the domain. When the user with a roaming user profile is authenticated, the roaming user profile copy stored on the shared network location is compared (by creation date and time) against the user's local user profile copy. If the network copy is the same as the user's local user profile, it is not copied from the network location to the client computer; the local copy is used instead. However, if the network copy is newer, it is copied from the network location to the client computer. When the user logs off, the user profile is copied back up to the defined network location.

Figure 10.5
A roaming profile can be defined for users who work at multiple locations throughout your company.

The next time the user logs on, if it is from a different network location, the roaming user profile is copied to the computer system at the location of the logon to the domain. If the user is logging on from the same location, the user profile will not be copied down from the network location if it is the same as the "locally cached copy" stored in the user's local profile folder.

NOTE

Only when changes occur is the user profile copied down to the location where the user is logging onto the network. However, at logoff, the roaming user profile is always copied back up to the server location.

The great news for Windows 2000 is that user profiles can be managed through Group Policy settings that define the folders that can roam; delete the profile if you are not logged onto your PC. See Chapter 12 for details. Steps to set up a roaming user profile are:

1. On the desired server, first create a shared folder using a UNC path in the format \\server_name\shared_folder_name.
2. Open the Active Directory Users and Computers snap-in and select the user account you wish to define as having a roaming user profile.
3. Selecting the Users properties, select the Profiles tab.
4. Enter the profile path in UNC format pointing to the shared folder location just created in Step 1, for example: \\server_name\shared_folder_name\logon_name.

Roaming User Profiles for Groups

Creating a roaming user profile for a group of users is usually handy for defining a specific profile for support or help desk personnel. The user account of each group member must have a path pointing to the shared copy of the shared roaming profile, as well as defining the permissions for access to the profile. Setting the permissions for a roaming user profile to a group is best done through the Control Panel using the System applet and the User Profile tab, as shown in Figure 10.6.

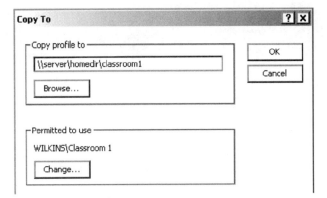

Steps for Creating a Roaming User Profile for Groups

1. First create a user profile template on a local Windows 2000 Professional workstation. This is done by creating a user account and configuring the desired desktop settings.
2. Next create a shared folder on the server that will hold the default roaming user profile.
3. On the local computer where the user profile has been created, in the Control Panel, open the System applet and select the User Profiles tab.
4. Highlight the user profile created in Step 1, and use the Copy To... button to copy the user profile to the shared network location. Also click the **Change** button to set the group permissions for the selected profile.
5. Open the Active Directory Users and Computers snap-in and select each user account you wish to define as having a roaming user profile.
6. Selecting the Users properties, select the Profiles tab.
7. Enter the profile path in UNC format pointing to the shared folder location just created in Step 1, for example: \\server_name\shared_folder_name\group_profile.

Mandatory User Profiles

For secure environments, we can go one step further and create a mandatory user profile. Changing the extension of the roaming user profile from .DAT to .MAN, as shown in Figure 10.7, changes the operation of the roaming user profile.

Figure 10.7
A mandatory user
profile is also a
roaming user profile
but the user can't
make any permanent
changes.

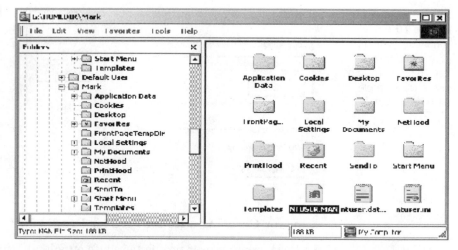

Figure 10.7
A mandatory user profile is also a roaming user profile but the user can't make any permanent changes.

All changes made by the end-user are discarded; the next time the user logs onto the domain, a fresh copy of the mandatory roaming user profile is sent down for the user during that session only. This type of roaming profile can be quite useful in training labs for groups of users where the settings rarely change. If changes were needed at some point, only one user profile would have to be maintained. To create a mandatory user profile, the user's NTUSER.DAT located on the server in the shared folder, or home folder location \\Server_name\Home_directory\ users_logon_name can be changed to a read-only format by changing the extension .DAT to MAN (NTUSER.MAN).

Home Directories

Creating a home directory on the server for your users is a great idea The home directory then becomes the default folder when the user selects File > Save from any software application. In Windows 2000, the home directory is not part of the roaming user profile; as a result its size won't be a concern during the logon process. Features of a home directory in a central location are:

- Central access to the home directory from any client computer on the network.
- Backing up of the important data documents stored in a central location to keep your job safer.

Steps for Creating Home Directories

1. First create and share a folder (directory) that will be the master folder for all directories on your network. All your user's home directories will be below this root folder.

2. For the shared root folder, remove the permission of Full Control from the Everyone group, and assign it instead to the Users group. Now all users with active domain user accounts will be able to access the shared folder.

3. Open the Active Directory Users and Groups snap-in and select the desired user account's properties.

4. Selecting the Profiles tab, click **Connect** and assign a drive letter to use.

5. In the To box, enter the UNC name as follows: \\Server_name\ Home_directory\%username%.

Home directories created on the NTFS volume using the %username% receive the benefit of each user's being assigned the NTFS Full Control permission on his own home folder. All other permissions are subsequently removed.

NOTE

The %username% variable will automatically name each user's home directory as the user's logon name. Note that this process does not create the directory—that is still a manual task.

Group Account Administration

Administration can be greatly simplified, since you can assign permissions and rights to a group of users rather than performing administration on each individual user account. Permissions mandate what users can do with the resource, typically a file folder, file, or printer. However, if several or many users need to read the same datafile, it makes sense to add the user accounts to a group and then give the group permission to read the file. User accounts, groups, contacts, and computers can be added to groups.

Groups: Types and Scope

There are two group types for Windows 2000: security and distribution groups. Security groups are the primary group type.

Security Groups

The Windows 2000 operating system uses security groups for assigning permissions to users or groups for access to network resources.

Distribution Groups

Future software applications including Exchange 2000 will be able to use distribution groups as lists for bulk communication or sending email.

Local Groups

For Windows 2000, a local group is normally used to assign permissions for resources on a local computer or the user's local domain. In mixed mode, local groups function just as in NT. In native mode, local groups created on a domain controller become domain local groups. Local groups can contain members anywhere in the forest, or from trusted forests. Local groups can only grant permissions to resources where they are created.

Figure 10.8
Local groups existed
in Windows NT 4.0.

A Local
Group

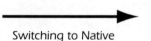

Switching to Native
Mode becomes...

A Domain
Local Group

Domain Local Groups

Domain local groups are only available in native-mode domains. Members can be from anywhere in the forest, or trusted forests. Permissions can be granted to resources within the domain where the domain local group resides. Domain local groups are used to combine members across the forest, assigning permissions to a resource in the domain. Domain local groups are listed in the global catalog, however their members are not. As a result, the global catalog does not, and cannot, use domain local group membership to build the user's access tokens. Instead the local domain where the user account was first created provides this information. In native mode, domain local groups can contain user accounts, computer accounts, universal groups, and global groups from any domain. Domain local groups within the domain can also be included.

Figure 10.9
Domain local groups
are available in native
mode.

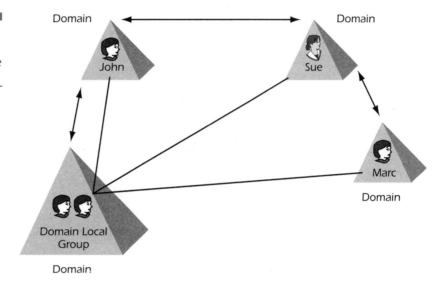

Global Groups

In native mode, global groups can contain user accounts and computer accounts from the same domain, as detailed in Figure 10.10. Global groups within the same domain can also be included. Permissions can be assigned to a global group for access to *any* resource located in the domain tree or forest. Global groups are listed in the global catalog, but their members are not.

Universal Groups

Universal groups can contain user accounts, computer accounts, universal groups, and global groups from any domain, as shown in Figure 10.11. All universal groups and their members are stored and listed in the global catalog. Members can be added to the universal group from any domain, and permissions can be assigned to gain access to a resource located in any domain. Universal groups can be used to define enterprisewide functions; memberships in large global corporations can now be defined nation- or worldwide. The downside of a universal group

286

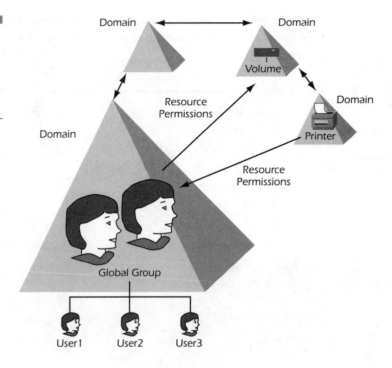

Figure 10.10
Global groups can contain users only from the domain where the global group is created.

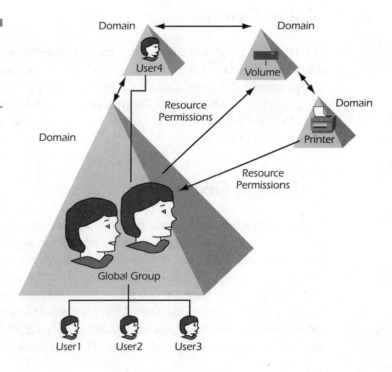

Figure 10.11
Universal groups are available only if you're running in native mode.

is the potential amount of replication required if the group membership is volatile. Static groups that rarely change members are ideal for universal groups.

Default Group Types: Predefined Global Groups

When a domain is created with dcpromo, the installation creates the predefined global groups in the Users container in Active Directory, as shown in Table 10.1.

TABLE 10.1 Predefined global groups.		
Domain Admins	Added to the Administrator's domain local group.
Domain Guests	Added to the built-in domain local group.
Domain Users	Added to the Users domain local group. Each new domain account is automatically made a member.
Enterprise Admins	Members have administrative control for the entire network. The Administrator account is a member.

These predefined groups have no inherent rights assigned to any user. Rights are assigned by adding global groups to domain local groups or by assigning users and rights to the predefined global groups.

Built-in Groups—Domain Local Groups

Several built-in domain local groups are created by the operating system for specific tasks, as listed in Table 10.2.

TABLE 10.2 Built-in domain local groups.		
Account Operators	Members can create, modify, and delete user and group accounts with the exceptions of the Administrator or Operator groups.
Administrators	These perform administrative tasks on all domain controllers and throughout the domain.
Backup Operators	Backup and restore domain controllers use the Backup utility.
Pre-Windows 2000 Compatible Access	The Everyone group is a member.
Print Operators	Members manage printers installed on domain controllers.

continued on next page

TABLE 10.2 Built-in domain local groups (continued).	Replicator	This supports replication services of the domain controller.
	Server Operators	Members can share hard disk resources and backup and restore files on a domain controller.
	Users	Authenticated users and the Domain Users global group are members.

Built-In Local Groups

The built-in groups listed in Table 10.3 are located in the Built-in folder found in the Active Directory Users and Groups console. These groups allow defined users to carry out specific tasks on domain controllers within Active Directory.

TABLE 10.3 Built-in local groups.	Administrators	The built-in Administrator account is a member. Once a member server or a Windows 2000 Professional joins a domain, the Domain Admins global group is added to the local Administrator group.
	Backup Operators	Windows backup can be used to backup and restore the computer.
	Guests	The built-in guest account is a member. Don't use this account.
	Power Users	Members can create and modify local user accounts, create groups, install printers, and share resources on the computer.
	Replicator	This supports directory replication.
	Users	Local user accounts that are created are added to this local group. The domain user's global group is added when a member server or a Windows 2000 Professional client joins a domain.

All defined standalone servers, member servers, and Windows 2000 Professional Clients have built-in local groups with certain preset permissions for all members. A local group gives users rights only on the local computer.

Changing Group Type

During the life of your network, certain users will be promoted to different departments or their roles may change. For these and other reasons, several group types can be changed. The domain must be running in native mode for group types to be changed.

- A distribution group can be changed to a security group.
- A domain local can be changed to universal as long as the domain local group does not *contain* a nested domain local group.
- A global group can be changed to a universal group, providing the global group is not a member of *another* global group.
- A universal group is always a universal group.

Nesting Groups in Native Mode

Nesting is the action of adding groups to other groups. For example, you could add the help desk personnel in each company division to a group that contains all help desk personnel in the state. Next, all the regional help desk groups could be added to a nationwide help desk group. Assigning resources is simpler, because permissions are assigned only to the nationwide help desk group. Although this example may make sense, troubleshooting permissions and setups gone awry is incredibly difficult with many levels of nested groups. Scenarios are listed for mixed and native mode in Table 10.4.

TABLE 10.4

Native and mixed nesting rules.

Group Scope	Native Mode Scope	Mixed Mode Scope
Global	User accounts and global groups from the same domain	Users from the same domain
Domain Local	User accounts, universal groups, and global groups from any domain. Domain local groups from the same domain	User accounts in global group from any domain
Universal	User accounts, other universal groups and global groups from any domain	N/A

Planning Group Membership

Before you sit down at the computer and start creating groups, proper planning should be carried out. Most of your initial planning will probably involve using global and domain local groups because your Windows 2000 server is probably running in mixed mode. Planning suggestions include:

- **Users that perform the same day-to-day tasks should be assigned to global groups**—For example: CAD operators are put in a global group called CAD; editors and copywriters go to a global group called Documentation.
- **Shared resources should be assigned to a domain global group**—Files, folders, printers, and other resources should be placed in separate domain local groups. Accounting spreadsheets go into Accounts; Color printers go into ColorPrinters.
- **Global groups that need access to the resource should be placed in the domain local group**—If the global group's Management, Sales, and Products all need access to color printers, all these global groups should be added to the local domain group ColorPrinters.
- **Allocate the required resource permissions to the domain local group**—All members of the domain global group will then receive the necessary permissions (Management, Sales, and Products) since they are members of the same domain local group ColorPrinters.

Planning for Universal Groups

Once all domain controllers are Windows 2000 domain controllers, universal groups will become more common. Universal groups are used for access to resources located in more than one domain. Permissions can also be assigned for resources in any domain in your network. A domain local group is limited to the domain where the resource is located. A universal group can be used to sign permissions for resources located anywhere. These groups have the utmost flexibility; possibly in the future, when we are all running in native mode, this will be the default group type.

Switching between User Contexts

Administrators should not log on with the administrator account unless absolutely necessary. Windows 2000 provides the Run As utility to allow administrators to execute administrator programs from an administrative context without having to log off and log back on. When you log in as a User or Power User, Run As allows you to execute administrative tools with either local or domain administrative rights while logged on as a normal user. This does not contravene the security of Windows 2000, since the appropriate username and password must be known in order to gain administrative access for the single task at hand. This allows you to log on as a regular user with defined permissions with the added ability of being able to carry out an administrative task without a full logout and login. Once the task started by Run As has completed, the administrative access is complete; you then continue with the active user account that was being used before Run As was invoked. Any MMC snap-in or administrative tool can also be executed with Run As.

How Do I Use Run As?

Using Windows Explorer, highlight and right-click the program or shortcut that you wish to execute with Administrative privileges; while pressing the **Shift** key.

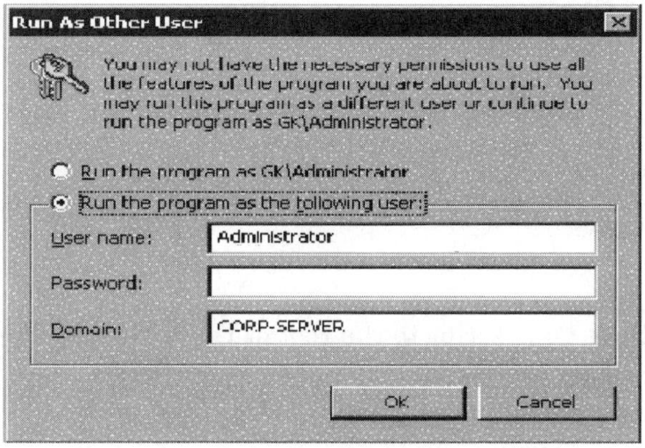

Figure 10.12
Using Run As helps
to maintain security.

1. Select the Run As menu option.
2. In the Run as Other User select the option "Run the program as the following user" and enter the username, password, and domain or local computer system.

If you wish to use the local Administrative account on the Windows 2000 computer, enter the name of the local computer. If you wish to use the domain Administrative account on the Windows 2000 computer, enter the name of the domain.

Administrator Tasks: Sample Scripting

1. Copy the utility ldifde.exe from \WINNT\system32 to the root of your local drive C:.
2. Next, open Active Directory Users and Computers and create an OU called Executive.
3. Type the following text into Notepad and modify the script, adding your domain or subdomain, as applicable, into each DN line and the last line UserPrincipalName.

```
#Create testuser1
DN:CN=testuser1,OU=Executive,DC=gk,DC=com
ObjectClass: user
sAMAccountname: testuser1
UserPrincipalName: testuser1@gk.com
#Create testuser2
DN:CN=testuser2,OU=Executive,DC=gk,DC=com
ObjectClass: user
sAMAccountname: testuser2
UserPrincipalName: testuser2@gk.com
#Create testuser3
DN:CN=testuser3,OU=Executive,DC=gk,DC=com
ObjectClass: user
sAMAccountname: testuser3
UserPrincipalName: testuser3@gk.com
```

4. Save your script to the root of Drive D: as bulkload.ldf. *Make sure to enclose the filename in quotations* ("bulkload.ldf").
5. At the command prompt at the root of D, enter the following command string:

```
ldifde -i -f bulkload.ldf
```

Syntax Notes:

-i Turn on Import Mode (the default is Export)
-f Input or Output filename

Your display should look similar to the following:

```
D:\>ldifde -i -f bulkload.ldf
Connecting to "corp-server.gk.com"
Logging in as current user using SSPI
Importing directory from file "bulkload.ldf"
Loading entries........................
25 entries modified successfully.
The command has completed successfully.
```

6. Check with Active Directory Users and Computers. Your test users should be in the OU Executive.

7. Select all the users in the OU Executive, right-click, and enable all of the user accounts.

Group Policy

This chapter provides details on group policy structure and configuration including:

- Creation and management of GPOs
- Assigning permissions
- Local, site, domain, and OU group policy
- Design of group policy

Group Policy

Group policy is *the* feature for Windows 2000 that management will be excited about. Also called Intellimirror, group policy provides an extra level of security to Windows 2000 and a host of new features such as the automatic assigning or publishing of software applications, folder redirection, and offline file synchronization. These features can only be taken advantage of by Windows 2000 Professional clients who are members of Windows 2000 sites, domains, and organizational units. It does not support any older down-level clients such as Windows 95/98/ME or Windows NT 3.51, or 4.0 clients. This is by design, to target the people who would otherwise not upgrade their client base as quickly to Windows 2000.

Before Group Policy

The name *group policy* is perhaps strange; you might think it would have something to do with groups, but it is deployed for users and computers. Although we can play some tricks with groups, users and computers are the usual components for group policy. Group policy began life as a system policy, as shown in Figure 11.1, which only adds to the confusion; if you actually deployed policies on Windows 95/98 and NT 4.0 as users, groups and computers were supported. If you still have some older Windows clients, system policies can still be executed on a Windows 2000 network for the older clients by using the System Policy Editor and storing the selected policy settings in NTCONFIG.POL in the NETLOGON share.

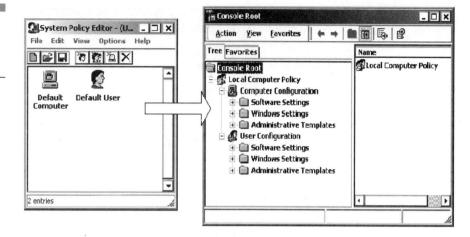

Figure 11.1
System policies have evolved into group policy.

Applying Group Policy

Group policy is applied through *group policy objects* (GPO) that are created using the group policy editor. They work well and the added bonus is that you don't have to save your settings in a specific location; this is done automatically for you in the SYSVOL folder on each domain controller. The group policy editor itself can be accessed directly by creating an MMC and populating it with the group policy editor or by selecting the properties of a site, domain, or OU, as shown in Figure 11.2.

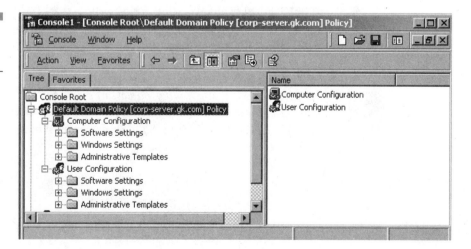

Figure 11.2
The group policy editor.

The group policy editor can be opened and used in several Windows 2000 locations, both at the local client and at the server. GPOs contain settings that can be linked with the following Active Directory containers: locally, sites, domains, and organizational units (LSDOU).

Local Windows 2000 Clients

Every Windows 2000 Professional client can be locally controlled by a local GPO. To open the local group policy editor, open the MMC and snap in the Group Policy to a new or existing console for the local computer.

Sites

To open the sites group policy editor, open the Active Directory Sites and Services. Choose the site to which you wish to apply policy and select its properties. Select the Group Policy tab.

Domains

To open the domains group policy, open the Active Directory Users and Computers. Choose the domain to which you wish to apply policy and select its properties. Select the Group Policy tab.

Organizational Units (OU)

To open an OU's group policy, open the Active Directory Users and Computers. Choose the OU to which you wish to apply policy and select its properties. Select the Group Policy tab. To edit the current policy settings, either select the policy from the Group Policy Object Links, or click New to define a new group policy object.

NOTE

There is also a group policy object, applied to the OU in each domain, where all domain controllers are installed. By default, user rights are enabled just as they were in NT 4.0; however, Windows 2000 User Rights are defined through group policy.

Predefined Group Policy Objects

After initial installation, there are three group policy objects that are predefined, as shown in Figure 11.3. Enabling additional choices in these GPOs applies to the specific scope of the GPO affecting users and computers or existing domain controllers hosting the domain.

Group policy objects installed by default are:

- **Local Computer Policy**—Every Windows 2000 computer (Servers, Workstations, and Domain Controllers) has a local computer policy.
- **Default Domain Controller Policy**—All domain controllers in the domain have an enabled set of user rights. Only the Administrator and Server operator can log on locally to the server by default.
- **Default Domain Policy**—This applies to all users and computers in the domain that authenticate to the domain.

Figure 11.3
GPOs installed by default.

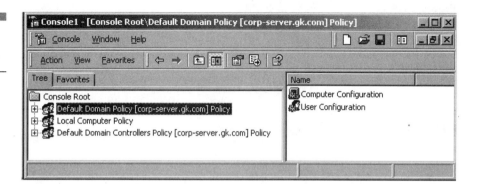

Group Policy Objects (GPO)

A group policy object can contain settings for the computer from which the user is logging onto the network, and settings for the particular user. In NT 4.0, system policy settings were stored in an ADM template and stored in a POL file. This structure remains intact, but the loading of the default GPO's settings and the saving of the POL file is an automatic operation carried out by the operating system. All GPO objects are stored in the Active Directory container for the domain. For example, in the domain gk.com they would be found at:

CN=Policies, CN=System, dc=windows, dc=gk, dc=com

A process called *linking* associates the GPOs with the selected locations in the tree that will receive the group policy. A GPO is divided into computer and user configuration headings with the subfolders of Software Settings, Windows Settings, and Administrative Templates.

Group Policy Architecture

The group policy container is an Active Directory container that stores the GPO properties and system information. Group policy templates are stored in the Policy subfolder in the SYSVOL volume folder of all domain controllers. Administrative policy templates, script files, security settings, and applications that have been tagged for automatic software installation are also stored in the SYSVOL folder, as detailed in Figure 11.4.

Figure 11.4
The SYSVOL folder is replicated to all domain controllers in the domain.

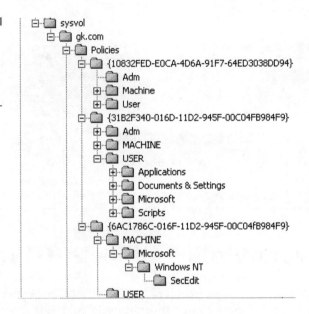

- **ADM**—This location holds the Administrative Templates.
- **SCRIPTS**—This folder holds all the user scripts.
- **USER**—This contains a REGISTRY.POL file holding Registry settings applied to users through HKEY_Current_User.
- **APPS**—These are advertisement files used by the Windows installer service.
- **FILES**—These are files to be deployed to the users.
- **MACHINE**—This contains a REGISTRY.POL file holding Registry settings applied to computers through HKEY_LOCAL_MACHINE.
- **APPS**—These are advertisement files used by the Windows installer that are applied to computers.
- **FILES**—This contains the files to be deployed to computers.

When does Group Policy Get Applied?

Group policy is applied to users and computer systems as shown in Figure 11.5. Computer policy is applied every time the computer boots or starts. User policy is applied every time the user logs into a computer system. Policies can also be applied at periodic intervals on a configurable timeline during the user's network session. A designated Windows 2000 server can be mandated to update the user and computer policy settings when changes have been updated through a configurable timeline, set within group policy without requiring the user to log on again.

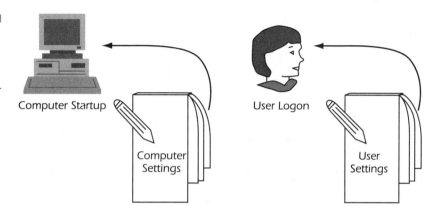

Figure 11.5
Computers and users have group policy applied.

Does Group Policy Affect Startup and Logon?

When a user logs onto a domain that has both Active Directory and group policy implemented, first the local group policy is found and deployed. If the local user/computer system has not logged onto a domain, then local group policy will have precedence.

The steps for the loading of group policy are:

1. The network and network services start on the local PC.
2. A list of applicable GPOs is acquired for the computer system depending on the answers to these questions:
   - Is the computer a member of a Windows 2000 domain and therefore group policy applies?
   - Where is the computer system located within Active Directory?

If the list of GPOs has not changed, the group policy in effect for the computer system remains in force with no additional processing required since the settings are already deployed. If processing is required, the computer settings are first reviewed and then applied in the following order: local GPO, site GPO, domain GPO, OUs GPOs.

3. The startup scripts (if present) are executed in synchronous mode, one after the other.

4. The user is presented the choice of logging in with **CTRL-ALT-DEL**.

5. The list of GPOs is acquired for the user depending on several factors:
   - Is the user a member of a Windows 2000 domain and therefore group policy applies?
   - Where is the user located within Active Directory?

   If the list of GPOs has not changed, the group policy in effect for the user remains in force with no additional processing. If processing is required, the user's group policy is reviewed and then it is applied in the following order: local GPO, site GPO, domain GPO, OUs GPOs.

6. The logon scripts (if present) are executed.

7. The Explorer shell is started.

How and Where Is Group Policy Applied?

GPO settings are obtained locally and then inherited from sites, domains, and parent and child organizational units (Figure 11.6). However, we can make changes to the default order of processing, for example:

- Group policy settings defined for a domain can override policy set in the site.
- Group policy settings defined for an OU can override policy set in the domain.

Site and domain group policy settings are intended for a wider base whereas OU settings are intended for more detailed control. They are applied specifically to users and computers and not to security groups, as was the case in NT 4.0 system policy.

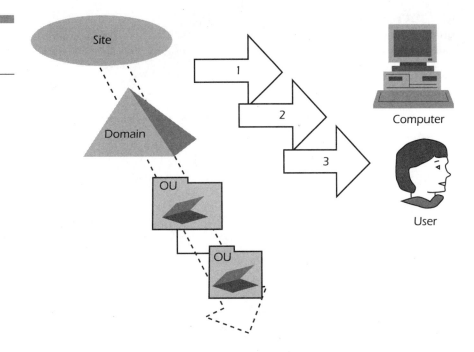

Figure 11.6
Group policy is cumulative.

The Processing Steps of Group Policy

- **Local GPO**—Each Windows 2000 computer system has one local group policy object; settings are deployed once enabled.
- **Site GPOs**—All GPOs that have been defined at the site level are processed next, one after the other.
- **Domain GPOs**—All GPOs that have been defined at the domain level are processed next, one after the other
- **Organizational Units GPOs**—GPOs associated with the organizational unit highest in the hierarchy are processed first, followed by any GPOs linked to the child OUs. Finally, the OU where the user or computer is located is processed.

Sales OU processing = A3, A1, A2, A5
Servers OU processing = A3, A1, A2, A4, A6

Figure 11.7
Group Policy is
applied in a logical
order usually starting
at the site level.

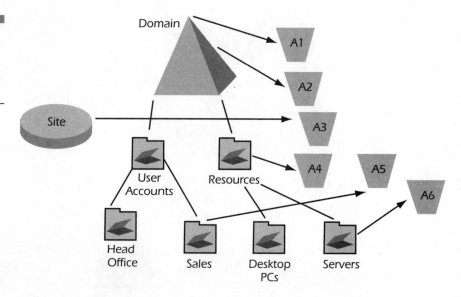

Reapplying Group Policy

By default, all group policy settings update their policy settings only when there are any new or changed settings. This is a departure from system policy settings in NT 4.0, where policy was reapplied at every logon. Group software policy settings are written to either the Local Machine or User portion of the Registry but the locations have changed for the Windows 2000 settings; HKLM and HKCU\Software\Policies is the new Windows 2000 path.

User policy settings are written to:
HKEY_CURRENT_USER\Software\Policies
HKEY_CURRENT_USER\Software\Microsoft\Windows
\CurrentVersion\Policies

Computer policy settings are written to:
HKEY_LOCAL_MACHINE\Software\Policies
HKEY_LOCAL_MACHINE\SOFTWARE\Microsoft\Windows
\CurrentVersion\Policies

The Windows 2000 operating system is no longer looking in the location where NT 4.0 settings were stored. This means that older Windows NT system policy settings will not be found and deployed. The NTCONFIG.POL file was used in the Windows NT 4.0 operating system for system policy whereas REGISTRY.POL is used for holding group policy.

Creating Group Policy Objects

Only domain administrators, enterprise administrators, and group policy administrators can create new group policy objects by default. Other groups or users must be added to the Group Policy Administrators security group before they can create group policy (Figure 11.8). However, once a nonadministrator gains the permissions to create a group policy object, he or she becomes the creator and owner of the GPO. By default the group policy objects allow Domain Administrators, Enterprise Administrators, the operating system, and the GPO creator full control; but the Apply Group attribute is not assigned. This makes sense; it means these users can edit and create the GPO but the policies contained in that particular GPO will not apply to them. A user who has successfully authenticated is defined as an Authenticated user and a member of the Authenticated group with read access to the Group Policy Objects with the "apply group" attribute assigned, as shown in Figure 11.9.

Figure 11.8
Click New to create a
new GPO.

Group Policy Options

The properties of each GPO shown in Figure 11.10 have several options for controlling the order of processing of group policy.

Figure 11.9
Authenticated users have group policy applied.

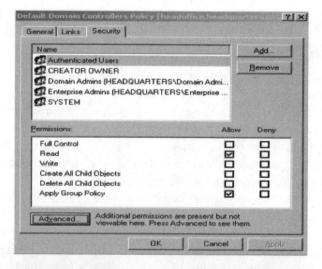

Figure 11.10
Property settings allow us to change the order of processing.

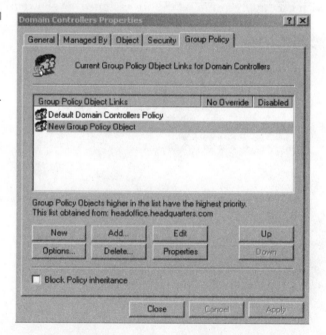

- **New**—Create new GPOs that are linked to the container when saved.
- **Add**—Link a site, domain, or OU container to this GPO.
- **Properties**—View and change the current GPO settings for users and computers.
- **Options**—No override–force these GPO settings to apply.
- **Disabled**—All ACLs applied to this GPO are ignored.

- **Block Policy Inheritance**—Any policies higher in the hierarchy will not be inherited at this point and lower in the tree.
- **Up/Down**—Set the priority of multiple GPOs defined for this container.

Exceptions to Group Policy Processing Order: No Override

No Override stops a particular policy from prevailing over a superseding policy set at a higher site, domain, or organizational unit (Figure 11.11). Any GPO linked to a site, domain, or organizational unit can be set to No Override so no policy settings can be overwritten. For example, the Headquarters domain policy could set No Override so policy settings defined at the domain level could not be overridden by any child container. If more than one GPO is set to No Override, the higher No Override in the hierarchy always takes precedence over the lower No Override.

Figure 11.11
No Override stops a policy setting from overriding another policy setting.

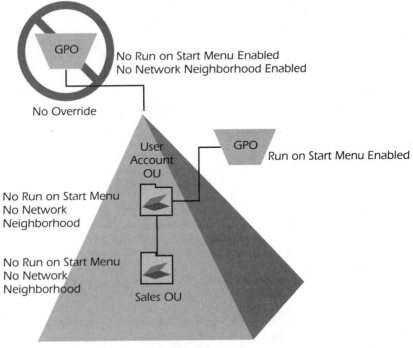

GPO

No Run on Start Menu Enabled
No Network Neighborhood Enabled

No Override

User Account OU

GPO

Run on Start Menu Enabled

No Run on Start Menu
No Network Neighborhood

No Run on Start Menu
No Network Neighborhood

Sales OU

Headquarters Domain

NOTE

No Override always takes precedence over a Block Inheritance Command.

Block Inheritance

Block Inheritance prevents the inheritance of all policy (Figure 11.12); lower-level OUs do not inherit the policy from a site, domain, or parent organizational unit. Block Policy Inheritance can be selected by selecting the properties of the site, domain or organizational unit. Block Inheritance is assigned to the site, domain, or OU; it is not applied to a group policy object. As a result, block policy ignores all group policy settings that arrive at the site, domain, or OU. Block inheritance is usually done at the OU level. For example the Sales OU could block all inheritance from the domain or the site, or any of the parent OU containers.

Figure 11.12
Block Inheritance stops the default deployment path of group policy.

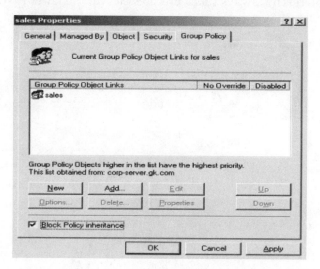

Loopback Processing

Loopback settings can be enabled to change the GPOs that are applied to a user at a particular computer system or systems by changing the default order for processing the user's GPOs. Loopback is a policy setting that is useful to apply in selected situations where security is crucial, such as a public area in a company where computer systems are used by many different types of users. The default is that the user's policy settings are assigned based on their location in Active Directory, that is, the site, domain, or organizational unit (OU). Loopback can be enabled to replace or merge, as shown in Figure 11.13. For any conflicting settings, the computer's GPO takes precedence since it is processed last. The setting of loopback mode is found in the group policy settings of the computer portion of any GPO under Administrative Settings\System\Group Policy, as shown in Figure 11.13.

- **In Replace mode**—The GPO list for the user is replaced completely by the computer's GPO list received at startup.
- **In Merge mode**—The GPO list received by the computer onto which the user is logging is added to the end of the user's GPO list.

Figure 11.13
Loopback processing can be useful for kiosk or public computer systems.

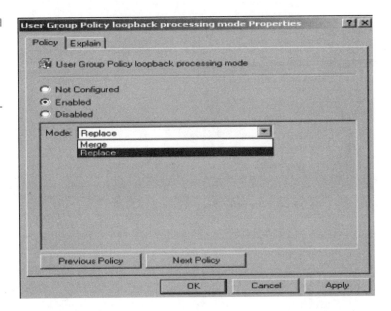

Defining the Refresh Cycle of Group Policy

By default, group policy is set to be processed and applied to every user logon. Through Administrative Settings\System\group policy, the refresh cycle can be changed to any value for both user and computer policy. A random value is then added to the selected refresh interval so that group policy won't be reapplied to a large number of clients at the same time. For testing purposes, setting the refresh value to 0 refreshes the policy every 7 seconds! Changing the refresh rate could be disastrous if not carefully thought out. For example, if a software installation were flagged to be uninstalled through a group policy setting, once auto-refresh executed, all users who might be using the software would have it uninstalled automatically.

Figure 11.14
Both the computer and user refresh cycles can be set from seconds to hours.

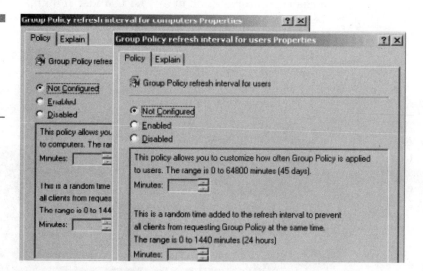

Multiple GPOs: Who Goes First?

Group Policy Objects for the larger containers are completely processed before GPOs defined for smaller containers. Within each site, domain, and organizational unit, group policy processing is dependent on the number of defined GPOs.

If multiple GPO's are linked to a site, domain, or organizational unit, apply in a prioritized order—from bottom to top and not from top to bottom as you might expect. The top GPO in Figure 11.15 is the highest in the list; therefore it has the highest priority, *therefore it is processed last*!

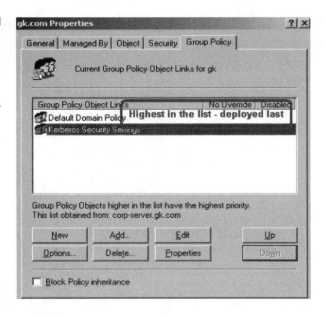

Disabling GPO Components

You can choose to disable either the computer or the user configuration through the properties of each group policy object, as shown in Figure 11.16. A very important detail contained in Figure 11.16 is called Revisions. This particular GPO has been revised 11 times for computer settings and once for user settings. When group policy is applied, GPOs with no revisions are skipped, since there are no new changes to apply. This information could be used in deciding to disable the computer or user portion of the GPO.

Linking Group Policy throughout the Forest

A policy "link" is similar to a "shortcut. Links can be used when policies don't inherit. Only one GPO can be maintained and settings could be applied to multiple sites, domains, or OUs from just one GPO. Using a link, one GPO could be used for multiple domains in a tree or forest for deploying software or any other group policy setting standard across the forest. However, using links across sites with slow connectivity could

Figure 11.16
Disabling unused
portions of group
policy will improve
the boot cycle.

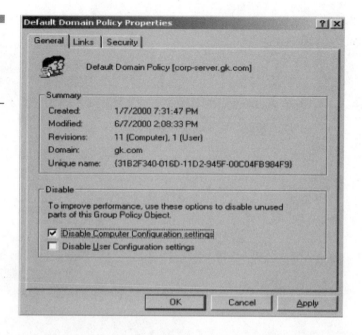

Figure 11.17
Links can be used to
assign policy settings.

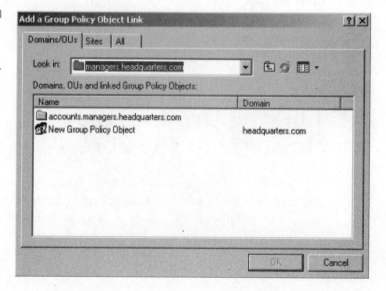

produce very slow logins since the objects in Active Directory and the SYSVOL holding the templates on the remote domain must be read.

Access Control Lists and Group Policy Objects

When a group policy object is created, it applies to most users and computers in the container to which it is linked. Since each GPO is an object stored in Active Directory, it also has an access control list (ACL) assigned. The group Authenticated Users is assigned the permissions of Read, and Apply Group policy. Local System, Domain Admins, and Enterprise Admins are assigned all permissions except for Apply Group Policy. Therefore we can also use the ACL to allow and deny access to the GPO based on security group membership. When a user is made a member of a domain, that user is automatically made a member of the Authenticated User global group. As shown in Figure 11.18, the Authenticated User has Read and Apply Group Policy. If the Apply Group Policy checkbox for the Authenticated User is unchecked, then the Authenticated Users group will not receive this group.

Figure 11.18
Groups can be used with the ACL to Deny Group Policy settings based on group membership.

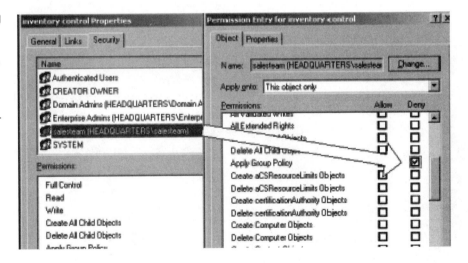

Therefore, security groups can be used to group users who will not receive specific group policy. Using the "Deny" Apply Group Policy option, control of group policy can be assigned to groups. For example, a

GPO is created for the Managers OU and the Accounts OU to install a custom inventory tracking software application. All users of these two OUs will now have that application installed through the Inventory Control GPO defined at the parent Managers OU when they next log on. However, the sales staff group in the Accounts child OU is not to receive this application. One solution is to create a security group for the sales staff called salesteam in the Accounts OU and then add an *access control entry* (ACE) to the Inventory Control GPO with a Deny Apply Group Policy checkbox. Every member of salesteam will now not have the Inventory Control GPO applied.

Delegation of Control

Through delegation of control, the control and maintenance of an organizational units group policy can be deferred to a nonadministrative user. A group of users (or a user) can select and manage existing Group Policy Objects.

1. In the Active Directory Users and Computers snap-in, right-click the Organizational Unit that you want to delegate, and select Delegate Control.
2. In the Delegation of Control wizard you will be asked to confirm the OU that you wish to delegate.
3. You will then be prompted for the names of the users and groups to which to delegate control.
4. Select a previously defined group (or user) and then click **Next**.
5. In the list of Predefined Tasks, select Manage Group Policy links, then click **Next**, as shown in Figure 11.19.
6. Click **Finish** to accept and complete the changes.

Software Settings (Computer and User)

Both the user and computer sections of each GPO can be utilized either to publish or to assign software applications using the Microsoft Windows Installer service either to a particular user or users or for a particular computer. This was a feature of SMS that has been merged into

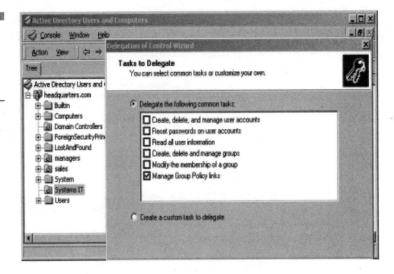

Figure 11.19
The Delegation of Control wizard can help delegate group policy.

Windows 2000. Microsoft will be providing software utilities to upgrade SMS 2.0 packages to be compatible with group policy packages.

Any software application that sports the "Designed for Windows 2000 Logo" ships with an installation procedure (MSI) that can call the Windows Installer service starting the installation. Office 2000, which was released before Windows 2000, was bundled with a predefined MSI package that can be used with group policy.

The installer service also self-repairs applications it has installed. Whenever the application executes after the initial installation, it performs a system check with the MSI script; if any components are missing, they will be reinstalled.

Assigning Applications for Computers and Users

Choosing the package option from the context menu of computer group policy launches a search for any compatible MSI packages, as shown in Figure 11.20. Choosing a package requires that we select a network path, since the package must reside on a shared volume accessible to the computer or user.

When a software package is deployed on a particular computer, once the package has been assigned, the next time the computer system is started, the package will install. Once an application is assigned to a user, the next time he or she logs onto the network the application is advertised on the Start Menu or canned to start when the user attempts to open a file associated with the application.

Figure 11.20
Software can be assigned or published to computers and users.

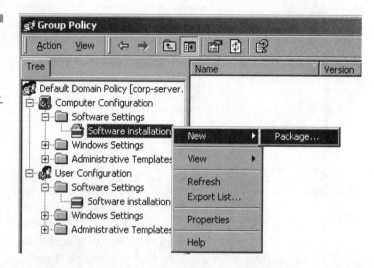

Figure 11.20
Software can be assigned or published to computers and users.

Publishing Applications for Users and Computers

Once an application has been published to a user or users, it is not visible to the end-user on the Start Menu. Instead, the user can choose to install the application from the Add/Remove Programs Applet in the control panel, or by selecting a document associated with the software application, such as a Microsoft Word document file which would then launch the installation of Microsoft Word.

Any applications that can be installed through group policy can also take advantage of the ability for additional customization called *transforms*. The software vendor may also supply additional templates or repackaging tools; for example, Office 2000 is bundled with a customization wizard that can help customize the installation of the key office components.

Using Group Policy Software Installation

Several key steps must be undertaken in order properly to install software through group policy. These steps are:

1. Planning the location and focus of the software installation
2. Defining a network location as the software distribution point
3. Deciding on the software installation defaults
4. Scheduling the deployment of software applications
5. Defining software application properties.

Planning the Location and Focus

There are several location choices for where the software could be installed. If all users in a particular site need the software, then a GPO can be created at the site level affecting all domains and OUs within the site. This can create problems if the application is large and bandwidth is limited. It is certainly a better choice to stage the installation of a massive software application such as Office 2000 at the OU level for small numbers of users, say 10 at a time. You could also decide to create a GPO with the dedicated task of installing software applications across the domain or site.

Define Your Software Distribution Point

A network share that is stable and always available must be chosen, or several locations, depending on the size and hierarchy of the network. Next copy or replicate the software packages to the network share and make sure to assign the minimum permissions to the folders.

Software Installation Defaults

Global software installation defaults are defined by selecting the properties of the Software Installation node in the group policy object, as shown in Figure 11.21.

The new package options in the General tab are:

- **Default Package Location**—Specifies the network share for the packages.
- **Display the Deploy Software Dialog Box**—Assigns, publishes, or configures the package properties.
- **Publish**—The publishing of applications can only be directed to users and not computer systems. The default package properties are assumed with this choice.

■ ■ ■

Figure 11.21
Package options for
assigning or
publishing with
group policy.

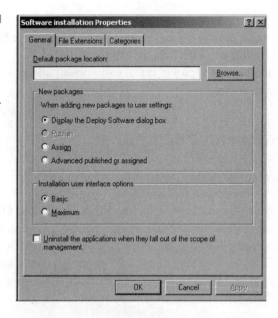

- **Assign**—When a new package is added, the default package properties are to be used when assigning to a computer or user.
- **Advanced Published or Assigned**—When a new package is added, you have the default choice of reviewing the Configure Package Properties.
- **Basic**—Provides minimum installation information.
- **Maximum**—Provides all installation messages.

■ ■ ■ ■ ■ ■ ■ ■ ■ ■ ■ ■ ■ ■ ■

NOTE

The checkbox at the bottom of the General tab allows you to have the application uninstalled when this particular group policy object no longer applies to either the user or computer. This could be a dangerous option if it is unchecked by mistake; "the scope of management" is a very vague term since management will not typically be creating group policy.

- **File Extensions**—This tab allows you to specify what extension will trigger for the installation of a software application.

Schedule the Deployment

Software can by either assigned or published to both users and computers, so a defined schedule is a must for proper software management. Table 11.1 lists the available options.

TABLE 11.1

Software deployment rules.

When Available	Publish to User	Assign to User	Assign to Computer
Software is available	Next logon	Next logon	When computer restarts
Software is installed	Add/Remove Programs Applet	Start menu or Desktop shortcut	Software is automatically installed at reboot
Extension is selected	Yes if auto-install was selected	Yes	NA
Can software be removed	Yes	Yes	No

Applications should be assigned when you want every computer system to have the application.

Applications should be published when you want the application to be available to clients managed by the GPO. Publishing an application lets the user decide whether or not to install the published application.

Defining Software Application Properties

Default global setting for all new packages was set previously on the properties of the Software installation; however, selecting the individual properties of each package allows you to change some of the global settings as shown in Figure 11.22.

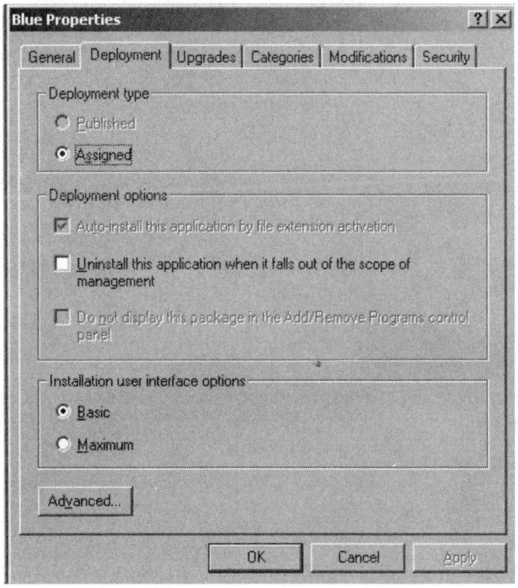

Figure 11.22
Package properties can overrule global settings.

Windows Settings for Computers

Windows settings for computers contain many features for centrally controlling the Windows 2000 computer systems on your network.

Control for any system process or backup procedure you want to mandate for your users can be scheduled via a *script* file.

The Windows Scripting Host (WSH) is now a standard with Windows 2000. WSH also integrates with VB and PERL script.

Security Settings are detailed in Table 11.2.

TABLE 11.2

Security settings for computer group policy.

Account Policies	Define ....
Password Policy	Password history, min/max age
Account Lockout Policy	Account lockout threshold and duration
Kerberos Policy	Ticket and computer clock sync details
Local Policies	
Audit Policy	Audit entries will be sent to the Event Viewer for certain items for example: account and system successes or failures
User Rights Assignment	Similar to User Rights in User Manager for Domains with additional choices
Security Options	Various security settings for computer systems
Event Log	Properties for the application, security, and system event logs
Restricted Groups	Include group members on any computer system, forcing group membership when this policy is enforced
System Services	The starting, stopping, and access to specific services
Registry	Registry settings to be added to any computer include access control, registry auditing, and ownership
File System	Add a file, or folder to any computer system as well setting its auditing and permissions
IP Security Policies on Active Directory	All characteristics of IPSec can be configured here
Public Key Policies	All public key settings for the domain can be configured

Administrative Templates
for Computers

The administrative templates are group policy settings defined through ADM template files stored in the SYSVOL folder for each GPO. These are then replicated to each domain controller in the domain.

Figure 11.23
There are many powerful settings to make administration of computers and users easier.

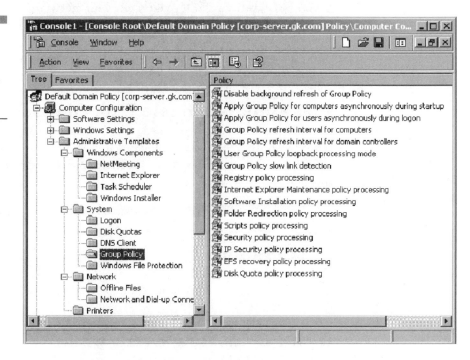

NOTE

Other custom ADM templates can be added by right-clicking Administrative Templates and selecting Add/Remove Templates.

The important settings are found under Administrative Template\Important Computer\Administrative Templates\System Settings.

Logon\Maximum Wait Time
for Group Policy Scripts

The default is 10 minutes, which gives an indication of a badly designed boot sequence. Users who wait more than a minute will get frustrated and turn their systems off and on. User education is essential if many group policy settings are to be deployed.

Logon\Delete Cached Copies of Roaming Profiles

If you have many roaming users on your network, this setting is a lifesaver, since any user profiles created on a computer system that is not the logged-on user's defined PC will be deleted when the user logs off. This is quite handy for users performing user support at their PCs.

Disk Quotas\Enable Disk Quotas

If you wish disk quota management to stay enabled and stop users from messing with the defined settings, then enable and mandate disk quotas through this group policy setting.

Disk Quotas\Enforce Disk Quota Limit

Use this setting to enforce any set disk quota limits.

Disk Quotas\Log Event when Quota Limit Exceeded

Track when users exceed their defined quota through system events in the Application log.

Group Policy\Group Policy Refresh Interval for Computers

If you wish to change the default mode of when group policy is refreshed, enable this setting

Group Policy\Loopback Processing Mode

Enable loopback processing in either merge or replace mode.

Group Policy\Registry Policy Processing

Registry settings can be mandated to be processed every logon.

Group Policy\Software Installation Policy Processing

The software installation features of group policy can also be mandated to be processed at every logon.

Windows Settings for Users

Windows settings will be among the most widely used group policy settings, because as they apply to the end user's day-to-day tasks using the Explorer shell and the Start Menu, as shown in Figure 11.24.

Figure 11.24
Windows settings control the user's Internet environment.

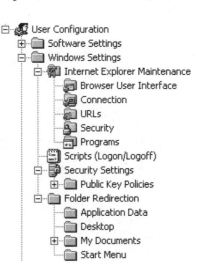

Internet Explorer

Internet Explorer allows you to define the user's IE environment as viewed in Tools\Internet Options. Connection and proxy settings can also be set and mandated.

Scripts

Scripts allow control of the user's logon and logoff scripts. Be aware that the location of these scripts has shifted from the NT 4.0 location to the SYSVOL folder, which then gets replicated to all other domain controllers in the domain.

Folder Redirection

Folder Redirection allows both global and specific redirection of Application Data, Desktop, My Documents My Pictures, and Start Menu folder to a network location. Folder redirection and software installation only happen during initial computer startup and user logon. You should take advantage of redirecting the My Documents folder as shown in Figure 11.25; a global location can be set for all users or can be defined by users group and defined network path.

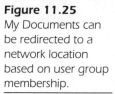

Figure 11.25
My Documents can be redirected to a network location based on user group membership.

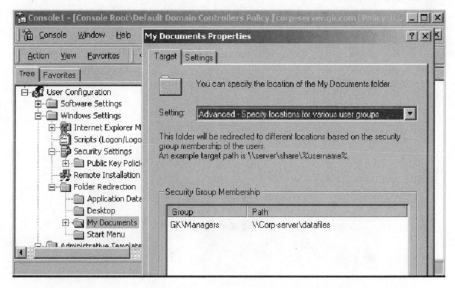

Administrative Templates for the User

These settings are an enhanced set of Explorer shell options that allow the user's Windows 2000 environment to be tailored, as shown in Figure 11.26.

Figure 11.26
Administrative templates provide many options for controlling the user's environment.

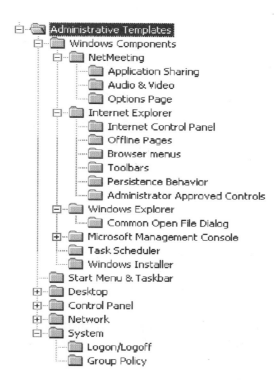

Most of these numerous settings are self-explanatory; there are hundreds of settings that could be enabled per user. The most important settings are found in Administrative Templates\System.

Administrative Templates\System Settings

Logon/Logoff \Disable Task Manger

If you wish to disable the user's ability to run Task Manager enable, this setting.

Logon/Logoff\Run these programs at user logon

This setting allows more granular control of the user's environment upon startup.

Administrative Templates\System\Group Policy Settings

Group Policy\Group Policy Refresh interval for users

This allows you to define the refresh cycle of group policy.

Group Policy\Group Policy domain controller selection

Define a specific domain controller that will be responsible for deploying group policy.

Group Policy\Exclude directories in roaming profiles

If you are using roaming user profiles, this setting allows you to mandate what won't roam.

Offline Files

Offline files is feature of Windows 2000 that may prove to be manageable and useful. Offline files can be enabled by users, as shown in Figure 11.27, and enhanced by group policy.

The idea is that when a user logs off the network, specific data files are automatically copied to the user's PC for use offline, or when the user is out of the office with her notebook. Once the user arrives back at work, the files are resynchronized with the network copies, and everything is fine. For the busy executive with zero patience, this feature could be a disaster waiting to happen if the user is not aware of why it is taking so long to log off the network. If that user knew that the data files needed for the business meeting next week were automatically being downloaded for use out of the office, perhaps she would think this feature useful. Again, the user needs to be educated before this feature is deployed. If you decide to deploy offline files, mandate the environment you have created with group policy settings.

Figure 11.27
Offline file caching may be a great idea if users are educated properly.

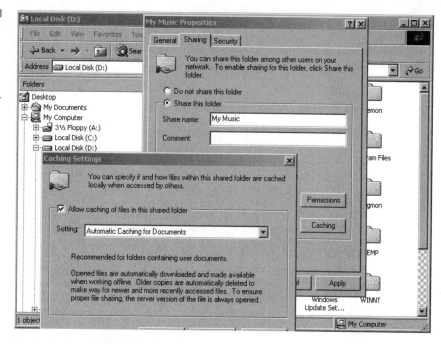

Planning and Designing Group Policy Objects

Careful planning should be carried out before deploying group policy (Figure 11.28). The size of your company could determine the complexity or simplicity of your design. The organizational chart that defines your company structure may be of some value in planning group policy.

Separate Policy Design—A GPO with Subject-Specific Settings

The goal with this design is to create separate GPOs that contain similar types of settings (Figure 11.29). For example, for a specific domain or OU, separate GPOs could be created as follows:

- **Scripts GPO**—Startup and shutdown user script
- **Software GPO**—Application software to be deployed
- **Security GPO**—Kerberos and IPSec settings
- **Internet GPO**—IE security settings

Figure 11.28
The org chart may be the place to start when planning group policy.

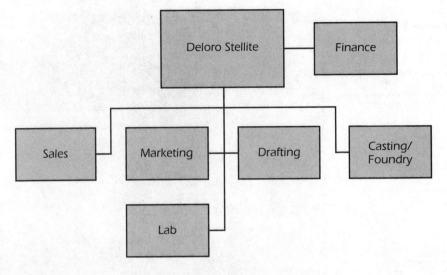

Figure 11.29
Subject-specific settings may be easier to manage and deploy.

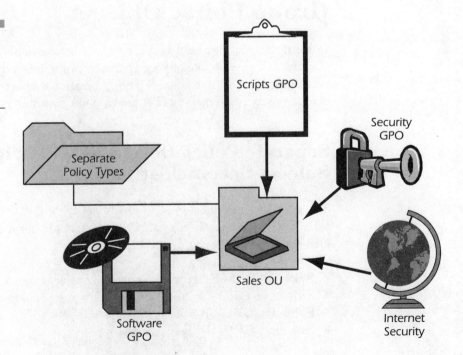

Multiple Policy Type—A Single GPO with Multiple Types of Settings

Include multiple types of group policy settings in a single GPO. This is useful for companies where administration is centralized.

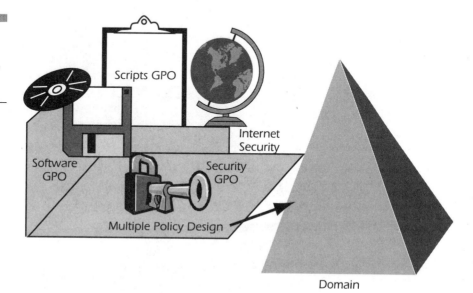

Scripts GPO

Internet Security

Software GPO

Security GPO

Multiple Policy Design

Domain

Dedicated Policy Type—GPOs with Dedicated User and Computer Settings

Include all user settings in one GPO. Include all computer settings in another GPO. Assign or deny the desired user and computer GPO components. Separation can aid in troubleshooting problems (Figure 11.31).

Layered GPO Design

For a layered GPO design, include specific group policy settings in a base GPO. Next, include required group policy settings in other lower-priority GPOs. The base GPO should contain as many generic settings as can be applied to all users and computers. The other GPOs created are then designed for the group of users, as shown in Figure 11.32.

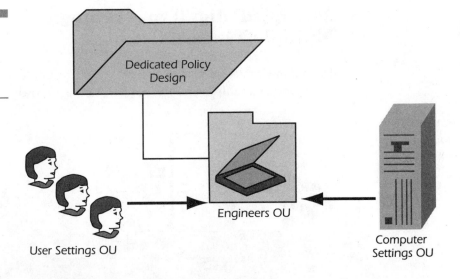

Figure 11.31
Separating user and computer settings can aid in troubleshooting.

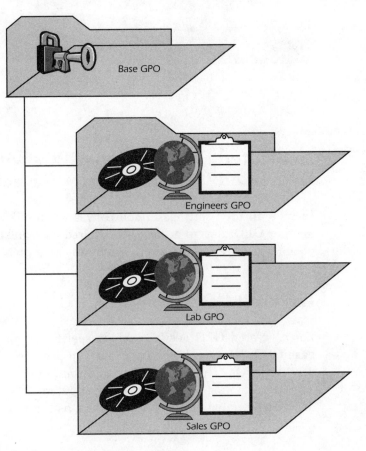

Figure 11.32
Layered design takes advantage of the order of precedence of the GPOs.

Monolithic GPOs

This design uses a minimum set of specific GPOs that are directly assigned to the OU where the users and computers are located.

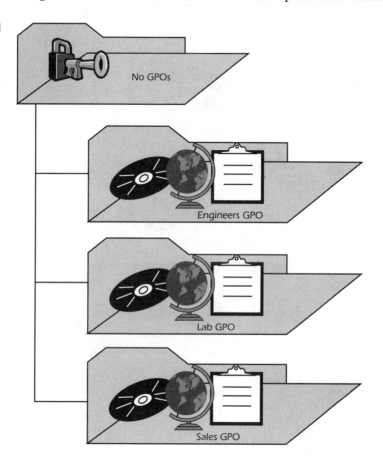

Figure 11.33
A minimum amount
of overhead.

Central Control

This design uses both central control and delegation of control to OUs. At the domain level, create a GPO with no override. This ensures all enabled settings will be enforced throughout the hierarchy. The settings in this GPO must be settings that everyone, including Administrators, can live with; for example, Change Password. All other GPOs could be delegated to an OU Administrator.

Figure 11.34
Central control for
the settings for
everyone.

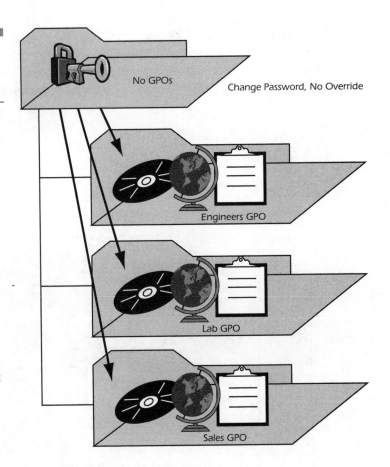

Backing Up and Restoring Active Directory

This chapter details the backing up and restoring of Active Directory and discusses:

- Defining the System State
- Backing up the AD database
- Using the Backup and Restore wizard
- Unauthoratitive and authoritative restore procedures
- Using Ntdsutil

Planning for Failure

Backing up, restoring, and general overall maintenance of the Active Directory database is essential for planning for eventual failure. Every domain controller should be backed up on a timely, efficient schedule and this means a lot of additional planning and system maintenance. Performing the most basic of backups using the Ntbackup tool uses over 230 MB. Once Exchange 2000 and other back-office components are added to the mix, the core system components will approach 400 MB, or more.

We have to plan for extra redundancy across our domains. Having additional domain controllers host each domain is a must. With two or more domains available, in-site replication takes care of the schema, configuration, and domain replicas within each domain, and schema and configuration across sites. However, don't become complacent; replication can't be assumed to be a backup. After all, what happens if everything goes down?

This is the worst-case scenario, and planning for the worst means you will come out on top when disaster strikes. This operating system is still very new and unproven; pay extra attention to backups.

This chapter deals with the system components called the system state, however regular data backup and other essential files that will be uniquely essential to your company must be backed up on a regular basis.

Active Directory File Structure

Each domain controller running Active Directory holds system files that include their portion of the Directory. The database and supporting log files that are the Directory are stored under the system root in the

WINNT\NTDS folder, as shown in Figure 12.1. The Active Directory database is composed of the following files stored on every domain controller:

- **NTDS.dit**—The database file itself.
- **Log files**—These are used to track and maintain transactions before they are written to the Active Directory database.

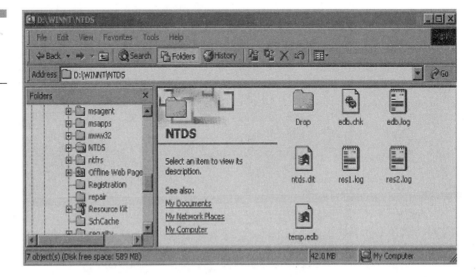

Figure 12.1
The Active Directory database and log files.

During the initial server installation, a default template called NTDS.DIT is stored on each Windows 2000 server in the location WINNT\SYSTEM32, removing the need to insert the Server CD during dcpromo. During the promotion process to a domain controller, NTDS.DIT is used to create the initial database file and copied into the C\WINNT\NTDS folder.

Database Transaction Steps

Active directory is a fault-tolerant transaction-based database; therefore all transactions take place in a particular and systematic order, as shown in Figure 12.2.

1. A user with Administrator rights creates an object that starts the transaction process.

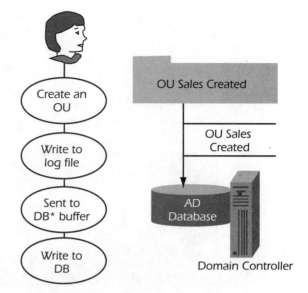

Figure 12.2
Precise steps are carried out when the database is updated.

2. First, the transaction is written to a log file.
3. Next, the transaction is deposited to a database buffer.
4. Finally, the database is written to complete the transaction.

Transaction Log Details

Transaction log files record all transactions carried out to the Active Directory database in either sequential or circular log format. The default method for recording log files is defined as "sequential," where no overwriting of log information is performed. Transaction log files can reach a maximum of 10 MB in size.

In sequential mode, the default transaction log file called EDB.LOG is stored in the same folder as NTDS.DIT and used until the 10 MB size limit is reached.

At this point, a log file is created called EDB00001.LOG and the contents of EDB.LOG are copied into this new log file. Then the log file is cleared and again continues to receive transactions.

Backup transaction log files are created and incrementally named EDB00001, EDB00002, and so on. In circular mode, which can be enabled through a Registry edit that is not recommended, incremental transaction log files are not created; instead EDB.LOG is overwritten. For accurate troubleshooting history, sequential logging should always be left in the enabled state; there is no space saving, because the log file is created with an initial and maximum size of 10 MB.

There are several types of transaction log files used with Active Directory.

Checkpoint Logs

The checkpoint log file called EDB.CHK is also stored in the same folder as NTDS.DIT and contains the pointers to the actual transactions in the transaction log files that have been written to the database.

Reserved Logs

Two reserve log files, each 10 MB in size, are stored in the same folder as NTDS.DIT and are called RES1.LOG and RES2.LOG. These files will be used in low hard disk conditions. If space falls below 10MB, a new log file cannot be created; as a result the reserved log files will be used by the operating system to store any outstanding transactions still being held in memory. Then the system will shut down with an "out of disk space" error.

Patch Logs

During a regular online backup, patch files are created and used to track transactions written to the Active Directory database during back-up. Patch log files have a .PAT extension.

Automated Database Cleanup

Automated database cleanup tasks are called *garbage collection*. By default, garbage collection, also called an *on-line defragmentation*, runs automatically on all domain controllers every 12 hours. This time frame can be changed using ADSI Edit; however I wouldn't recommend it unless you have security needs that require levels of secrecy that most businesses will not require. As we shall see, the ability to restore objects that have been deleted by mistake is a big bonus.

The following three tasks are performed by garbage collection:

- **Deletion of old log files**—Under normal circumstances there will be incremented transaction log files that will be removed.
- **Deletion of Tombstones**—When an object is removed from the database, the directory service tags the object as being in the "tomb-

stone state." Objects tagged to this state alert all domain controllers during replication that they have been deleted. Objects deleted are not immediately removed from the database; they are just flagged for deletion with a tombstone tag. Deleted objects tagged as tombstones are moved to the Deleted Objects container, and at the end of the defined tombstone lifetime, the garbage collection process finally removes them. The default tombstone lifetime is 60 days, so even if you delete a large number of objects from the database, the size of the database will not change; in fact it could increase as objects are added. An object flagged for deletion can be restored within the tombstone lifetime through a process called an *authoritative restore*. This is discussed later in this chapter.

- **The database file is defragmented**—The database is automatically rearranged into a more compact format; however, any disk space freed up is not released to the file system. To release the free space, the system must be restarted in Directory Services Repair Mode and defragged in offline mode; DSRM can be selected by pressing F8 during the reboot.

Granting Backup and Restore Rights

You must have proper permissions to perform backup and restore operations for domain controllers. Backup and restore rights are granted independently through group policy setting for the domain controllers in the domain. This is easy to miss; User Rights are set through group policy settings accessed by right-clicking the Domain Controllers folder in Active Directory Users and Computers, as shown in Figure 12.3. The Domain Security Policy snap-in defines the users and groups permitted to backup and restore files and folders. There must be a company so large that there are personnel who get hired just to do backups, and restores. The Administrator also can perform backup and restore tasks.

What is the System State?

The term used to define essential system files on all Windows 2000 systems, servers, and clients is the system state. Backing up the AD data-

Figure 12.3
Backup and restore rights are set through local security policy.

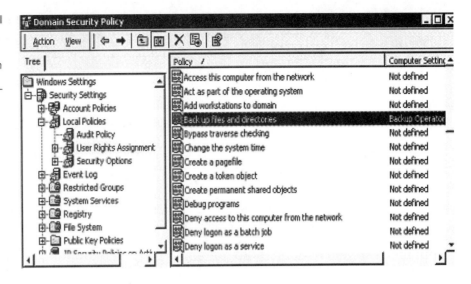

base is just one component of the system state. The term "system state" refers to the collection of files required to start and run Windows 2000, as shown in Figure 12.4.

Figure 12.4
The entire system state must be selected for backup.

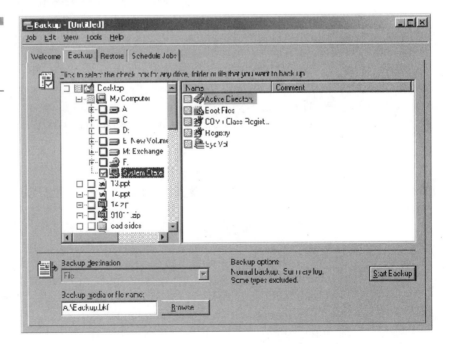

Just backing up the Active Directory database file and log files is not a full system backup; the backups you perform must also be useful for complete restore purposes. There are many other essential components, depending on your server's configuration. Be sure that the system state is completely selected when a backup is performed; partial backups and restores of the system state are not an option.

What Does a System State Backup Contain?

System state components for Windows 2000 domain controllers will always be a minimum size of 250 MB and include:

- Boot files, including %system root %\WINNT system files
- Files protected by Windows File Protection (WPF)
- Active Directory
- SYSVOL (for domain controllers only)
- The Registry
- The component services class registration database
- Certificate Services database (if the server is running Certificate Services)
- Cluster service (if the server is running Cluster service)

For Windows 2000 member servers (and Windows 2000 Professional clients) system state components include:

- Boot files, including %system root %\WINNT system files
- The Registry
- The component services class registration database

Using the Backup Wizard

The first thing you should know about Ntbackup, the Windows backup wizard, is that only local Active Directory backups at the server console are supported. Remote backups are not supported at this time, and if you want this flexibility, you will have to buy the full Seagate solution. The backup utility is found at Start > Programs > Accessories > System Tools > Backup. Choices are to back up, restore, or create an emergency repair disk.

When you use the backup wizard, the system state can be backed up to a disk, supported tape system, or network share. If you choose the

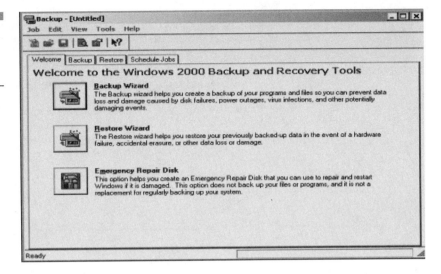

Figure 12.5
Ntbackup and ERD
are combined in the
Backup Utility.

network share option, make sure that the network share is NTFS version 5 in order successfully to back up and restore all Windows 2000 features you may have deployed, including the Encrypting File System (EFS), permissions, disk quotas, and Remote Storage information.

The system state can be included in your daily backup; however, I recommend that a separate system state also be performed on a weekly schedule and removed to a safe off-site location. Any time a change is to occur on your Windows 2000 network, perform a system state backup. Then write down the details in your network log. Proper documentation habits combined with timely backups are skills that all too often get left undone—that's where I come in most of the time.

Creating a Emergency Repair Disk

Remember the fun we had with the Emergency Repair Disk in NT? I'm going to miss it... sometime. The fact is, it still exists, and it can be just as important, depending on the age of the software applications you are using. If the software was written for Windows 95/98, or NT 4.0, then the Registry will be certainly used for storage of essential information. In fact, Active Directory employs the Registry for storage of essential system information used in safe mode, and during regular online mode as well. Investigate the path HKEY_LOCAL_MACHINE\SYSTEM\ControlSet002\Services\NDTS\Parameters for settings on DNS, replication, and the global catalog. (These settings are covered in the Troubleshooting chapter.)

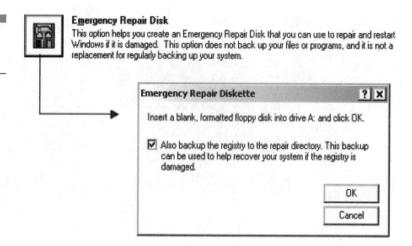

Figure 12.6
Creating an ERD is
still essential.

The Windows 2000 ERD is *not* the same as NT 4.0's when you consider what gets written to the floppy disk. Compressed registry hive backup to a floppy disk is not supported by Windows 2000, yet by checking the option "Also backup the Registry to the Repair directory," as shown in Figure 12.8 a compressed registry hive backup is maintained.

The ERD contains the MS-DOS environment initialization files autoexec.nt, config.nt, and setup.log detailing the current installation and necessary CRC information used during the repair process. The ERD is still a vital part of the regular maintenance of Windows 2000 and should be performed before and after system hardware and software changes because the CRC information may be required for a system restore. If it's an option, it will be required at some point in the repair process.

NOTE

When you back up your system state, the Registry hives are backed up to the \%systemroot%\repair\regback folder. Registry hives in the Regback folder could then be used to replace a corrupted Registry without a complete system state restore.

The repair process involves booting with the four Windows 2000 setup floppy disks that can be created with the command bootdisk\makebt32 from the NT Server CD, or by using the Directory Services Restore Mode after pressing **F8** from the Boot menu.

Performing a Nonauthoritative Restore

The backup wizard Ntbackup always operates in nonauthoritative mode when performing a restore of the system state. The term "Nonauthoritative" means that the restored domain controller is not the authority on the present state of the online Active Directory database. Once the restored domain controller is brought on-line, the replication process will bring the restored domain controller's system state up to date with any changes made while the failed server was offline, as shown in Figure 12.7.

Figure 12.7
The replication process will update the restored server if changes have occurred.

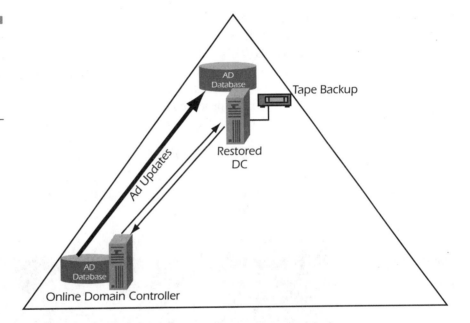

The information that needs to be updated will be obvious to the replication service, since the *update sequence numbers* (USN) of the restored server will be lower than the USN values of any other domain controller that resides in the domain. This underscores the value of having at least two domain controllers in each domain.

If any of the following conditions are not met, the system state is not restored:

- The drive letter for the %systemroot% folder must be the same as when it was backed up.

- The %systemroot% folder must be the same folder as when it was backed up.
- If SYSVOL was located on another volume, it must exist and have the same drive letters.

Verifying the Nonauthoritative Restore Process

After the database is first restored from backup media, it is not yet in usable format. To cause the Active Directory service to make the database usable, the backup tool adds RestoreInProgress to the registry subkey HKEY_LOCAL_MACHINE\SYSTEM\CurrentControlSet\Services\NTDS. This value notifies the Active Directory service to perform a consistency check and then to reindex the database files when Active Directory is restarted. The RestoreInProgress entry is automatically deleted when the process is finished.

To check the status of a nonauthoritative restore, run the Ntdsutil tool at the command prompt before the domain controller is started in normal mode and brought online for the first time. Type Files to display the Files menu, and then type Info. If the Active Directory database files are successfully recovered, Ntdsutil displays the information screen shown in Figure 12.8.

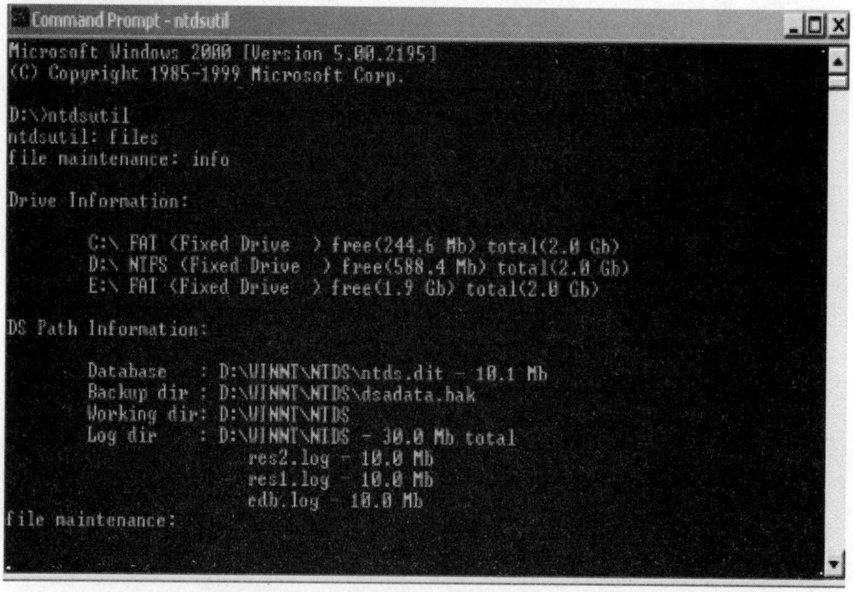

Figure 12.8
Ntdsutil can be used to verify the restored database and log file integrity.

```
Command Prompt - ntdsutil                                    _ □ X
Microsoft Windows 2000 [Version 5.00.2195]
(C) Copyright 1985-1999 Microsoft Corp.

D:\>ntdsutil
ntdsutil: files
file maintenance: info

Drive Information:

        C:\ FAT  (Fixed Drive ) free(244.6 Mb) total(2.0 Gb)
        D:\ NTFS (Fixed Drive ) free(588.4 Mb) total(2.0 Gb)
        E:\ FAT  (Fixed Drive ) free(1.9 Gb) total(2.0 Gb)

DS Path Information:

        Database   : D:\WINNT\NTDS\ntds.dit - 10.1 Mb
        Backup dir : D:\WINNT\NTDS\dsadata.bak
        Working dir: D:\WINNT\NTDS
        Log dir    : D:\WINNT\NTDS - 30.0 Mb total
                        res2.log - 10.0 Mb
                        res1.log - 10.0 Mb
                        edb.log   10.0 Mb
file maintenance:
```

Performing an Authoritative Restore

An authoritative restore means that you do not want replication to update the restored domain controller; the restored domain controller becomes authoritative to its replication partners. An authoritative restore would be used when objects have been deleted from Active Directory and the deletions have then been replicated to other domain controllers. A specific object or subtree of objects can be selected from an archived Active Directory database and restored to the domain controller. All selected objects restored will then be assigned an update sequence number (USN) greater than the current set of online objects. The USNs will be increased by 100,000 to ensure that the update sequence numbers are definitely authoritative.

Figure 12.9
Using Ntbackup in DSRM starts the restore process.

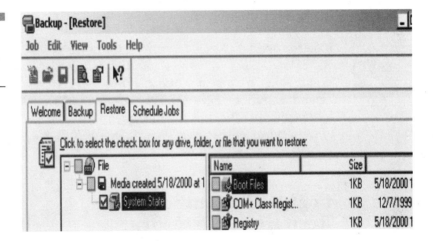

Once online, the restored server will update the other domain controller(s) in the domain, replicating the restored state from the restored domain controller's database to all domain controllers in the domain and the forest, and overwriting the current contents.

Only the domain and configuration domain directory partitions are marked as authoritative. The schema cannot be authoritatively restored.

Authoritative Restore Steps

1. Boot the domain controller and at the Windows 2000 Boot menu press **F8** and from the choices presented choose Directory Services Restore Mode.

2. Next select the Windows 2000 installation to recover, and then press **Enter**.

3. At the logon prompt, supply the Directory Services Restore username and password used when the domain controller was promoted, using DCPROMO.

4. Click **OK** to confirm that you are using the offline Safe mode.

5. Select Start >Programs > Accessories > System Tools and select Backup to start the backup utility.

6. Select the **Restore** tab and choose the backup media and the system state to restore.

7. Restore the System State data to its original location and also to an alternate location.

8. Using Ntdsutil, mark the entire Active Directory database as authoritative. (The discussion on Ntdsutil is just ahead.)

9. Restart the computer in normal mode.

NOTE

After the SYSVOL share is published, check to make sure that your group policy settings are intact. If necessary, copy the SYSVOL directory from the alternate location over the existing SYSVOL share. This backup and copy procedure ensures the integrity of the computer's group policy, since replication between domain controllers may overwrite the group policy.

Completing Authoritative Restore with Ntdsutil

Ntdsutil is a command-line utility provided for performing Active Directory maintenance on Windows 2000 domain controllers.

It is installed by default in the WINNT\SYSTEM32 folder. Active Directory database restore is but one of many tasks it can perform.

NOTE

Using this command for an authoritative restore is usually performed at the Safe mode command prompt; however you can override the default and restore active directory on an online server.

At the Safe mode command prompt type Ntdsutil and press **Enter**.

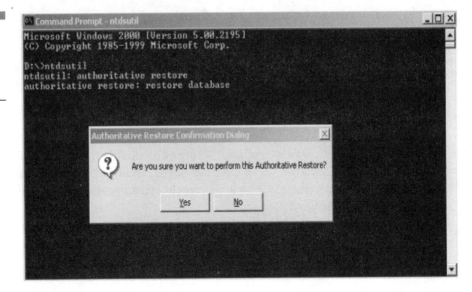

Figure 12.10
Ntdsutil is the final step in the authoritative restore process.

Next, type Authoritative restore and press enter. To use authoritative restore for the entire directory, type **restore database** and press **Enter**, as shown in Figure 12.10.

Ntdsutil Restore Steps

During the authoritative restore Ntdsutil, carries out the following tasks, as shown in Figure 12.11.

Figure 12.11
Ntdsutil finishes the authoritative restore process.

```
authoritative restore: restore database

Opening DIT database... Done.

The current time is 05-18-00 23:09.09.
Most recent database update occured at 05-18-00 22:12.04.
Increasing attribute version numbers by 100000.

Counting records that need updating...
Records found: 0000001436
Done.

Found 1436 records to update.

Updating records...
Records remaining: 0000000000
Done.

Successfully updated 1436 records.

Authoritative Restore completed successfully.

authoritative restore:
```

1. Opens the Ntds.dit file
2. Increases the version numbers
3. Counts the records that need updating
4. Verifies the number of records updated and reports completion. (You need not specify an increased version number size, since Ntdsutil does this automatically).

For authoritative restoration of a portion, or subtree of the directory, such as a grouping of organizational units (OUs), type Restore subtree <subtree distinguished name> and then press **Enter**. For example, to restore the Sales OU in the Headquarters.com domain, the commands are as follows:

1. Ntdsutil
2. Authoritative restore
3. Restore Subtree OU=Sales,DC=Headquarters,DC=COM.

If you want to restore an OU that is nested, the distinguished path must be enclosed in quotations marks.

Checking Authoritative Restore

To check that the authoritative restore was successful, you can use the command line utility Repadmin.exe at the command to check the metadata. The metadata listing details when each attribute was given its current value. Version number increases can also be checked.

To use Repadmin.exe, the syntax to check the condition of the container in the headquarters domain would be:

Repadmin /showmeta cn=Configuration,dc=headquarters,dc=com. The results are shown in Figure 12.12.

Tombstone Lifetime

When restoring system state, the age of the backup must not exceed the Active Directory tombstone lifetime (the length of time that deleted objects are maintained in Active Directory before the system permanently removes them). The default is 60 days. If an attempt is made to restore a tape or file-set older than the tombstone, the restore APIs will reject all the data as out of date and restore will not complete.

Figure 12.12
Ntdsutil is used to verify meta data.

10 entries.

Loc.USN	Originating DSA Org.USN	Org.Time/Date Ver Attribute
=======	=============== ======	============ === ========
1157	Default-First-Site-Name\HEADOFFICE	1157 2000-05-16 15:30.43 1 objectClass
3081	8c457981-a97f-4546-94ef-baabe51a23b6	3081 2000-05-18 23:09.10100001 cn
3081	8c457981-a97f-4546-94ef-baabe51a23b6	3081 2000-05-18 23:09.10100001 instanceType
3081	8c457981-a97f-4546-94ef-baabe51a23b6	3081 2000-05-18 23:09.10100001 whenCreated
3081	8c457981-a97f-4546-94ef-baabe51a23b6	3081 2000-05-18 23:09.10100000 isDeleted
3081	8c457981-a97f-4546-94ef-baabe51a23b6	3081 2000-05-18 23:09.10100001 showInAdvancedViewOnly
3081	8c457981-a97f-4546-94ef-baabe51a23b6	3081 2000-05-18 23:09.10100001 nTSecurityDescriptor
1157	Default-First-Site-Name\HEADOFFICE	1157 2000-05-16 15:30.43 1 name
3081	8c457981-a97f-4546-94ef-baabe51a23b6	3081 2000-05-18 23:09.10100001 wellKnownObjects
3081	8c457981-a97f-4546-94ef-baabe51a23b6	3081 2000-05-18 23:09.10100001 objectCategory

NOTE

The tombstoneLifeTime attribute is set on the object.cn=Directory Services,cn=Windows Nt,cn=Services,cn=Configuration,dc=DomainName.

Utilities that can be used to change the tombstone lifetime are ADSI Edit and Ldp. Changing this attribute is not necessary unless extreme security measures are required.

Restoring Trust and Member Server Passwords

Trust relationships and computer account passwords for member servers are negotiated every seven days by default by the security subsystem. When authoritative restore is used on a domain controller there is the possibility that a previously used obsolete password for trusts and computer accounts could also be restored.

If this happened, communications between domain controllers in the same domain and member servers would be disrupted until the security subsystem changed the passwords again, as detailed in Figure 12.13.

Primary Restore

A primary restore is a last resort when all domain controllers in the domain are lost and you want to rebuild a domain controller from backup. The steps for performing a primary restore are:

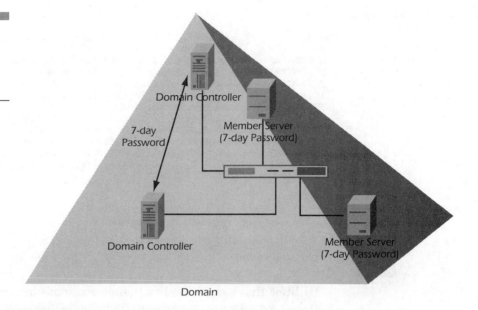

1. Use primary restore for the first domain controller, selected from Ntbackup advanced restore options, as shown in Figure 12.14. Select the checkbox "When restoring replicated data sets, mark the restored data as the primary data for all replicas."

Figure 12.14
Restore options.

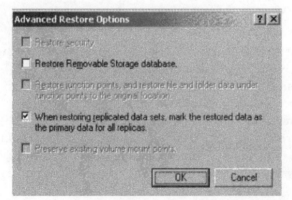

2. Use nonauthoritative restore for all other domain controllers.

A primary restore also builds a new *file replication service* (FRS) database by loading the data present in the SYSVOL folder onto the local domain controller.

Recovery without Restore

By demoting a domain controller with dcpromo and then promoting it back again, you may be able to rebuild the required system state information. This is not a procedure to be relied upon, since there may be replicated items that were not updated when your server failed, for example:

- Software applications installed on one domain controller
- Data files stored on one domain controller
- Tape backup hardware installed on a remote server.

The other reality is that dcpromo is not a utility that does a great job in demoting a domain controller. After demotion, system components may still remain to inhibit the repromotion of the domain controller. This metadata must be removed from the root domain's domain controller using Ntdsutil and a process called *metadata cleanup*. Details on metadata cleanup are discussed in Chapter 15.

Administrative Solutions: Create an Emergency Repair Disk

Start Backup from Start\Programs\Accessories\System Tools.

A. Click the button **Emergency Repair Disk**.
B. Insert a floppy disk into drive A.
C. Once the backup is completed, view the information that makes up the ERD for Windows 2000.

Backing up the System State

Start Backup from Start\Programs\Accessories\System Tools.

A. Click the **Backup** tab and check System State.
B. Double-click **System State** to see what has been chosen for the system state backup.

C. Click the **Browse** button and change the Backup media or file name path to a local hard drive or network share, for example C:\w2000.bkf, and click Open.

D. Click the **Start Backup** button.

E. At the Backup Job Information screen review the Advanced options: note what is not being backed up by default.

F. Click the **Start Backup** button.

G. After the backup has completed, review the backup log.

H. Exit the Backup wizard.

Nonauthoritative Restore of the System State

Reboot your computer and at the Boot menu select "Windows 2000 Server" and Press F8 for advanced options.

A. Select Directory Services Restore Mode (Windows NT domain controllers only) and press **Enter**; at the bottom of the screen in blue the selected option "Directory Services Restore Mode Windows NT domain controllers only" will be displayed.

B. The computer will boot into a safe mode—Directory Service Repair, and will not start the Directory Service. During this time, your computer will not be running as a domain controller and will only authenticate with local SAM account information.

C. Log on to your computer as Administrator, using the password with which the server was promoted, and accept the Safe mode warning.

D. Start the Backup wizard and select the Restore tab.

E. Expand File; select the "media created" and check the System State checkbox.

F. Restore files to Original location.

G. Accept the Warning and click **OK**.

H. At the Confirm Restore dialog box click **OK**.

I. Accept the backup file presented, for example: C:\> w2000.bkf, and click **OK**.

J. Review the restore log and then close the Restore Progress dialog box.

K. Restart your computer at the prompt.

Authoritative Restore of Deleted Objects

Reboot the computer and at the Boot menu select "Windows 2000 Server" and press **F8** for advanced options.

A. Select Directory Services Restore Mode (Windows NT domain controllers only) and press **Enter**.

B. Log on to your computer as Administrator, no password, and accept the Safe mode warning.

C. Start the Backup wizard and select the Restore tab.

D. Expand File; select the "media created" and check the System State checkbox.

E. Restore files to Original location.

F. Accept the Warning and click **OK**.

G. At the Confirm Restore dialog box, click **OK**.

H. Accept the backup file presented, for example C:\>w2000.bkf), and click OK.

I. Restart your computer at the prompt.

J. From the Boot menu, boot into Directory Services Restore Mode.

K. Run Ntdsutil, and at the prompt; enter the following example commands:

  : authoritative restore

  : restore subtree ou=<ouname>,dc=<yourdomain>,dc=gk,dc=com

NOTE

If you deleted a nested OU, quotation marks must be enclose all syntax after restore subtree "ou= .... Dc=gk,dc=com".

L. Confirm the authoritative restore by clicking **Yes**.

M. Ntdsutil will then open the DIT database and count, and update the records that need updating, as shown in Figure 12.12.

N. Reboot the computer.

O. Check in ADUC; the Office OU should have been restored successfully.

P. Use repadmin /showmeta to check the version number increase. Repadmin/showmeta OU=,ouname>,DC=<yourdomain>,DC=gk, DC=com.

Performing Offline Defragmentation

By default, Windows 2000 servers running directory services will perform a directory online defragmentation every 12 hours as part of the garbage collection process. This defragmentation only rearranges data in the database file (NTDS.DIT) but does not reduce its size. Offline defragmentation can be performed to create a smaller NTDS.DIT as follows:

Reboot the server, select the OS option and press **F8** for advanced options.

A. Select the "Directory Services Restore Mode" option and press **Enter**. Press **Enter** again to start the operating system.
B. Windows 2000 will start in Safe mode with no directory service running. Log on using the Administrator account and password stored in the local Registry SAM hive.
C. Exit to the command prompt.
D. Make a folder called temp in drive C.
E. Start Ntdsutil, and at the prompt, enter the following commands:
   : files
   file maintenance: info
F. Write down your ntds.dit size: _____ , which is displayed in the info screen.
G. Enter the command: file maintenance: compact to c:\temp.
H. After the defragmentation has completed, type **Quit** twice to return to the command prompt.
   Now replace the old NTDS.DIT with the new compressed version.
I. Look in C:\temp and write down the size of ntds.dit _____.
   Copy c:\temp\ntds.dit to C:\WINNT\NTDS.
J. Delete all log files in C:\WINNT\NTDS.
K. Restart the computer and boot Windows 2000 Server.

Using ADSI Edit to Change the Tombstone

Objects marked as "tombstoned" are actually deleted 60 days after their original tombstone status setting; modifying the tombstone lifetime can change this time.

Changing the Default Tombstone Life of 60 Days

Log on to your domain as Administrator.

A. Open ADSI Edit from Start\Programs\Windows 2000 Support Tools\Tools.
B. Highlight the Domain NC and from the Action menu select Settings.
C. In the Connection dialog box select a Naming Context of Configuration container.
D. Navigate to CN=Configuration/CN=Services/CN=Windows NT/CN=Directory Service.
E. Highlight CN=Directory Service and from the Action menu select Properties.
F. From the "Select a property to view," select tombstone Lifetime.
G. To change the default value, type in a number in the Edit Attribute box and click **SET**.

To change the default garbage collection period of 12 hours:

A. From the "Select a property to view," select: garbageCollPeriod.
B. To change the default value, type in a number in the Edit Attribute box and click **SET**.

Schema Fundamentals

This chapter provides details on the schema in the following areas:

- Understanding the role of the schema
- Object classes and attributes
- Editing the schema
- Using Ntdsutil to transfer or seize the schema role

What Is the Schema?

The schema is a confusing concept to master in Windows 2000. It is mentioned many times in numerous white papers and Windows 2000 documentation as "containing definitions for the objects and attributes" that can be created, stored, and searched for in Active Directory. Information in the schema is defined as object classes, attributes, and syntaxes.

- An **object class** is a collection of mandatory and optional attributes that define each specific class of Active Directory object or objects.
- An **attribute** elaborates, or provides additional information about, the object.
- **Syntax** is the allowed structure of the data the attribute will accept, such as string or binary.

Schema Basics

When a user, group, or computer account is first created in a Windows 2000 member server using the Computer Management console, these objects can be created because the operating system has a predefined base set of object classes and attributes it knows about. Once the member server is promoted to a domain controller, the number of objects and attributes that a DC must understand greatly increases, to over 1,000 values.

When Active Directory is installed, the default objects and attributes are dumped into the database (NTDS.DIT) from a file called schema.ini, which can be found in the %SYSTEMROOT\SYSTEM32 folder. Figure 13.1 shows the schema.

The base schema in Windows 2000 contains all the class and attribute definitions used, and to be used, by Windows 2000, Windows 2000 components, and Windows 2000 software applications.

Figure 13.1
The schema is
viewed with the
Schema console.

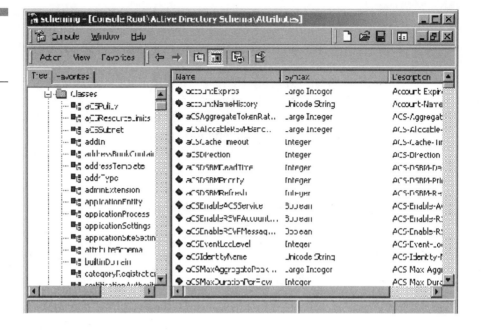

NOTE

There is only one schema for each Active Directory tree or forest. All objects created in the forest must obey the same rules for database structure and content enforced by the schema.

Schema Details in English

The above details are cryptic, to say the least, so here is an explanation in English. You decide to build a house and you know nothing about house construction so you ask your friends about where you can obtain information on how to start learning. One of your friends recommends that you read something called a building code. You obtain a copy of this building code and it's huge and almost unreadable to the novice builder. It describes all the rules and regulations for building a house, the wood types you can use, the size and length and width. The building code is the "schema" for the construction industry, in effect the exact rules that must be followed. Following this analogy and applying it to a Windows 2000 DC, the schema is almost unreadable (at first) and the schema sets the rules about what objects and attributes the operating system understands and will allow you to use to build each domain controller.

When a software application or a hardware device supported by Active Directory is installed into Windows 2000, the schema must be modified to include the new objects and attributes that the new application or device requires in order to be installed and then execute. The best example at this time is Exchange 2000; it performs a massive update to the schema. In fact, it more than doubles the size of the schema once it is installed through a process called a *forest prep*. Each forest adheres to one forest, therefore each domain controller in a forest will receive schema updates through the normal replication process.

Schema Location

The schema is located in the schema container as part of the *Directory Information Tree* (DIT), as shown in Figure 13.2. The relationship of the schema partition to the other directory partitions is essential, since the schema contains all the object class and attribute type definitions used when defining or creating objects, or searching for information.

Figure 13.2
Where is the schema located?

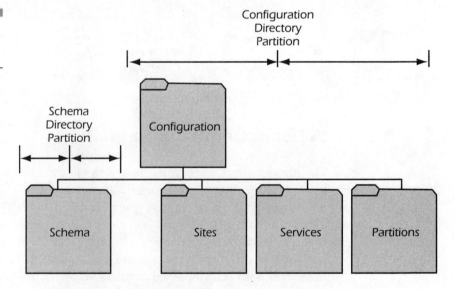

The contents of the schema can be viewed with the Active Directory Schema console or with ADSI Edit.

NOTE

Object Classes Defined

Users, groups, computers, and organizational units are examples of object classes defined in the schema. Every user account object created is part of the object class User, as shown in Figure 13.3. When a new user account is created, the defined mandatory attributes such as user name, user principal name, and SID account identifier are defined and then stored in the Users container, or the defined OU. When a user account is created (for example the user account Mark), Mark is now a defined object in the Directory, and is an instance of the object class User.

Figure 13.3
The User object class.

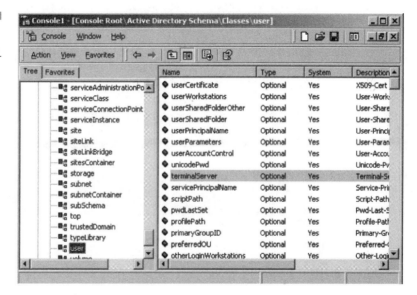

The object Mark may also have defined one of the optional attributes defined for the User object class called telephoneNumber. The telephoneNumber attribute for the object Mark of the object class User has the value 343-6787.

In addition, the attribute telephoneNumber could be defined as a syntax value String (numeric) that mandates that the telephoneNumber value can only accept the digits 0–9.

The attributes and classes used in Active Directory are stored in the schema container as the blueprint for what can be added or searched for within the forest.

- Every group account object created is part of the object class Group.
- Every computer object created is part of the object class Computer.

■ Every OU object created is part of the object class Organizational Unit.

Another example of an object class could be a computer, which could belong to the following classes:

■ PCs
■ Mainframes
■ Notebooks, and so on

A computer can be described by its make, model, and speed—these are the *attributes* of the computer. The possible values for the model of the computer could be Compaq, Apple, or Dell. The syntax for each model could be the registered manufacture's corporate number or some other unique identifier.

The local root administrator is added to the Schema Administrator group by default as shown in Figure 13.4.

Figure 13.4
Members of the Schema Administrator's group can edit the schema.

Schema Objects

The schema is the skeleton framework of all objects and attributes created in the domain. When a domain is first created, a default schema is installed and defined; it contains characterizations and details for the objects currently existing in the directory including users, groups, and containers. Classes are collections of attributes, and the attributes hold the information stored in the Directory. The default schema definition is defined in the SCHEMA.INI file that also contains the initial structure for the NTDS.DIT database.

Any new objects or attributes created must conform to the rules of the schema, as detailed in Figure 13.5.

Figure 13.5
Object classes and attributes define the contents of the Active Directory database.

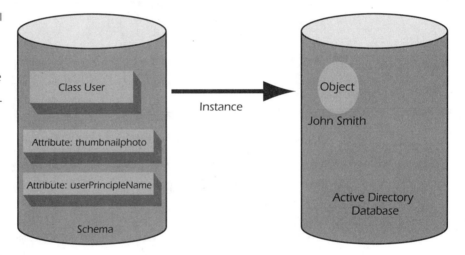

Object Identification

Active Directory is based upon the X.500 naming standards; these mandate that all object classes be uniquely defined. Microsoft has included the entire X.500, X.501, and X.520 schema elements within Active Directory—therefore AD is said to be X.500 based. In Figure 13.6, the properties of the volume object show the unique OID assigned to a volume within the Active Directory schema.

A hierarchical Object Identifier (OID) uniquely identifies each object. The first part of the OID indicates the path to the branch where the object is located in the X.500 tree hierarchy. The second part locates the object uniquely in the defined branch.

Figure 13.6
The Volume object class is uniquely identified with a X.500 OID.

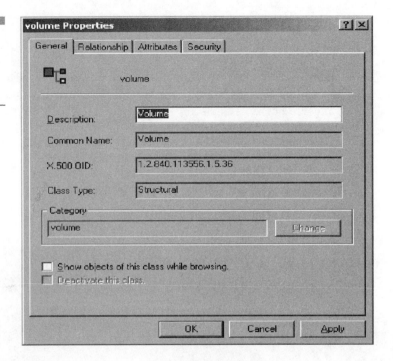

Object Identifier (OID) Details

OIDs are also used in SNMP, OSI, and X.500 environments to identify data components and unique parts in a distributed environment.

The first four identifiers **1.2.840.113556** are assigned as follows:

- 1 is the ISO (International Standards Organization)
- 2 is ISO member organizations
- 840 is for the United States registration body ANSI (American National Standards Institute)
- ANSI assigned 113556 to Microsoft

Microsoft manages object identifiers from this point downward in the branch for the base schema.

Table 13.1 details the OID assignments for Microsoft and Active Directory.

To obtain a valid OID your country, you must contact local registration body.

NOTE

TABLE 13.1	1	ISO
Old assignments for Microsoft and Active Directory.	2	ANSI
	840	USA
	113556	Microsoft
	1	Active Directory
	5	Active Directory classes
	4	Built-in classes

attributeSchema Objects

Attributes are stored in the schema container as a "global list" of attributes allowing any attribute definition to be applied to many classes. Attributes are defined as attributeSchema objects, which define the rules for new class objects and attributes. Each attributeSchema object is an instance of the attributeSchema class. Contained in the properties of each object is information for unique identification of each attribute.

On each object class the four tabs General, Relationship, Attributes, and Security, as shown in Figure 13.6, define the attributeSchema object attributes that must be entered during creation of a class object, including:

- The common name of the class
- The LDAP display name of the attribute
- The object identifier for the attribute
- The GUID for the attribute
- The syntax of the attribute
- The range of the attribute
- Whether this is a single or multivalue attribute

Single or Multivalue Attributes

The object class defines the attributes each entry is allowed to contain. Attributes are defined as mandatory or optional and single or multivalue.

A single value attribute can be TRUE or FALSE. A multivalue attribute can contain multiple values of uniform syntax.

Figure 13.7
Objects can be single- or multivalued.

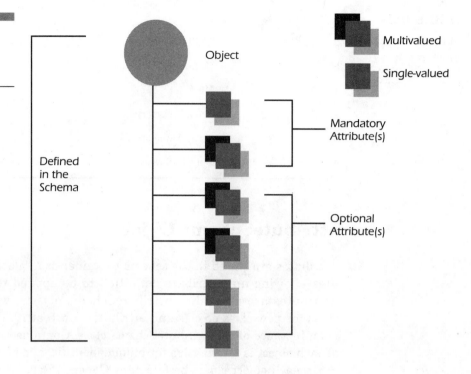

Multivalue attributes are an example of Microsoft's changing the X.500 standards as applied to the reading of multivalue attributes, as detailed in Figure 13.7. LDAP reads a multivalue attribute as a single entry. An Internet draft titled "Incremental Retrieval of Multivalued Properties" is before the IETF for consideration.

Examples of defined attributes for the attributeSchema class are detailed in Table 13.2.

TABLE 13.2

Defined attributes for the attributeSchema class.

Attribute	Syntax	Mandatory	Multivalue	Description
cn	Unicode	Yes	No	Descriptive relative distinguished name for the schema object
attributeID	Object identifier	Yes	No	Object identified that uniquely identifies this attribute
DAPDisplayName	Unicode	Yes, but filled in automatically	No	Name by which LDAP clients identify this attribute

continued on next page

TABLE 13.2

Defined attributes for the attributeSchema class (continued).

Attribute	Syntax	Mandatory	Multi8value	Description
schemaIDGUID	String (octet)	Yes	No	GUID that uniquely identifies this attribute
MAPIID	Integer	No	No	Integer by which Messaging Application Programming Interface (MAPI) clients identify this attribute
attributeSecurity GUID	GUID	No	No	GUID by which the security system identifies the property set of this attribute
attributeSyntax	Object identifier	Yes	No	Syntax object identifer of this attribute

Syntax

Syntax is the variety of data that can be stored in an attribute. Every attribute of every object class is associated with precisely one syntax. Examples are integers, strings, or numeric string, as detailed in Table 13.3.

TABLE 13.3

Every attribute of every object class is associated with precisely one syntax.

Syntax	OID
Distinguished Name	2.5.5.1
Object OID	2.5.5.2
Case-sensitive string	2.5.5.3
Case-insensitive string	2.5.5.4
Printable string	2.5.5.5
Numeric string	2.5.5.6
X.400 mail address	2.5.5.7
Boolean	2.5.5.8
Integer	2.5.5.9
Octet String	2.5.5.10
Time	2.5.5.11
Unicode	2.5.5.12
SID	2.5.5.17

classSchema Objects

Each classSchema object details the various attributes it is associated with, including the list of mandatory attributes and the list of optional attributes.

TABLE 13.4

classSchema Ojects attributes.

The common name of the class	Must be unique
The LDAP display name of the class	Needed for searching
The object identifier for the class	
The GUID for the class	
Mandatory attributes that must be present for an instance of the class	
Optional attributes that can be present	
The class to which the parent of instances of this class may belong	
The superclass from which this class inherits its characteristics	All mandatory and optional characteristics
Other auxiliary classes from which this class inherits attributes	
The type of class: abstract, structural, or auxiliary	
The default hiding state for the class	Is the class visible to the end-user or hidden

The three types of class that can be created are:

- **Structural**—The most common type.
- **Abstract**—Inherits from other classes.
- **Auxiliary**—Stores attributes that other objects can inherit.

Using ADSI to View the Schema

The schema container is bound to the top of the LDAP search tree called rootDSE. The attribute schemaNamingContext points to the location of the schema.

To identify the Schema directory, partition by using ADSI Edit:

1. Start the ADSI Edit console in MMC by installing the Admin tools Adminpak.msi.
2. Right-click ADSI Edit at the top of the console tree, and click **Connect to....**

3. For Connection Point options, select Naming Context and select RootDSE from the Naming Context box; then click **OK**.
4. At the bottom of the Console Tree, click **RootDSE** to display the RootDSE folder.
5. Right-click the RootDSE folder, and click **Properties** as shown in Figure 13.8.
6. From the Select property to view dialog box, select schemaNaming-Context from the list of properties (attributes) shown.
7. In the Attribute Values section, view the Value(s) box; the distinguished name of the schema directory partition will be listed.

Figure 13.8
Properties tab selected.

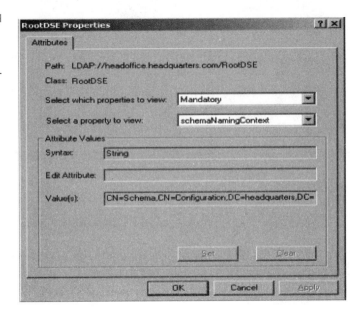

Modifying the Schema

By default, schema modification is disabled on all Domain controllers. You must be a member of the Schema Administrators group to change the FSMO role where modifications will be made. The Active Directory Schema console can be used to permit write access to the schema, as shown in Figure 13.9. Only one domain controller in the forest is allowed to write to the schema.

The following four modifications can be made to the schema as shown in figure 13.10 and listed below:

Figure 13.9
The Schema console can be used to permit write access to the schema.

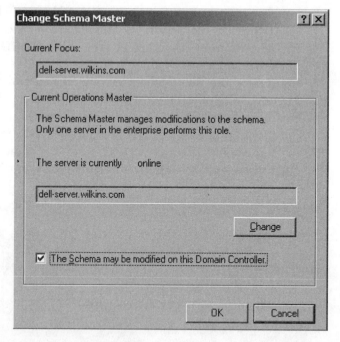

Change Schema Master

Current Focus:

dell-server.wilkins.com

Current Operations Master

The Schema Master manages modifications to the schema.
Only one server in the enterprise performs this role.

The server is currently   online

dell-server.wilkins.com

Change

☑ The Schema may be modified on this Domain Controller.

OK   Cancel

Figure 13.10
Schema modifications.

Create New Schema Class

Identification

Common Name: asset tags

LDAP Display Name: asset tags

Unique X500 Object ID: 1.2.840.113556.1.4.7000.233.28788.2008

Inheritance and Type

Parent Class: user

Class Type: Structural

< Back   Next >   Cancel

- Creating classes
- Modifying classes
- Creating attributes
- Deactivating classes and attributes

Using Ntdsutil to Change the Schema Master

1. Start Ntdsutil by typing ntdsutil at the command prompt.
2. At the Ntdsutil prompt, type: **roles**.
3. At the FSMO maintenance prompt, type: ntdsutil.
4. To do a graceful transfer of the Schema FSMO, type: **transfer schema master**.
5. To perform a forced transfer of the Schema FSMO, type: **seize schema master**, as shown in Figure 13.11.

To return to the FSMO maintenance prompt, type: **quit**.

Figure 13.11
Using ntdsutil the Schema master can be transferred.

Order of Processing When Extending the Schema

If the schema is extended with scripts or ADSI, perform the update as follows:

1. Aim your update at the FSMO Role Owner domain controller. Bind to the schema on that domain controller which is the schema master, as shown in Figure 13.12.

Figure 13.12
You must connect to the current schema master before transferring the FSMO role using the Schema console.

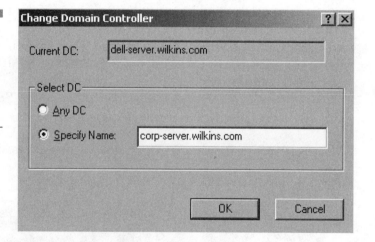

2. Make sure beforehand that you have sufficient administrative privileges to perform the schema update. Only members of the Schema Administrators group are allowed to change the contents of the schema. You must ensure that your user account is a member of this group. By default, all Administrators are members of the Schema Administrators groups.

3. Create the registry entry, known as the *safety interlock*, that allows write access to the schema. By default, access to the schema is read-only. This entry is located in the registry on the FSMO role owner at HKEY_LOCAL_MACHINE\SYSTEM\CurrentControlSet\Services\NTDS\Parameters\Schema Update Allowed. This entry must exist and its value must be a DWORD of 1 for schema updates to take place.

4. Add your new attributes and classes.

5. Add attributes to classes.

Each domain controller updates its schema cache 5 minutes after a schema change. If the extensions are going to be used within 5 minutes, you must trigger a cache reload.

Adding Object and Attributes to the Schema

Add the Active Directory Schema Console to a MMC

Log on to the root domain or to the location where the FSMO role for the schema master is assigned as Administrator.

A. Start the MMC through Start\Run and type **mmc** and click **OK**.
B. From the Console menu select Add/Remove snap-in and click **Add**.
C. Select the Active Directory Schema snap-in, click **Add** and then **OK**.
D. Save the MMC console to the Desktop as Schema.msc.

Check the Current Operations Master through the Schema Console

Start the Active Directory Schema console from the Desktop.

A. Right-click the Active Directory schema icon and select Operations Master.
B. Verify that the Current domain controller assigned to manage the schema is the correct location.

Check that Write Operations are Permitted to the Schema

Right-click the Active Directory schema icon and select Operations Master.
    Choose "The Schema may be modified on this domain controller." The checkbox must be checked on the current schema master before editing can be carried out.

Creating a New Attribute

Before you can create new attributes and classes you must first generate unique base object identifiers. A new Resource Kit utility OIDGEN.EXE is an OID Generator. It generates a pair of unique base-object identifier values for use in extending the Active Directory schema. One object identifier is for use in defining new Attributes, the other is used for defining new Classes.

Before you run OID Generator, setting the following cmd window properties will make it much easier to copy the generated object identifiers into a document or source code.

A. Click Start | Run and enter cmd and click **OK.**
B. Click the top left-hand corner and select **Properties**.
C. Select the **Layout** tab and set the window size width to 100.
D. Select the **Options** tab and click the **QuickEdit Mode** checkbox to enable copy and paste.
E. Close the command-prompt, and then re-open it.
F. Type OIDGEN and press **Enter** to generate class and attribute base identifiers.

OIDGEN Notes

Use the generated object identifier pair as the root of your object identifier space and assign new object identifiers by adding an element to the end of each object identifier.

Increasing the Value for Each New Class or Attribute Desired

If the Attribute Base OID is:
1.2.840.113556.1.4.7000.233.28688.28684.8.174127.1287321.272966.218 134

then your first attribute should be increased by 1, as shown below.
1.2.840.113556.1.4.7000.233.28688.28684.8.174127.1287321.272966.218 134**.1**

Your second attribute should again be increased by 1, as shown below:
1.2.840.113556.1.4.7000.233.28688.28684.8.174127.1287321.272966.218 134**.2**

If the generated Class Base OID is:
1.2.840.113556.1.5.7000.111.28688.28684.8.115800.1245096.756946.145 477

then your first new class should be increased by 1, as shown below.

1.2.840.113556.1.5.7000.111.28688.28684.8.115800.1245096.756946.145
477.**1**

Add Your New Attribute

Expand the Active Directory Schema tree in the left pane.

A. From the left pane in the Schema console, highlight the Attributes folder.
B. From the Action menu, select **Create Attribute**.
C. Accept the warning that creating schema objects is a permanent operation that cannot be undone and click **Continue**.
D. In the Create a New Attribute Object dialog box, enter the two assigned objects and syntax from the Create a New Attribute Parameter and the Attribute Chart.
E. Use your generated base attribute OID and increase twice to create the two unique OID values for each attribute (Created with OIDGEN).
F. Use Cut and Paste from the command prompt to enter the values.
G. Click **OK** after each attribute is created.

Entering New Attribute Parameters

Value	Type this text
Common Name	From Classes Chart below
LDAP Displayname	From Classes Chart below
Unique X.500 Object ID	Generated by OIDGEN
Syntax	Case Insensitive String

Creating a New Class

From the left panel in the Schema console, highlight the Classes folder.

A. From the Action menu select Create Class.
B. Accept the warning and click **Continue**.
C. Create the new class with the required values and then click **Finish**.

Managing Users and User Services

This chapter provides details on Active Directory management of users and network services designed for easier user management, including:

- Assigning NTFS and share permissions
- Object permissions
- Auditing
- Using the Distributed File System
- Delegating administration
- Deploying the Remote Installation Service (RIS)

Windows 2000 Object Types

Maintenance of Windows 2000 objects is both a daily and weekly task involving Active Directory and Windows 2000 objects. Table 14.1 shows each type of object, its object manager, and the management tool used to perform maintenance. The Active Directory Users and Computers console (ADUC) is one of the most popular AD utilities, since adding users, group, organizational units, and defining group policy are performed using this utility. If your network is a mixed bag of Windows operating systems, users may not be using Windows 2000 Professional, but instead NT 4.0; in this case, NT 4.0 administrator tools will still be used. The NT 4.0 tools are included on the Windows 2000 Resource Kit for this very purpose.

In addition, you may not wish to share all folders, printers, and user information across the entire Directory; for these situations, the local server utilities are used in place of AD utilities. For example, to share a folder for user access, the Explorer shell is still used to share the desired folder and assign permissions.

TABLE 14.1

Objects and their associated utilities.

Object Type	Object Manager	Utility
Active Directory objects	Active Directory	Active Directory Users and Computers
Folders and files	NTFS	Windows Explorer
Shares	Server service	Windows Explorer
Printers	Print spooler	Start | Settings then Printers
Services	Service controllers	Security Templates, Security Configuration and Analysis
Registry keys	The Registry	Regedit32

NTFS Standard Folder Permissions

NTFS permissions are used to specify which users and groups of users, can access network folders and files (Figure 14.1). Permissions are defined by selecting the desired folder or file and, through its properties, selecting the Security tab. Although NTFS permissions were used in NT 4.0, Windows 2000 has many more permissions that can be used for a much finer, granular level of control.

Figure 14.1
Standard NTFS permissions are either assigned or denied.

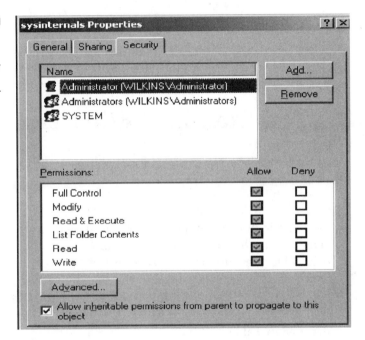

Windows 2000 permissions are now defined as standard and special; most of the time standard permissions will be more than adequate for security needs.

The main concept to grasp when defining which files and folders your users will be allowed to access is that the permissions set on a folder apply to the folder and also to the files in the folder. If you have subfolders beneath the folder where permissions have been defined, the default is that all defined permissions will flow down to the lower-level folders in the tree unless specifically stopped. NTFS version 5.0 permissions are the same for Windows 2000 Professional Clients and Windows 2000 Server products. Standard NTFS folder permissions are detailed in Table 14.2.

TABLE 14.2

NTFS standard folder permissions.

NTFS Folder Permissions	Allows the User ...
Full Control	Change permissions, take ownership, delete subfolders and files plus all other folder actions
Modify	Write, Read, Execute, and Delete
Read and Execute	Read, list folder contents, and move through unpermitted folders to other subfolders
List Folder Contents	See the names of files and subfolders in each folder
Read	See files and subfolders, view folder ownership permissions and attributes
Write	Create new files and subfolders change folder attributes, view folder ownership

NTFS Standard File Permissions

File permissions are set on the individual files in each folder, as shown in Figure 14.2. File permissions should be used sparingly, since they can be difficult to troubleshoot if file permissions are not documented. If a file within a folder needs special permissions, it should be moved to a new folder and folder permissions assigned. The major concept to be considered when assigning file permissions is that they take priority over folder permission. A user with file permissions to a file can access that file even without access to the folder containing the file. However, that user must know the full UNC path to the file location. Standard NTFS file permissions are listed in Table 14.3; special permissions are detailed in Table 14.4.

TABLE 14.3

Standard NTFS file permissions.

NTFS Folder Permissions	Allows the User ...
Full Control	Change permissions, take ownership, plus all other NTFS file permissions
Modify	Modify, Delete, Write, Read, and Execute
Read and Execute	Read and run applications
Read	Read the file and view ownership, permissions, and attributes
Write	Overwrite the file and change file attributes, view folder ownership and permissions

Figure 14.2
NTFS file permissions are assigned to the individual files.

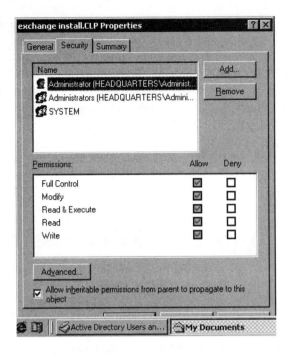

TABLE 14.4	Transverse Folder/Execute File	Move or deny moving through folders where access has not been granted; execute File applies just to file permissions
Assigning special permissions—allow or deny.	List folder/Read data	Read or deny reading files and folders in the folder; read data applies just to file permissions
	Read Attributes	Read or deny reading the attributes of a file or folder
	Read Extended Attributes	Allow or deny; extended attributes are defined by each program
	Create Files/Write Data	Create or deny the creation of files within a folder; write data apply just to file permissions
	Create Folders/Append Data	Create or deny the creation folders within a folder; append data apply just to file permissions
	Write Attributes	Change or deny the changing of attributes of a file or a folder
	Write Extended Attributes	Allow or Deny; extended attributes are defined by each program
	Delete Subfolders and Files	Delete or deny the deletion of subfolders and files even when the Delete permission has not been granted

continued on next page

TABLE 14.4

Assigning special permissions—allow or deny (continued).

Delete	Allow or deny the deletion of a file or a folder
Read Permissions	Read or deny the reading of file or folder permissions
Change Permissions	Change or deny the changing of the file or folder permissions
Take Ownership	Take ownership or deny taking ownership of the file or folder
Synchronize	Allows or denies different threads of a multithreaded program to synchronize with other worker threads

Assigning NTFS Permissions

Defining and assigning NTFS permissions should be discussed as part of security planning. Groundwork first has to be done, preferably on a large whiteboard in the presence of everyone involved with security. NTFS permissions are tricky and complicated, and it is easy to mess up and assign more access than you planned.

Here are some rules to help you succeed with assigning permissions:

1. Utilize the User group rather than the Everyone group for assigning global permissions. The User group contains users whom you personally created; the Everyone group contains users plus the users created by the operating system for system tasks. For the viewing of public files and executing software, assign Read and Execute permissions to the Users group, if possible. This reduces the possibility of file deletion.

2. When a volume is first formatted with NTFS, the Everyone group is assigned the permission of Full Control, as shown in Figure 14.3.

    There are still some glaring weaknesses in the default security system for Windows 2000 that must be addressed for a secure network environment. This default setting should be changed immediately after the volume has been created and formatted. Although the Everyone group is not as widely used in NT 4.0, it is still present in several cases: at the volume root level and when assigning shares through the Explorer shell.

3. Group files into application, data, and home folders for easier assignment of permissions at the folder level and greater ease when backing up data and personal files. If public data folders are to be

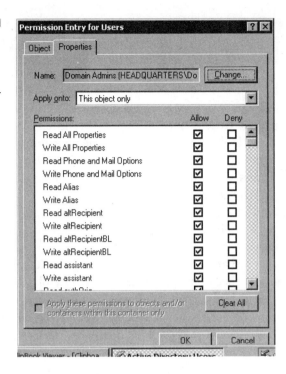

Figure 14.3
The Everyone group is still sometimes present.

used, assign the permissions Read and Execute, and Write to the Users group. Then assign the Full Control permission to the Create Owner identity group. This ensures that the person who created the file is assigned as creator and owner of the file, and not the Users group.

4. In mixed mode where NT 4.0 and Windows 2000 servers co-exist, global groups and local groups should be used just like NT 4.0 network setup and configuration. Your older NT clients will not understand or be able to use the newer NTFS permissions or universal groups or the advanced nesting features of a native Windows 2000 network.

5. Always assign permissions to groups of users and not individual users, unless a specific user is to be entrusted with administrative duties. Domain local groups should be located on the server where the resource is located, with the desired permissions assigned to the local group. The users should then be placed in domain global groups that are added to the desired local group. Understanding this concept of nesting groups is essential for deploying a manageable security system.

In native mode, you have the choice of using universal groups as well as domain local and global groups.

6. Design your group permissions for a minimum of repetition. Creating groups with a bare minimum of rights is very efficient in the long run. If your users need the permissions Read and Write but only some need the Modify permission, the best solution is to create two groups, one with the permissions of Read and Write and another group with the single permission of Modify. You may want to go further and create three groups: one for Read, one for Write, and one for Modify. Then add the groups to the resource creates the group permissions you desire.

7. Use the Advanced button only when it is absolutely required. The properties sheet for each object opened displays an Advanced button where permissions can be allowed or denied to a particular characteristic of an object, rather than the entire object, as shown in Table 14.5.

TABLE 14.5

Special permissions related to file and folder permissions.

Special Permission	Full Control	Modify	Read and Execute	List Folder Contents	Read	Write
Transverse Folder/ Execute File	✔	✔	✔	✔		
List folder/ Read data	✔	✔	✔	✔	✔	
Read Attributes	✔	✔	✔	✔	✔	
Read Extended Attributes	✔	✔	✔	✔	✔	
Create Files/ Write Data	✔	✔	✔			
Create Folders/ Append Data	✔	✔	✔			

continued on next page

TABLE 14.5

Special permissions related to file and folder permissions (continued).

Special Permission	Full Control	Modify	Read and Execute	List Folder Contents	Read	Write
Write Attributes	✔	✔	✔			
Write Extended Attributes	✔	✔	✔			
Delete Subfolders and Files	✔					
Delete	✔	✔				
Read Permissions	✔	✔	✔	✔	✔	✔
Change Permissions	✔					
Take Ownership	✔					
Synchronize	✔	✔	✔	✔	✔	✔

An example of required Advanced options would be the denying to a particular group access to personal information such as telephone numbers or personal addresses of other workers. In these early stages of Active Directory, not much thought will be given to the wealth of information stored in the Directory—several years from now the complaint will probably be that there is too much information accessible to the average network user. If your network is already a very large corporate entity unto itself, reviewing the wealth of permissions that can be set on the Users group in these early stages of AD, as shown in Figure 14.3, is a idea you should consider as a heads-up toward the future.

8. Allow inheritance of permissions. Unless absolutely necessary not to, allow the inheritance of permissions by subfolders and files. Changing the flow of permissions is incredibly hard to undo, and even harder to troubleshoot. If a subfolder requires specific permissions different from its parent folder above it and subfolders below, the best solution is to move the folder up to the root of the drive, creating a new subtree of folders starting with the newly moved folder.

Figure 14.3
Advanced
permissions for Users.

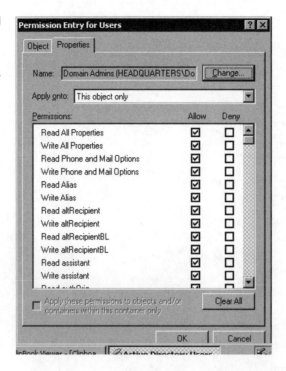

9. Document all nonstandard changes. In your company, you may have reasons or rules that define how folder permissions must be assigned. If you must break one of these rules, make sure that you document the reasons and your solution the old-fashioned way, on paper. This is a habit you must force yourself to carry out—trying to solve problems with undocumented permissions.

Effective Permissions Define Access

A network user is usually a member of the Domain Users group, as shown in Figure 14.4, and many other groups; therefore permissions that apply to a user are typically a combination of the user's assigned permissions and the assigned permissions of the group to which the user is a member. The user's effective permissions are a combination of the user and group permissions. If the user was assigned the Read permission for an object and is also a member of a group with Write permissions to the same object, the user's effective permission for the object is Read and Write.

Figure 14.4
All network users are
members of the
Domain Users group.

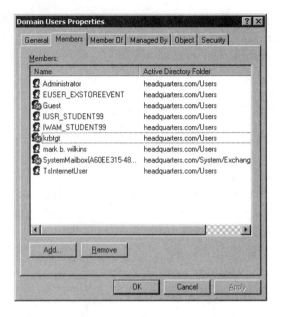

Deny Means Deny

NTFS Permissions can be either allowed or denied. Deny takes priority over any permission assigned to a user or group account. If a user is denied permission to an object, for example a printer, even if the user is also a member of a group with the permission to access that particular printer, the deny permission takes precedence, denying the user access to the printer.

- If Mark allowed the Sales group to read the sales analysis spreadsheet, then only the members of the Sales group will be able to read his spreadsheet file.
- If Mark decided that John, a member of the Sales group, should not be able to read the sales analysis spreadsheet, then John can be explicitly denied access to read the file.

Change Permissions and Take Ownership

Change permission allows the user to change permissions on a file or folder without requiring full control. Permissions can be changed on a file or folder; however the file can't be modified or deleted. Any user with the full control permission assigned can assign the Full Control or Take Ownership permission to any user or group, allowing a user or a member of a group to take ownership.

An administrator can always take ownership of a file or folder and then change the permissions. The assigning of ownership cannot be done, only the ability to take ownership. The user must select his name from the access control settings for the specific file or folder through the Owner tab, selecting the Change Owner To list.

A common reason for taking ownership of files or folders is when an employee has moved within the company or has been let go.

The administrator could then take ownership of the files or folders, reassign permissions, or transfer the right to take ownership to another user or group of users.

Copying Files and Folders

Several problems you may have with users migrating from Windows 95/98 involve their understanding of how files and folder permissions respond when NTFS is added to the mix. Copying or moving files from one hard drive location to another may change the assigned file or folder permissions.

Figure 14.5
Copying files is different with NTFS partitions.

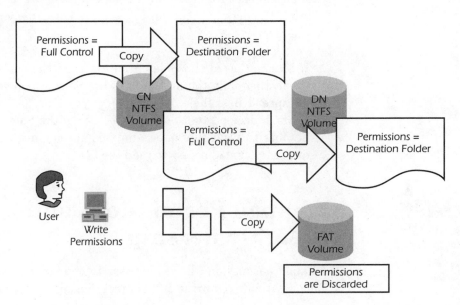

- When a file or folder is copied within a single NTFS volume, or between NTFS volumes, the file assumes the permissions of the folder or volume it is copied to—the destination.
- When a file or folder is copied from an NTFS volume to a FAT or FAT32 volume, the NTFS permissions are discarded.

You must have the Write permission assigned for the destination folder to copy files and folders. Once the copy process has been completed, the person who performed the process becomes the Creator Owner of the file. A savvy user could use a FAT volume to strip permissions from files and folders, breaking apart security assumed to be in place. If the user's Windows 2000 Professional workstation partitions are not all NTFS, security can be easily compromised.

Moving Files and Folders

When a file or folder is moved within a single NTFS volume, the file or folder retains its original permissions, as shown in Figure 14.6. When a file or folder is moved between separate NTFS volumes, the file or folder assumes the permissions of the destination folder. In moving files or folders to FAT or FAT32 volumes, the NTFS permissions are also discarded. A user must also have the Write permission for the destination folder in order to move files and folders to that location. The Modify permission must be assigned to the source file or folder. After a successful move operation, Windows 2000 deletes the file or folder from its original location and the user performing the move also becomes the Creator Owner.

Using Shared Folders

Shared folders provide network access to required files across the network. Shared folder permissions apply to folders, not individual files. Keep in mind that shared folder permissions are only in force across the network and not at the local node where the folder is stored. The default shared folder permission is Full Control assigned to the Everyone group when the folder is initially shared. Shared folders should be grouped into Software application and Data folders for easier management.

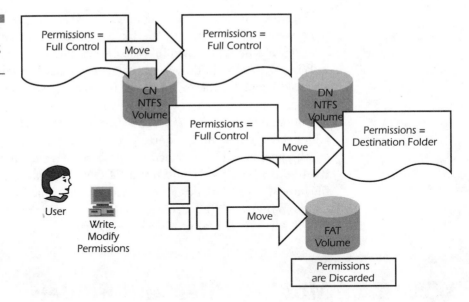

Figure 14.6
Moving files on NTFS partitions.

If a user is a member of multiple groups, the effective permissions for each user are the combination of assigned user and group permissions. The permissions that can be assigned or denied with shared folders are shown in Table 14.6. Deny overrides all other assigned permissions assigned for both users and groups.

TABLE 14.6

Shared folder permissions.

Shared Folder Permission	Allows the User To...
Read	View files and subfolders, view data in files, traverse to subfolders and execute programs
Change	Add files and folders to the shared folder, change data in files and folders, delete, and read
Full Control	Change file permissions, take ownership of files and carry out all tasks granted with the change permission

Application Folders

Application folders are used for software applications installed at a server location. For easier network management, create a software application folder with subfolders for all installed network applications, assigning Full Control at the root folder to the Administrator and removing

Full Control from the Everyone group. Next, assign the Read permission to the Users group that contains all users created by network administration. For support staff who need to support end-users and perform software maintenance and upgrades, grant the Change permission.

Public Data Folders

The public data folder structure should be separate from the application folders used for applications. It is possible to locate the public data folder on a separate volume from the operating system. The Administrator, not the Everyone group should be granted Full Control to the root data folder. The Change permission should be assigned to the Users group, as shown in Figure 14.7, allowing users to read, write, and change files.

Figure 14.7
Assigning permissions to the Users group.

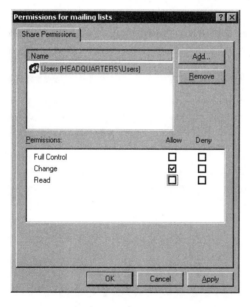

Working Data Folders

Working data folders are data files related to a specific group or software application. The Administrator, not the Everyone group, should be granted Full Control to the root data folder. Subfolders should then be assigned the Change permission for the groups of users who need to access the specific data.

Combining Shared Folder and NTFS Permissions

When shared folder permissions and local NTFS permissions are combined, the more restrictive permission is applied. This is a huge concept to grasp. Assigning local NTFS permissions is only half the battle, since the folder must be shared in order to be available across the network to your users. Sharing of folders can be performed at two network locations; the most common is user access to a network share created on a share; the least common is users accessing their files from their own workstations.

Assigning Full Control to the Everyone group when a share is first created might seem excessive until you remember how local NTFS and share permissions work together.

Even with the Everyone group assigned full control to a network share, the users' effective permissions (created by their user permissions and group permissions assigned) will almost always be more restrictive than Full Control. Therefore the Everyone group does not pose a problem. However, it is still a better procedure to remove Full Control from the Everyone group and assign the Change permission to the User group, since these are the users you have created. At the local level, the Everyone group is not assigned Full Control to a local folder.

Each user must have NTFS permissions for the files and folders plus shared folder permissions.

NOTE

Publishing Resources in Active Directory

With the use of the Active Directory Users and Computers console (ADUC), as shown in Figure 14.8, resources can be published in Active Directory. Resources that can be published in the Directory include users, computers, printers, folders, files, and network services. Any resource published in the Directory should be required by a majority of users across the forest; if users requiring a network resource are local to

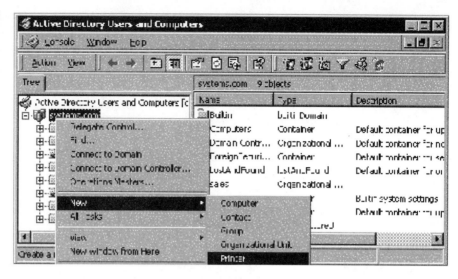

Figure 14.8
Using ADUC to publish AD resources.

the domain, then the sharing of the printer, files, or folders should be carried out using the Explorer shell.

Users and Computers

When a user joins a domain, the user account for the user must first be created; however the computer workstation will be automatically added to the Computers container.

Folders and Files

Publishing a shared folder or files in the directory is accomplished using the ADUC console. Select the organizational unit or domain where the folder is to be published; from the Action menu select New and Shared Folder. Enter the name and the UNC network path to the shared folder.

Printers

When a printer is installed on a Windows 2000 server, the choice can be made to publish the printer in the Directory. The choice to publish Windows 2000 printers in the Directory can be controlled through the printer Properties, by selecting the Sharing tab. NT 4.0 printers can also be published in the Directory using ADUC.

Every printer need not be published in the Directory. If your network consists of several domains, it may not be logistically relevant or necessary for a user in Europe to attempt to print to a color printer in North America.

Network Services

The network services published in the Directory depend on your user status and the network design. Corporate servers are an example of a network service that can be published in the Directory using Active Directory Sites and Services.

NOTE

An Administrator may also decide to store DNS, WINS, and DHCP settings in the Directory; in effect they are published for the existing Domain Controllers. Universal and global groups also use the Directory for storing certain user information. In the near future, Exchange 2000 will take advantage of distribution groups and other required, services such as IIS and NNTP (Network News Transport Protocol).

Using the Distributed File System (DFS)

DFS for Windows 2000 Server provides a new way of managing shared files across a network hierarchy, as shown in Figure 14.9. Files can be automatically replicated and distributed across multiple servers, yet appear to the end-user to be located in one location. The user attached to a DFS shared folder does not have to know the physical location or the name of the server where the share is located as a shared DFS folder through an Active Directory search. The links of the DFS root point to shared folders that can reside on different computers. Domain DFS roots and a standalone DFS root can both be used; however standalone is not a fault-tolerant option, since the shared files are stored on a single computer and replication is not supported.

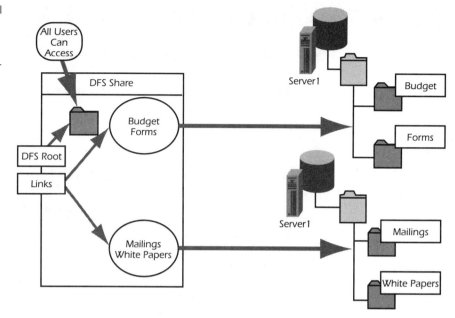

Figure 14.9
DFS shares help
manage shared files.

DFS Provides Transparent Access to Resources

DFS uses a hierarchy of server shares called DFS shares. In order to create a DFS share, a container called a DFS root is first created, containing files and optional links that point to other shared folders. The optional links point to folders that can each be physically located on different servers. The links can also point to multiple identical shared folders; this provides a level of fault tolerance the Explorer shell shared folder can't duplicate.

Windows NT 4.0 and Windows 98 both include a DFS client; Windows 95 clients can download the DFS client for Windows 95 from Microsoft.

Using DFS shares, a user does not need to know the actual location of the shared folders, and the drive letter is not used to reference the folders, just the folder link. This is a first step away from referencing files through drive letters. The permissions required to access a shared folder through DFS are no different from the basic folder access. The server the DFS root inhabits is called a host server. When roots on other servers in the domain are created, the shared files hosted by DFS can be replicated automatically. The DFS topology is automatically published in Active Directory; once there are multiple DFS roots created on multiple servers, the DFS topology is synchronized through the Directory.

Deploying DFS

The basic tasks required to set up DFS are:

1. Create a DFS root, as shown in Figure 14.10.
2. Establish a DFS link.
3. Opt to include DFS shared folders.
4. Set the replication policy.

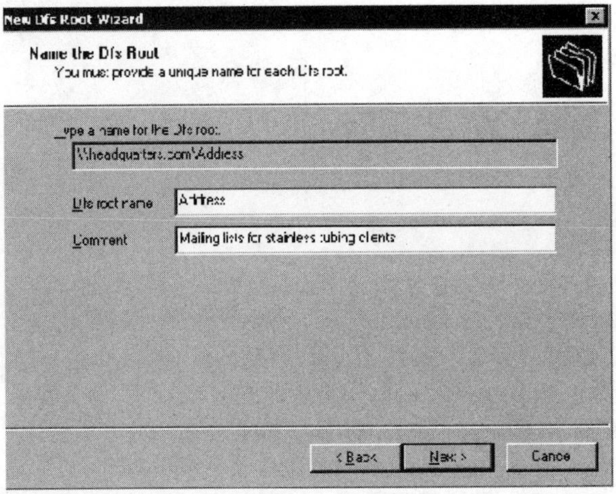

Figure 14.10
Create the DFS root.

Creating the DFS Root

The DFS root can be created on both FAT and NTFS partitions and on a standalone DFS root or at the Domain level for fault tolerance.

From Administrative tools, select the Distributed File System to launch the DFS Root wizard. It will prompt you for the DFS root type, host domain, host server, and the DFS root share.

Creating a DFS Link

Once the DFS root has been created, links can be created up to a current maximum of 1,000. Open the distributed file system and highlight the DFS root where the DFS link is to be attached; from the Action menu select New DFS Link.

In the Create a New DFS link splash screen, enter the link name that identifies the link to the end-users, the shared folder location, and the time each client will cache the link information; the default is 1,800 seconds (30 minutes).

Adding DFS Shared Folders

For each DFS link, a set of DFS shared folders that the link points to can be added. The first folder to be added to the set uses the Distributed File System console selecting Create a New DFS link.

The next folder is added to the set by your selecting "Create a New Replica." The maximum number of DFS shared folders supported in a set is 32.

Once you create a set, replication should be defined. In the Add a New replica splash screen, select Automatic replication to allow the files stored in the DFS set to participate in replication. Only Windows 2000 servers using NTFS version 5 can participate in the automatic replication process.

Setting the Replication Policy

The contents of DFS roots and DFS shared folders can take part in the replication process. Replication copies the contents of the DFS root or share to the linked DFS share folder or folders, depending on the number of defined DFS roots or defined DFS shared folder sets.

Selecting automatic replication, the file replication service (FRS) works in the background performing updates across any folders that have been selected for replication. The default for replication is 15 minutes.

When replication policy is defined, one of the DFS shared folders is defined as the initial master; it then replicates any changes to the other DFS shared folders in the defined set. Replication policy is defined using the Distribution File System console. Selecting the DFS shared folder to define replication, select Replication Policy from the context menu. After you define the master using the Set Master button, each of the other shared folders in the set must be added to the replication chain by highlighting each folder and clicking the **Enable** button.

Controlling Access to Active Directory Objects

Object-based security is also used by Windows 2000 for implementing access controls for all directory objects in the Directory. Each Active Directory object has a binary value called a security descriptor that defines who has the permission to gain access to the object and what type of access is allowed. Permissions are held in access control lists (ACLs) inside the security descriptor, as shown in Figure 14.11. The SACL (system-audit access control list) defines the permission events that will generate audit messages. The DACL (discretionary access control list) classifies the permissions that users or groups have to the object.

Figure 14.11
ACL details for AD objects.

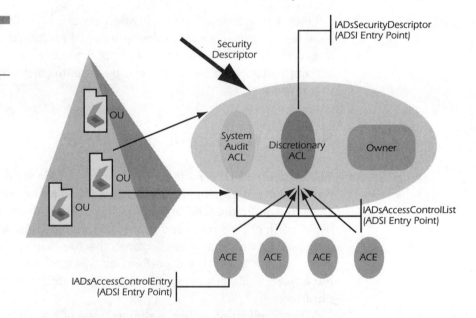

Both the SACL and DACL can contain numerous access control entries (ACEs) that match the audit and/or permission entries.

Across Active Directory, permissions provide security for the published network resources, allowing controlled access to the individual objects or the object attributes. The Administrator or the owner of an object must assign permission to an object before a network user can gain access. The authenticated user will normally have Read access to most objects, though there may be situations where even Read access to certain objects maybe not acceptable. The need for object control may be more pronounced when there are several or many Administrators performing support. In this situation, you would want to limit access to many objects. A partial listing of the objects available for a Windows 2000 Domain Controller is shown in Figure 14.12.

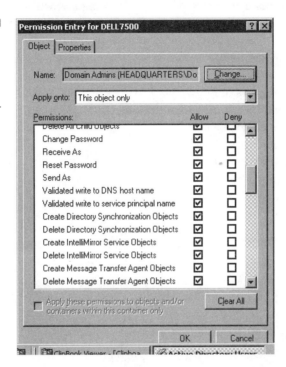

Figure 14.12
Objects and properties are advanced permissions.

Access Control Lists

Access control lists can apply to the entire object or to the individual properties of the object. Therefore, the administrator can control the users who can see an object, and what properties of the object users can see. The type of object will determine which permissions you can select; for example, you can assign the Reset Password to a user but not to a printer object.

Active Directory does not assign full object permissions to the Everyone group, as NTFS shares and folders does. Instead, the Everyone group is used to assign limited global object permissions; for example, for all created User objects the Everyone group is only assigned the permission to Change Password. Since this is a task assigned to the enduser, this permission, by default, is globally assigned to the Everyone group, and therefore to all users.

The Everyone group is also used for printing objects; the global default is Print and Read Permissions, and Auditing objects. A partial listing of objects that can be defined using ADUC is found below; there are hundreds of objects defined by Microsoft that are not yet deployed. Over the next few years, as Exchange 2000 and other Active Directory applications are released, these other objects will become more commonly deployed.

- This object only
- This object and all child objects
- Child objects only
- ADC Connection Agreement objects
- ADC Service objects
- Administrative Group objects
- Computer Policy objects
- Directory Replication Connector objects
- Exchange Container objects
- GroupPolicyContainer objects
- IntelliMirror Group objects
- Organizational Unit Objects
- Printer Objects (if shared through AD)
- User Objects
- Shared Folder objects (if shared through AD)
- Site objects
- Trusted Domain objects

NOTE

Permissions used in securing Active Directory objects are assigned differently when they are applied directly to folders and files. NTFS permissions for files and folders shared on a Domain Controller using the Explorer shell still use the Everyone group, assigning Full Control to the share and to the local folder by default.

Using ADUC to Manage Permissions

If ADUC is used to review and manage permissions, the Security tab is not initially shown until you select the View button and select Advanced Features, as shown in Figure 14.13. When you select any object's properties in the details or value pane of ADUC, the current security can be viewed. The highlighted user or groups permissions are shown in the Permissions section. The Security tab displays the complete list of Users and Groups that have some defined level of permission for the selected object. This first level of permissions is called the *standard level*. The Advanced button is where *special permissions* can be set in much greater detail.

Figure 14.13
Showing Advanced
features.

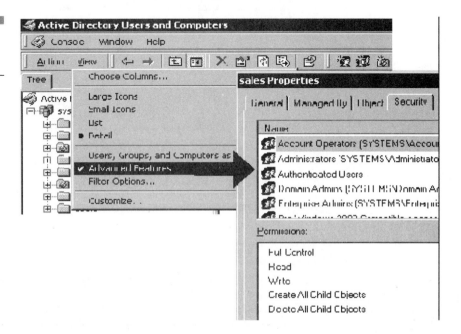

Standard and Special Object Permissions

Both standard and special permissions can be set on all objects. Standard permissions are groupings of special permissions.

Reviewing special permissions shows all permissions for complete granular access control. Standard permissions are usually adequate for sharing folders and printers but may not be enough for defining member servers and organizational units. The standard Write permission is made up of the individual special permissions Write All Properties, Add/Remove Self as Member, and Read. The standard object permissions available for assignment to most objects, for example an OU, are listed in Table 14.7.

Figure 14.14
Object permissions
for all objects.

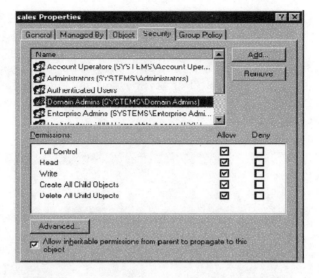

Table 14.7
Standard object
permissions.

Object Permission	Allows the User
Full Control	Full control plus change permissions and take ownership
Read	List Contents, Read All Properties, and Read Permissions
Write	Change the objects attributes
Create all child objects	Add any type of child object to an OU
Delete all child objects	Remove any type of child object to an OU

Depending on the type of specific object created, the available permissions that can be assigned can be more or fewer than the listing in Table 14.7. For example, the default standard permissions that can be assigned to a shared folder in Active Directory are Full Control, Read, and Write.

For a printer, the default standard permissions that can be assigned are Print, Manage Printers, and Manage Documents. Printers are also published in AD, but not through ADUC; instead the Sharing tab on an installed printers property sheets allows you to list the printer in the directory. Keep in mind that object permissions set through Active Directory are for the delegation of administrative tasks.

Inheritable Object Permissions

By default, access control entries (ACEs) are propagated from the parent object ACL to a child object ACL, as shown in Figure 14.15. Inheritable ACLs are propagated when a new child object is created. ACEs are also propagated from the parent to the child object when the DACL or the SACL on the parent object is modified. Unchecking the inheritance checkbox allows you to remove the flow of permissions from one object to another. The three options available after the checkbox is cleared are:

- **Copy**—Copies the previously inherited permissions to the object.
- **Remove**—Removes all inherited permissions, keeping only permissions that were explicitly specified on the object.
- **Cancel**—Stops and rechecks the inheritance checkbox.

Figure 14.15
Permissions are
inherited by default.

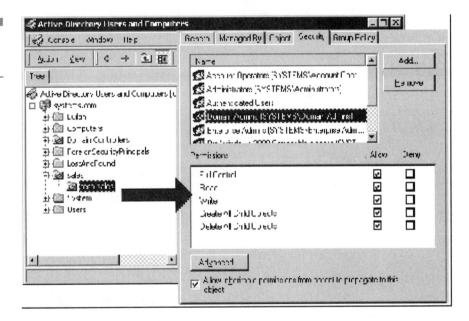

NOTE

The checkbox "Allow inheritable permissions from parent to propagate to this object" is usually an available option depending on where the object is created in the Active Directory tree. However, the Security tab of a domain does not show this option, since we are at the top of the domain tree.

Assigning Special Permissions

Inherited permissions are shown in Figure 14.16, to indicate inheritance.

- The Add button allows you to add a user or group to the current grouping of users and groups that have permissions on this object.
- View/Edit allows you to edit any existing permissions shown and also permits access to permissions that can be set on the object and the properties of the object.

Figure 14.16
Special permissions.

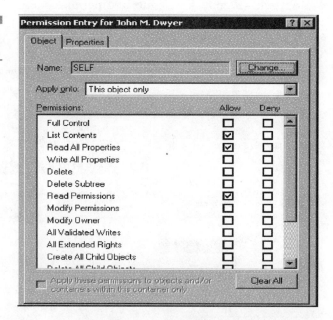

Object and Property Permission Entries

Permissions can be managed for Active Directory objects at the object or property level, as shown in Figure 14.17. Permissions allowed or denied at the object level apply to the entire object; however permissions allowed or denied at the property level apply only to the specific properties. Note that while the permissions that are inherited cannot be unchecked or changed in the Allow column of the child object, Deny can still be applied to an Allow permission.

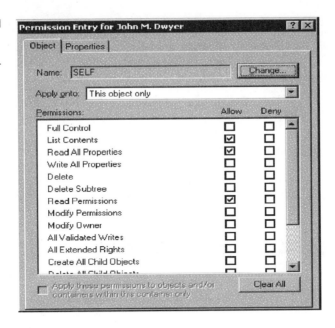

Figure 14.17
User permissions.

Object and Attribute Types

The Objects and Properties tab does not show all available options for an object. The list for filtered object types and properties is stored in %system root% \SYSTEM32\DSSEC.DAT, as shown in Figure 14.18. Adding or removing items from the list can modify the filter. If the object type shown in square brackets is followed by @=7 [container], for example, as shown in Figure 14.18, then the object type is filtered. If the object class is filtered by the attribute in the object class, for example, canonical name=7, changing 7 to 0 stops the filtering, as well as the showing of the attribute when the object's special permissions are again viewed.

Delegating Administrative Control

Windows 2000 includes a utility called the Delegation of Control wizard. It allows Administrators to delegate management of five predefined types of objects to single users or groups at the container level, as shown in Figure 14.19. Table 14.8 lists the choices allowed by the delegation of Control wizard.

Figure 14.18
Filtered object types.

Figure 14.19
Objects available to
single users or
groups at the
container level.

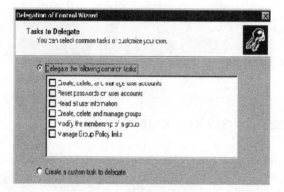

TABLE 14.8

Choices allowed by
the delegation of
the Control wizard.

Using the DOC Wizard	You can delegate these tasks
At the site level	Manage group policy links
At the domain level	Join a computer to a domain
Manage group policy links	
At the OU level	Create, delete, and manage user accounts
	Reset passwords on user accounts
	Read all user information
	Create, delete, and manage groups
	Modify the membership of a group
	Manage group policy links

Although the DOC wizard is handy for assigning permissions at the container level, it cannot be used for denying specific permissions or removing control previously delegated with the DOC.

Auditing

The process of monitoring user and operating system activities is called auditing and is shown in Figure 14.20. Auditing results are called events, which are written to the security log in the Event Viewer on all Windows 2000 nodes.

Figure 14.20
The Event Viewer is used to view auditing.

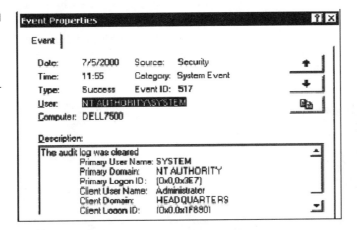

An audit entry contains three key pieces of information:

- The action that was executed.
- The user that carried out the action.
- The success or failure of the event and when it occurred.

By defining an audit policy you can define what events are logged to the security log on every NT and Windows 2000 computer. All client activity on a Windows 2000 domain controller can be logged, regardless of the age of the Windows client. The success and failure of domain logons, file access, and security access can all be monitored through an audit policy. Auditing is turned off by default.

Defining an Audit Policy

System trends can be tracked over time through archiving event logs for analysis. Security logs should be reviewed as part of daily or weekly maintenance. Audit only what you can reasonably review and manage. Audit resource access using the Everyone group: the access may be from a system process rather than a user and the Everyone group contains everything. Audit administrative activity using the Administrative group.

For domain controllers, the definition of the audit policy is enabled through the group policy object for the domain. For a local computer, a local group policy for that particular node is configured. The user right Manage Auditing and Security Log must be granted to the user or group of users on the computer node where auditing is to be set up and reviewed. The Administrator group is assigned this right by default. Files and folders you wish to audit must be on an NTFS volume; FAT volumes are not supported.

NOTE

User rights are not permissions; they are defined by using the administrative tool ADUC, selecting the domain controller, and editing the GPO for that domain controller.

Events Audited by Windows 2000

Success, failure, or both of these options define each category of audited events in Windows 2000, as shown in Figure 14.21. Audit policy is defined by editing the group policy object for the site, domain, organizational unit, member server, or standalone workstation. Table 14.9 details the event categories Windows 2000 can audit.

TABLE 14.9

Windows 2000 event audit categories.

Event Category	Details (Success/Failure)
Account logon	User account validation request
Account management	User or group account, or a password was modified, created, changed, or deleted
Directory service access	An Active Directory object was accessed
Logon events	Logon or logoff details

continued on next page

TABLE 14.9

Windows 2000 event audit categories (continued).

Event Category	Details (Success/Failure)
Object access	Access to a file, folder, or printer
Policy change	Changes to user security, user rights, or audit policy
Privilege use	A user performed a defined right while logged onto the network
Process tracking	A software application or service performed an action
System events	Computer and network services details

Figure 14.21
Group policy defines audit policy.

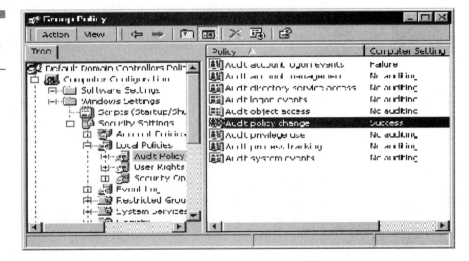

File and Folder Auditing

File and folder auditing is defined through the Explorer shell. Select the file or folder; select Advanced to define the audit options available. Select either success or failure, or both, to define the events to audit. Table 14.10 details the audit options for files and folders.

TABLE 14.10 Audit options for files and folders.		
Transverse Folder/Execute File	Moving through folders even when access has not been granted; executing file when permissions have not been granted
List Folder/Read Data	Reading files and folders in the folder or reading data in files
Read Attributes/Read Extended Attributes	Reading the attributes of a file or folder
Create Files/Write Data	Creating files in a folder or changing contents of a file
Create Folders/Append Data	Creating folders within a folder; appending data to a file
Write Attributes/Write Extended Attributes	Changing the attributes of a file or a folder
Delete Subfolders and Files	Deleting a file or subfolder
Delete	Deleting a file or folder
Read Permissions	Reading file or folder permissions
Change Permissions	Changing file or folder permissions
Take Ownership	Taking ownership of a file or folder

Auditing Active Directory Objects

To enable auditing of Active Directory objects, the Audit Directory Service Access must be set. Using ADUC, select the properties of any object and select the Security tab. Click the Advanced button and select the Auditing tab. Choose View/Edit to define the audit for the Everyone group or New to define a user or group to audit.

Select success, failure, or both options for the audit policy.

Auditing Printer Access

To audit printers, Audit Object Access must be set in the audit policy. Auditing is then defined through each printer's properties, selecting the Auditing tab, as shown in Figure 14.23.

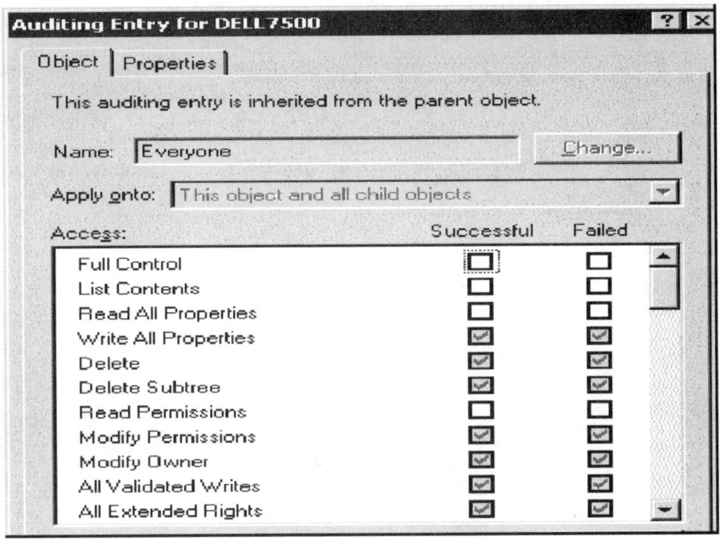

Figure 14.22
Setting audit options.

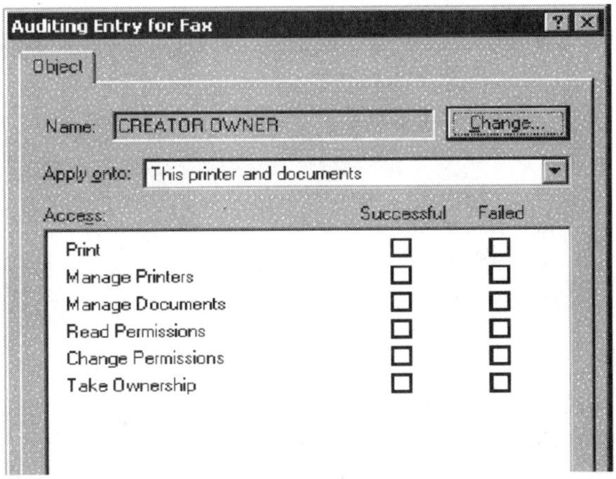

Figure 14.23
Access choices for auditing.

Remote OS Installation

Automated installation of Windows 2000 Professional can be deployed on remote boot-enabled clients from an Remote Installation Service (RIS) servers, as shown in Figure 14.24. RIS supports clients with no operating system installed or whose current OS is damaged.

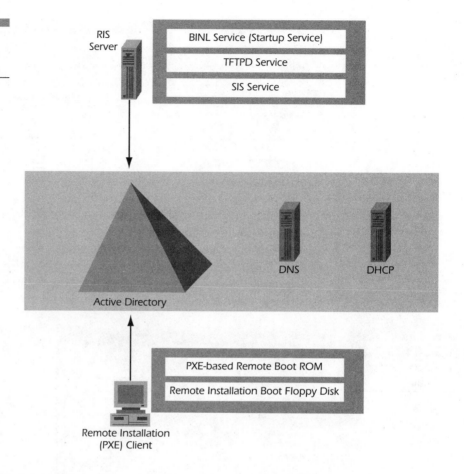

Figure 14.24
RIS components for Windows 2000.

NOTE

RIS cannot currently be used to upgrade any Windows-based OS; for these cases, SMS, SysPrep.EXE, or a bootable CD can be used. RIS requires several essential hardware and software components to operate.

Boot Information Negotiation Layer (BINL)

The Boot Information Negotiation Layer (BINL) service listens for and answers to DHCP (PXE) and Client Installation wizard requests. BINL also communicates with Active Directory to confirm credentials.

Trivial File Transfer Protocol Daemon (TFTPD)

The RIS server uses TFTP to download the initial files needed to begin the remote installation process to the client. The first file downloaded to the client is Startrom.com, and exhibits the prompt "Press F12 for Network Service Boot". After F12 is pressed, the Client Installation wizard is downloaded to start the remote installation process.

Single Instance Store (SIS)

SIS is the service that manages the file space required by RIS, also removing file duplicates on the RIS volume.

Remote Install Server Software Components

Remote Installation Service (RIS)

RIS is an optional Windows 2000 server software component providing remote installation of Windows 2000 Professional.

Domain Name Service (DNS)

RIS servers depend on DNS for locating AD services and domain controllers.

Dynamic Host Configuration Protocol (DHCP)

RIS requires a DHCP server to be available, since the RIS client receives its IP address from DHCP before communicating with the RIS server.

Active Directory

The RIS service must be installed on either a Windows 2000 member server or a Windows 2000 domain controller. Active Directory is utilized to locate needed network services and any existing RIS clients.

RIS Server and Client Requirements

Windows 2000 Remote OS Installation requires the following server hardware:

- Pentium or Pentium II 200 megahertz (MHz) or faster processor (Pentium 166 MHz minimum).
- 96–128 megabytes (MB) of RAM, needed when services such as Active Directory, DHCP, and DNS are installed.

- 2 GB disk space for the Remote Installation Services server's folders.
- 10 MB network adapter (100 MB recommended).
- CD-ROM drive (or access to a network share) containing Windows 2000 Professional.

The drive from which RIS will operate must be formatted with NTFS. In addition, RIS cannot be installed on the same hard drive as the system volume. DFS shares are also not supported.

Windows 2000 Remote OS Installation requires the following client hardware:

- Pentium 166 MHz or faster processor, Net PC PXE-based remote boot-enabled client.
- 32 MB of RAM minimum (64 MB recommended).
- 800 MB or larger disk drive.
- DHCP PXE-based boot ROM version .99c or later or a network adapter supported by the RIS boot floppy disk.

There is a limited list of manufacturers who support the PXE-ROM code. Therefore a RIS client boot floppy can be created that connects to the RIS server through a PCI Ethernet adapter. To review the list of supported adapters, execute RBFG.EXE located after installing the RIS service in \\RISservername\Reminst\Admin\i386 folder.

Installing RIS

To add the RIS service to the desired server, use the Control Panel applet Add/Remove Components to install the Remote Installation Services, as shown in Figure 14.25. Once the RIS components have been installed from the server CD, you will need to reboot your computer.

From the Administrative Tools menu, when you click on the Configure Your Server option and select "Finish Setup", the RIS wizard will prompt you through the remaining installation options.

Two RIS components will be installed to allow you to configure and implement RIS:

- **Remote Installation Preparation Wizard**—RIPrep allows you to create a customized image of Windows 2000 Professional.
- **Client Installation Wizard**—OSChooser is the client-side wizard downloaded to the RIS client to guide the installation procedure.

Figure 14.25
RIS requires DHCP
and DNS.

Authorizing RIS Servers

A RIS server must first be authorized through the DHCP service before
servicing clients can proceed, as shown in Figure 14.26. Open the DHCP
console and highlight the DHCP server that will attend to RIS client
requests. From the Action menu, select Manage Authorized Servers and
select Authorize. Type the name or IP address of the RIS server to be
authorized and click **OK**; close all dialog boxes.

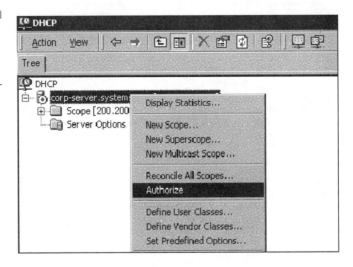

Figure 14.26
RIS servers must be
authorized through
DHCP.

Setting RIS Server Properties

From the Administrative Tool ADUC, select the RIS server's properties, as shown in Figure 14.27. Select the Remote Install Tab and choose from the two available options:

- Respond to Client Computers Requesting Service
- Do not respond to Unknown Client Computers

Figure 14.27
RIS configuration is set through Active Directory Users and Computers console.

From the Advanced Settings button there are three tabs to configure:

- **New client**—Define the computer naming format and the AD location for the client computer account.
- **Images**—Windows 2000 Client Images available for installation.
- **Tools**—Remote administrative tools for managing Windows 2000 servers.

Creating an RIPrep Image

From the client workstation, run the RIPrep utility from the RIS server, as shown in Figure 14.28. The Remote Installation Preparation wizard will step you through the prompts, including:

- **Server Name**—The RIS server where the image will be copied
- **Folder Name**—The name of the folder on the RIS server where the image will be copied
- **Friendly Description and Help Text**—Descriptors of the OS image.

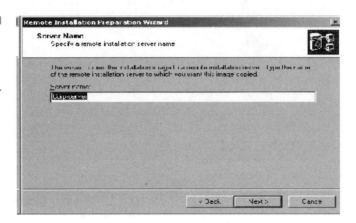

All unique Registry settings, SIDs, computer name, and any unique characteristics are removed before the image is created.

RIP supports Windows 2000 Professional installed to Drive C: only. The size of the RIS server's hard drive will be used as the default image size; if the RIS server partition is 2 GB, then the image will be 2 GB and the hard drive size of a new RIS client must also be 2 GB.

NOTE

If images are created from retail copies of Windows 2000 Professional rather than the OEM copies, then the product identification number must be added to RIPREP.SIF located in \RemoteInstall\Setup\ Images\Image_name\i386\Templates.

Creating a RIS Boot Disher

A boot disk must be created for client computers that do not have a PXE-based remote boot-enabled ROM but have a supported NIC, as shown in Figure 14.29. The Adapter List details the supported network adapters. The RBFG utility creates the RIS boot disk located in the \\RIS_server\RemoteInstall\Admin\i386 folder.

Figure 14.29
Creating a RIS boot
disk.

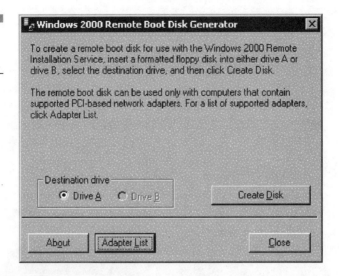

Figure 14.29
Creating a RIS boot
disk.

Prestaging RIS Client Computers

Prestaging is the process of predefining a computer account that is authorized to use an RIS server to install Windows 2000 Professional. The computer's GUID is used as the unique identification number, as shown in Figure 14.30.

When the RIS client first boots, the GUID will be checked to make sure the client has been preauthorized, as shown in Figure 14.30.

Figure 14.30
The GUID uniquely
identifies the
computer that can
use RIS.

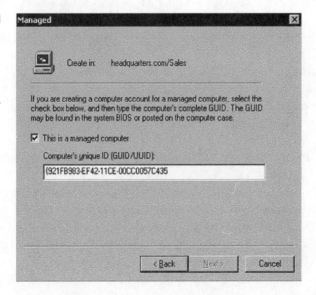

The Remote OS Installation Process

The RIS client boots using a boot disk or boot PROM and attempts to connect to the network by sending a network service request for an client IP address and the IP address of the nearest RIS server.

1. The RIS server checks in Active Directory for a prestaged client computer account that matches, using the client's GUID, a key component of the PC98/Net PC specifications.
2. The Client Installation wizard is then downloaded to the client, prompting the user to log onto the network.
3. Once logon is successful, the RIS server checks to see what group policy settings and OS image the client is to be offered.
4. If there is only one option, the installation is automatic; if the user is allowed a choice, then choices will be displayed.
5. Once the user accepts the installation settings, the selected OS installs as an unattended installation.

Troubleshooting Active Directory

This section provides an introduction to troubleshooting, covering topics including:

- Troubleshooting DNS, Domains and Connectivity
- Changing FSMO operation with NtdsUtil
- Troubleshooting replication
- Monitoring with performance monitor
- Using log files

Why Has My Network Stopped Working?

Windows 2000 with Active Directory is the sum of many parts that have to work together precisely, or failures can start to take their toll. When Active Directory begins to fail, most of the time the failures occur in small steps that are not very noticeable. There are three main areas that must be diagnosed and analyzed when troubleshooting an Active Directory network: name resolution, network connectivity, and domain controllers.

Name Resolution

If computers or network resources cannot be queried, it is possible that DNS names are not being resolved to IP addresses. Several TCP/IP commands can be used to test the status of DNS, including the Event Log, Ping, Nslookup, and NetDiag. When a Windows 2000 domain controller is first started, it registers its DNS domain name with the DNS service plus additional domain controller SRV records, including A records and/or CNAME records. These records allow servers to be located by the service they provide (for example LDAP), and the supported protocols (for example TCP and UDP). Both these types of records should be checked where the DNS server is installed using the DNS console after the promotion of a server to an Active Directory domain controller.

Verify name resolution problems by viewing the Event Log by viewing the DNS Server log. The system log can also provide details of any possible problems—a common error logged to the System log is the Net Logon event error 5781, indicating that the domain controller is having problems dynamically updating DNS records for the domain controller.

DNS name resolution must be working successfully to connect to Active Directory. If DNS fails, everything fails, since the network location of network services such as DNS itself, global catalog servers, sites, and domain controllers cannot be located without DNS working properly.

Troubleshooting steps for DNS are:

1. Run Nslookup at the command prompt to see if DNS is working. You should see DNS resolved to a DNS server on the network as shown in Figure 15.1.

Figure 15.1
Nslookup is the reliable tool for checking DNS operation.

2. Check to make sure that the client or server is pointed to the correct DNS server in the local area connection properties of TCP/IP. It is the simplest of errors but that's all it takes to stop Active Directory from functioning.

3. Using the DNS Console as shown in Figure 15.2, clear the DNS server's cache using the context menu; or after checking that the forward and reverse lookup zones are OK, update the server data's files; perhaps some records are corrupted in RAM or at the server.

Figure 15.2
The DNS console can be used to refresh the server's DNS records.

4. Check to make sure that periods are at the end of the FQDN of each and every resource record. This is a problem for NT and Windows 2000 DNS. Sometimes, when forward and reverse lookup zones are created with the wizard, the all-important periods at the end of the fully qualified domain names are left off. The start of authority, name servers, and host records in the forward lookup zone should be checked for proper DNS namespace and periods at the end of the FQDN, as shown in Figure 15.3. In the reverse lookup zones, check all start of authority, name server, and pointer records. Believe it or not, the missing periods can bring a DNS server to its knees.

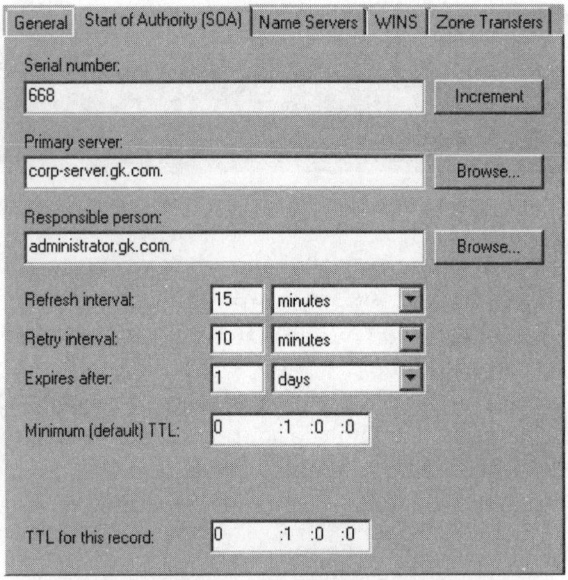

Figure 15.3
The periods at the end of the primary server must be present—sometimes they are missing.

Network Connectivity

If the network infrastructure is broken or hardware and software components fail, Active Directory fails. At the command prompt, type ipconfig /all and check the screen output for the essential components as listed in Figure 15.4.

- What is the current IP address assigned?
- What is the current default gateway?
- What is the current DHCP server?
- What DNS information is known?

Figure 15.4
Network
connectivity: using
Ipconfig.

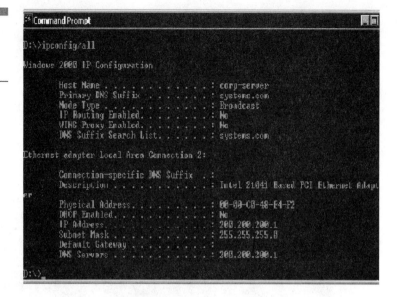

Ipconfig information can also be sent to a text file by using the command ipconfig /all > winnt\ipconfig.txt.

Using Ipconfig with no additional syntax displays the DNS information for the local adapter. As Table 15.1 shows, several options are available.

TABLE 15.1

Ipconfig syntax.

Ipconfig Command Options	Details
ipconfig/ all	Gives full DNS details including the FQDN and DNS search list
ipconfig/ flushdns	Flushes and resets the resolver cache
ipconfig/ displaydns	Displays the contents of the resolver cache
ipconfig/ registerdns	Refreshes all DCHP leases and registers any DNS names
ipconfig/ release	Releases all DHCP leases
ipconfig/ renew	Refreshes all DCHP leases and dynamically updates DNS records

Testing Client Network Connectivity with NetDiag

NetDiag is included on the Windows 2000 Server CD support tools. The NetDiag command-line utility can be used to test the network functionality of all computers, including your clients'. NetDiag examines the current network configuration and connections by reviewing current registry, DLLs, and log settings. The beauty of NetDiag is that no additional syntax is required for a full testing of the local host (see Figure 15.5). NetDiag reports on the options detailed in Table 15.2.

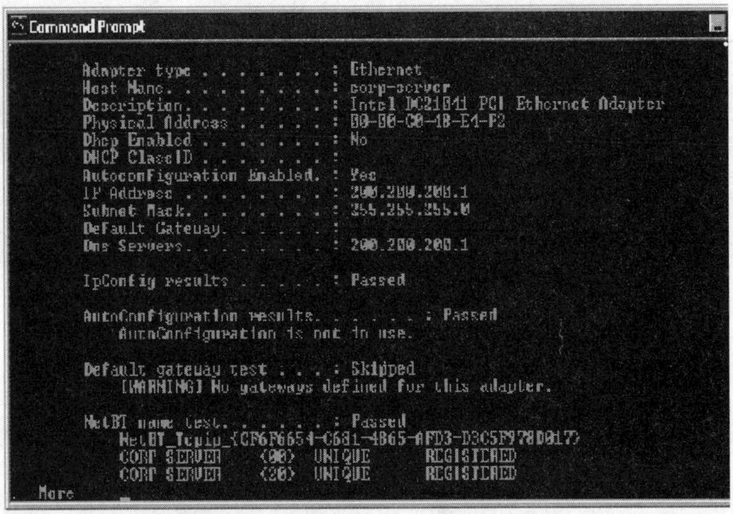

Figure 15.5
NetDiag tests network functionality.

TABLE 15.2

NetDiag test details.

Test Name	Purpose	Details
NDIS	Adapter status	Gives complete network adapter details
IPConfig	IP configuration	Similar to ipconfig /all
Member	Domain membership	Gives primary domain details including computer role, domain, and domain GUID
IPLoopback	IP loopback ping	Pings the IP loopback address 127.0.0.1
DefGw	Default gateway	Pings the default gateway
NbtNm	NetBt name test	Checks that the workstation's service name is equal to the computer name and other stats

continued on next page

TABLE 15.2

NetDiag test
details.

Test Name	Purpose	Details
DNS details	DNS test	Checks the DNS cache and DNS registration
Browser	Redirector and Browser test	Makes sure the workstations service is running and tests the browser and redirector
DsGetDc	DC discovery test	Uses the directory service to find a generic DC, then a PDC, and, and next a Windows 2000 DC
DcList	DC list test	Obtains a list of DCs in the domain from the directory services
Trust	Trust relationship test	Tests trust relationships, SIDs, and secure channels
Kerberos	Kerberos test	Tests Kerberos protocols and displays TGT / session ticket details
LDAP	LDAP test	Tests LDAP searches on all active DCs found in the domain
Route	Routing test	Displays the static and persistent entries in the routing table
NetStat	NetStat test	Displays statistics of protocols and current TCP/IP network connections
Bindings	Bindings test	Displays bindings statistics
IPSec	IP Security Test	Tests whether IP security is enabled and shows active IPSec policies

NOTE

NetDiag can also be executed in /V (for verbose) and /DEBUG modes for additional details.

Troubleshooting Domain Controllers with DcDiag

Another command-line tool useful for revealing the current state of domain controllers within a tree or forest is DcDiag. This scrutinizes the state of the domain controllers in a tree or forest, reporting any problems found. The domain controller can be tested for verifying many software components and services, including replication and connectivity. The syntax for Dcdiag.exe in verbose mode is Dcdiag /S:server /V Dcdiag. Replication tests include:

- Topology integrity
- Inter-site health
- Replication latencies
- Directory partition permissions
- Trust object replication
- File replication service
- Critical services check
- FSMO roles check

Using Ntdsutil for FSMO Maintenance

FSMO roles can be managed and changed with Ntdsutil, the powerhouse command-line utility. When domain controllers become unavailable due to hardware problems, certain FSMO roles may have to be transferred manually. If a server with a defined FSMO role is not available, another server is not automatically promoted to assume the role. The needed FSMO role must be moved to a new server and owner manually. Changes can be made through the GUI and the correct MMC when everything is working, however when failure occurs, safe mode and command prompt, recovery console, or directory services restore mode must be available to transfer the desired role. When the first Windows 2000 domain controller in a forest is created, the five roles are assigned to the first domain controller.

The roles of each DC in a domain should be documented in the network log for disaster recovery.

NOTE

From the administrator's viewpoint:

- The inability to add users may indicate that the RID master has failed.

- The inability to make changes to the schema even with proper permissions may indicate that the schema master has failed.
- The inability to add or remove domains may indicate that the Domain naming master has failed.

From the user's viewpoint:

- On a native-mode network, the loss of the PDC Advertiser would mean that changing passwords on a large network may cause authentication failures until the changes are replicated to all domain controllers.
- In mixed mode, a client not using an Active Directory client installed will not be able to change his/her password.
- Replication between NT 4.0 BDCs will also fail and system events would be posted in the event log.

Viewing FSMO Roles

The FSMO roles can be viewed using the UI or the command-line utility Ntdsutil. Log into your domain as Administrator and start Active Directory Users and Computers from the Administrative Tools menu. From the Action menu select Operations Masters; the three domain FSMO roles are shown, each with their own tab.

The two forest-wide FSMO roles, the schema, and domain-naming master are assigned to a domain controller in the forest. Log onto the forest as Administrator and start Active Directory Domains and Trusts. From the Action menu select Operations Masters to review the domain-naming FSMO role. Use the schema console and select the Operations Masters option to review and change the location of the schema operations masters role.

Using Ntdsutil to Transfer or Seize FSMO Roles

Ntdsutil can be used at the command prompt, in safe mode, or in directory services restore mode to change the FSMO roles as required. In order to transfer or seize the roles, you must be logged on as an Administrator. From Start\Run enter Ntdsutil and press **OK**.

Your prompt should look like **ntdsutil.exe**:

Now type Roles and press **Enter**.

Your prompt should look like **FSMO maintenance**:

Type **?** and press **Enter**. Your prompt should look like the listing below:

```
?                                 —Print this help information
Connections                       —Connect to a specific domain
                                   controller
Help                              —Print this help information
Quit                              —Return to the prior menu
Seize domain naming master        —Overwrite domain role on
                                   connected server
Seize infrastructure master       —Overwrite infrastructure role
                                   on connected server
Seize PDC                         —Overwrite PDC role on connected
                                   server
Seize RID master                  —Overwrite RID role on connected
                                   server
Seize schema master               —Overwrite schema role on
                                   connected server
Select operation target           —Select sites, servers, domains,
                                   roles and Naming Contexts
Transfer domain naming master     —Make connected server the
                                   domain naming master
Transfer infrastructure master    —Make connected server the
                                   infrastructure master
Transfer PDC                      —Make connected server the PDC
Transfer RID master               —Make connected server the RID
                                   master
Transfer schema master            —Make connected server the
                                   schema master
```

In order to transfer an FSMO role, you first have to connect to the domain controller holding that role. Type Connections and press Enter; your prompt should look like: **server connections**:

Type connect to <your server> and press **Enter**;

The message "**Binding to < your-server > ...**" should first appear and then the message:

"**Connected to sales-server using credentials of locally logged on user.**"

You can now change or seize the desired FSMO role(s), assuming you had the proper authority; the syntax is listed below.

Transfer the Schema Master

C:\> ntdsutil
ntdsutil: roles

```
fsmo maintenance: connections
server connections: connect to server <server name>
server connections: quit
fsmo maintenance: transfer schema master
```

Transfer the RID Master

```
C:\> ntdsutil
ntdsutil: roles
fsmo maintenance: connections
server connections: connect to server <server name>
server connections: quit
fsmo maintenance: transfer rid master
```

Transfer the PDC Master

```
C:\> ntdsutil
ntdsutil: roles
fsmo maintenance: connections
server connections: connect to server <server name>
server connections: quit
fsmo maintenance: transfer pdc
```

Transfer the Infrastructure Master

```
C:\> ntdsutil
ntdsutil: roles
fsmo maintenance: connections
server connections: connect to server <server name>
server connections: quit
fsmo maintenance: transfer infrastructure master
```

Transfer Domain Naming Master

```
C:\> ntdsutil
ntdsutil: roles
fsmo maintenance: connections
server connections: connect to server <server name>
server connections: quit
fsmo maintenance: transfer domain naming master
```

Troubleshooting Replication Problems

Replication problems can stop domain controllers from receiving directory updates. These problems can be within a domain, within a site, or across sites. The event viewer can provide an amazing amount of detail for tracking how replication is performing at any given time; however, the default setting for the event logs does not show much detail. The reasoning behind this is influenced by the extra bandwidth required, depending on the choices checked. To properly troubleshoot replication, you first must get used to the cryptic messages, then it becomes quite readable. We'll proceed to the section on the Event Viewer and then the details on how to produce a lot of detail in the event logs.

Using the Event Viewer

As you know, the event viewer categorizes and stores error codes identifying potential problems, to assist with troubleshooting and analysis. Event Viewer event logs are sometimes dismissed as a utility that doesn't provide enough readable information to be useful; that criticism can be true. However, Windows 2000 has greatly increased the amount of default system reporting that ends up in any event log. As services and network components carry out their tasks across the Windows 2000 network, informational messages are also stored in the system log folder as a network audit trail. Information is stored as Informational, Warning, and Errors, as shown in Figure 15.6, although it could be argued that many informational messages deposited into an event log are errors. For example, when a domain controller is also made a global catalog server, an information message will be generated and sent to the Directory Service log. It may be successful, or it may say that an attempt was made to add global catalog duties to the domain controller but it couldn't right away—both of these messages are considered information, and the second message is an error. Another example, detailed in Figure 15.7, shows that replication has failed for 124 successive attempts, or 15,053 minutes, yet it is still rated as only information. Is it an error, or is the server in question down for major maintenance?

Figure 15.6
The event viewer
should be reviewed
every day.

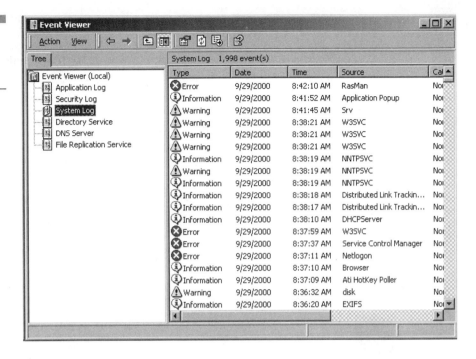

Figure 15.7
Information message
may in fact be errors.

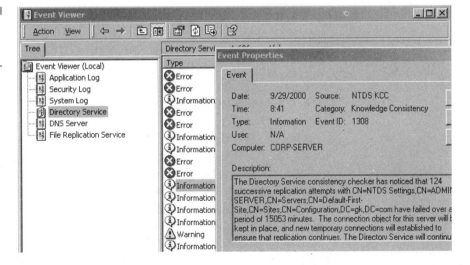

*The point is that you must check the event logs regularly in order to keep
on top of your active directory network.*

NOTE

What Do the Event Logs Monitor?

- **Applications**—Includes warnings, errors, and information provided by installed applications.
- **Security**—Includes information about the success or failure of audited events set through an audit.
- **Directory Service**—Includes warnings, errors, and information generated by Active Directory as it executes.
- **File Replication Service**—Includes warnings, errors, and information generated by the file replication service.
- **System**—Includes warnings, errors, and information generated by the Windows 2000 operating system.
- **DNS**—The DNS log is added to the event viewer when the DNS is installed.

NOTE

If an error code is supplied, use the net helpmsg command to view further details of the error code.

Changing the Amount of Detail Sent to the Event Viewer

By default, the Event Viewer doesn't use great detail to track and report on how Windows 2000 and Active Directory are operating. This may be a surprise to you. However, using the Registry, we can choose the amount of reporting detail reported to the event logs. This will create more work for the local domain controller, but if you are trying to trace replication details, KCC operation, and update sequence numbers successfully, then the detail is needed. Here's how to wake up the Event Log.

Open Regedt32 and navigate to HKEY_LOCAL_MACHINE\ SYSTEM\CurrentControlSet\Services\NTDS\Diagnostics.

Double-click the following DWORD values, shown in Figure 15.8, and change the value from 0 to 5, depending on what detail you require.

The value of the entry specifies the level of detail of the events logged to the event log: 0 is the default setting and 5 is the highest setting, where all activity and detail is recorded. The value of each DWORD is provided in Table 15.3.

Figure 15.8

Using Regedt32, we can set the amount of detail sent to the Event Viewer logs.

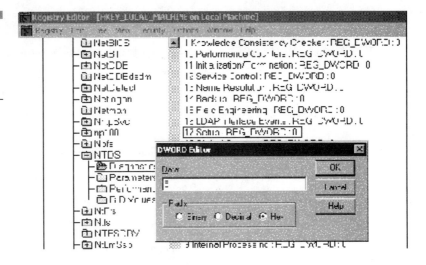

TABLE 15.3

DWORD values.

DWORD Option	Detail
0 None (default)	Only critical events and error events are logged
1 Minimal	All major tasks performed by a service are logged
2 Basic	Events with a logging level of 2 are logged
3 Extensive	Events with a logging level of 3 are logged; each step taken to run a task is logged
4 Verbose	Events with a logging level of 4 are logged
5 Internal	All events are logged

The default logging level of 0 should be left at 0 unless a problem needs to be solved. Setting the Directory Services log file properties to overwrite events as needed is recommended until log size can be determined. Table 15.4 details the registry values you can change, with the amount reporting detail reported.

The registry key HKEY_LOCAL_MACHINE\SYSTEM\Current ControlSet\Services\NTDS\Parameters has many valuable entries for determining what server roles are current on the local host.

NOTE

TABLE 15.4

Registry values.

Registry Value	Event(s) created from
Knowledge Consistency Checker KCC	Sites, site links, and server errors
Security Events	Accessing objects or attributes without sufficient rights
ExDS Interface Events	Communication between AD and Exchange clients
Replication Events	Outbound replication details about what objects and attributes are replicated and why
Garbage Collection	When objects marked for deletion are actually deleted
Internal Configuration	Directory Service operation details
Directory Access	Reading and writing to directory objects from all sources
Internal Processing	From AD processing for Microsoft troubleshooting
Performance Counters	NTDS performance counter details
Initialization/Termination	Starting and stopping AD
Service Control	AD service events
Name Resolution	Resolution of addresses and Active Directory names
Backup	Backup of AD
LDAP Interface Events	LDAP processing
Setup	Using the AD Installation wizard
Global Catalog	Global catalog details
Inter-site messaging	The ISM service replication messages and site routes for the KCC

Using the Windows 2000 Support Tools

On the Windows 2000 Server CD are some powerful support tools you should not be without. Why they are not on the Administrators Tools menu is a mystery to me. The path to locate the tools is \I386\ SUPPORT\TOOLS\2000RKST.MSI. Once installed, they will be on the Programs menu under Windows 2000 Support Tools. The one tool you should definitely know about is the Active Directory Replication Monitor.

Using the AD Replication Monitor

This tool can tell you almost anything you want to know about in-site replication. After launching the ADRM and right-clicking the Monitored Server Icon, you can add your server; it then displays the naming contexts your server is hosting, as shown in Figure 15.9, as well as a wealth of other goodies.

Figure 15.9
The replication monitor details every nuance of replication within a site.

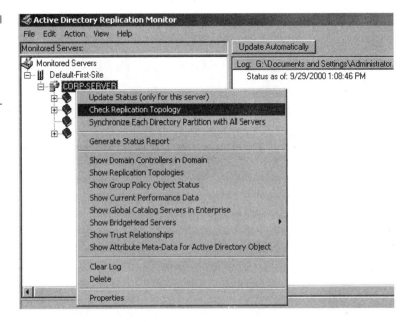

Right-click on your server icon and selecting its properties; you can check many aspects of your server's current replication and replication partners. From your server's properties:

1. Select the FSMO Roles tab to display the current FSMO role owners in your forest
2. Query each role owner to verify proper that the ADRM can resolve, connect, and bind.

Now, selecting your server, right-click, and from the Context menu:

1. Check Replication Topology to trigger the KCC; now check the event log.
2. Generate a Status Report; save the file as rep.log and review.
3. Show Domain Controllers in Domain.

4. Show Replication Topologies. From the dropdown View menu, select Connections Objects Only. Right-click on each server shown and select Show Intra-Site Connections. Review the current replication architecture in your domain and site. There should be connections shown for your replication partners within the domain and for replication within the site.

5. Show global catalog servers in Enterprise.

6. Show trust relationships.

Using Resource Kit Utilities for Troubleshooting

These tools are part of the Windows 2000 Resource Kit and are useful for troubleshooting Active Directory.

- **ADDIAG.EXE**—Software installation diagnostics utility providing user and system status through Active Directory
- **DELPROF.EXE**—Deletes user profiles either locally or remotely
- **ENUMPROP**—Displays Properties on any AD object
- **GPOTOOL**—Validates the health of GPO objects
- **GPRESULT.EXE**—Lists all the GPOs applied to a specific computer and user and also when they were last refreshed
- **KERBTRAY.EXE**—A Tray tool that lists the Kerberos ticket information
- **NETDIAG**—A multiuse diagnostic tool for checking many network parameters
- **DNSCMD**—Full DNS control at the command prompt (/info, /zoneinfo, /enumzones, etc.)
- **PATHPING**—Tracerlike information in a ping package

Using Repadmin

Repadmin is a command-line interface for troubleshooting Active Directory replication that is part of the Windows 2000 Server Resource Kit. Using Repadmin, you can determine a domain controller's direct replication partners. First, exit to the command prompt and type the following command:

```
repadmin /showreps dc=<yoursubdomain>,dc=domain,dc=com
```

Once the target server is reached, it will display a similar output, as shown in Figure 15.10. You should be able to see the domain controllers hosting each local domain.

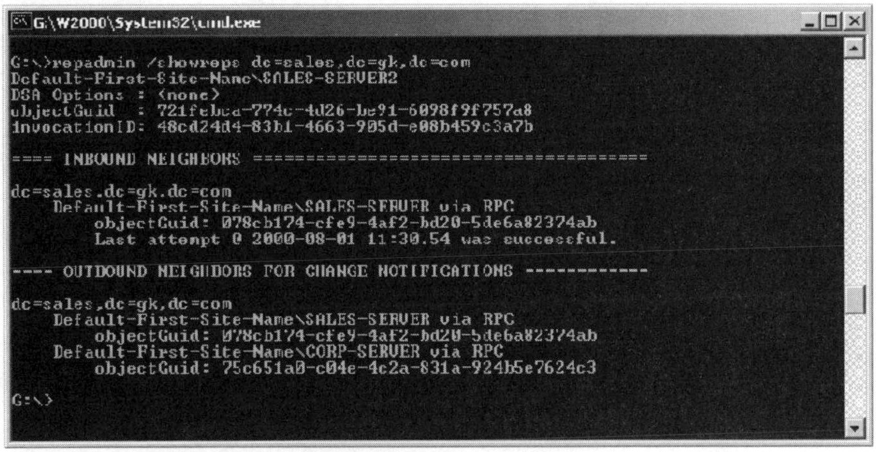

Figure 15.10
Repadmin can show replication details.

Under the Inbound Neighbors section of the output, the direct replication partner's for each directory partition will be identified, along with the status of the last replication. You can also use Repadmin.exe to get the changes that have been replicated within the domain. Exit to the command prompt and type the following command to save all changes seen by this domain controller to a text file called changes.txt:

```
repadmin /getchanges dc=<yoursubdomain>,dc=domain,dc=com >
changes.txt
```

Edit changes.txt with EDIT—you will see the groups, and users you have created.

Log Files used for Active Directory Troubleshooting

The default location for log files is the %System Root%\ Debug folder, as shown in Figure 15.11. You should be aware that many system tasks are logged to log files; the details you are seeking may be right under your nose.

Figure 15.11
Many powerful log
files are found in the
WINNT\Debug
folder.

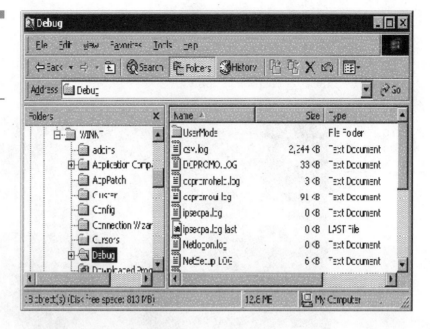

Active Directory Installation

Active Directory installation and removal is logged to DCPromoUI.log.
In addition, the dcpromoui.log file details the source domain controller
and directory partitions that were replicated.

NT 4.0 DC Promotion

When an NT 4.0 domain controller is promoted to a Windows 2000
domain controller, the process is logged in DCPromos.log. Details on the
creation of the AD database, the SYSVOL structure, and the installation
of services is logged to Dcpromo.log.

Joining a Computer to a Windows 2000 Domain

When a computer is joined to a Windows 2000 domain, the netsetup.log
records the details, both successes and failures. When the Net Logon
service is used for network logon requests, the netlogon.log file is
updated.

Active Directory Removal

Replication problems that may occur during the removal of Active Directory are logged to Ntfrsapi.log. When a user logs onto a Windows 2000

domain, details on the processing of the user's profile and group policy processing are logged to the Userenv.log

Monitoring NTDS.DIT with Performance Monitor

Figure 15.12 shows performance counters in the NTDS object that are for use with Performance Monitor to help provide statistics about real-time database replication performance. These counters can also be used to help determine your server's performance capacity by defining events that execute whenever the defined baseline is exceeded. Counters defined by Microsoft for capacity planning are provided in three categories:

- **Statistics**—Total actions per second
- **Ratio**—Percentage of total activity
- **Accumulative**—Activity since the computer was started

A sampling of NTDS counters can be found in Table 15.5. DRA is short for Directory Replication Agent; DS is short for Directory Service.

Figure 15.12
Performance Monitor has counters for NTDS.

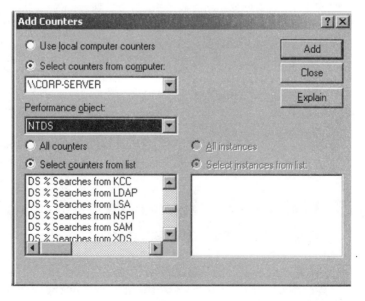

TABLE 15.5

Active Directory
NTDS performance
counters.

NTDS Counters	Details
DRA Inbound Bytes Compressed (Between Sites, After Compression)/sec	Sizes of compressed replication data inbound from directory system agents (DSAs) from other sites
DRA Inbound Bytes Not Compressed (Within Site)/sec	Size of replication data not compressed at the source—that is, inbound from other DSAs in the same site
DRA Inbound Bytes Total/sec	Total number of bytes received through replication
DRA Outbound Bytes Compressed (Between Sites, After Compression)/sec	Size of compressed replication data outbound to DSAs in other sites
DRA Outbound Bytes Not Compressed (Within Site)/sec	Size of replication data outbound to DSAs in the same site
DRA Outbound Bytes Total/sec	The total number of bytes sent per second
DS Threads in Use	The current number of threads in use by the directory service
LDAP Client Sessions	The number of sessions of connected LDAP clients
LDAP Bind Time	The time in milliseconds required for the completion of the last successful LDAP binding
Kerberos Authentications/sec	The number of times per second that clients use client tickets to authenticate to this domain controller
NTLM Authentications/sec	The number of NTLM authentications (per second) serviced by this domain controller
LDAP Successful Binds/sec	The number LDAP bindings (per second) that occurred successfully
LDAP Searches/sec	The number of search operations (per second) performed by LDAP clients

Using the Recovery Console's Advanced Features

With the recovery console, you can access the NTFS, FAT, and FAT32 volumes on each server without starting the Windows 2000 graphical interface. Using the recovery console you can:

- Use, copy, rename or replace operating system files and folders.
- Enable or disable the start of services or devices when you next start your computer.
- Repair the file system boot sector or the Master Boot Record (MBR).
- Create and format partitions on drives.

However, there's a catch. The default operation of the recovery console is that only system folders are viewable and you can't copy files from removable media or use wildcards.

Changing the Recovery Console's Default Operation

Before you can change any of the default environment variables to TRUE, you must enable the set command option using the Domain Controller Security Policy. This will then allow you full use of the recovery console, as it should have been designed to do in the first place. Log into your domain as Administrator, start ADUC, and highlight the Domain Controller container. Select the Properties of the Domain Controllers container and click the default domain controller's group policy. Next, click the Edit button and navigate to Computer Configuration\Windows Settings\Security Settings\Local Policies\Security Options, as shown in Figure 15.13.

Locate the following policy: Recovery Console: Allow floppy copy and access to all drives and all folders. Select the Properties of the policy, check the box "define this policy setting", and click the enabled option; click **OK.** Close the group policy option and click **OK**. Now run the following command to force an immediate refresh of your local computer's local security policy: C:\ >secedit /refreshpolicy machine_policy.

To test the recovery console's operation, reboot your computer system and from the boot menu select Microsoft Windows 2000 Recovery Console. After you start the Recovery Console, you receive the following message:

```
Microsoft Windows NT Recovery Console
Type 'exit' to leave the command prompt and reboot the system.
1: C:\WINNT
Which Windows NT installation would you like to logon to (enter
to abort)?
```

Enter the number for the Windows 2000 installation and the Administrator account password. Now you can use the Set command in the

Figure 15.13
Domain controller's
security policy
settings.

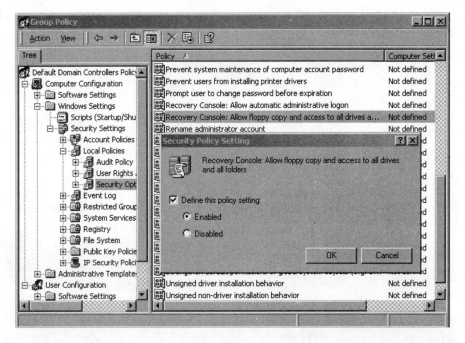

recovery console to display or modify certain environment variables. If each of the listed environment variables is set to TRUE, the variable is enabled. FALSE is disabled and is always the default setting. The syntax for the Set command is: set <variable> = true or false; make sure you leave spaces before and after the "=" sign.

Once the variables are set to TRUE, you will have the following results:

set allowwildcards = true:	Allows you to use wildcards
set allowallpaths = true:	Allows you to change directories to all folders on all drives
set allowremovablemedia = true:	Allows you to copy files from the hard disk to a floppy or other recognized removable medium

Start your domain controller into Recovery Console, then type the following command at the command prompt for full copying of files to and from removable media, the use of wildcards, and the ability to see all folders on the local hard drive.

- set allowremovablemedia = true
- set allowallpaths = true
- set allowwildcards

Administrator Tasks

Using Performance Monitor to Monitor Local and Remote Performance Counters

Click Start\Programs\Administrative Tools\Performance

A. Highlight System Monitor and on the details pane, right-click and select **Add Counters**.
B. Make sure your computer is selected in "Select counters from computer".
C. From Performance Object, select the NTDS performance object.
D. Add 3 counters to your monitor.
   DS % Reads from KCC
   DC % Directory Reads /sec
   DS Threads in Use
E. Click the **Explain** button for further details about each counter.

Creating a Counter Log

Click Start\Programs\Administrative Tools\Performance

A. Double-click **Performance Logs and Alerts** and select **Counter Logs**.
B. Right-click the details pane and select **New Log Settings**.
C. Name the New Log Settings LDAP Monitor and click **OK**.
D. In the General tab, note the path to the log file (C:\PerfLogs).
E. Click **Add** and select the NTDS performance object.
F. Select the counter LDAP Searches/sec and click **Add** and then **Close**.
G. Click the Log Files tab and set the following parameters:
   – Start numbering At: 1
   – Log file type: CSV
   – Log file size: Maximum Limit
H. Select the Schedule tab and set the following parameters and then click **OK**:
   – Start Log at: a time 2 minutes from now.
   – Stop Log after: 3 minutes.
 I. When the log file time starts, open ADUC and explore existing users and OUs.
J. After the log has stopped you can view the log file from C:\Perflogs.

Creating an Alert

Double-click Performance Logs and Alerts and select Alerts.

A. Right-click the **Alert Settings** in the details pane and select New Alert Settings.
B. In the New Alert Settings dialog box, enter LDAP Searches and click **OK**.
C. In the General tab, enter a comment "Alert when searches are over 5 seconds".
D. Add the counter from your computer LDAP Searches /sec.
E. Set the Alert to Over and the Limit to 5.
F. Set the Sample data to every 3 seconds.
G. On the Action tab, log an entry in the application event log.
H. On the Schedule tab, set the following parameters and click **OK**:
   – Start scan: a time 2 minutes from now
   – Stop scan after: 3 minutes
 I. When the log file starts, open ADUC and explore existing users and OUs.
J. After the log has stopped, you can view the alerts in the application log in Event Viewer.
K. Right-click My Computer and select Manage\Event Viewer.

Install All the Administrator Tools to the Administrator Program Group

When Windows 2000 is first installed, a default number of administrative tools is installed into the Administrative Tools Program group. Here's how to install all the tools.

Open the Control Panel and select the Add/Remove Programs applet.

A. One of the programs available should be the Windows 2000 Administration Tools.
B. Highlight the Windows 2000 Administration Tools and click the **Change** button; this will launch the Administrative Tools Setup wizard. Click **Next**.
C. Select the option "Install all of the Administrative Tools" and click **Next**.
D. Once the installation has completed, open the Administrative Tools menu from the Start menu and review the new additions.

Database Sizing and Replication Traffic

This chapter provides details on properly sizing the AD database and an analysis of network traffic, discussing such topics as:

- ESE database architecture
- Database performance
- Adding users and objects
- Network traffic analysis

Calculating the Database Size

The directory database architecture is divided into three levels: the directory system agent at the top, the database layer in the middle, and at the bottom, the extensible storage engine. The Active Directory runs as part of the trusted domain on the server. Once you promote your server using Dcpromo, Active Directory services including the database run as part of the service called LSSAS.EXE; you won't find a separate service called Active Directory showing in the Windows Task Manager. Several files represent the *extensible storage engine* (ESE) as shown in Figure 16.1.

- The database: NTDS.DIT file
- Several log files: (.LOG)
- The checkpoint file: (.CHK)

Figure 16.1
The database is comprised of log files and NTDS.DIT.

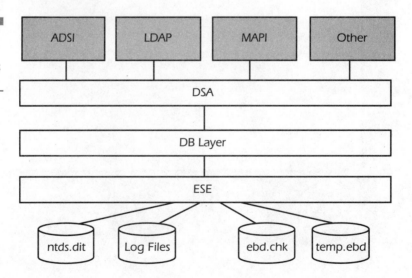

AD Write Operation

When a write operation is performed to the directory it is manipulating or changing an attribute on an existing object or creating a new object. The following steps are performed each time a write operation occurs:

1. The requestor starts the transaction.
2. The new value is written into the Memory Log Buffer.
3. At the same time the new value is written to the Memory Cache (this is a cached version of the A/D database), the log file is updated with the changes made.

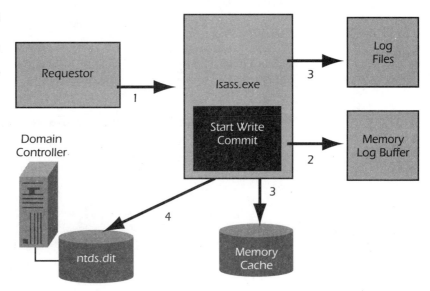

Figure 16.2
The write operation is fault tolerant.

Once the change has been written to the log file, the transaction is said to have been committed. At some point in the future, the change will also be written to the actual database file when the system is idle. After the write operation has completed, the checkpoint in the database is moved ahead, signifying a change has been made.

Database and Log Files: Performance

The log files and the database file (NTDS.DIT) should be located on different spindles for mid-size to large domain controllers. The completely different types of hard disk access mandate that performance will be poor unless separate drives are used. For the best performance on large domain controllers with several thousand users, separation of system components is the key. Yet the most important factor is fault tolerance using several domain controllers rather than just one large system.

- The Database file NTDS.DIT is almost entirely read access and is accessed randomly. Write operations, when they occur, are asynchronous and multithreaded.
- A log file, in comparison, is almost all write access and is accessed sequentially. Write operations, when they occur, are synchronous and are single threaded.

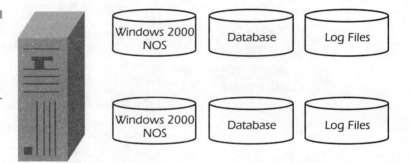

Figure 16.3
The database is mostly read access and the log files are mostly write access.

Hardware Minimums

The minimum RAM for a well-working server should be 1 Gig with a Pentium III processor. Why put in a server that will have to be upgraded in a year or so? Adding RAM of a different type to a production server is not a good idea, especially if it is a Microsoft server.

The number of CPUs should be reviewed; at a minimum 2 CPUs are necessary for any servers supporting over 1,000 users. Hard drive space can be miscalculated easily. The base Windows 2000 server requires 750 MB of hard drive space. Active Directory requires a minimum of 200 MB so let's use 1 Gig as the minimum requirement for a Domain Controller. An additional minimum 1 Gig of free space is also recommended by Microsoft for growth; we have not added any groups, OUs, or user objects and we are at 2 Gig. Add the support tools and the full Administrative Tools, the Resource Kit and Service Pack 1 and we are up to 2.5 Gig without breaking a sweat.

The swap file should be 600 MB minimum, and space should be added for use in case of a system crash. Since RAM is at 1 Gig, at least 2 Gig should be added for BSODs. Now, we're up to 5.3 Gig. If the server is to be a global catalog server, then the size of the database could almost double again, depending on the other domains' security principles and universal groups.

It's safe to say that the root domain controller should have an initial hard drive size of approximately 10 Gig. Yet we haven't considered the distributed file system, data files, Exchange 2000, and email.

Garbage Collection

Garbage collection is a housekeeping process that tunes the Active Directory database in an ongoing process (detailed in Chapter 12). The garbage collection process runs on each domain controller independently and, over time, space is freed up in the database from deleted objects, called tombstones. The garbage collection interval is set by default to every 12 hours.

Online Defragmentation

Garbage collection also removes old log files and defragments the database while it is online. The process of defragmentation is the movement of data in order to repopulate the database pages efficiently. When Active Directory is first set up and many objects are added to the database, because of the inherent design, storage is usually not as efficient as it could be. The history of the AD database is Access. Also keep in mind that the database is potentially being populated from several or many domain controllers through the replication process. There are two ways to defragment the active directory database, by either online or offline defragmentation. Online defragmentation runs as part of the gabage collection carried out every 12 hours on a domain controller. Offline defragmentation requires that the domain controller be taken off line and rebooted into Directory Services Repair Mode. Ntdsutil, a command line utility, is then executed to defragment the database and also reduce the size of the database file. It is important to realize that the database size does not shrink after online defragmentation, even though space has been freed up for new objects. However, the online defragmentation is just as efficient as the offline method. We humans prefer to see the size reduction of the database file, confirming that something has been done, but this involves rebooting the server. Offline defragmentation can be used for a number of scenarios including restoring the database back to a previous state and converting a global catalog DC to a DC.

NOTE

For testing purposes, the offline defragmentation of the database is fundamental for finding out how large the database really grows over time.

Database Sizing: Adding Users

In order to determine how large the database will grow, its important to view database storage capabilities. For testing purposes the best common object would be a user account with just the mandatory user attributes: username, SAM account name, and password. The size of the user account with these attributes is approximately 3.6 KB. In reality, you would be adding many additional attributes.

Database Sizing Steps

1. Begin by loading a fixed set of user accounts.
2. Next measure the size of the database growth.
3. Take the domain controller offline and perform an offline defragmentation with Ntdsutil.exe.
4. Measure the database size and document the results.
5. Load another fixed set of objects and repeat steps 1–4.

Analysis

If users were added in bulk, 100,000 at a time up to 500,000, and at each step the domain controller were taken offline and defragmented, the growth pattern and the size of the database would remain linear up to millions of user accounts added.

Database Sizing: Adding OUs

Adding objects that are not security principles is less space intensive, since there can be less mandatory attributes. Users and groups are common security principles to deploy and have many attribute choices, whereas an OU is not a security principle and therefore much smaller. The size of an OU, computer, printer, or empty groups, is approximately 1.1KB.

OU Database Sizing

1. Begin by loading a fixed set of OUs.
2. Next measure the size of the database growth.
3. Take the DC offline and perform an offline defragmentation with Ntdsutil.exe.
4. Measure the database size and document the results.
5. Load another fixed set of objects and repeat steps 1–4.

Analysis

If OUs were added in bulk to one domain, 2,000 at a time up to 16,000, and at each step the DC were taken offline and defragmented, the growth pattern and the size of the database would still remain linear up to 16,000 OUs in one domain and beyond.

Forecasting a Company's Database Size

Microsoft has come up with some simple guidelines based on their testing of Active Directory. This formula was devised for planning database growth with common objects.

User Size + 30 Attributes *100 Bytes per string attributes * # of users = DB Store

Database Sizing Example

In this example a medium-size company was used for analysis. Testing was based on common objects (OUs, users, groups, workstations, and volumes). The size of the sample company's objects was: 2,000 OUs, 100,000 users, 90,000 workstations, 30,000 groups, 2,000 printers, and 2,000 volumes.

- Users had 30 attributes assigned (first name, last name, etc.)

- Workstations had 6 attributes assigned (Name, OS Version etc.)
- Groups had 8 attributes assigned plus 100 members
- Volumes had 3 attributes assigned
- Printers had 8 attributes assigned
- All string attributes were set to a random length from 1 to 100 characters

Analysis

Ten percent of the sample company's objects were added in steps until 100 percent of the objects were added. The final database store size, with 100,000 users and the various attributes, was 1.6 GB. This store size can be handled easily by the database; the AD database used in Exchange 5.5 configurations handled in excess of 60 GB.

How Do You Use this Information?

1. Find the number of users of your company to calculate an initial database size for your company.
2. Add additional objects that your company has using these rules.
   - Consider all security objects (users, groups, and computers) the size of a user object (add 3.6KB per object).
   - Consider all non-security objects the size of an OU (add 1.1KB per object).
3. Add 100 Bytes per string attribute of 10 characters.
4. When a binary store is added (Picture ID, Certificate) add 50% to the data size.
5. To be safe, at a minimum *double* your estimated size.

   Example: A large ISP in California created a 5.88 million user store with 30 additional attributes per users: 3,600 KB + 30 * 100 Bytes * 5.88 Users = 38,808.000.000 Bytes. Actual Size = 39.4 GB.

Global Catalog and Replication Size

The global catalog is also a factor in the traffic levels on an Active Directory network; 15–25 percent of the local domain controller database is replicated to the global catalog server. As we know, the GC contains a partial replica of all objects in the enterprise. The global catalog is usually required for user logins using UPNs and searches throughout the directory; universal groups also publish their members in the GC. Object creation(s) made at any domain controller in the tree or forest are replicated to the global catalog.

To test the amount of replication and network traffic, tests can be performed to analyze the global catalog factor in replication. If a root domain was created, the domain controller in the root domain is also a global catalog by default. Next, creating a child domain and leaving the DC in the child domain as a domain controller, the same number of objects could be created in both domains with just the mandatory objects. As global and universal groups are also created, more information will be stored in the global catalog. Replication of the objects and a subset of the attributes created in the child domain between the child domain and the root domain would then be carried out because the global catalog was in the root domain. Finally, measuring the size of the database files in both the root and child domain would show the size of replication required to maintain the global catalog. The measurements would show that the child domain's database is much smaller than the root domain controller's database.

Deleting Objects Creates Replication

When an object is deleted from the database, it is not deleted at once. Instead, the object is called a tombstone; its attributes are stripped and it is sent to the lost-and-found container. Replication of the tombstone alerts the other domain controllers that the object has been deleted from everyday usage but still remains in the database. The lifetime of a tombstone object is set to 60 days; after this time garbage collection automatically deletes the object. The tombstone value has implications for the database size for the first 60 days of life of a domain controller. The database will continue to grow for the first 60 days unless the tombstone value is changed to a shorter time frame. Even if deletions take place, the objects remain; they are just not viewable.

After 60 days, online defragmentation will free up space in the database; however the size of the database will not change to indicate the newly available free space.

Scalability Testing

Scalability testing of the Active Directory database is best done with the creation of user accounts; they are the largest objects we can create with multiple attributes. The addition of many users to Active Directory shows that the database grows in a linear fashion regardless of size, as detailed by these features measured when creating users with a minimum set of attributes:

- 10,000 users = 62.2 MB
- 100,000 users = 454 MB
- 1,000,000 users = 4.1 GB
- 10,000,000 users = 41.9 GB
- 16,000,000 users = 68.6 GB

Domain Controller Hardware Selection

Having many objects on just one powerful domain controller will strain the capabilities of the entire network—the load must be spread among multiple domain controllers. Compaq Corporation has tested in excess of 40 million objects, comprising 100 GB of replicated domain partitions, using RAID 5 controllers to determine the proper mix of hardware for the best performance. Testing found that the hardware for the server was not as important as the storage hardware required for both data storage and replication both in and across sites. The most important statistic found during testing was that hard drive input and output (I/O) was the trigger for performance. RAID was found to be essential, in fact almost mandatory, for a medium to large implementation of Active Directory. RAID is used to increase the number of platters available to process the I/O requests. On-board caching must also be used to reduce the response time; the RAID controller can write the I/O request to memory, which is the fastest method, and then synchronize the writing to the database.

Extensible Storage Engine I/O Patterns

In order to increase the performance of Active Directory, the number of I/Os per second must increase. As your Active Directory hierarchy grows, the number of users will increase and therefore the number of sequential searches of the database using the global catalog and domain controllers will also increase. The goal is to maintain the same response time as your network increases in size. Hard drives are sold advertising MB per second, yet for AD the important benchmark is the number of I/Os per seconds. The Active Directory database file has an input/output speed of 8 KB per second. The input/output per second is a constant value for hard drives. Increasing the number of drives increases concurrent access and improves performance.

Case Study

Let's say that through testing and calculations the database store required for your company within three years is calculated to be 360 GB, and RAID 5 is to be used for improved I/O performance and fault tolerance. If the largest drive available on the market were 47 GB, then eight platters would be required to hold the database store. However, when we look at Figure 16.4, the maximum I/O that can be achieved is 70 I/Os over the entire drive or 560 I/Os per second.

Figure 16.4
Hard drives performance for AD should be measured in total I/Os per second.

Drive (GB)	Form Factor	Number of Supplies	I/O per Drive	Total I/O per Second
47	5 1/4	8	70	560
18	3 1/2	20	100	2,000
9	3 1/2	40	100	4,000
4.3	3 1/2	84	100	8,400
2.1	3 1/2	172	100	17,200

If 2.3 GB drives were used, 180 platters would be required to hold the database store. Although this is technically impossible, and not practical, this would be a much better solution for Active Directory, since the I/O across the drive has increased to 100. Most important, the I/Os per second have increased to 17,200 per second, an increase of 3,025 percent. The best solution would be either 4.3 or 9 GB drives; the I/Os are still much faster than the larger drives at 4.3 GB 8,400 I/Os and 9 GB 2,000 I/Os respectively.

Tuning your domain controllers in this fashion changes the dynamics of your processing cycle.

- If the I/O of your servers is too low, then your processors will be waiting on the hard drive so CPU processing will be low.
- If your I/O is properly tuned, then your processor workload will greatly increase, since the processors now have lots of concurrent work to do.

RAID Decisions: Database and Log File Considerations

The question is not, should we use RAID, but rather what type of RAID should we use? RAID provides load balancing across multiple disks, increases performance and storage, and protects against downtime and hardware failure.

- Log files are stored in RAM so that the action performed on the hard drive is Write to the physical log files. Log files should be stored on RAID-1 drives, which use mirrored volumes.
- The database file NTDS.DIT is mostly Read. The RAID-level storage system for the database should be at a minimum RAID-1 and preferably RAID-5.

RAID Details

Concurrent reads can be accomplished across RAID-5 arrays. With properly selected hard drives, RAID-5 is the best solution for Active Directory. There is both hardware and software RAID; Windows 2000 supports software

RAID internally, but hardware RAID is always better. Use hardware raid if at all possible; for performance details visit **http://www.adaptec.com**.

RAID-1

In Windows 2000, RAID-1 is mirrored volumes: all data written to a primary volume are also written to a secondary volume. Double the hard drive space is required, since each file is stored in two locations.

RAID-5

In Windows 2000, RAID-5 volumes share data across all the disks in the array, writing parity information across all the disks. RAID-5 requires a minimum of three disks to store the same amount of information that would be stored on JBOD (Just a bunch of disks) drives; the additional parity takes up the additional space.

Intra-Site Replication Traffic

Creating users, groups, and volumes with just the minimum attributes generates significant one-time replication traffic at creation. Depending on your network, these may be one-time, monthly, or daily tasks. Look at the test numbers in Figure 16.5; if a single user object is created, 13 K of information will be replicated within the site—the extra 10 K or so is used setting up the initial replication connection. When 10 user objects are created, the overhead is reduced as the connection is established and then the information is replicated. When 500 objects are created, over 1.9 MB of data must be replicated. Intra-site data are not compressed; the assumption is made that local site connectivity is good at 100MB Ethernet.

Replicating Users with Additional Attributes

Adding additional attributes once the connection object is taken into account takes approximately 100 bytes per attribute, as shown in Figure 16.6.

# Objects	Users	Global Groups	Universal Groups	Volumes
1	13,019	11,309	11,145	10,277
10	47,037	26,902	26,823	22,848
100	386,148	187,754	185,606	149,736
500	1,914,087	905,015	906,079	715,577
1,000	3,818,256	1,815,170	1,803,090	1,436,085
5,000	19,123,820	8,9858,915		

Intrasite Domain Replication in Bytes
"Overhead per Attribute"

# Users	Mandatory Attributes	Plus 1 Attributes	Plus 3 Attributes	Plus 5 Attributes
1	13,019	13,233 "214"	13,439 "30"	13,451 "82"
10	47,037	47,917 "88"	49,923 "96"	51,765 "96"
100	386,148	396,308 "102"	416,107 "99"	435,496 "96"
500	1,914,087	1,966,967 "106"	2,064,423 "102"	2,160,454 "94"
1,000	3,818,256	3,919,177 "101"	4,123,535 "103"	4,328,794 "107"
5,000	19,123,820	19,619,815 "99"	20,628,381 "102"	21,611,973 "95"

Group Replication within a Site

The baseline for testing replication was first measured with no group members. Next members were added to the groups; the average size of an added group member is 180 bytes. The result for very large groups of 500 with 100 members each is over 19 MB.

Figure 16.7
Group replication within a site.

Object Replication in Bytes
"Overhead per Group Member"

# Groups	No Members	10 Members	20 Members	100 Members
1	11,309	13,023 "171"	15,028 "186"	29,212 "179"
10	26,902	45,180 "183"	36,199 "191"	206,193 "179"
100	187,754	370,333 "183"	549,351 "181"	2,007,563 "182"
500	905,015	1,822,257 "183"	2,745,787 "184"	9,956,677 "181"
1,000	1,815,170	3,633,795 "182"	5,458,848 "182"	19,920,866 "181"

Replicating Password Changes

The frequency of password changes across your network and the size of your user pool will determine the size of password data being replicated. Machine accounts and trusts also change their passwords on a seven-day interval. A password change averages 500 bytes. Remember the replication is per attribute; so only the changes are replicated, not the entire object.

Figure 16.8
Intra-site password replication size.

Intrasite Password Changes in Bytes

# Users	Bytes	Bytes per User
1	10,805	1,842
10	12,811	385
100	59,856	509
500	275,422	533
1,000	444,085	435
5,000	3,014,610	601

Intra-Site Global Catalog Replication

The global catalog is a partial replica of all the objects in the enterprise. The number of attributes stored in the global catalog is minimal. Editing the schema can change the attributes stored in the GC. Each object has a definition of whether or not it is included in the global catalog. The type of groups you decide to deploy has a large importance in the amount of replication and querying that involves the GC. Universal groups publish group membership listings in the global catalog, whereas global groups and local domain groups do not. Figure 16.9 shows intersite replication for the domain controllers and the global catalog. The boldface numbers show the size of the global catalog replication. The numbers in regular typeface show the normal domain replication. Adding 5,000 user objects shows a domain replication size of 19 MB. The global catalog is about 30 percent less at 13 MB.

Figure 16.9
Global catalog replication in the domain.

Object Replications in Bytes

# Objects	Users	Global Groups	Universal Groups	Volumes
1	12,401 "13,019"	11,601 "11,309"	11,437 "11,145"	11,101 "10,277"
10	35,595 "47,037"	26,783 "26,902"	26,862 "26,823"	23,011 "22,848"
100	272,877 "386,148"	183,123 "187,754"	183,205 "185,606"	145,199 "149,736"
500	1,323,177 "1,914,087"	897,828 "905,015"	879,990 "906,079"	690,042 "715,577"
1,000	2,640,974 "3,818,256"	1,750,665 "1,815,170"	1,751,239 "1,803,090"	1,370,457 "1,436,085"
5,000	13,189,354 "19,123,820"	8,735,103 "8,995,915"	8,745,150	6,860,815

Intra-Site Global Catalog and Universal Group Replication

Global and universal groups with no members are very similar. Once group membership are increased, the universal group size becomes much larger. If 100 global groups with 100 members is created, the size is 183 KB. If 100 universal groups with 100 members is created the data size replicated is 2.2 MB. Global catalog replication is smaller than domain replication within the site since the global catalog has fewer attributes to replicate.

Figure 16.10
Global catalog and
universal groups are
compared.

Global Groups in Bytes

# Groups	0	10	20	100
1	11,601	11,519	11,437	11,437
10	26,783	26,783	26,783	26,783
100	183,123	183,369	183,367	183,041

Universal Groups in Bytes

# Groups	0	10	20	100
1	11,437	13,491	17,149	31,731
10	26,862	46,816	67,256	245,908
100	183,205	388,725	593,623	2,207,641

Inter-Site Domain Replication

Inter-site replication uses RPC over IP, as shown in Figure 16.11. Schema, global catalog, and configuration replication support RPC and SMTP. There is no notification for inter-site replication; instead it is based on time intervals—the default is 15 minutes. Compression is used; the data can be compressed down to 10–15 percent of original size.

Inter-Site and Intra-Site Domain Replication

When we compare the inter-site and intra-site domain replication we see that the ability to compress the data between sites is significant. Inter-site replication compresses the data efficiently. If a WAN connection is part of your network, sites should be used; sites should never cross the WAN link. For the creation of 100 user objects within the site, the data replicated equal 386K. From one site to another the data size is compressed to 39K. For the creation of 1,000 user objects within the site, the data replicated equal 3.8 MB. From one site to another the data are compressed to 291 K.

Figure 16.11
Replication between sites.

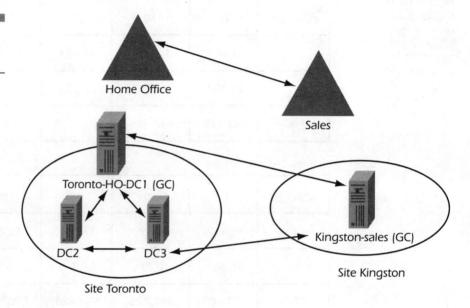

Figure 16.12
Domain replication compared.

Objects Replications in Bytes
"Intrasite Domain Replication"

# Objects	Users	Global Groups	Universal Groups	Volumes
1	14,108 "13,019"	10,437 "11,309"	11,227 "11,145"	9,667 "10,277"
10	45,563 "47,037"	25,683 "26,902"	26,741 "26,823"	21,691 "22,848"
100	39,583 "386,148"	28,743 "187,754"	29,675 "185,606"	22,602 "149,736"
500	173,105 "1,914,087"	102,404 "905,015"	119,180 "906,079"	81,691 "715,577"
1,000	291,041 "3,818,256"	194,926 "1,815,170"	199,054 "1,803,090"	151,989 "1,436,085"

Inter-Site GC RPC Replication

Figure 16.13 shows that compression greatly reduces the size of data being replicated between sites and global catalog servers. Compression figures are in white and the intra-site data are shown in orange. If SMNP were used for replication in place of RPC, compression of data between sites is used, but the compression ratio is 50 percent less.

In addition, RPC is synchronous compression and SMTP is asynchronous and not as reliable—it uses the mail transport rather than TCP/IP.

Figure 16.13
Global catalog inter-site replication.

Object Replications in Bytes
"Intrasite GC Replication"

# Objects	Users	Global Groups	Universal Groups	Volumes
1	12,565 "12,401"	11,471 "11,601"	11,389 "11,437"	11,183 "10,277"
10	36,018 "35,595"	26,895 "26,783"	26,813 "26,862"	23,171 "23,011"
100	32,391 "272,877"	28,600 "183,823"	28,379 "183,205"	24,598 "145,199"
500	121,481 "1,323,177"	101,858 "879,823"	102,200 "877,990"	83,099 "690,042"
1,000	233,503 "2,640,974"	104,047 "1,750,665"	194,357 "1,751,239"	170,918 "1,370,457"

Replication Traffic Summary

In summary, the behavior of the Active Directory database is linear and easy to predict. The hard drive used for the database should be at least three times the size of the directory sizing estimate. The I/O specs per second of the selected hard drive are the most important statistic to consider. Replication is also very predictable both in-site and between sites: if 2,000 users a day were added this would create 582,000 bytes per day, which would work out to 1/10 of 1 percent of a 28.8-KB modem connection. The operating system replication is manageable, for now.

Figure 16.14
Replication data
between a site is
minimal.

# Users	Domain Intrasite	Domain Intersite	GC RPC	GC SMTP
1	13,019	14,108	12,565	22,253
10	47,037	45,563	36,018	52,887
100	386,148	39,583	32,391	59,675
1,000	3,818,256	291,041	233,503	440,165

Administrative Tasks: Using the Active Directory Sizer (ADSIZER)

One software tool Microsoft has made available for the planning of Active Directory is a utility called ADSIZER. We can use ADSIZER for several scenarios, including finding out approximately how big the Active Directory database for the company will be. The tool can be found at **http://www.Microsoft.com/windows2000/library/planning/ activedirectory/adsizer.asp**

1. Install ADSIZER per instructions.
2. Click **Start\Programs** and **Active Directory Sizer**.
3. From the File menu select **New**.
4. Using the wizard and the chart below, enter the suggested values.

The default uses the Default-First-Site, however you could add several sites to mimic your real site scenario. By distributing your users among the sites, ADSIZER would tell you the amount of network traffic to expect between the domain controllers in and between each site.

Number of Users	300	300	1000	5000
% of user active during peak hours	60	60	60	60
Additional Attributes	25	25	30	30
Average # of groups belonged to	10	10	30	40
Interactive Users Calculation: 1 hour 60 X 60 = 3600 seconds 300 users / 3600 0. 083 per second	.083	0.278	1.389	

Batch (Client Server App)	1	5	10
Network (Printers, Network Services)	10	50	100
Passwords Expire	30	30	30
Additional ACEs for each user	25	25	25
Windows 2000 computers	200	400	3000
Other computers	100	600	1000
Other published objects	50	100	150
CPU Utilization rate	75	50	50
Processor type	Pentium III 600	Same	Same
# of processors	Uni	2	4
Administration (Weekly)	10,2,20	100,20,40	200,40,80
Exchange 2000	15,10	40,60	80,100
DNS	Yes	Yes	Yes
Dial in Connections	10	20	100
DHCP lease interval	8	8	8
DNS aging and scavenging parameter	7	7	7
Services Search/sec Add/sec Delete/sec Modify/sec	None	None	None

5. Using the chart below enter the domain database size and the global catalog size.

Save results as:	Mydomain	Largecorp	Enterprise	Company
Domain Name	MyDomain	LargeCorp	Enterprise	Your Company
# of Users	300	1000	5000	
Domain Database Size:				
Global Catalog Size:				

Using ADSI Edit to Change the Default Tombstone

Objects marked as "tombstoned" are actually deleted 60 days after their original tombstone status setting; modifying the tombstone lifetime can change this time. To change the default tombstone life of 60 days:

Log onto your domain as Administrator.

1. Open ADSI Edit from Start\Programs\Windows 2000 Support Tools\Tools.
2. Highlight the Domain NC and from the Action menu select **Settings**.
3. In the Connection dialog box, select a Naming Context of Configuration Container.
4. Navigate to:
   CN=Configuration/CN=Services/CN=Windows NT/CN=Directory Service
5. Highlight CN=Directory Service and from the Action menu select **Properties**.
6. From the Select a property to view, select: tombstoneLifetime.
7. To change the default value, type in a number in the Edit Attribute box and click **Set**.

Using ADSI Edit to Change the Default Garbage Collection

1. From the "Select a property to view" select: garbageCollPeriod.
2. To change the default value, type in a number in the Edit Attribute box and click **Set**.

APPENDIX A

ACRONYMS

ACE	access control entry
ACL	access control list
AD	Active Directory
ADSI	Active Directory Service Interfaces
ANSI	American National Standards Institute
API	application programming interface
ATM	asynchronous transfer mode
BDC	backup domain controller
CAD	computer-aided design
CN	common name
CNAME	canonical name
COM	Component Object Model
CRC	cyclical redundancy check
DAP	Directory Access Protocol
DB	database
DC	domain controller
DCOM	Distributed Component Object Model
DDE	Dynamic Data Exchange
DEN	directory enabled networks
Dfs	Distributed File System
DHCP	Dynamic Host Configuration Protocol

DISP	Directory Information Shadowing Protocol
DIT	directory information tree
DLG	domain local group
DLL	dynamic link library
DN	distinguished name
DNS	Domain Name System
DOP	Directory Operational Binding Management Protocol
DRA	directory replication agent
DSA	directory system agent
DSP	Directory System Protocol
EFS	Encrypting File System
ERD	Emergency Repair Disk
ESE	Extensible Storage Engine
FQDN	fully qualified domain name
FRS	File Replication Service
FSMO	flexible single masters operations
FTP	File Transfer Protocol
GB	gigabyte
GC	global catalog
GPO	group policy object
GUI	graphical user interface
GUID	globally unique identifier
HINFO	host information
HTTP	Hypertext Transfer Protocol
IETF	Internet Engineering Task Force
IIS	Internet Information Server
IMAP	Internet Message Access Protocol
IP	Internet Protocol
IPv4	Internet Protocol version 4
IPv6	Internet Protocol version 6

ISDN	Integrated Services Digital Network
ISO	International Organization for Standardization
ISP	Internet service provider
ISTG	Inter-Site Topology Generator
IT	Information Technology
ITU	International Telecommunication Union
IXFR	incremental zone transfers
JBOD	just a bunch of disks
PDC	primary domain controller
PERL	Practical Extraction and Reporting Language
POP	Post Office Protocol
PTR	pointer
R	read
RAID	redundant array of inexpensive disks
RAM	random access memory
RDN	relative distinguished name
REPL	replication
RID	relative identifier
RP	responsible person
RPC	remote procedure call
RR	resource record
RW	read-write
RWD	read-write-delete
SAM	Security Accounts Manager
SASL	Simple Authentication and Security Layer
SID	security identifier
SMTP	Simple Mail Transfer Protocol
SNMP	Simple Network Management Protocol
SOA	start of authority
SRV	RR service resource records

SSL	Secure Sockets Layer
SYSVOL	System Volume
TCP	Transmission Control Protocol
TCP/IP	Transmission Control Protocol/Internet Protocol
TGT	ticket-granting ticket
TTL	Time to Live
UDP	User Datagram Protocol
UNC	universal naming convention
UPN	user principal name
USN	update sequence number
VB	Visual BASIC
WAN	wide area network
WFP	Windows File Protection
WINS	Windows Internet Naming Service
WSH	Windows Script Host

APPENDIX B

ACTIVE DIRECTORY COMMAND-LINE UTILITIES

MoveTree—Allows you to move some objects from one domain to another. User accounts in OUs, and user accounts in the Users containers can be moved, however populated groups cannot.

SIDWalker—Allows you to set the access control lists on objects previously owned by accounts that were moved, orphaned, or deleted.

LDP—Allows many LDAP operations to be performed against Active Directory.

DNSCMD—The dynamic registration of DNS resource records can be checked, as can the deregistration of resource records.

DSACLS—Allows you to modify or view the access control lists of active directory objects.

NETDOM—Provides the ability to perform batch management of trusts, joining computers to domains, and verifying existing trusts and secure channels.

NETDIAG—Checks end-to-end network and distributed services functions.

NLTest—Tests and verifies that the locator and secure channel are functioning.

REPAdmin—Checks replication consistency between replication partners and monitors the replication status of partners or selected servers; displays replication metadata, forces push and pull replication events, and provides knowledge consistency checker (KCC) recalculation.

REPLMon—Displays replication topology, monitors replication status, and group policies, forces push and pull replication events, and checks FSMO and knowledge consistency checker recalculation.

DSAStat—Compares directory information on domain controllers and detects differences.

ADSIEdit—MMC snap-in used to view all objects in the directory, including schema and configuration information, to modify objects and set access control lists on objects.

SDCheck—Tests whether access control lists are being inherited properly, and also checks if access control lists are properly replicated from one domain controller to another.

ACLDiag—Checks and verifies if a user was granted or denied access to an active directory object.

DFSCheck—For managing the feature Distributed File System (DFS) by checking the configuration concurrency of Dfs servers; also displays the DFS topology.

APPENDIX C

ADMINISTRATIVE TASKS: VERIFYING SRV RECORDS

One method of verifying that your domain created with dcpromo is working is to check for the SRV records created during the promotion process.

1. At the command prompt execute Nslookup.

   A. At the Nslookup prompt type:

   ```
   > set type=srv
   > _ldap._tcp.<your sub domain name here>
   ```

   B. You should get a response as shown below in Figure C.1.

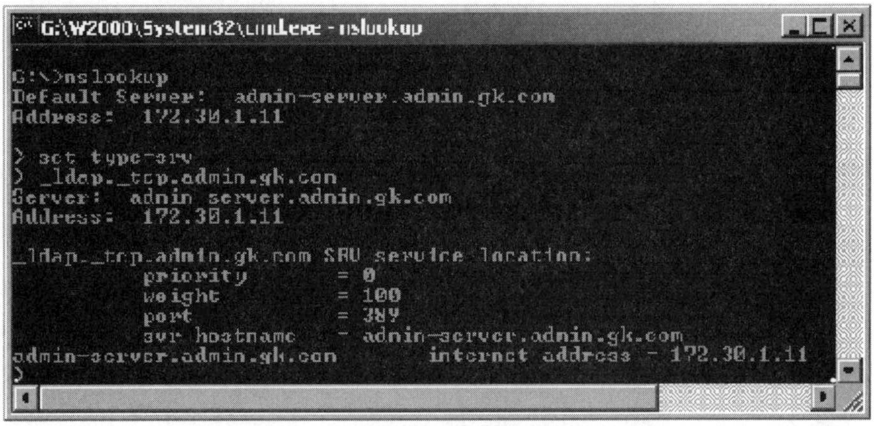

Figure C.1
Nslookup details SRV records.

2. Now use Nslookup to view the other created SRV records on your domain controller and also at your root domain.

   A. At the Nslookup prompt use the server command to set the search to your domain controller, for example; admin-server.

```
> server admin-server
```

B. Now enter the following SRV locations inserting your domain for the syntax

```
<domain controller> or <domainname>
```

   – This SRV allows clients to find LDAP servers for a specific domain.

```
_ldap._tcp. <domain name>
```

   – This SRV allows clients to find Kerberos Key Distribution Center (KDC) services for the domain.

```
_kerberos._tcp.<domainname>
```

   – This SRV allows clients to find Kerberos Change Password services in the domain.

```
_kpasswd._tcp.<domainname>
```

   – This SRV allows clients to find the global catalog servers using the Active Directory root domain.

```
_gc._tcp.<forestname>
```

Creating and Managing User Profiles

If you have not had a lot of experience in User Profiles and Windows 2000, these steps will help. First create a local user account.

1. Log onto your domain as Administrator and launch Active Directory Users and Computers.
   A. Right-click the domain icon and select the **Users** folder.
   B. From the Action menu, select **New** and then **User**.
   C. Create a new user in your domain with these parameters:

First Name	Last Name	User Logon Name	Password
Local	user	luser@yourdomain	None

D. Log off Windows 2000 and test this user's ability to log onto your domain.

E. Right-click on a blank area of the Desktop and select **Properties**.

F. Change the background to Boiling Point and change the picture display to Tile and apply.

G. Log off and back on as Administrator and open the Windows Explorer.

H. Navigate to C:\Documents and Settings and view the local user profile. How much space does the user profile take?

I. Close the Windows Explorer and from the desktop right-click **My Computer** and select **Properties**.

J. Select the User Profiles tab. What types of user profile was created?

K. Log off and log on as luser. How can you tell that you are using a different user profile?

Before creating roaming user profiles, first create and share the network folder that will store the roaming user profiles.

2. Logon to your domain as Administrator
   A. In drive C: create a new folder called profiles.
   B. Right-click the profiles folder and select **Properties**.
   C. Select the Sharing tab and share the profiles folder.
   D. Click the **Permissions** button and make sure that the Everyone group is present with Full Control. Click **OK** twice to return to Explorer.
   E. Create a folder in Profiles called uone.

Next, create a user profile template.

3. Log onto your domain as Administrator and launch Active Directory Users and Computers.
   A. Right-click the **Users** folder and select **New** and then **User**.
   B. Create a new user in your domain with these parameters:

First Name	Last Name	User Logon Name	Password
roaming	profile	rprofile@yourdomain	None

    C. Log off and back on as rprofile.

    D. Right-click on a blank area of the Desktop and select **Properties**.

    E. Change the background to Coffee Bean with the picture display to Tile.

    F. Click **OK** and log off.

Next create a user profile template and then copy that template to a shared network location.

4. Log onto your domain as Administrator and launch Active Directory Users and Computers.

    A. Right-click the **Users** folder and select **New** and then **User**.

    B. Create a new user in your domain with these parameters:

First Name	Last Name	User Logon Name	Password
user	one	uone@yourdomain	None

    C. Open the Control Panel; open the System Applet and select **User Profiles**.

    D. Highlight the local profile rprofile and then click the **Copy To** button.

    E. In the Copy To dialog box, enter the path \\yourservername\ profiles\uone.

    F. Click **OK** and accept the message.

    G. Check in the C:\profiles folder you created—there should be a new folder for the roaming user profile.

    H. Start Active Directory Users and Computers; in the Users folder select the user account for uone and double-click to view its Properties; select the **Profile** tab.

    I. Add the path to the Profile path: \\yourservername\profiles\ uone and click **OK**.

    J. Test the roaming profile by logging into your computer as user uone.

    K. Check the User Profile tab in the System Applet in Control Panel. Are you using a roaming profile? You should be.

Now change the roaming user profile to a mandatory user profile.

6. Log on as Administrator and open Windows Explorer.
   A. Navigate to the Profiles\uone folder.
   B. Change the name of NTUSER.DAT to NTUSER.MAN.
   C. Log off and test the mandatory user profile.
   D. Make changes to the Desktop and log off and back on. Are the changes saved?
   E. Open the Control Panel and select the System applet. Select the User Profile tab.
   F. Are you using a mandatory user profile?

Using LDP to View LDAP Operation and AD Structure

LDP can carry out a wealth of LDAP operations. Here are a few examples to get you started with LDP. The first task to perform is an LDAP _open operation.

1. Click Start | Program Tools | Windows 2000 Support Tools | Tools | Active Directory Administration Tool.
   A. Select the Connection dropdown menu and select **Connect**.
   B. Fill in the Connect dialog box with the following information and click **OK**.
      – Server: <servername> for example: sales-server
      – Port: 389
      – Connectionless: DO NOT CHECK (We will use TCP rather than UDP)
   C. Use the scroll bar to scroll the righthand pane back up to the top. Note the ldap_open, as shown in Figure C.2.

Figure C.2
LDAP open operation.

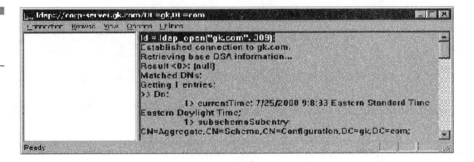

Perform an LDAP _bind operation.

2. Click the **Connection** menu and select **Bind**.

    A. Fill in the Bind dialog box with the following information and click **OK**.

        – User: administrator

        – Password: no password

        – Domain: <yourdomain> for example: admin.gk.com

        – (NTLM/Kerberos) Checkbox: Checked

    B. Use the scroll bar to scroll the right-hand pane back until the line res=ldap_bind is located, as shown in Figure C.3 ; this shows that your bind operation is successful.

Figure C.3
LDAP bind operation.

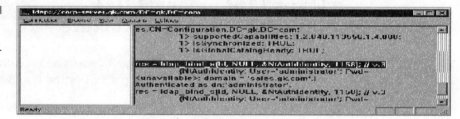

Next display the directory information tree of your domain.

3. Select the **View** dropdown menu and select **Tree**.

    A. Fill in the Tree dialog box with the following string, as it applies, and press **OK**.

```
DC=<yoursubdomain>,DC=domain,DC=com
```

    B. In the right pane scroll up until the line Expanding base 'dc=<yoursubdomain>, dc=domain,dc=com'... is found, as shown in Figure C.4.

Figure C.4
Viewing the tree.

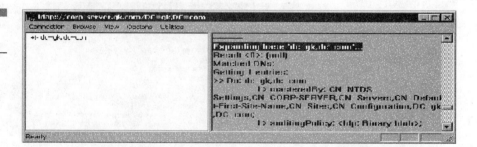

C. In the lefthand pane click the plus sign to expand the tree. The information shown is the same information displayed during use of Active Directory Users and Computers.

D. Minimize LDP, and open ADUC and compare.

E. Now, using LDP, double-click CN=Users and then expand.

F. Double-click the user CN=Administrator and then scroll the righthand pane to the line Expanding base 'CN=Administrator,CN=Users,...as, shown in Figure C.5.

Figure C.5
Reading metadata with LDP.

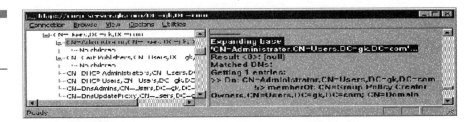

Finally perform an unbind operation.

4. Select the Connection menu and select **New**; this should clear your details pane.

A. From the Connection menu select **Disconnect**.

B. The details pane should show the unbind operation (0x0 = ldap_unbind(ld)).

Using LDP to Add a User

To add a user using LDP, you must first connect and bind to the desired domain and server.

Using the Connection menu, select Connect and connect to your server, port 389.

A. Use the Connection menu and again bind as administrator to your domain, making sure that the Domain checkbox is checked.

B. From the Browse menu, select **Add**; the Add splash screen should be displayed, as shown in Figure C.6.

C. Enter the DN: of the new user as follows.
   CN=testuser,CN=Users,DC=<your subdomain name>,DC= domain,DC=com

Figure C.6
Adding a user with
LDP.

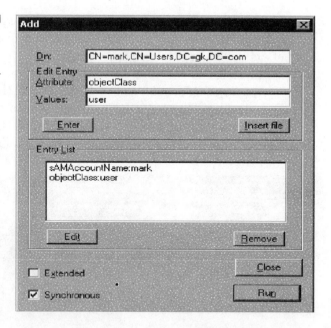

Two attributes with proper values must be added to each user account when it is first created.

Edit Entry Attribute	Values
SAMAccountName	Testuser
ObjectClass	User

D. Each attribute and value are added together, first one attribute with the corresponding value and then the next; press **Enter**, as shown in the previous figure.
E. Clicking the **Run** button executes the process and adds the user testuser to the Users folder.
F. Use ADUC to check the creation of the user account. The user account will have a red X and won't be automatically activated, since we have not added all of the required attributes.
G. Right-click and select **Activate**.

▄▄▄ ▄▄▄ ▄ Delegating Administrative Control

Open Active Directory Users and Computers from the Administrative Tools menu.

A. Double-click the Domain node, and then right-click the container whose control you want to delegate; choose Delegate Control from the shortcut menu. This starts the Delegation of Control wizard. Click **Next**.

B. Log onto your domain as Administrator and open ADUC.

C. Select an OU and a user within the selected OU to which to delegate control.

D. Highlight the OU and from the Action menu select Delegate Control.

E. Once the Delegation of Control wizard starts, click **Next**.

F. Click **Add** to add the user to which to delegate control and then click **Next**.

G. From the tasks to delegate, check "Create, delete and manage user accounts" and click **Next**.

H. Read the summary screen and click **Finish**.

Test Delegated Permissions

Log onto your domain as the delegated user for the selected domain.

A. Open ADUC from the Administrative Tools menu.

B. Expand the domain and select the OU to which you assigned delegation.

C. Try to change the logon hours for one of the other users in the delegated OU.

D. Were you successful? You should have been.

E. Try to change the logon hours for one of the other users in the Users container.

F. Were you successful? Why not?

APPENDIX D

KNOWLEDGE BASE ARTICLES

INDEX

Note: Boldface numbers indicate illustrations; italic t indicates a table.

ABOUT THE AUTHOR

Mark Wilkins is a course director and technical instructor for Data Tech Institute, a provider of technical seminars and video-based training materials for Fortune 500 companies. He is the author of *Windows System Policies* and *Administering SMS*.